VOLUME
10

HAVEN'T SEEN THE PRINCIPAL AROUND LATELY.

Silver Spoon

HIROMU ARAKAWA

Chapter 80:
Tale of Winter ⑰

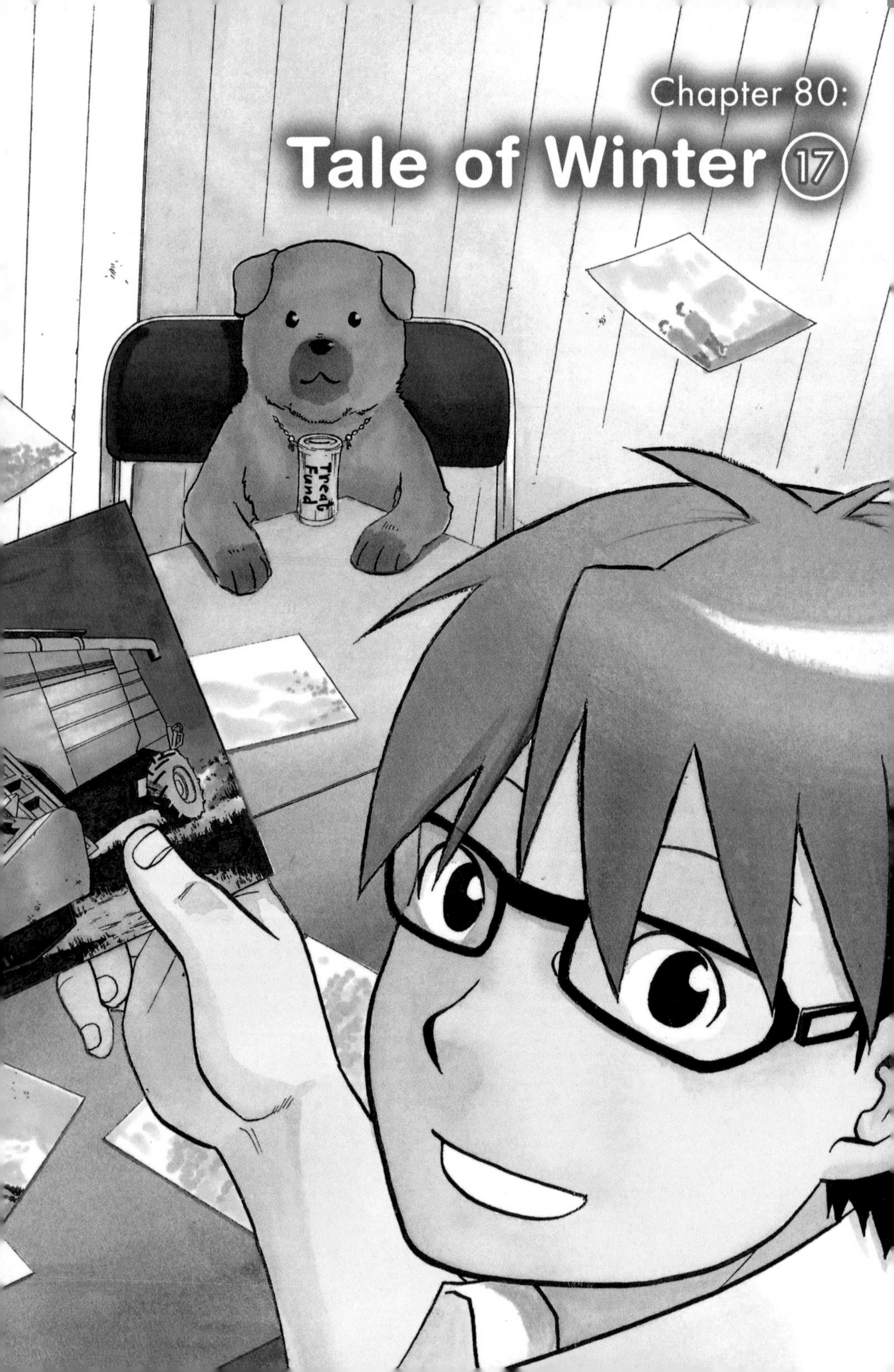
Treat Fund

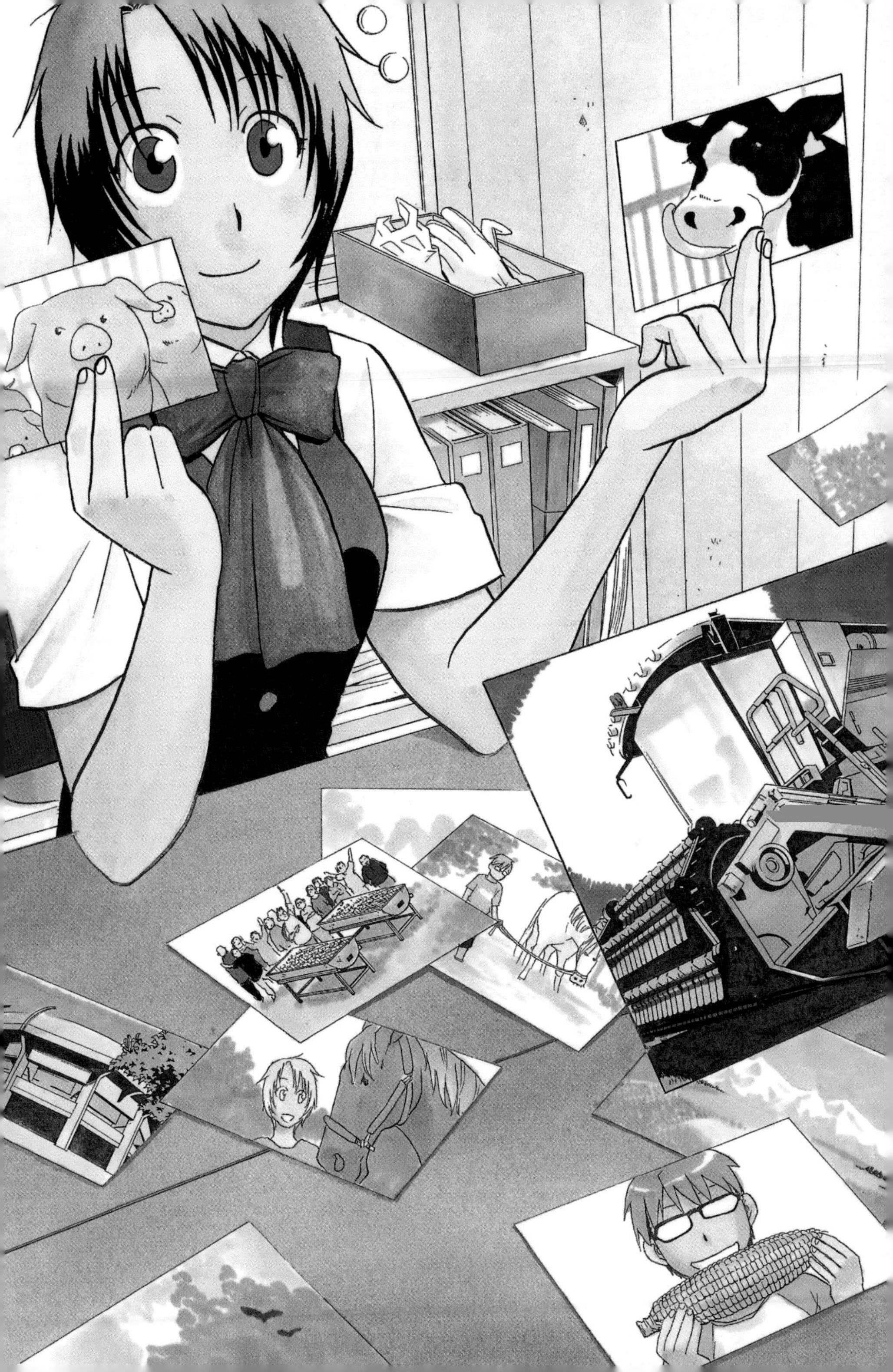

STORY & CHARACTERS

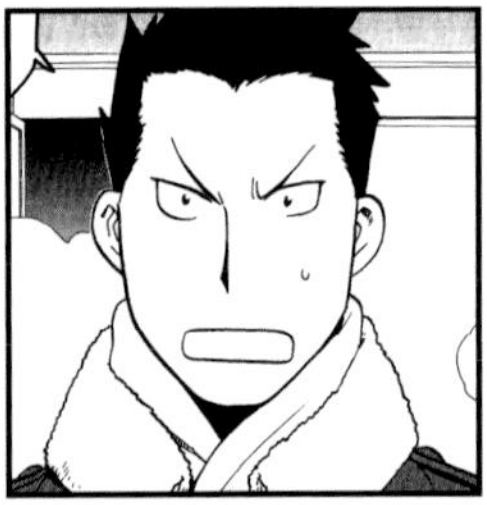

ICHIROU KOMABA

A former first-year student at Ooezo Agricultural High School who enrolled in the Dairy Science Program. He had planned on taking over the family farm after graduation, but it went out of business.

AKI MIKAGE

A first-year student at Ooezo Agricultural High School, enrolled in the Dairy Science Program. Her family keeps cows and horses. While her family has accepted that their only daughter won't carry on the family business, now she has to get into college...

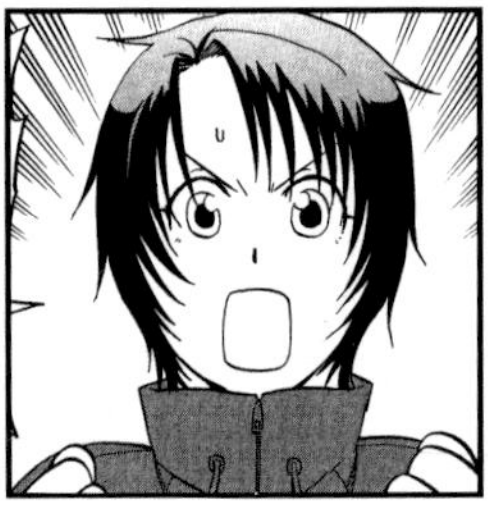

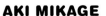

YUUGO HACHIKEN

A first-year student at Ooezo Agricultural High School, enrolled in the Dairy Science Program. A city kid from Sapporo who got in through the general entrance exam. He's finally started to see both the fun and the harshness of the agriculture industry...

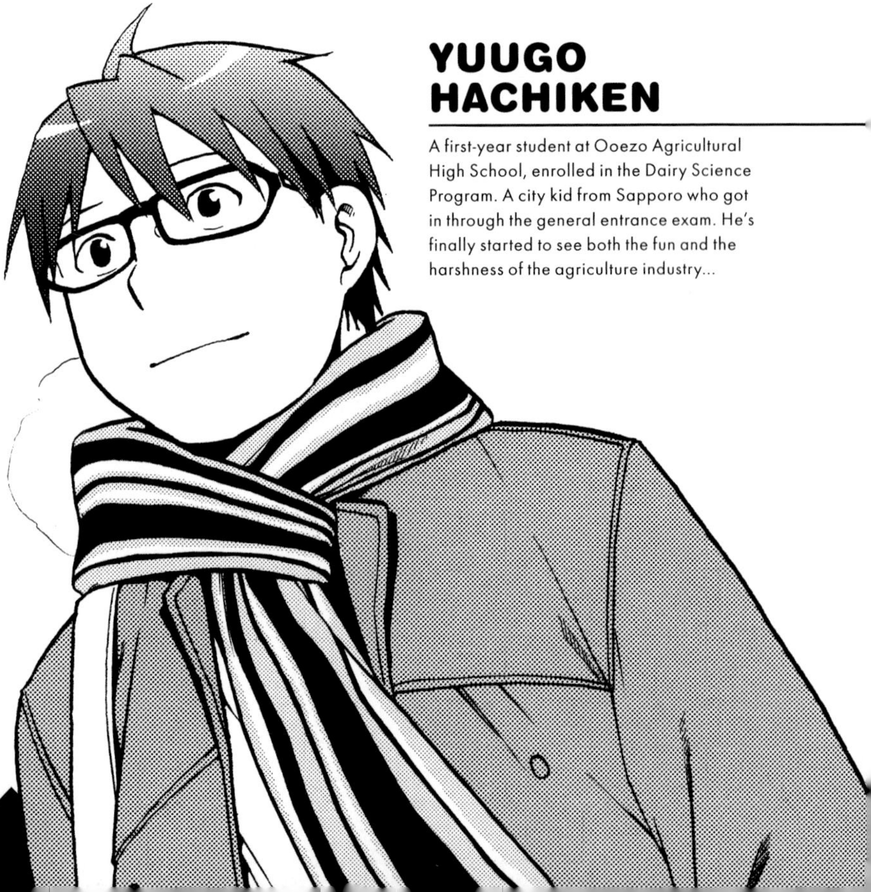

TAMAKO INADA

A first-year student at Ooezo Agricultural High School, enrolled in the Dairy Science Program. Her family runs a megafarm. A complete enigma.

The Story Thus Far:

Hachiken gives Aki Mikage the push she needs to muster her courage and confess her true feelings at a Mikage family meeting. What she really wants is to find a job working with horses, not to carry on the family business. Her family's answer: She has to go to college. Hachiken promises the Mikage family he'll take responsibility by supervising Aki's studies. As a result, Hachiken finds himself back at his own family home in search of his older brother's "studying cheat sheets"... and there Hachiken begins to change himself...by confronting his father...

SHINNOSUKE AIKAWA

A first-year student at Ooezo Agricultural High School, enrolled in the Dairy Science Program. His dream is to become a veterinarian, but he can't handle blood.

KEIJI TOKIWA

A first-year student at Ooezo Agricultural High School, enrolled in the Dairy Science Program. Son of chicken farmers. Awful at academics.

CONTENTS

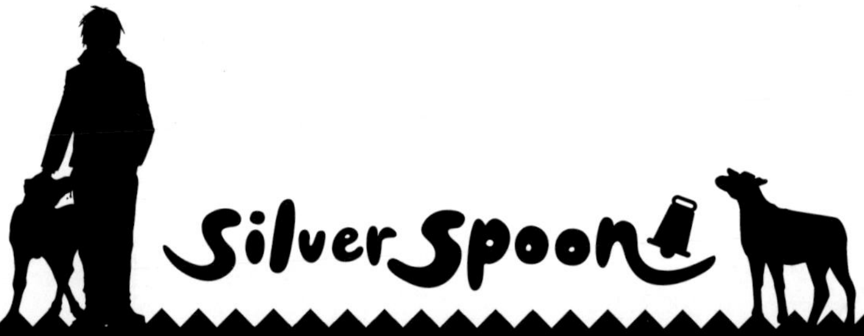
Silver Spoon

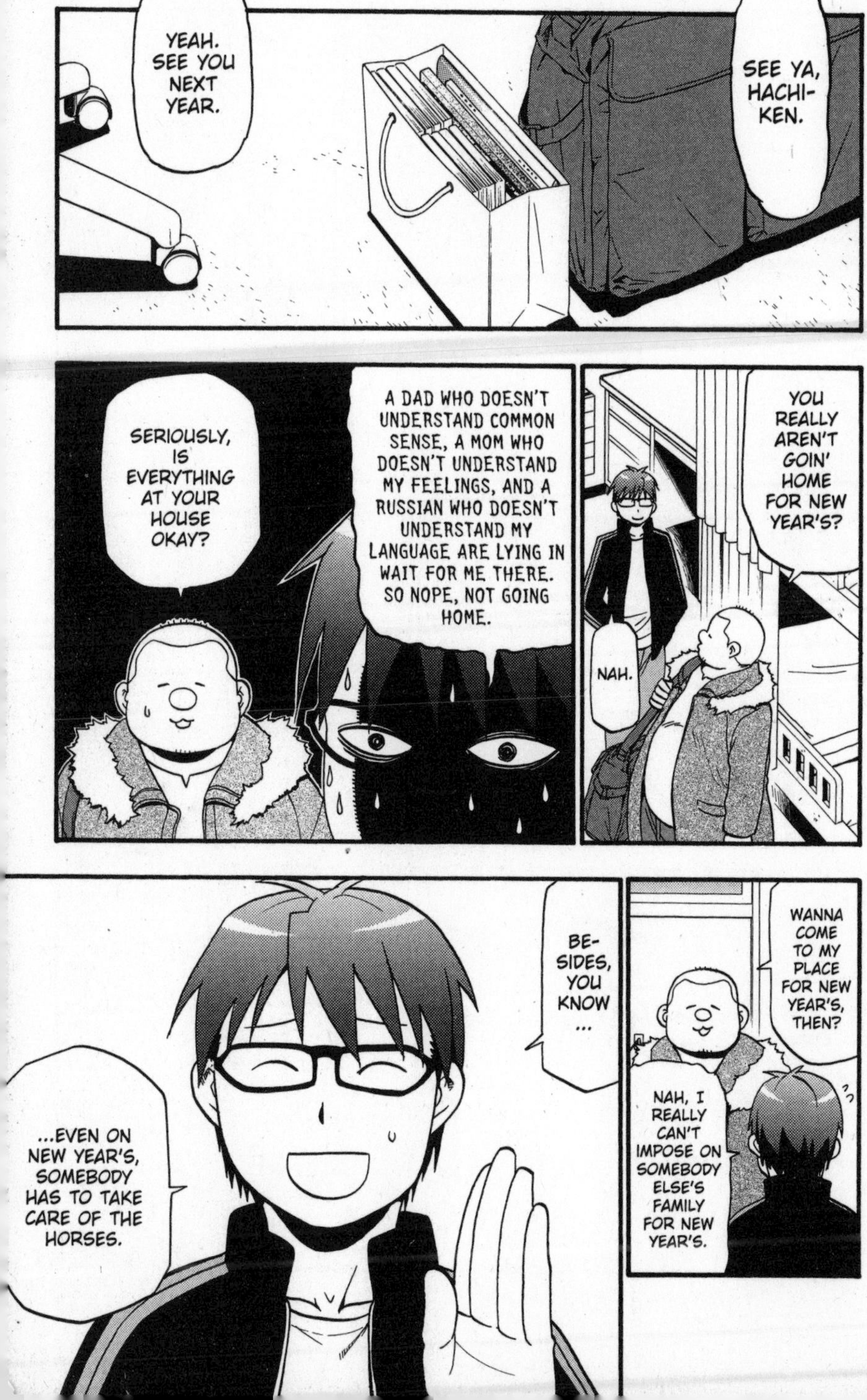
SEE YA, HACHIKEN.
YEAH. SEE YOU NEXT YEAR.
YOU REALLY AREN'T GOIN' HOME FOR NEW YEAR'S?
NAH.
A DAD WHO DOESN'T UNDERSTAND COMMON SENSE, A MOM WHO DOESN'T UNDERSTAND MY FEELINGS, AND A RUSSIAN WHO DOESN'T UNDERSTAND MY LANGUAGE ARE LYING IN WAIT FOR ME THERE. SO NOPE, NOT GOING HOME.
SERIOUSLY, IS EVERYTHING AT YOUR HOUSE OKAY?
WANNA COME TO MY PLACE FOR NEW YEAR'S, THEN?
NAH, I REALLY CAN'T IMPOSE ON SOMEBODY ELSE'S FAMILY FOR NEW YEAR'S.
BESIDES, YOU KNOW...
...EVEN ON NEW YEAR'S, SOMEBODY HAS TO TAKE CARE OF THE HORSES.

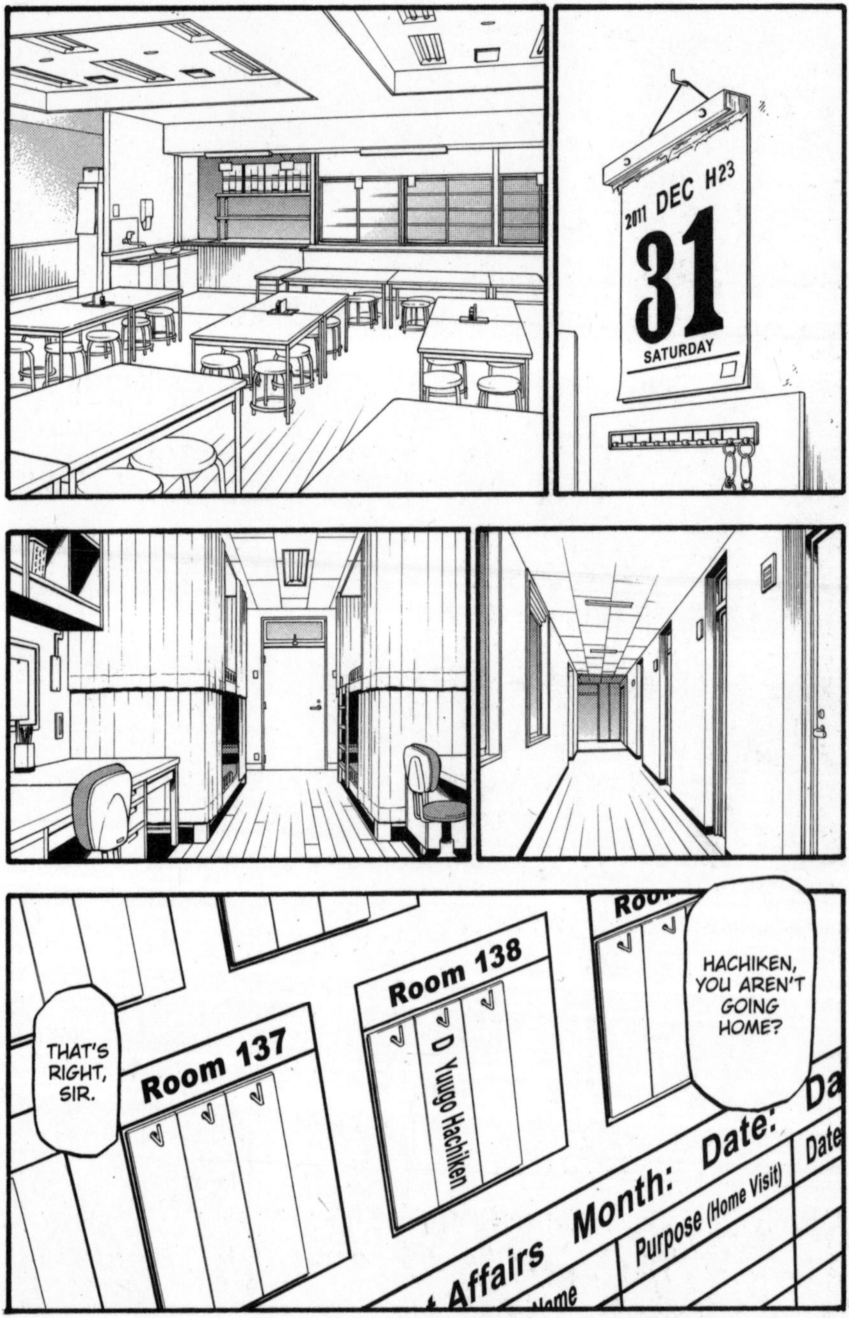
2011 DEC H23
31
SATURDAY
HACHIKEN, YOU AREN'T GOING HOME?
Room 138
D Yuugo Hachiken
THAT'S RIGHT, SIR.
Room 137
Affairs Month: Date:
Purpose (Home Visit)

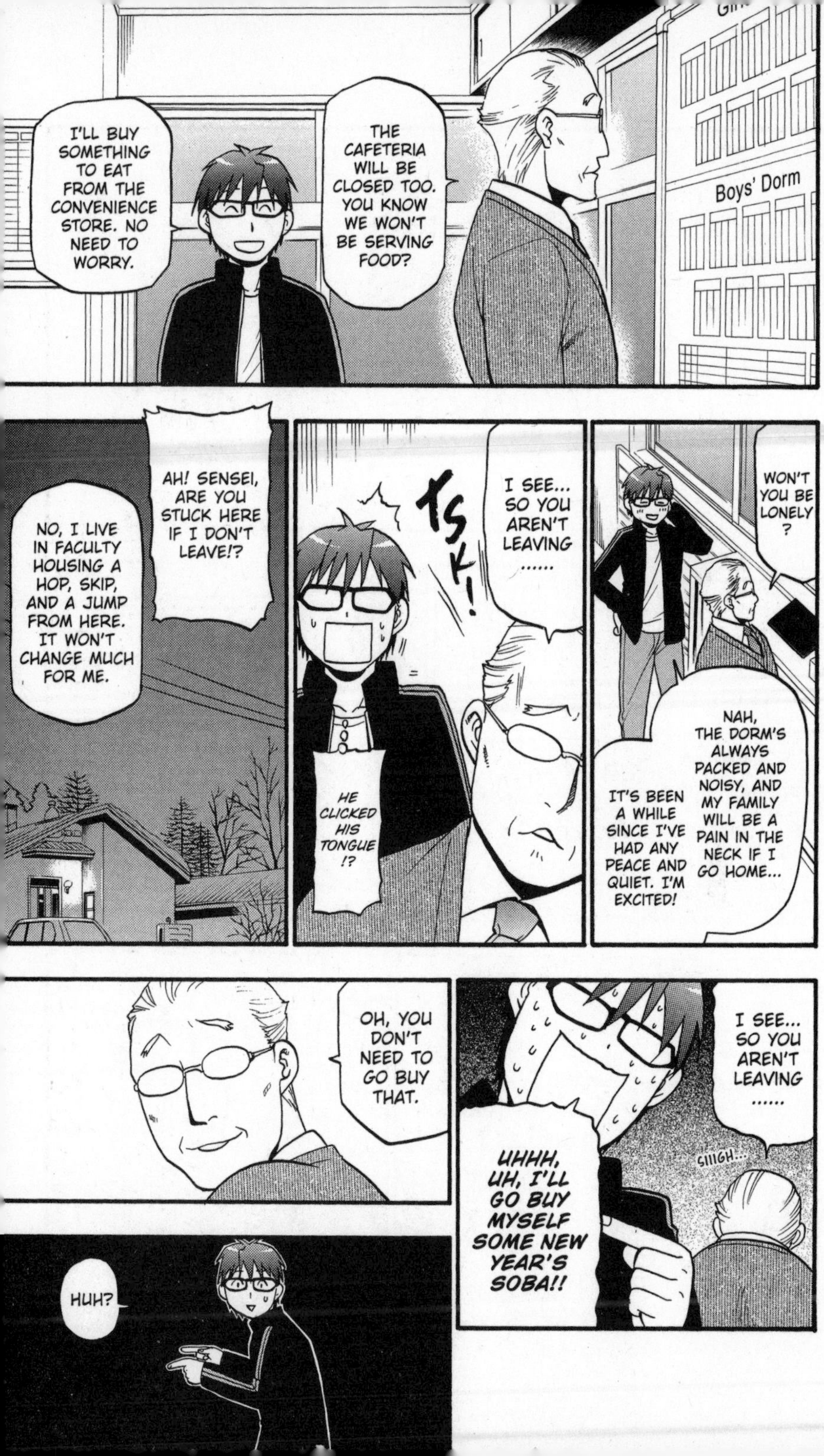
Boys' Dorm
THE CAFETERIA WILL BE CLOSED TOO. YOU KNOW WE WON'T BE SERVING FOOD?
I'LL BUY SOMETHING TO EAT FROM THE CONVENIENCE STORE. NO NEED TO WORRY.
WON'T YOU BE LONELY?
NAH, THE DORM'S ALWAYS PACKED AND NOISY, AND MY FAMILY WILL BE A PAIN IN THE NECK IF I GO HOME...
IT'S BEEN A WHILE SINCE I'VE HAD ANY PEACE AND QUIET. I'M EXCITED!
I SEE... SO YOU AREN'T LEAVING......
TSK!
HE CLICKED HIS TONGUE!?
AH! SENSEI, ARE YOU STUCK HERE IF I DON'T LEAVE!?
NO, I LIVE IN FACULTY HOUSING A HOP, SKIP, AND A JUMP FROM HERE. IT WON'T CHANGE MUCH FOR ME.
I SEE... SO YOU AREN'T LEAVING......
SIIIGH...
UHHH, UH, I'LL GO BUY MYSELF SOME NEW YEAR'S SOBA!!
OH, YOU DON'T NEED TO GO BUY THAT.
HUH?

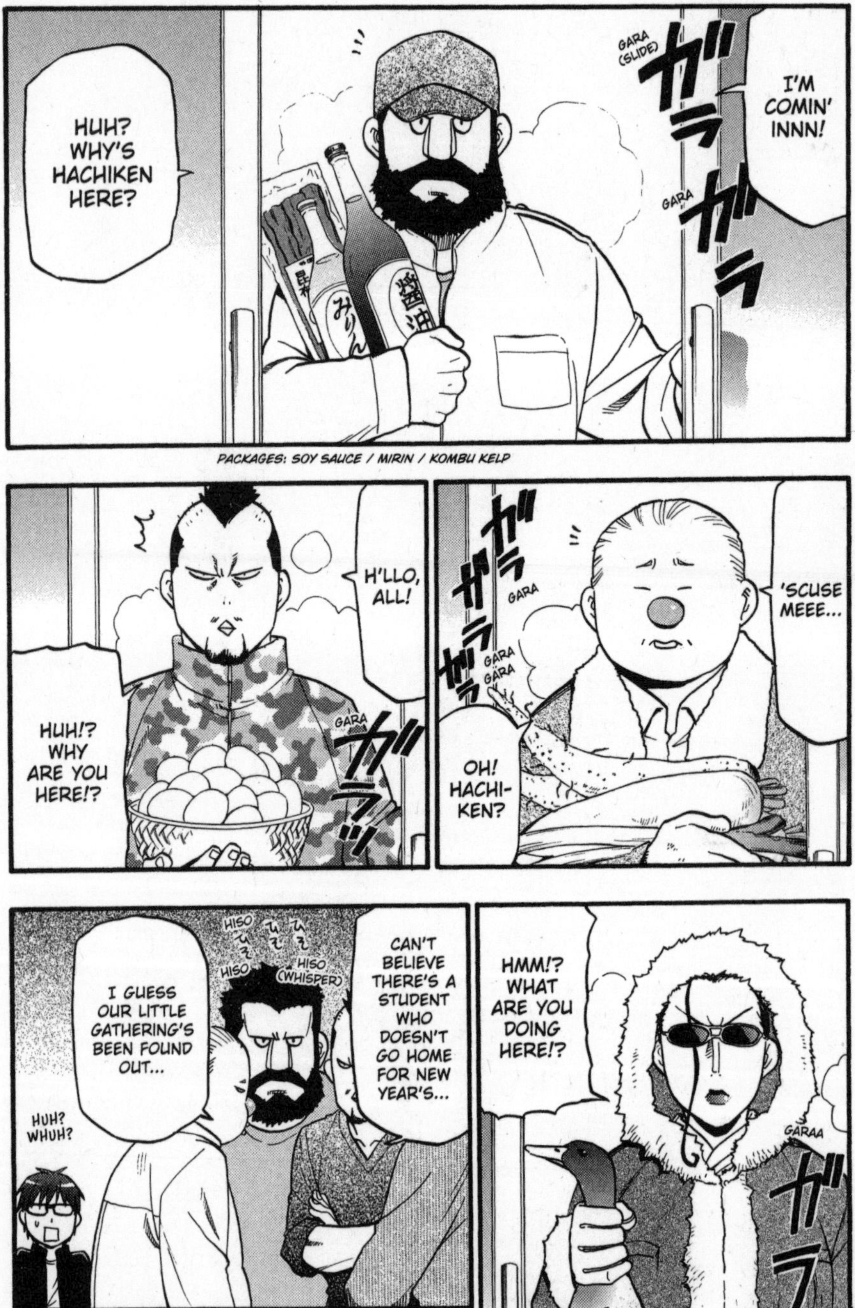

I'M COMIN' INNN!
GARA (SLIDE)
GARA
HUH? WHY'S HACHIKEN HERE?
PACKAGES: SOY SAUCE / MIRIN / KOMBU KELP
'SCUSE MEEE...
GARA
GARA GARA
OH! HACHI-KEN?
H'LLO, ALL!
GARA
HUH!? WHY ARE YOU HERE!?
HMM!? WHAT ARE YOU DOING HERE!?
GARAA
CAN'T BELIEVE THERE'S A STUDENT WHO DOESN'T GO HOME FOR NEW YEAR'S...
HISO HISO HISO (WHISPER)
I GUESS OUR LITTLE GATHERING'S BEEN FOUND OUT...
HUH? WHUH?

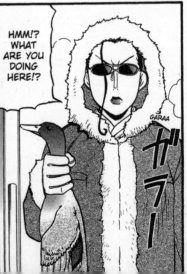

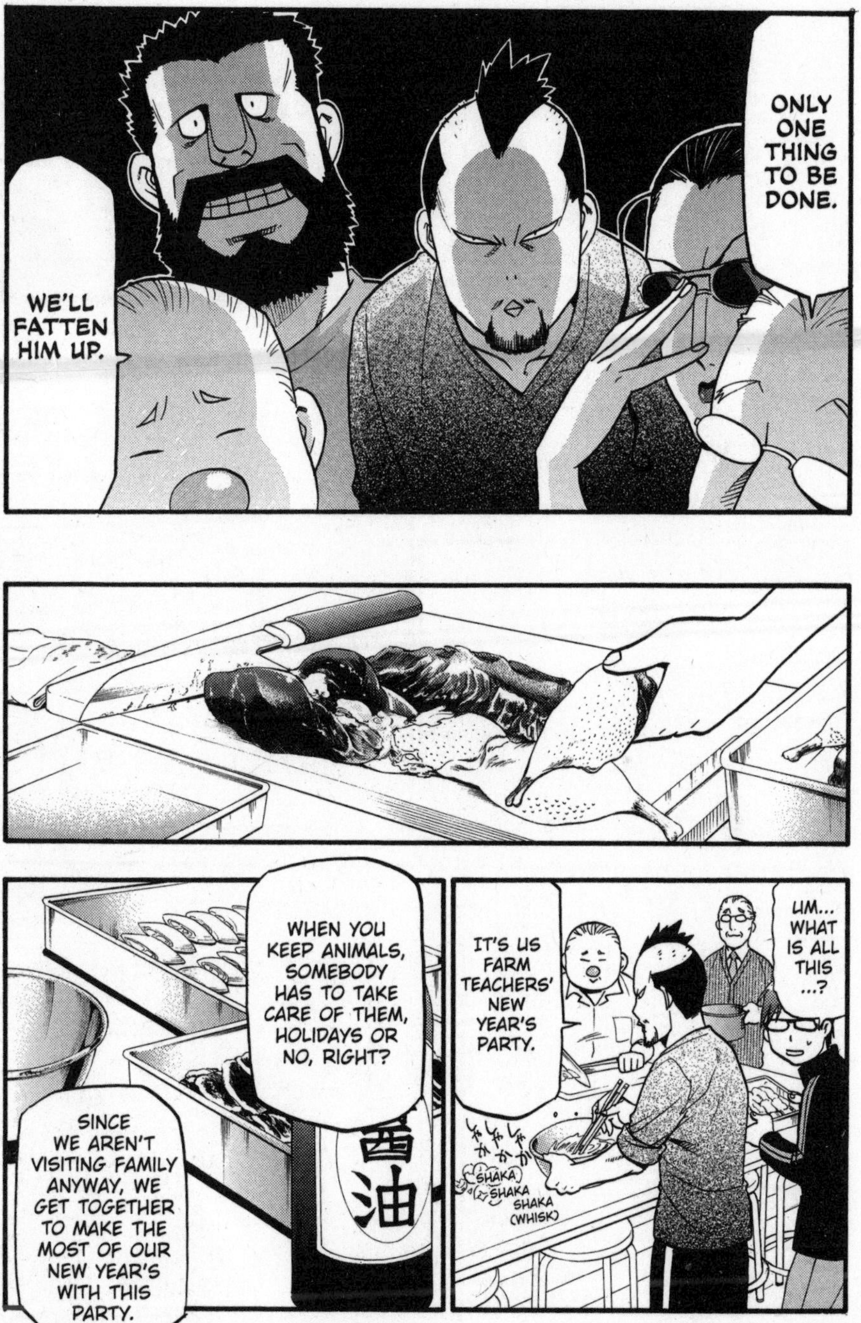
ONLY ONE THING TO BE DONE.
WE'LL FATTEN HIM UP.
UM... WHAT IS ALL THIS ...?
IT'S US FARM TEACHERS' NEW YEAR'S PARTY.
SHAKA SHAKA SHAKA (WHISK)
WHEN YOU KEEP ANIMALS, SOMEBODY HAS TO TAKE CARE OF THEM, HOLIDAYS OR NO, RIGHT?
SINCE WE AREN'T VISITING FAMILY ANYWAY, WE GET TOGETHER TO MAKE THE MOST OF OUR NEW YEAR'S WITH THIS PARTY.
醤油

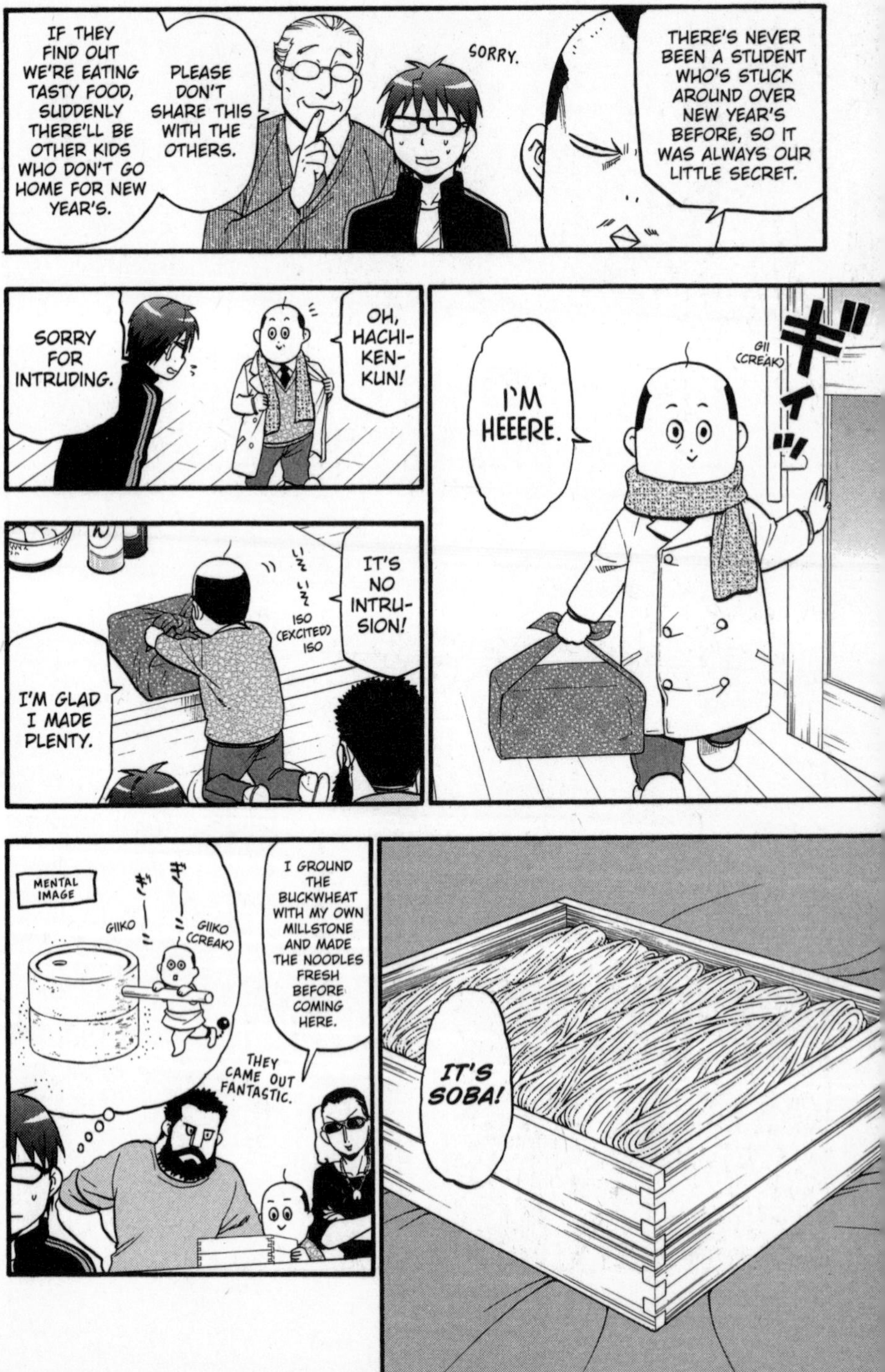
THERE'S NEVER BEEN A STUDENT WHO'S STUCK AROUND OVER NEW YEAR'S BEFORE, SO IT WAS ALWAYS OUR LITTLE SECRET.
SORRY.
PLEASE DON'T SHARE THIS WITH THE OTHERS.
IF THEY FIND OUT WE'RE EATING TASTY FOOD, SUDDENLY THERE'LL BE OTHER KIDS WHO DON'T GO HOME FOR NEW YEAR'S.
GII (CREAK)
I'M HEEERE.
OH, HACHI-KEN-KUN!
SORRY FOR INTRUDING.
IT'S NO INTRU-SION!
ISO (EXCITED) ISO
I'M GLAD I MADE PLENTY.
IT'S SOBA!
I GROUND THE BUCKWHEAT WITH MY OWN MILLSTONE AND MADE THE NOODLES FRESH BEFORE COMING HERE.
GIIKO (CREAK)
GIIKO
MENTAL IMAGE
THEY CAME OUT FANTASTIC.

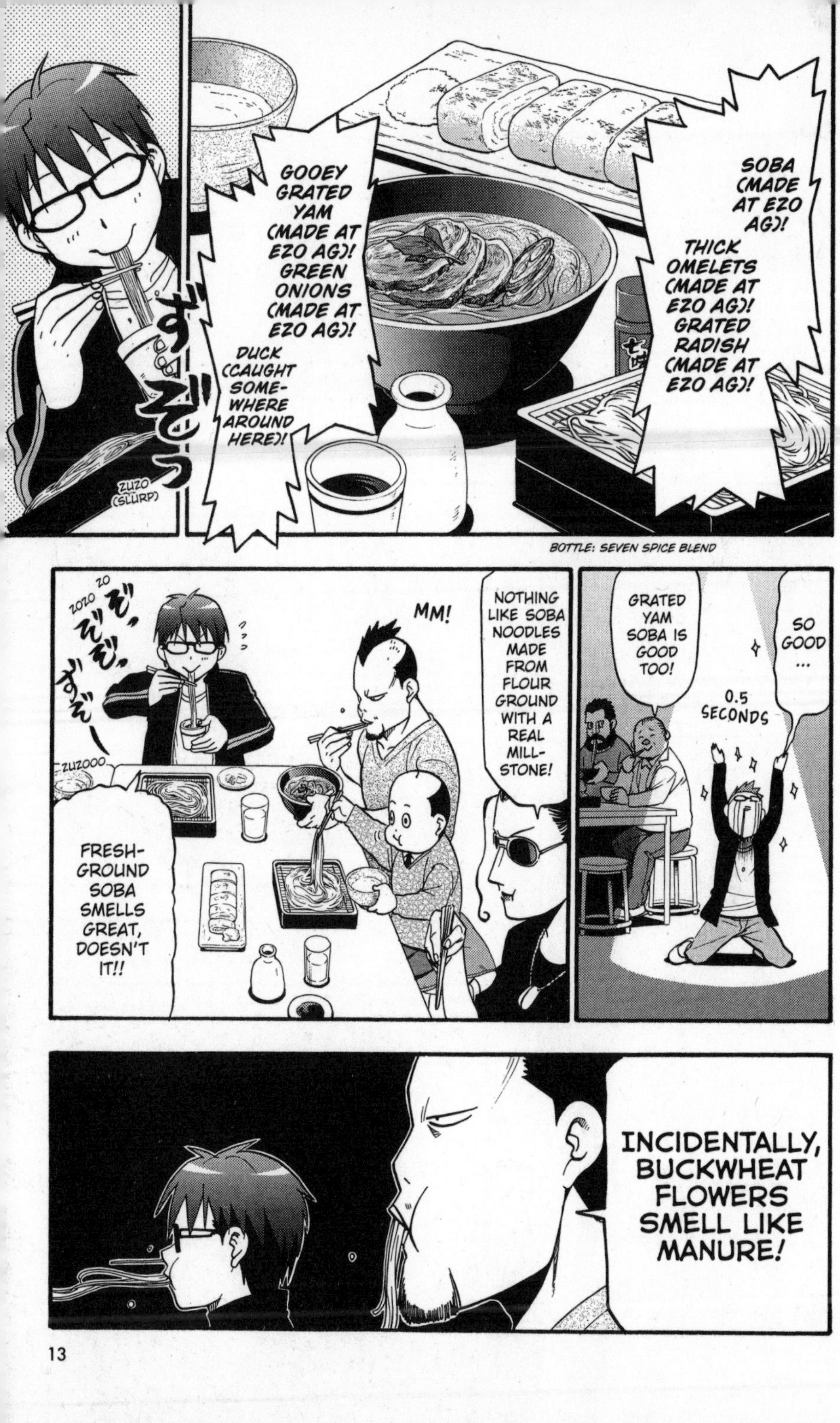
SOBA (MADE AT EZO AG)! THICK OMELETS (MADE AT EZO AG)! GRATED RADISH (MADE AT EZO AG)!
GOOEY GRATED YAM (MADE AT EZO AG)! GREEN ONIONS (MADE AT EZO AG)!
DUCK (CAUGHT SOME-WHERE AROUND HERE)!
ずぞっ
ZUZO (SLURP)
BOTTLE: SEVEN SPICE BLEND
SO GOOD ...
GRATED YAM SOBA IS GOOD TOO!
0.5 SECONDS
NOTHING LIKE SOBA NOODLES MADE FROM FLOUR GROUND WITH A REAL MILL-STONE!
MM!
ぞぞぞ、ぞぞぞ、ずぞー
ZOZO ZO
ZUZOOO
FRESH-GROUND SOBA SMELLS GREAT, DOESN'T IT!!
INCIDENTALLY, BUCKWHEAT FLOWERS SMELL LIKE MANURE!

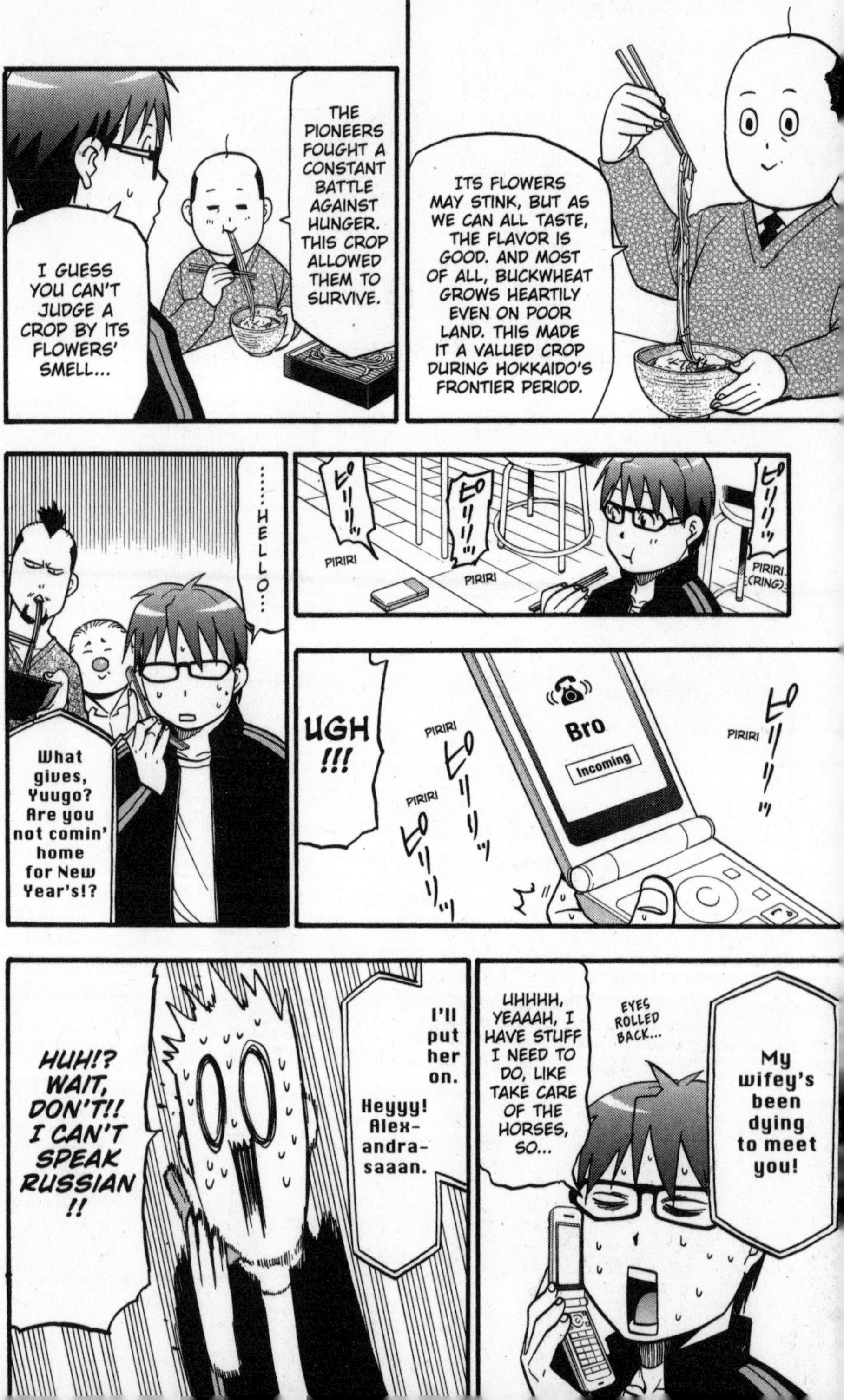
ITS FLOWERS MAY STINK, BUT AS WE CAN ALL TASTE, THE FLAVOR IS GOOD. AND MOST OF ALL, BUCKWHEAT GROWS HEARTILY EVEN ON POOR LAND. THIS MADE IT A VALUED CROP DURING HOKKAIDO'S FRONTIER PERIOD.
THE PIONEERS FOUGHT A CONSTANT BATTLE AGAINST HUNGER. THIS CROP ALLOWED THEM TO SURVIVE.
I GUESS YOU CAN'T JUDGE A CROP BY ITS FLOWERS' SMELL...
PIRIRI (RING)
PIRIRI
PIRIRI
PIRIRI
Bro
Incoming
PIRIRI
PIRIRI
UGH !!!
...HELLO...
What gives, Yuugo? Are you not comin' home for New Year's!?
My wifey's been dying to meet you!
EYES ROLLED BACK...
UHHHH, YEAAAH, I HAVE STUFF I NEED TO DO, LIKE TAKE CARE OF THE HORSES, SO...
I'll put her on.
Heyyy! Alex-andra-saaan.
HUH!? WAIT, DON'T!! I CAN'T SPEAK RUSSIAN !!

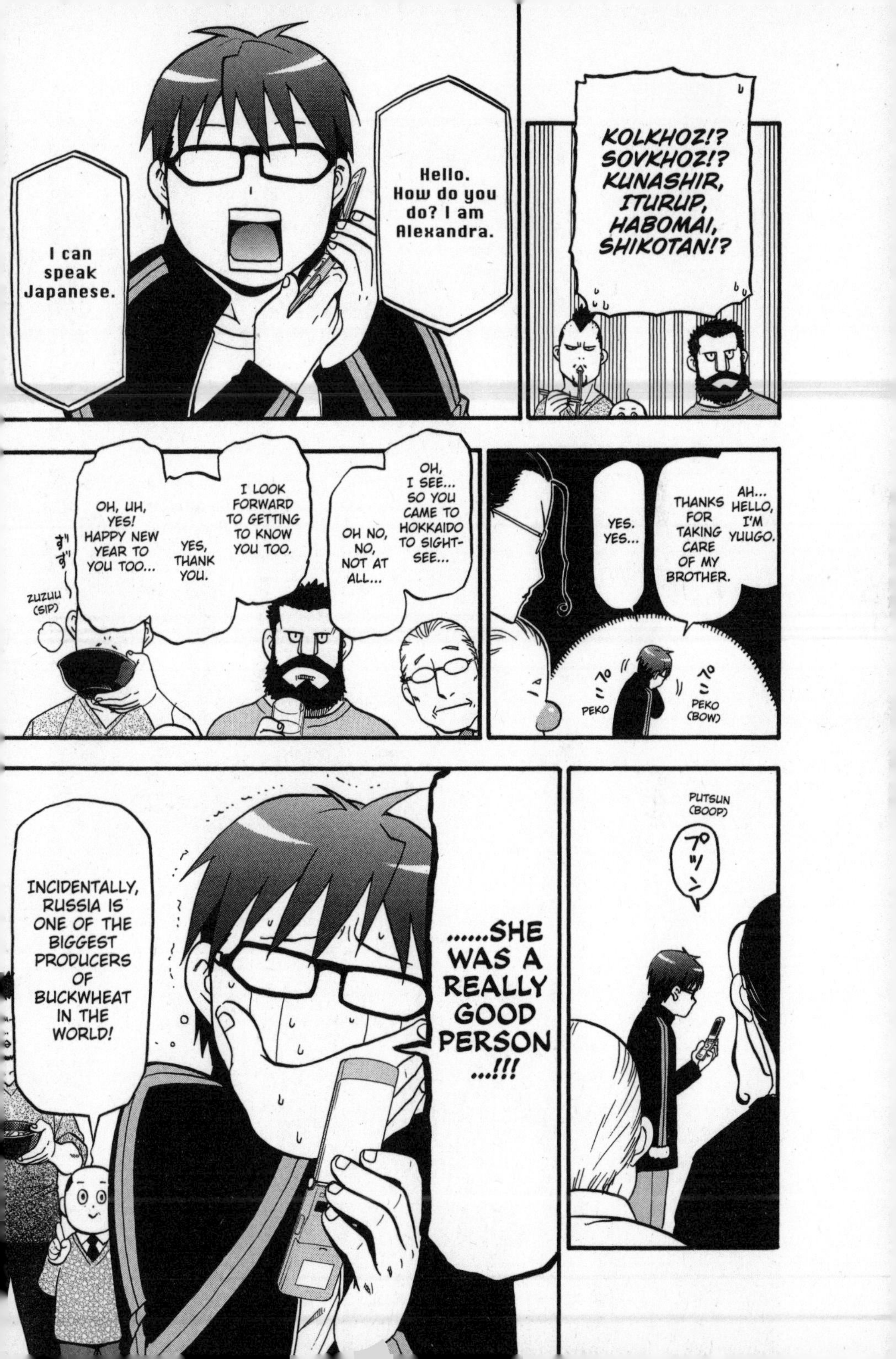
KOLKHOZ!? SOVKHOZ!? KUNASHIR, ITURUP, HABOMAI, SHIKOTAN!?
Hello. How do you do? I am Alexandra.
I can speak Japanese.
AH... HELLO, I'M YUUGO.
THANKS FOR TAKING CARE OF MY BROTHER.
YES. YES...
ぺこ
PEKO (BOW)
ぺこ
PEKO
OH, I SEE... SO YOU CAME TO HOKKAIDO TO SIGHT-SEE...
OH NO, NO, NOT AT ALL...
I LOOK FORWARD TO GETTING TO KNOW YOU TOO.
YES, THANK YOU.
OH, UH, YES! HAPPY NEW YEAR TO YOU TOO...
ずず
ZUZUU (SIP)
PUTSUN (BOOP)
プツン
......SHE WAS A REALLY GOOD PERSON ...!!!
INCIDENTALLY, RUSSIA IS ONE OF THE BIGGEST PRODUCERS OF BUCKWHEAT IN THE WORLD!

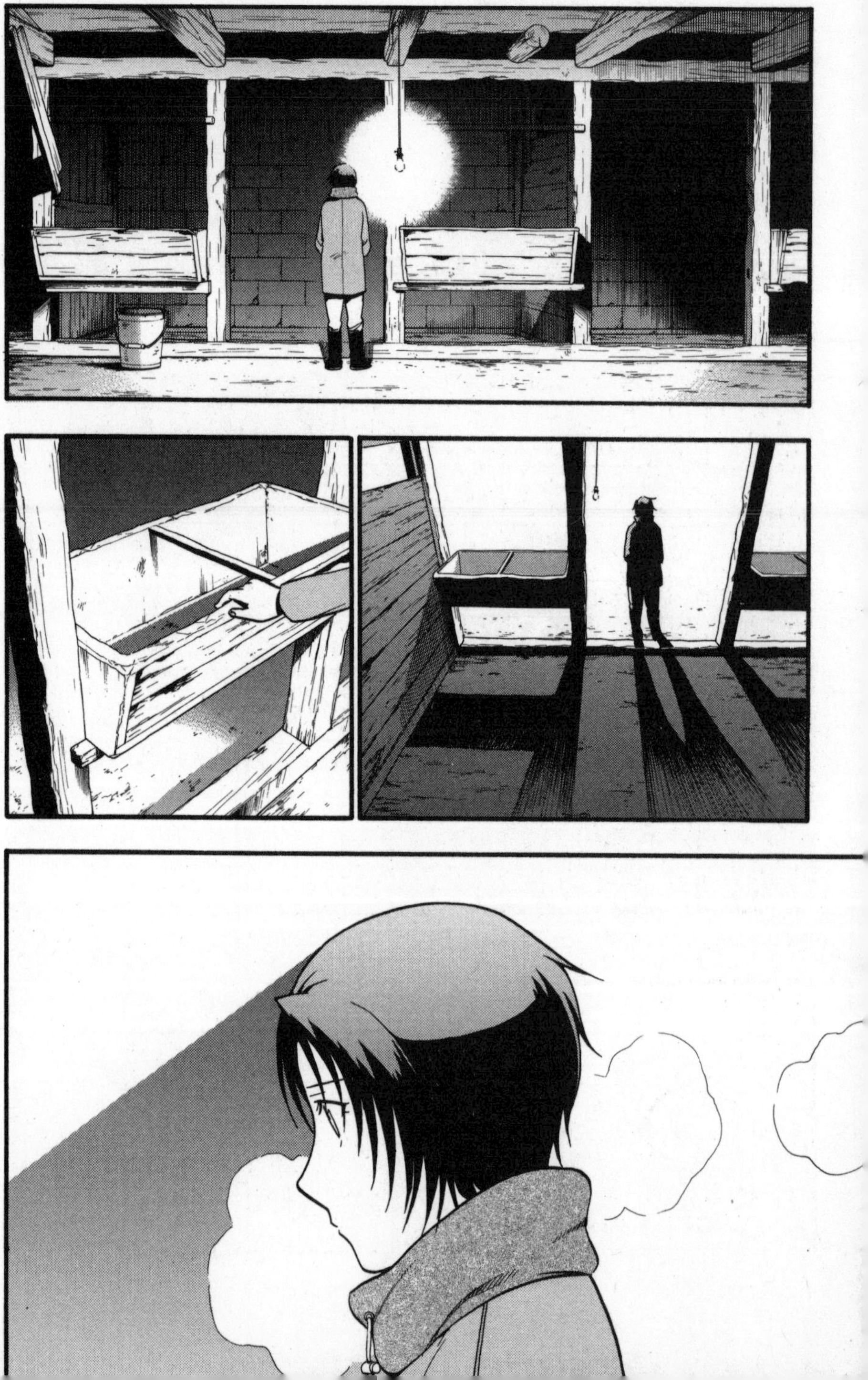

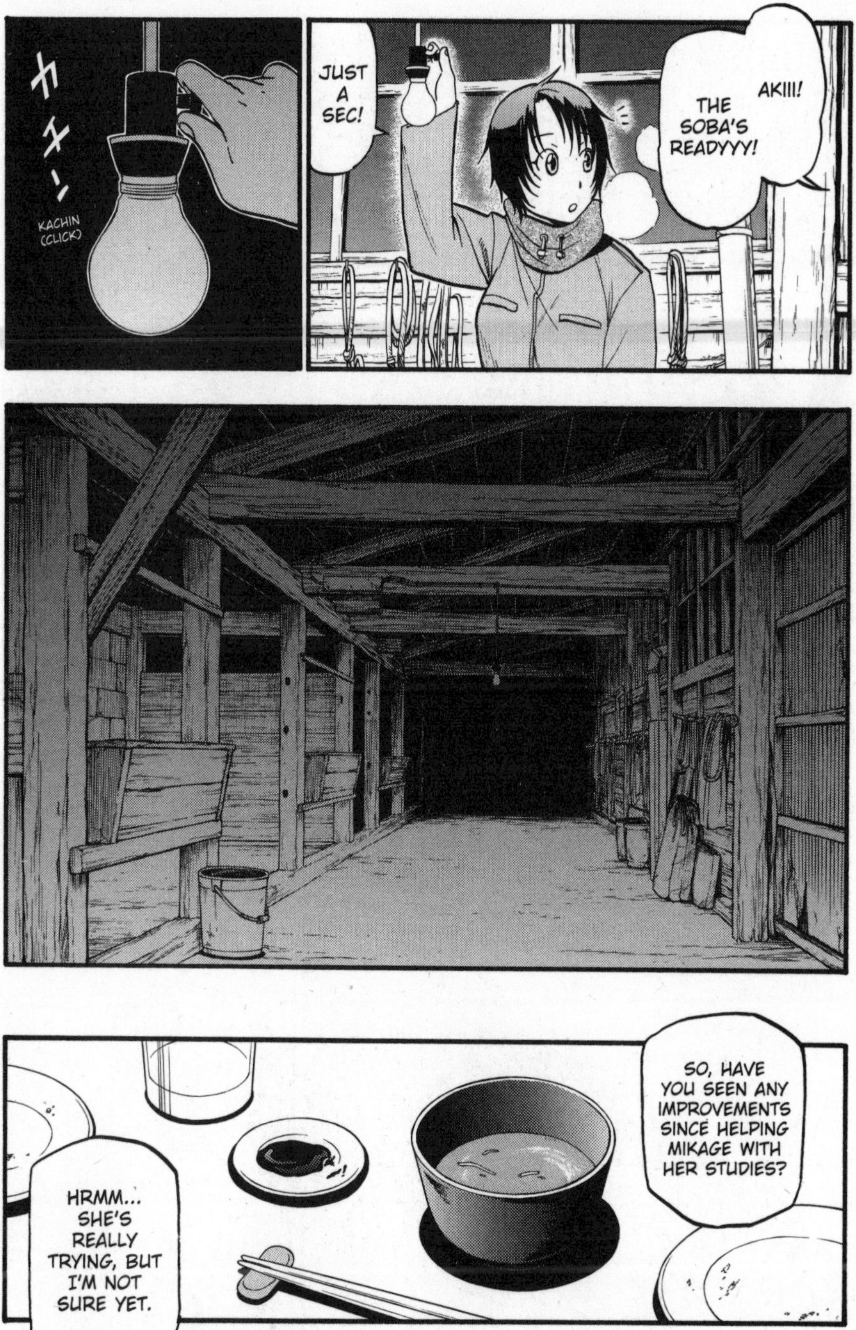
AKIII! THE SOBA'S READYYY!
JUST A SEC!
KACHIN (CLICK)
SO, HAVE YOU SEEN ANY IMPROVEMENTS SINCE HELPING MIKAGE WITH HER STUDIES?
HRMM... SHE'S REALLY TRYING, BUT I'M NOT SURE YET.

BOTTLE: OH! RICE TEA

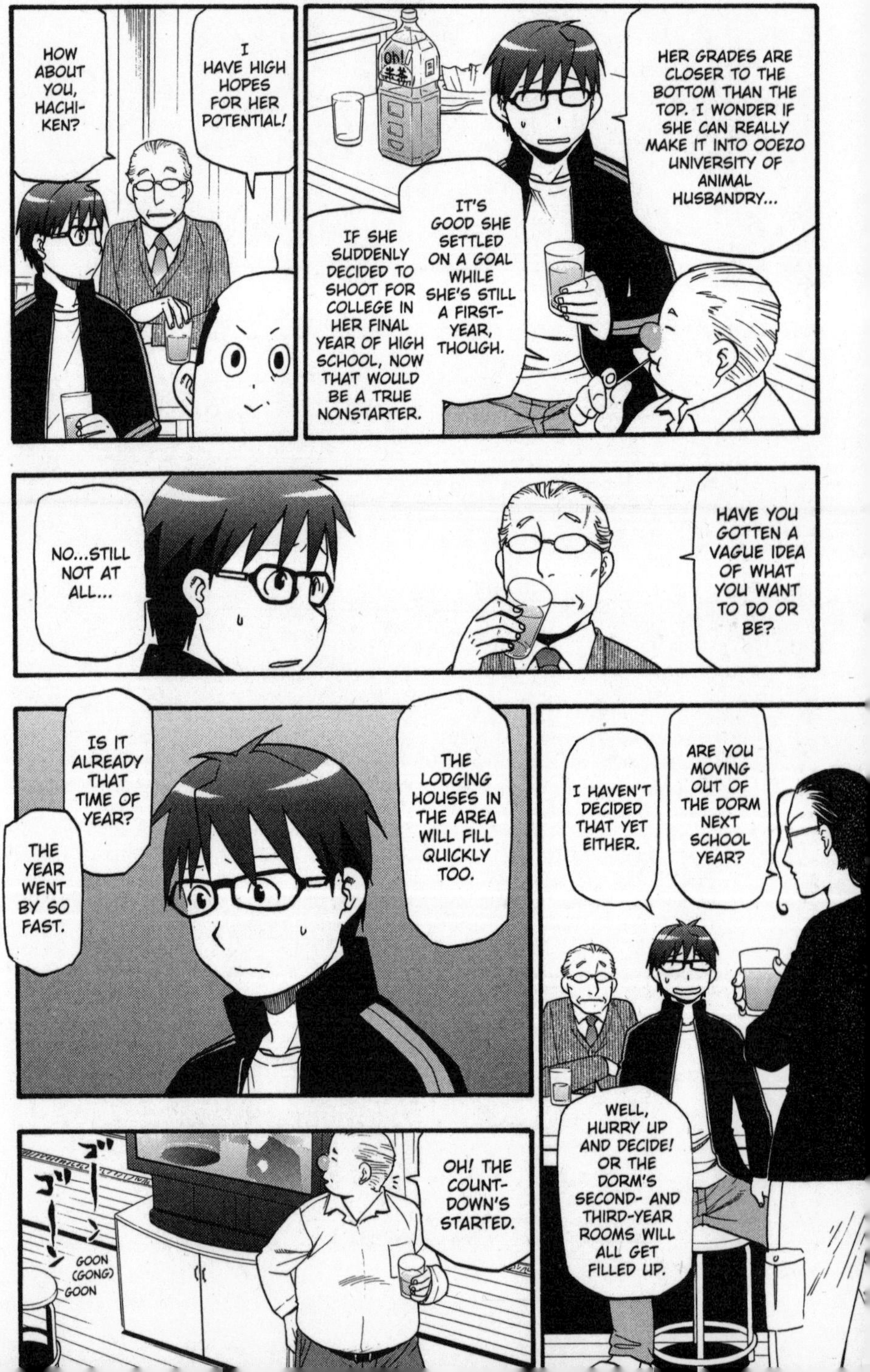
Oh! 米茶
HER GRADES ARE CLOSER TO THE BOTTOM THAN THE TOP. I WONDER IF SHE CAN REALLY MAKE IT INTO OOEZO UNIVERSITY OF ANIMAL HUSBANDRY...
IT'S GOOD SHE SETTLED ON A GOAL WHILE SHE'S STILL A FIRST-YEAR, THOUGH.
IF SHE SUDDENLY DECIDED TO SHOOT FOR COLLEGE IN HER FINAL YEAR OF HIGH SCHOOL, NOW THAT WOULD BE A TRUE NONSTARTER.
I HAVE HIGH HOPES FOR HER POTENTIAL!
HOW ABOUT YOU, HACHI-KEN?
HAVE YOU GOTTEN A VAGUE IDEA OF WHAT YOU WANT TO DO OR BE?
NO...STILL NOT AT ALL...
ARE YOU MOVING OUT OF THE DORM NEXT SCHOOL YEAR?
I HAVEN'T DECIDED THAT YET EITHER.
WELL, HURRY UP AND DECIDE! OR THE DORM'S SECOND- AND THIRD-YEAR ROOMS WILL ALL GET FILLED UP.
THE LODGING HOUSES IN THE AREA WILL FILL QUICKLY TOO.
IS IT ALREADY THAT TIME OF YEAR?
THE YEAR WENT BY SO FAST.
OH! THE COUNT-DOWN'S STARTED.
GOON (GONG) GOON

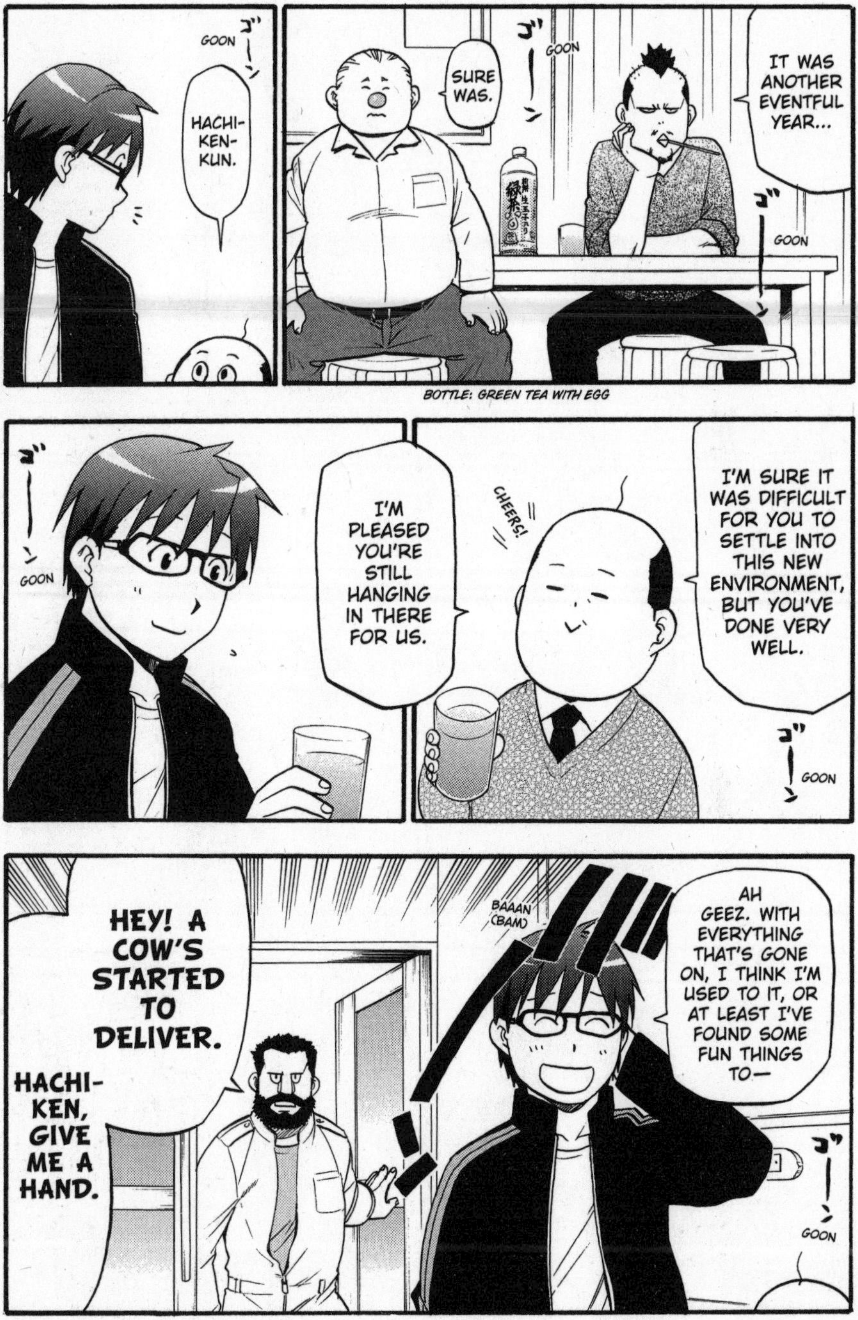
IT WAS ANOTHER EVENTFUL YEAR...
GOON
SURE WAS.
GOON
HACHI-KEN-KUN.
GOON
BOTTLE: GREEN TEA WITH EGG
I'M SURE IT WAS DIFFICULT FOR YOU TO SETTLE INTO THIS NEW ENVIRONMENT, BUT YOU'VE DONE VERY WELL.
GOON
CHEERS!
I'M PLEASED YOU'RE STILL HANGING IN THERE FOR US.
GOON
AH GEEZ. WITH EVERYTHING THAT'S GONE ON, I THINK I'M USED TO IT, OR AT LEAST I'VE FOUND SOME FUN THINGS TO—
GOON
BAAAN (BAM)
HEY! A COW'S STARTED TO DELIVER.
HACHI-KEN, GIVE ME A HAND.

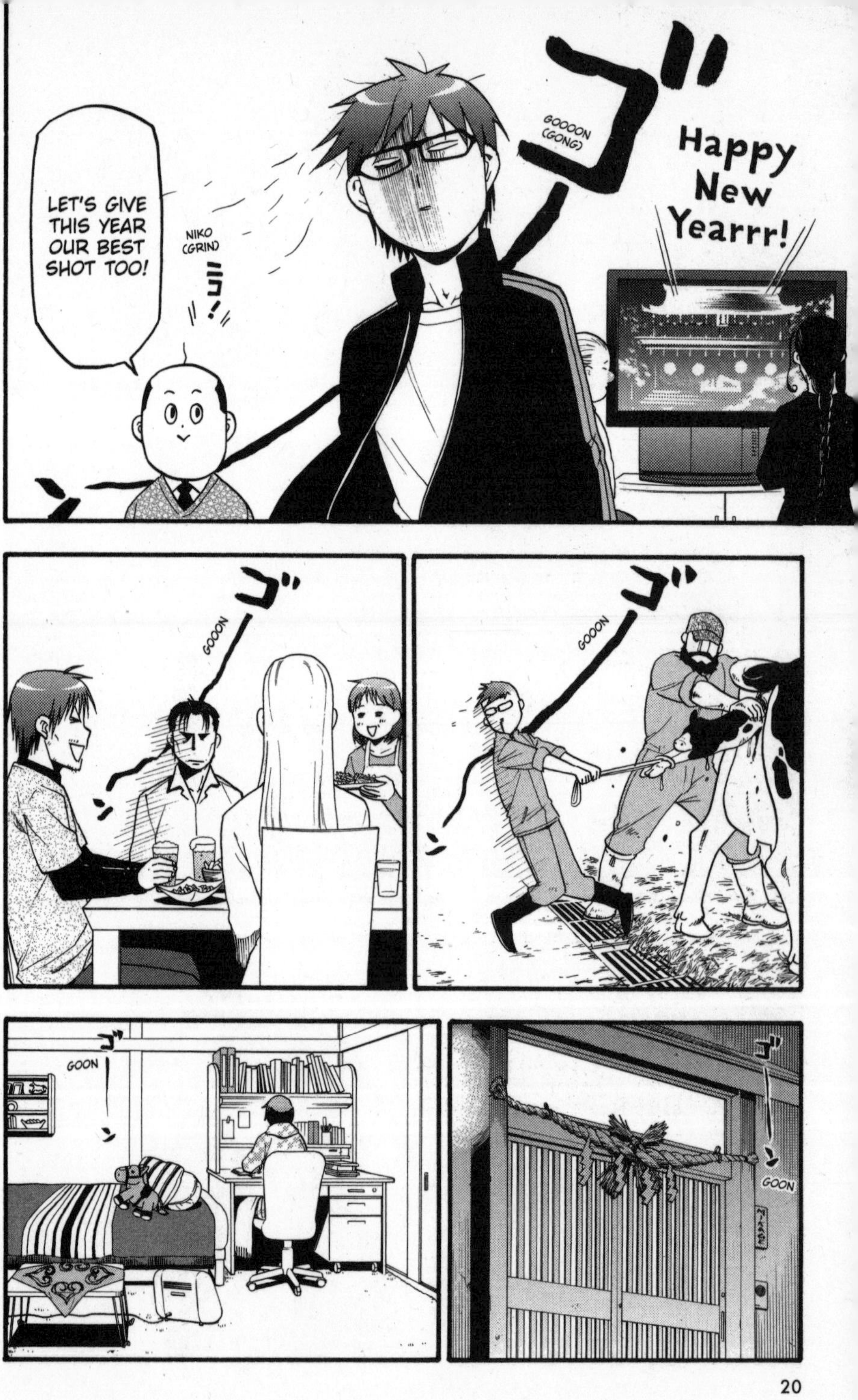
Happy New Yearrr!
GOOOON (GONG)
NIKO (GRIN)
LET'S GIVE THIS YEAR OUR BEST SHOT TOO!
GOOON
GOOON
GOON
GOON

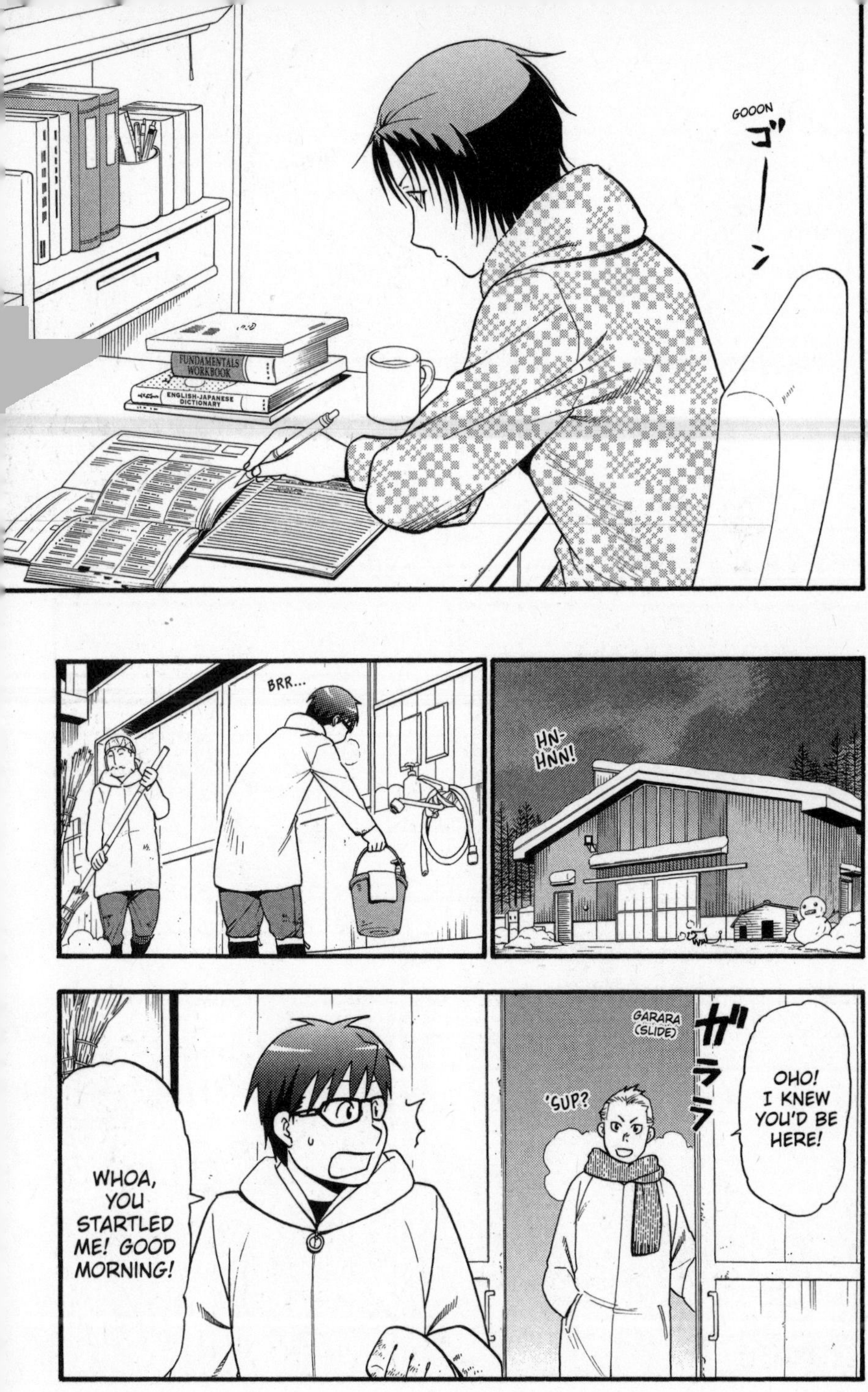
GOOON
ゴーン
FUNDAMENTALS WORKBOOK
ENGLISH-JAPANESE DICTIONARY
HN-HNN!
BRR...
GARARA (SLIDE)
ガラララ
OHO! I KNEW YOU'D BE HERE!
'SUP?
WHOA, YOU STARTLED ME! GOOD MORNING!

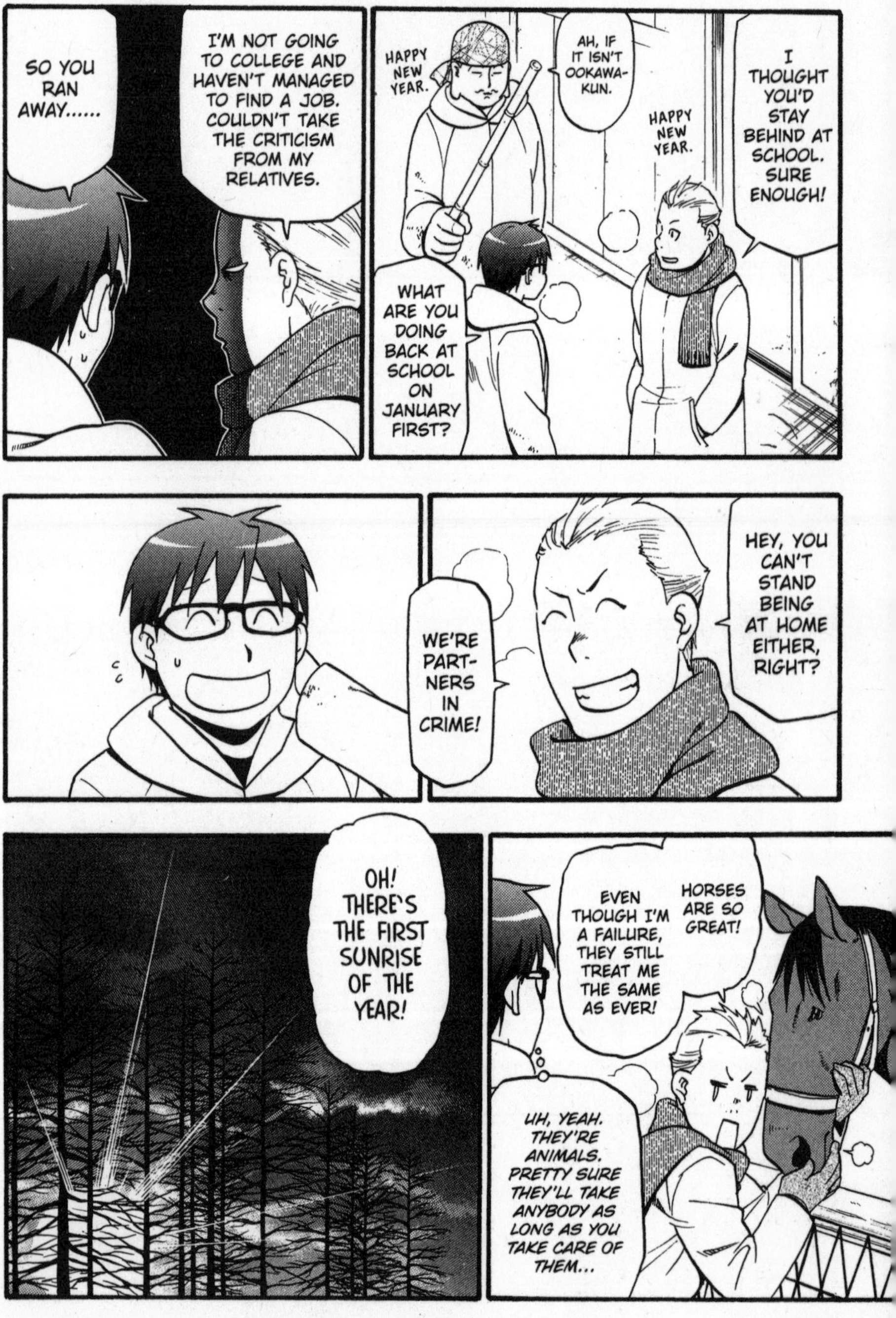
I THOUGHT YOU'D STAY BEHIND AT SCHOOL. SURE ENOUGH!
HAPPY NEW YEAR.
AH, IF IT ISN'T OOKAWA-KUN.
HAPPY NEW YEAR.
WHAT ARE YOU DOING BACK AT SCHOOL ON JANUARY FIRST?
I'M NOT GOING TO COLLEGE AND HAVEN'T MANAGED TO FIND A JOB. COULDN'T TAKE THE CRITICISM FROM MY RELATIVES.
SO YOU RAN AWAY......
HEY, YOU CAN'T STAND BEING AT HOME EITHER, RIGHT?
WE'RE PARTNERS IN CRIME!
HORSES ARE SO GREAT!
EVEN THOUGH I'M A FAILURE, THEY STILL TREAT ME THE SAME AS EVER!
UH, YEAH. THEY'RE ANIMALS. PRETTY SURE THEY'LL TAKE ANYBODY AS LONG AS YOU TAKE CARE OF THEM...
OH! THERE'S THE FIRST SUNRISE OF THE YEAR!

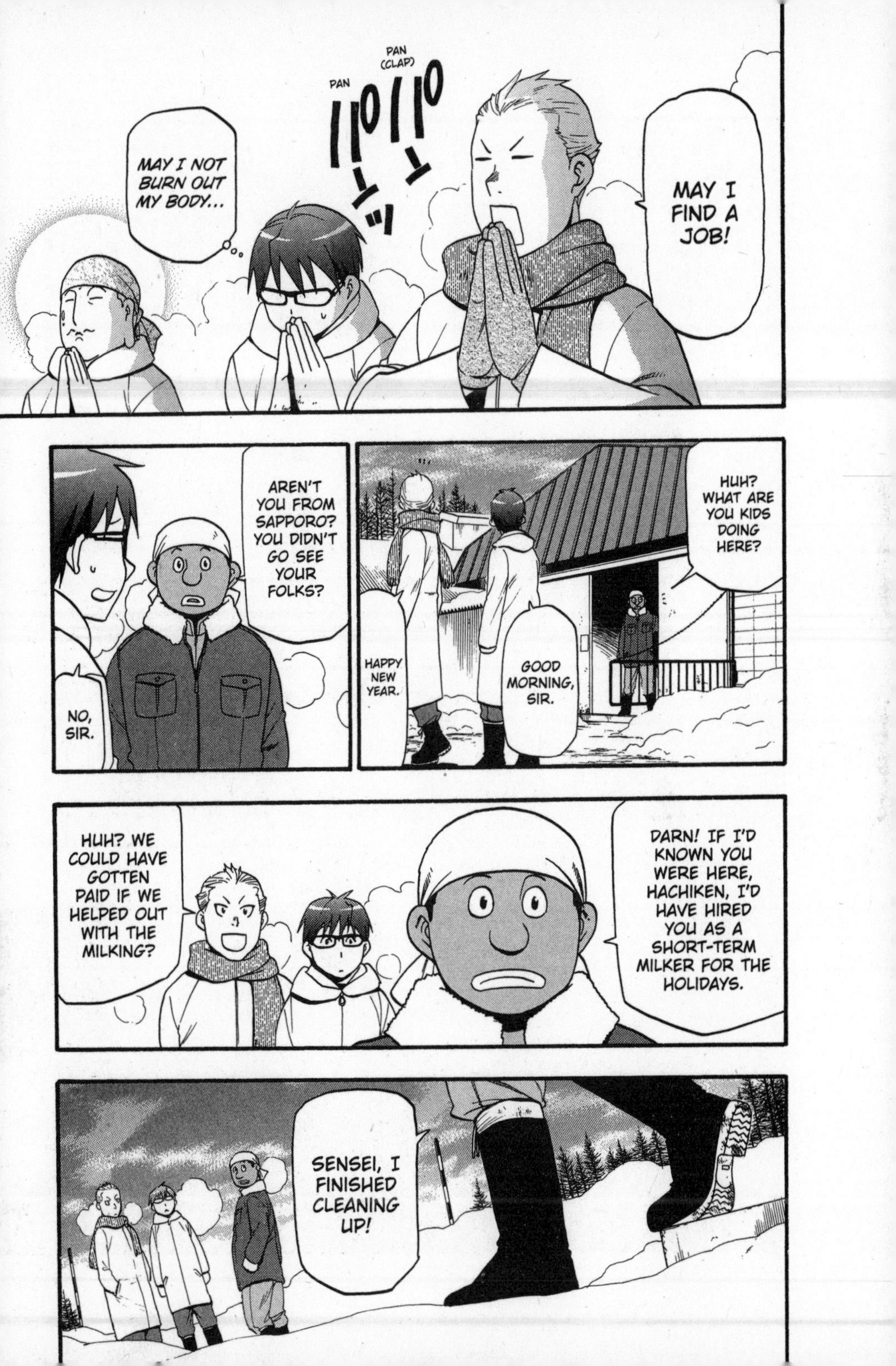
MAY I FIND A JOB!
PAN (CLAP)
PAN
MAY I NOT BURN OUT MY BODY...
HUH? WHAT ARE YOU KIDS DOING HERE?
GOOD MORNING, SIR.
HAPPY NEW YEAR.
AREN'T YOU FROM SAPPORO? YOU DIDN'T GO SEE YOUR FOLKS?
NO, SIR.
DARN! IF I'D KNOWN YOU WERE HERE, HACHIKEN, I'D HAVE HIRED YOU AS A SHORT-TERM MILKER FOR THE HOLIDAYS.
HUH? WE COULD HAVE GOTTEN PAID IF WE HELPED OUT WITH THE MILKING?
SENSEI, I FINISHED CLEANING UP!

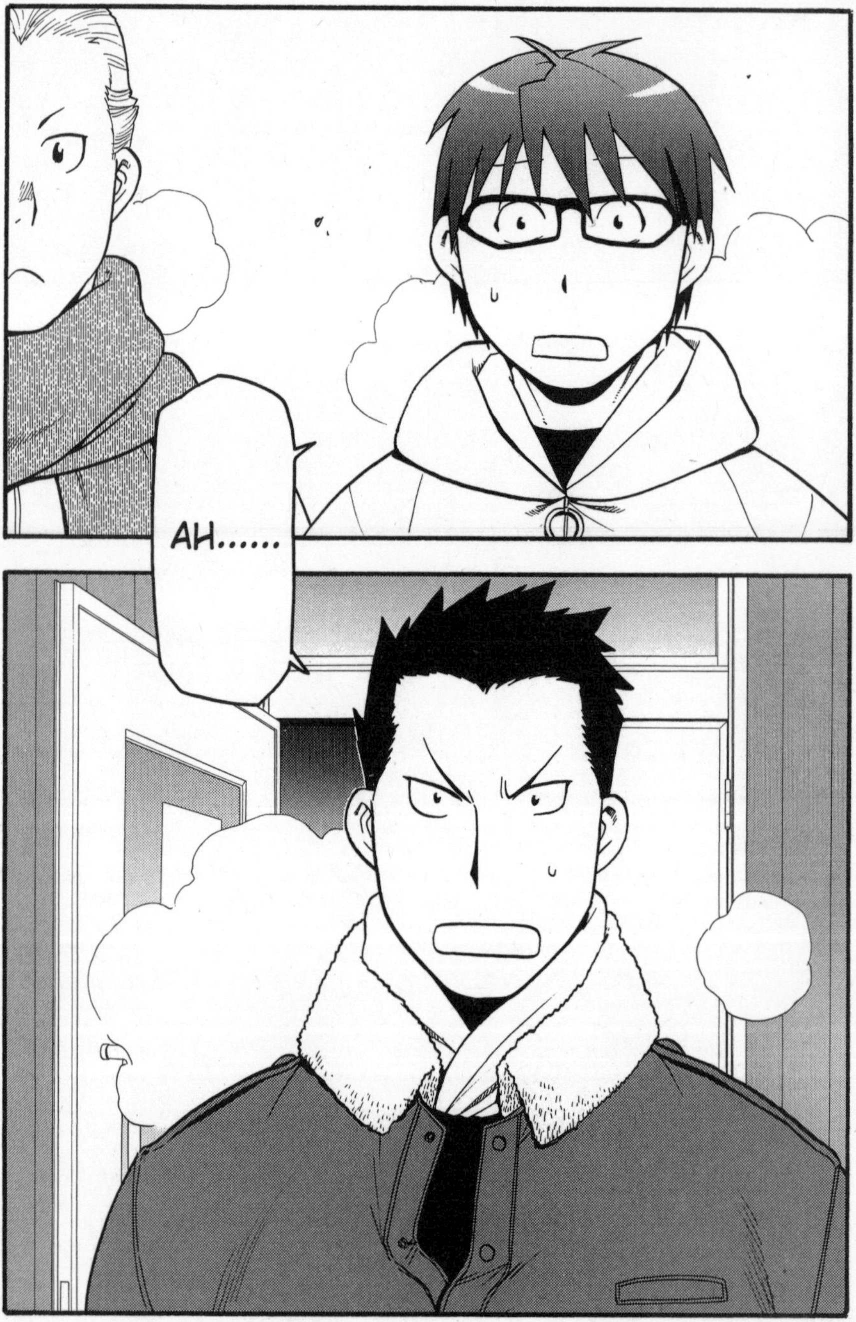
AH......

Silver Spoon

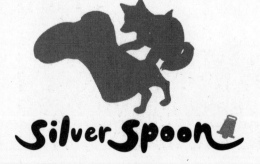

BLACK KING

JAPANESE
DRAFT HORSE

OWNED BY
EZO AG

Chapter 81: Tale of Winter ⑱

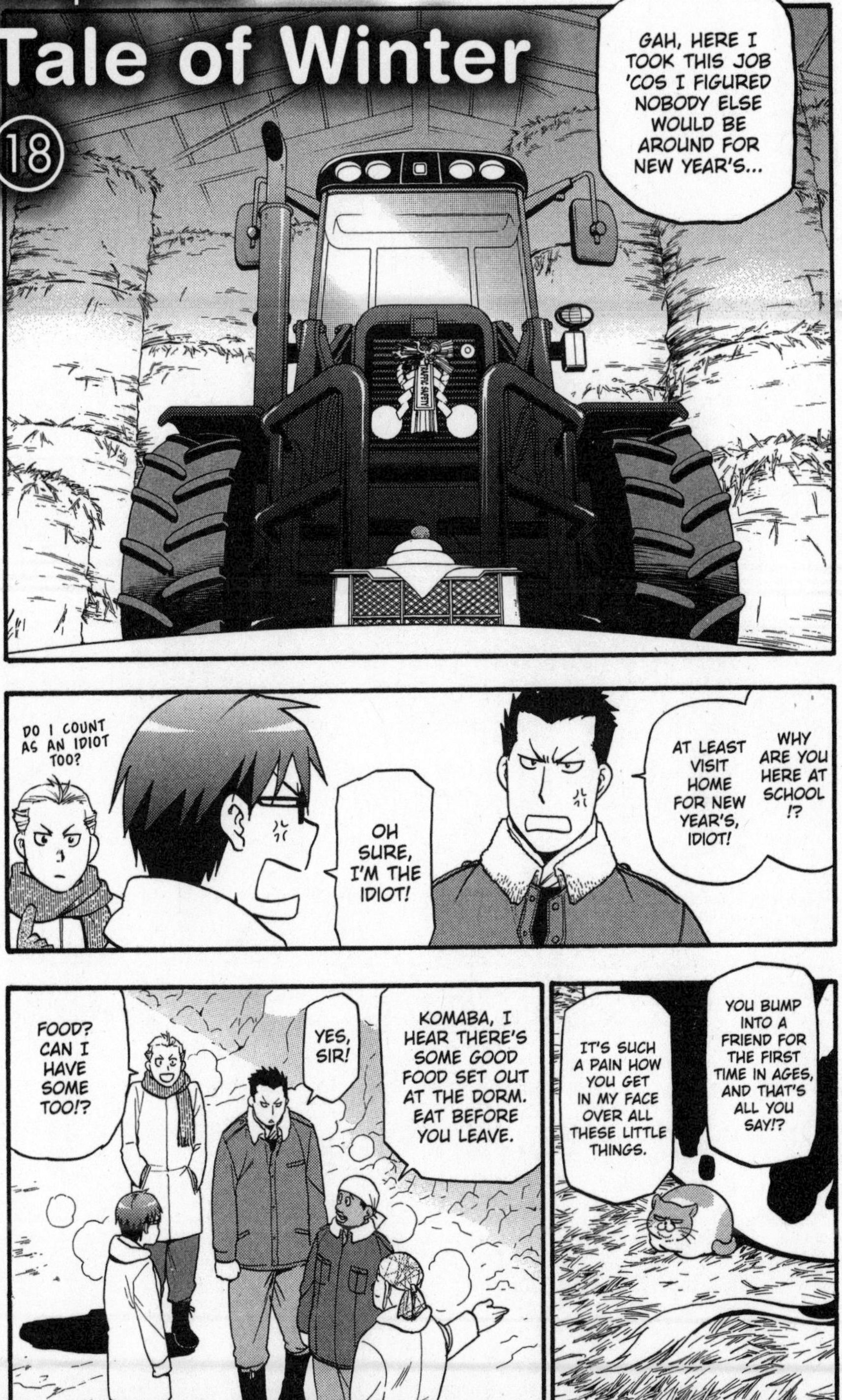
GAH, HERE I TOOK THIS JOB 'COS I FIGURED NOBODY ELSE WOULD BE AROUND FOR NEW YEAR'S...
WHY ARE YOU HERE AT SCHOOL!?
AT LEAST VISIT HOME FOR NEW YEAR'S, IDIOT!
OH SURE, I'M THE IDIOT!
DO I COUNT AS AN IDIOT TOO?
YOU BUMP INTO A FRIEND FOR THE FIRST TIME IN AGES, AND THAT'S ALL YOU SAY!?
IT'S SUCH A PAIN HOW YOU GET IN MY FACE OVER ALL THESE LITTLE THINGS.
KOMABA, I HEAR THERE'S SOME GOOD FOOD SET OUT AT THE DORM. EAT BEFORE YOU LEAVE.
YES, SIR!
FOOD? CAN I HAVE SOME TOO!?

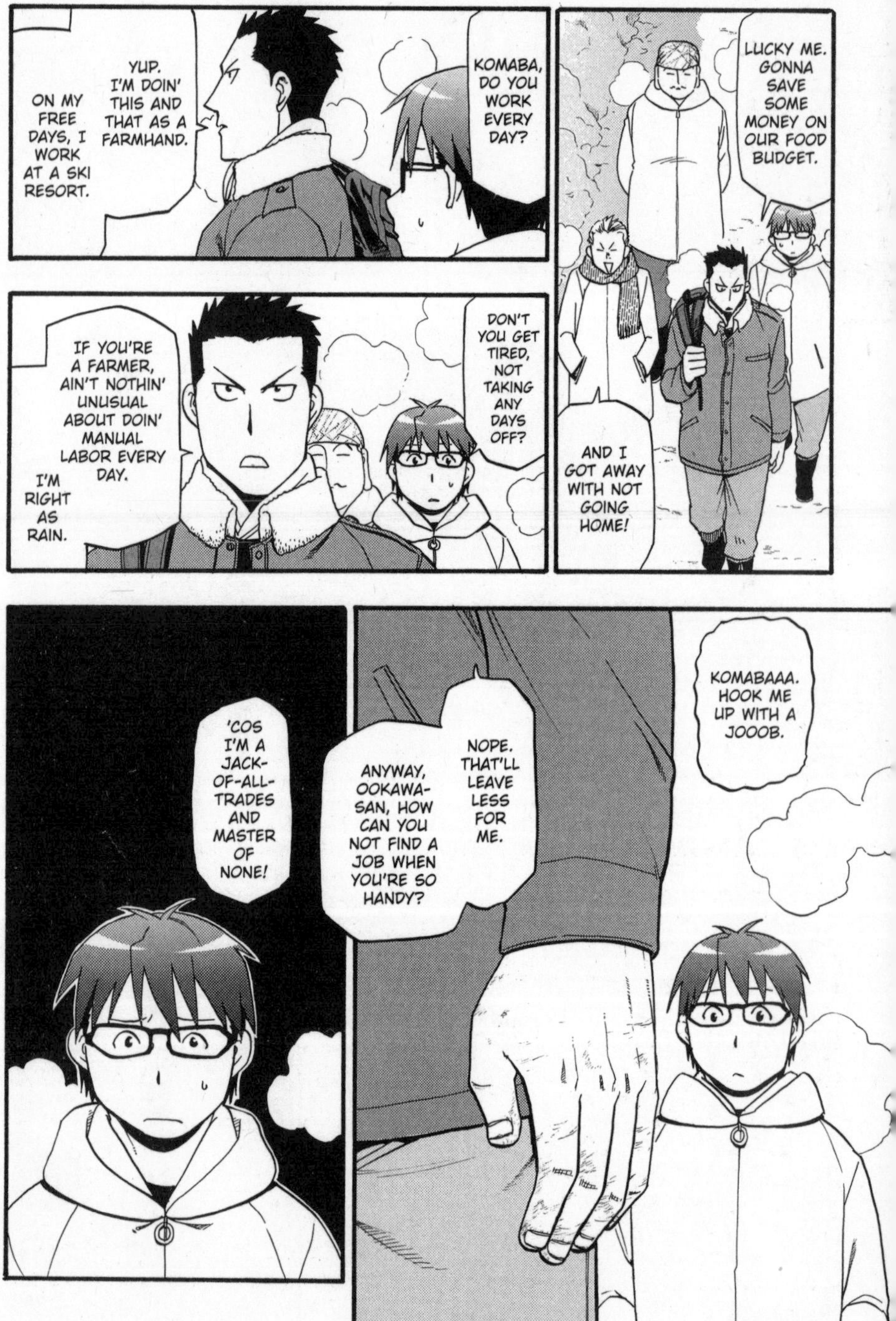
LUCKY ME. GONNA SAVE SOME MONEY ON OUR FOOD BUDGET.
AND I GOT AWAY WITH NOT GOING HOME!
KOMABA, DO YOU WORK EVERY DAY?
YUP. I'M DOIN' THIS AND THAT AS A FARMHAND.
ON MY FREE DAYS, I WORK AT A SKI RESORT.
DON'T YOU GET TIRED, NOT TAKING ANY DAYS OFF?
IF YOU'RE A FARMER, AIN'T NOTHIN' UNUSUAL ABOUT DOIN' MANUAL LABOR EVERY DAY.
I'M RIGHT AS RAIN.
KOMABAAA. HOOK ME UP WITH A JOOOB.
NOPE. THAT'LL LEAVE LESS FOR ME.
ANYWAY, OOKAWA-SAN, HOW CAN YOU NOT FIND A JOB WHEN YOU'RE SO HANDY?
'COS I'M A JACK-OF-ALL-TRADES AND MASTER OF NONE!

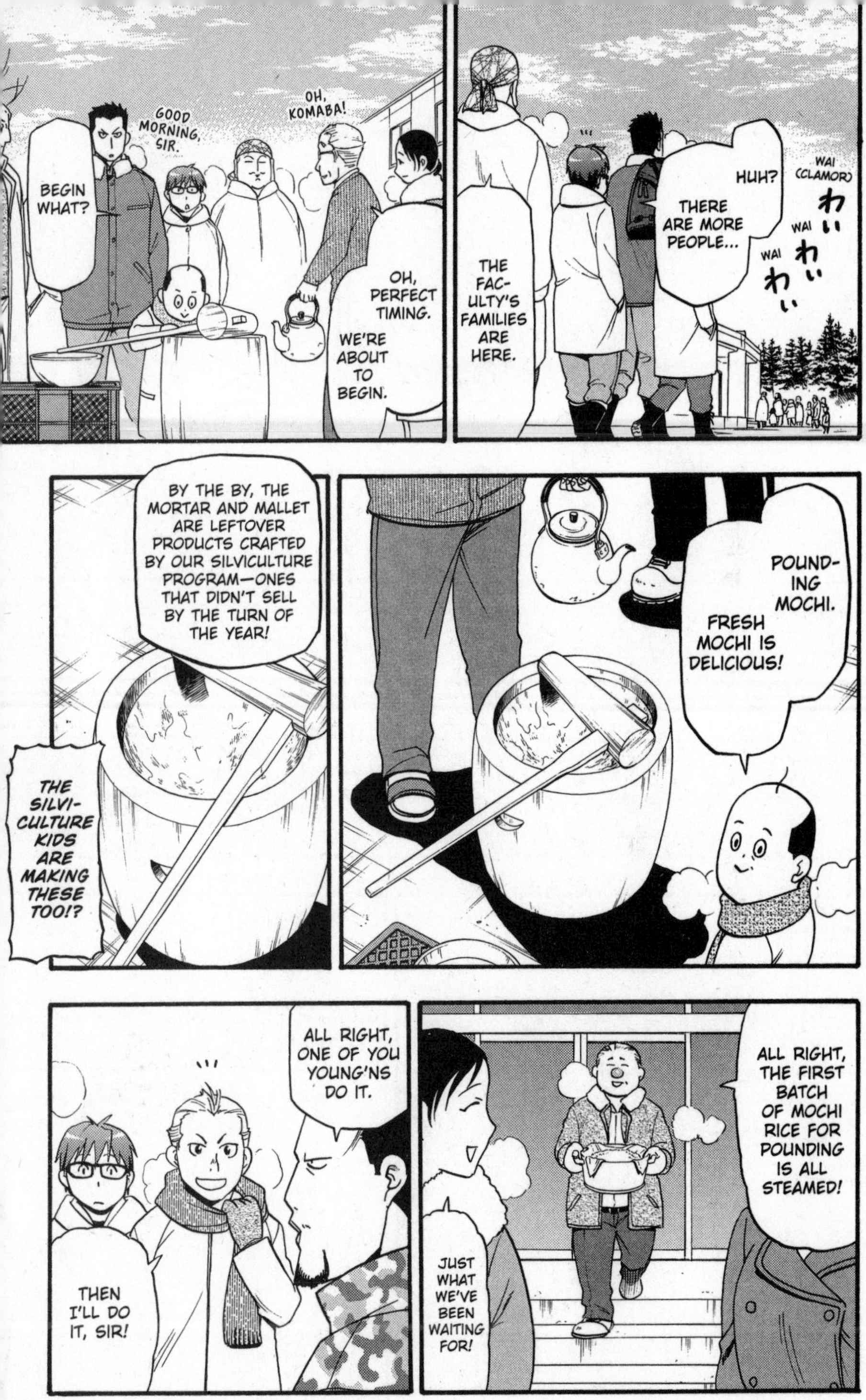
WAI (CLAMOR) わい
WAI わい
WAI わい
HUH?
THERE ARE MORE PEOPLE...
THE FAC-ULTY'S FAMILIES ARE HERE.
OH, KOMABA!
GOOD MORNING, SIR.
OH, PERFECT TIMING.
WE'RE ABOUT TO BEGIN.
BEGIN WHAT?
POUNDING MOCHI.
FRESH MOCHI IS DELICIOUS!
BY THE BY, THE MORTAR AND MALLET ARE LEFTOVER PRODUCTS CRAFTED BY OUR SILVICULTURE PROGRAM—ONES THAT DIDN'T SELL BY THE TURN OF THE YEAR!
THE SILVI-CULTURE KIDS ARE MAKING THESE TOO!?
ALL RIGHT, THE FIRST BATCH OF MOCHI RICE FOR POUNDING IS ALL STEAMED!
JUST WHAT WE'VE BEEN WAITING FOR!
ALL RIGHT, ONE OF YOU YOUNG'NS DO IT.
THEN I'LL DO IT, SIR!

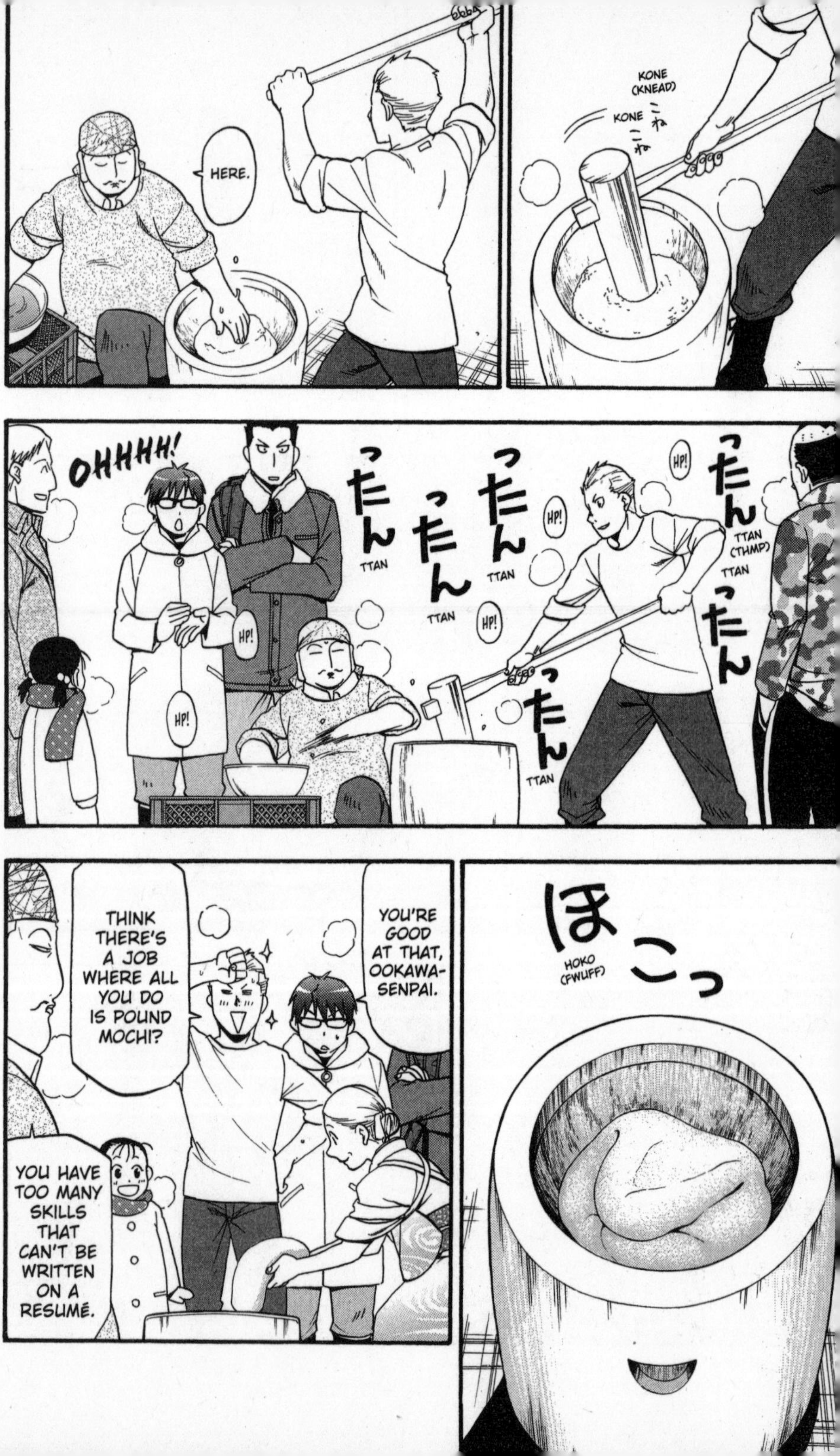

KONE (KNEAD)
こね
KONE
こね
HERE.
HP!
ったん
TTAN (THMP)
TTAN
ったん
ったん
TTAN
ったん
TTAN
HP!
ったん
TTAN
HP!
ったん
TTAN
HP!
HP!
OHHHH!
ほこっ
HOKO (FWUFF)
YOU'RE GOOD AT THAT, OOKAWA-SENPAI.
THINK THERE'S A JOB WHERE ALL YOU DO IS POUND MOCHI?
YOU HAVE TOO MANY SKILLS THAT CAN'T BE WRITTEN ON A RESUMÉ.

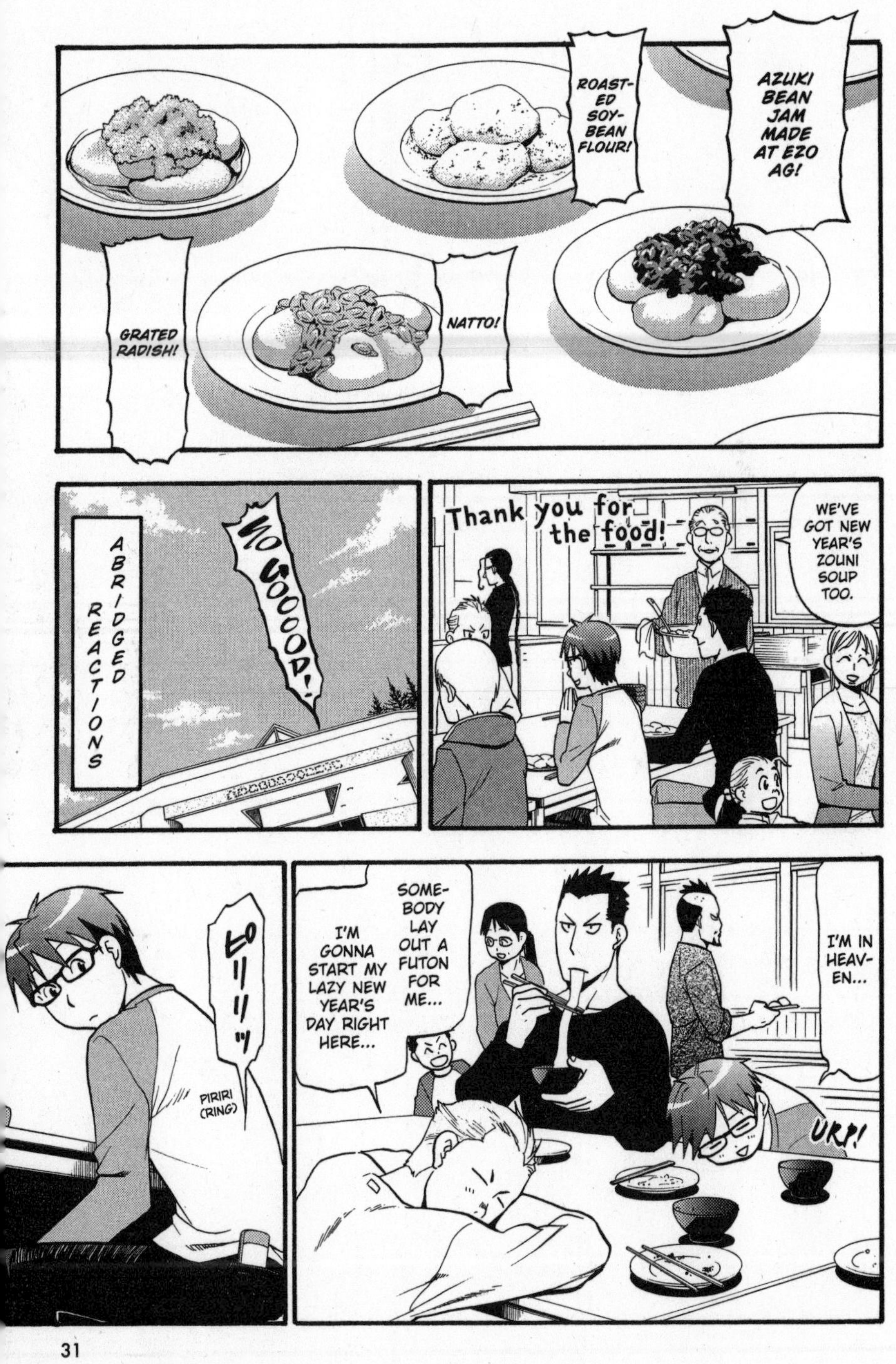
AZUKI BEAN JAM MADE AT EZO AG!
ROASTED SOYBEAN FLOUR!
NATTO!
GRATED RADISH!
WE'VE GOT NEW YEAR'S ZOUNI SOUP TOO.
Thank you for the food!
SO GOOOOOD!
ABRIDGED REACTIONS
I'M IN HEAVEN...
URP!
SOMEBODY LAY OUT A FUTON FOR ME...
I'M GONNA START MY LAZY NEW YEAR'S DAY RIGHT HERE...
ピリリッ
PIRIRI (RING)

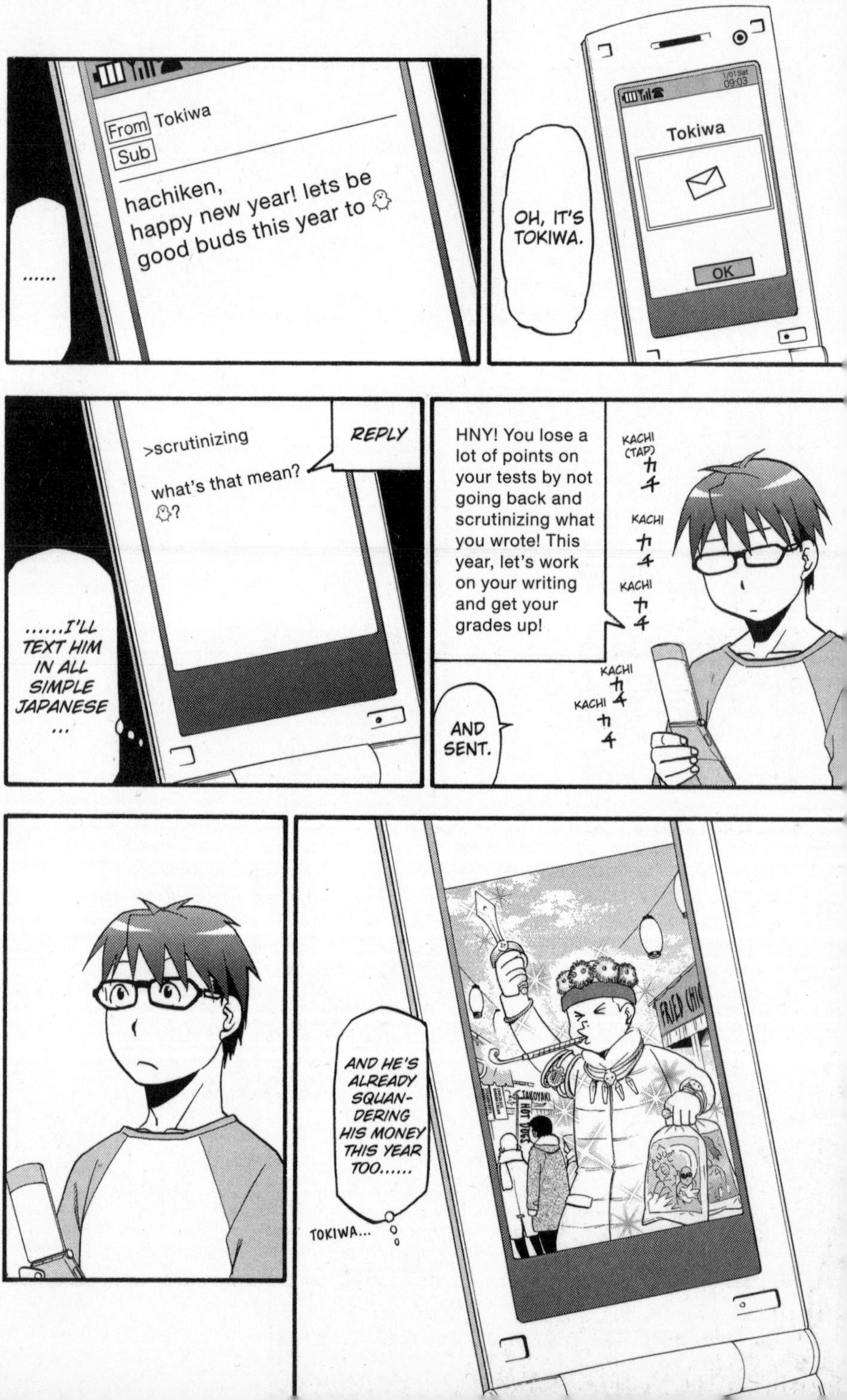
1/01 Sat
09:03
Tokiwa
OK
OH, IT'S TOKIWA.
From Tokiwa
Sub
hachiken,
happy new year! lets be good buds this year to
......
HNY! You lose a lot of points on your tests by not going back and scrutinizing what you wrote! This year, let's work on your writing and get your grades up!
KACHI (TAP)
KACHI
KACHI
KACHI
KACHI
AND SENT.
REPLY
>scrutinizing
what's that mean?
?
......I'LL TEXT HIM IN ALL SIMPLE JAPANESE ...
AND HE'S ALREADY SQUANDERING HIS MONEY THIS YEAR TOO......
TOKIWA...
TAKOYAKI
HOT DOGS

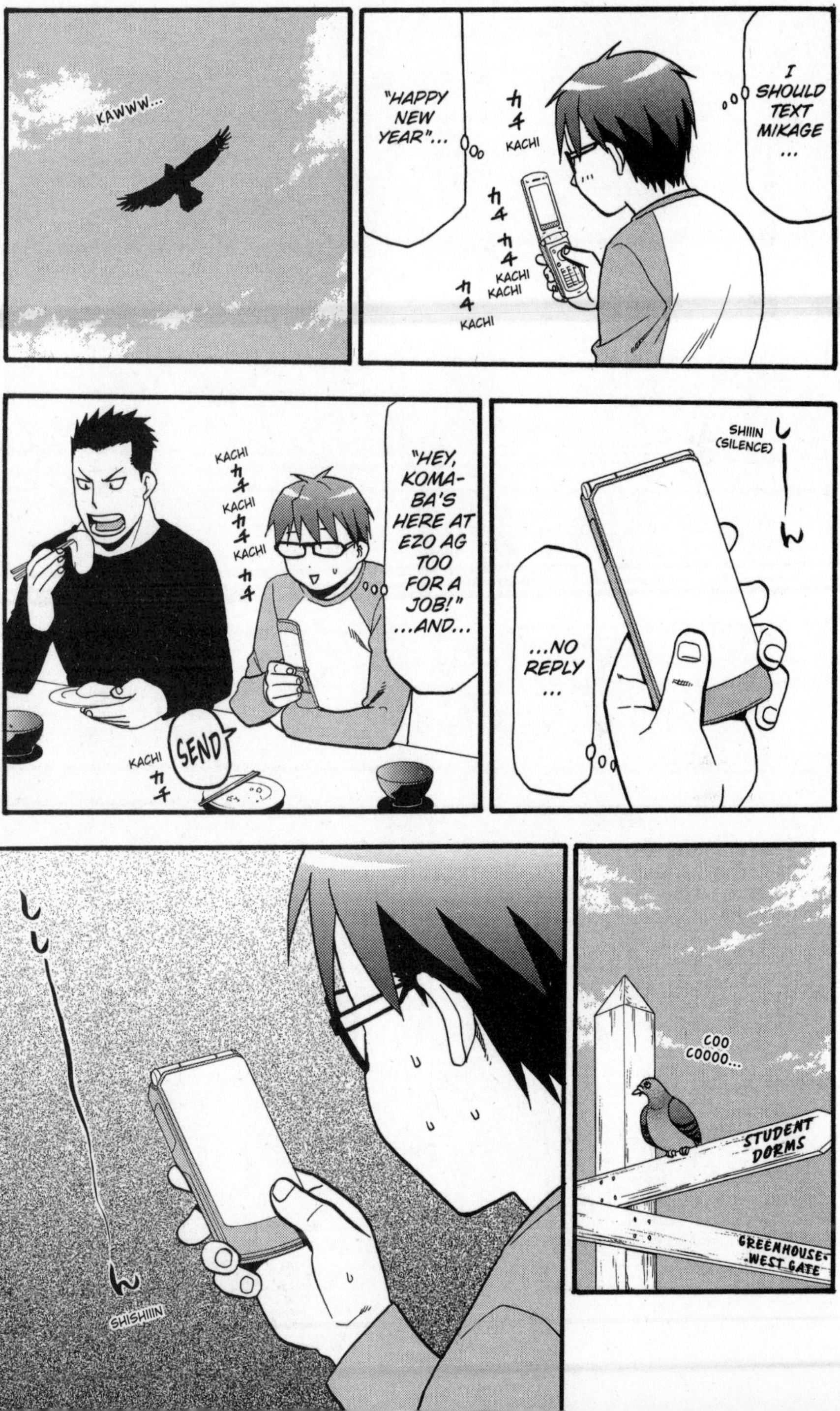
I SHOULD TEXT MIKAGE ...
"HAPPY NEW YEAR"...
カチ
KACHI
カチ カチ
KACHI KACHI
カチ
KACHI
KAWWW...
しーん
SHIIIN (SILENCE)
...NO REPLY ...
"HEY, KOMA-BA'S HERE AT EZO AG TOO FOR A JOB!" ...AND...
KACHI
カチ
KACHI
カチ
KACHI
カチ
SEND
KACHI
カチ
COO COOOO...
STUDENT DORMS
GREENHOUSE WEST GATE
しいいーん
SHISHIIIN

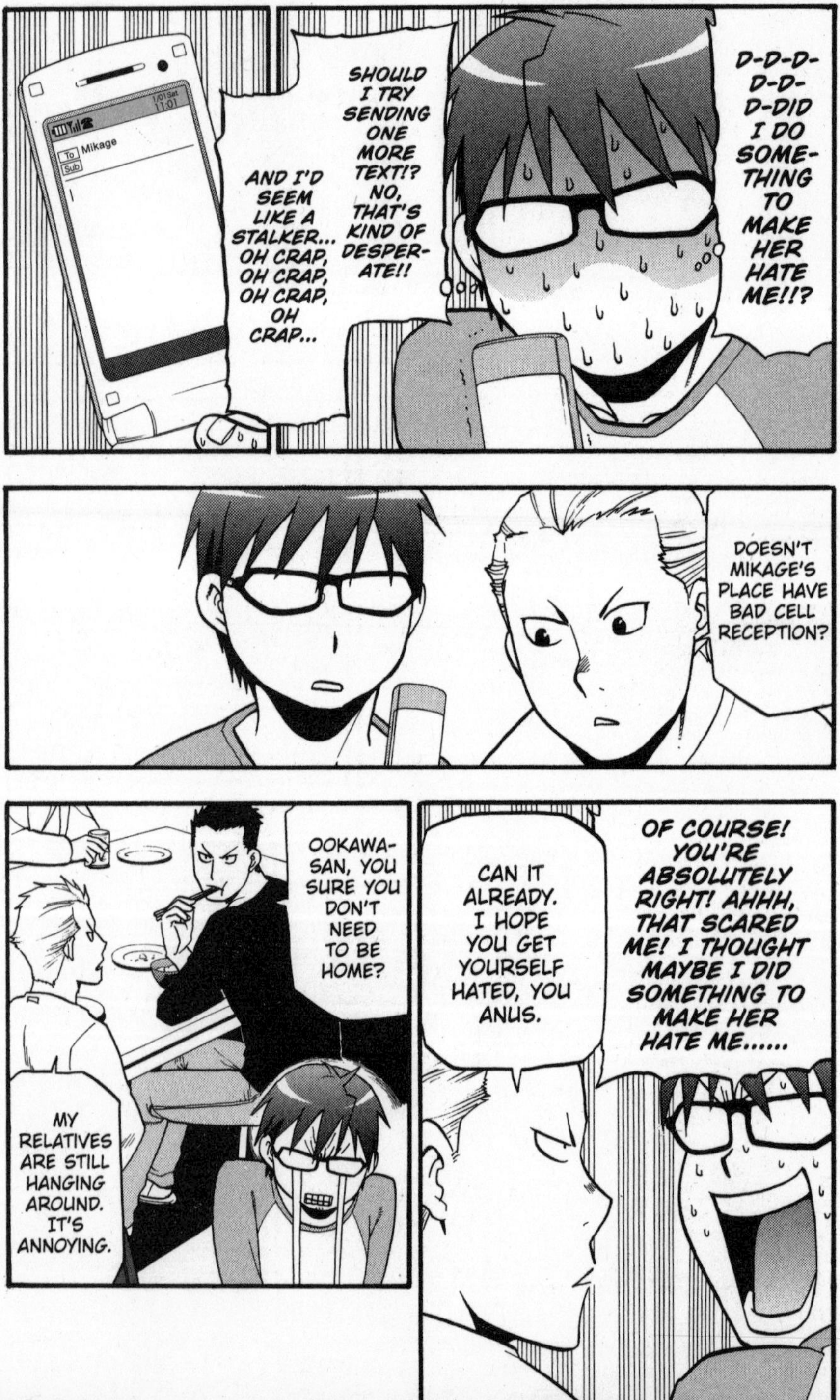
D-D-D-D-D-D-DID I DO SOMETHING TO MAKE HER HATE ME!!?
SHOULD I TRY SENDING ONE MORE TEXT!? NO, THAT'S KIND OF DESPERATE!!
AND I'D SEEM LIKE A STALKER... OH CRAP, OH CRAP, OH CRAP, OH CRAP...
To
Mikage
Sub
DOESN'T MIKAGE'S PLACE HAVE BAD CELL RECEPTION?
OF COURSE! YOU'RE ABSOLUTELY RIGHT! AHHH, THAT SCARED ME! I THOUGHT MAYBE I DID SOMETHING TO MAKE HER HATE ME......
CAN IT ALREADY. I HOPE YOU GET YOURSELF HATED, YOU ANUS.
OOKAWA-SAN, YOU SURE YOU DON'T NEED TO BE HOME?
MY RELATIVES ARE STILL HANGING AROUND. IT'S ANNOYING.

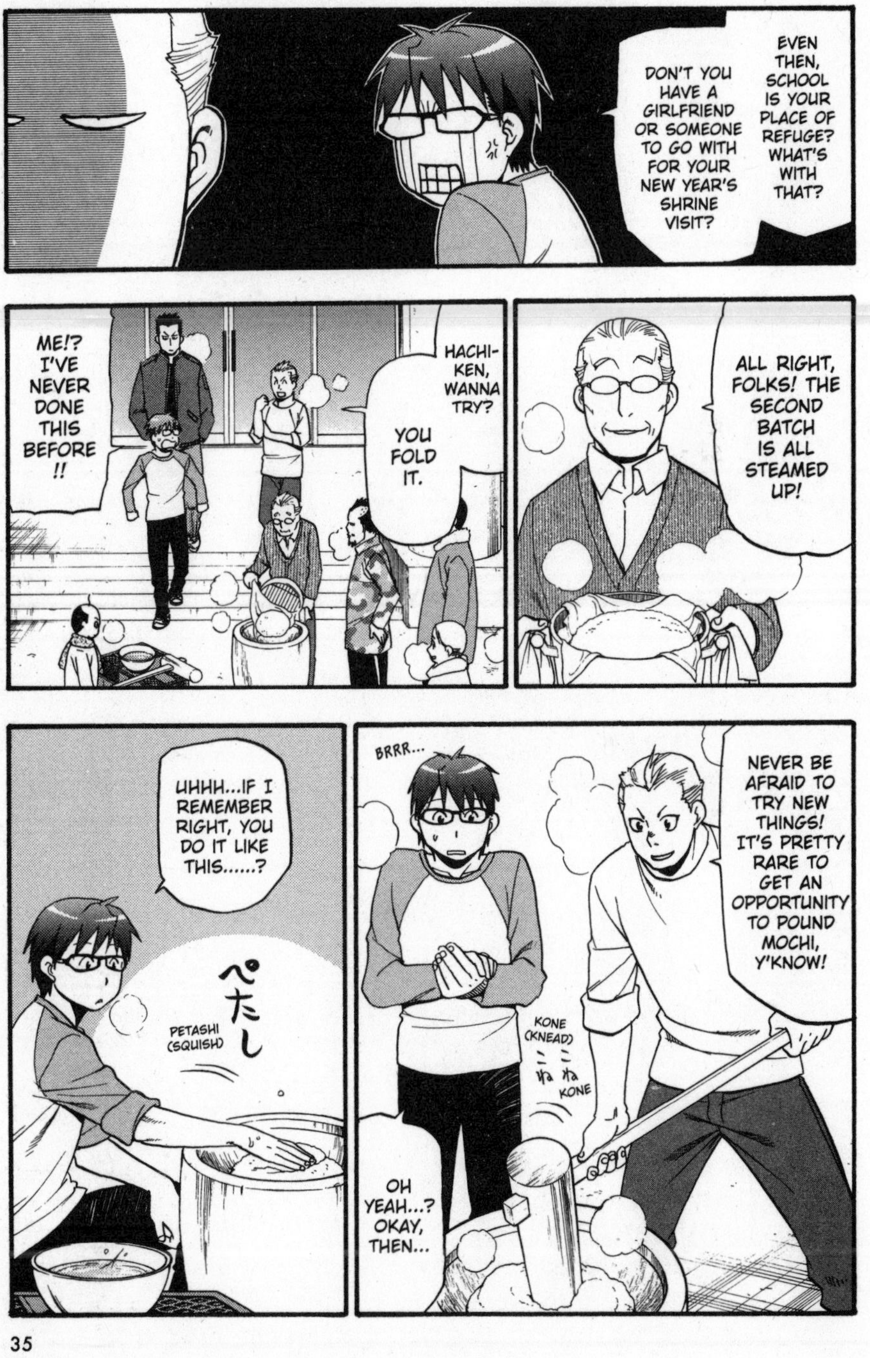
EVEN THEN, SCHOOL IS YOUR PLACE OF REFUGE? WHAT'S WITH THAT?
DON'T YOU HAVE A GIRLFRIEND OR SOMEONE TO GO WITH FOR YOUR NEW YEAR'S SHRINE VISIT?
ALL RIGHT, FOLKS! THE SECOND BATCH IS ALL STEAMED UP!
HACHI-KEN, WANNA TRY?
YOU FOLD IT.
ME!? I'VE NEVER DONE THIS BEFORE !!
NEVER BE AFRAID TO TRY NEW THINGS! IT'S PRETTY RARE TO GET AN OPPORTUNITY TO POUND MOCHI, Y'KNOW!
BRRR...
こね こね
KONE (KNEAD) KONE
OH YEAH...? OKAY, THEN...
UHHH...IF I REMEMBER RIGHT, YOU DO IT LIKE THIS......?
ぺたし
PETASHI (SQUISH)

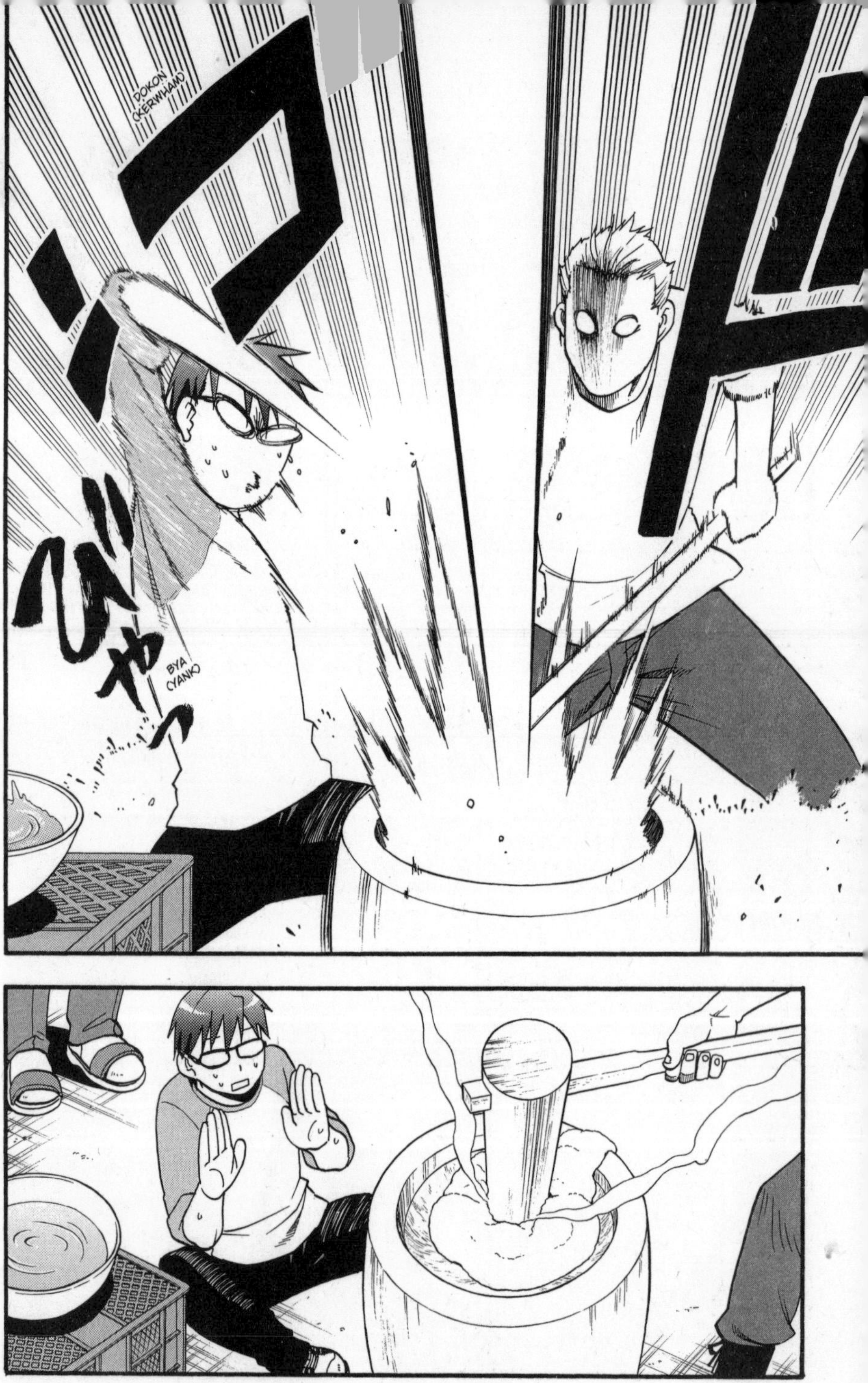
DOKON (KERWHAM)
BYA (YANK)

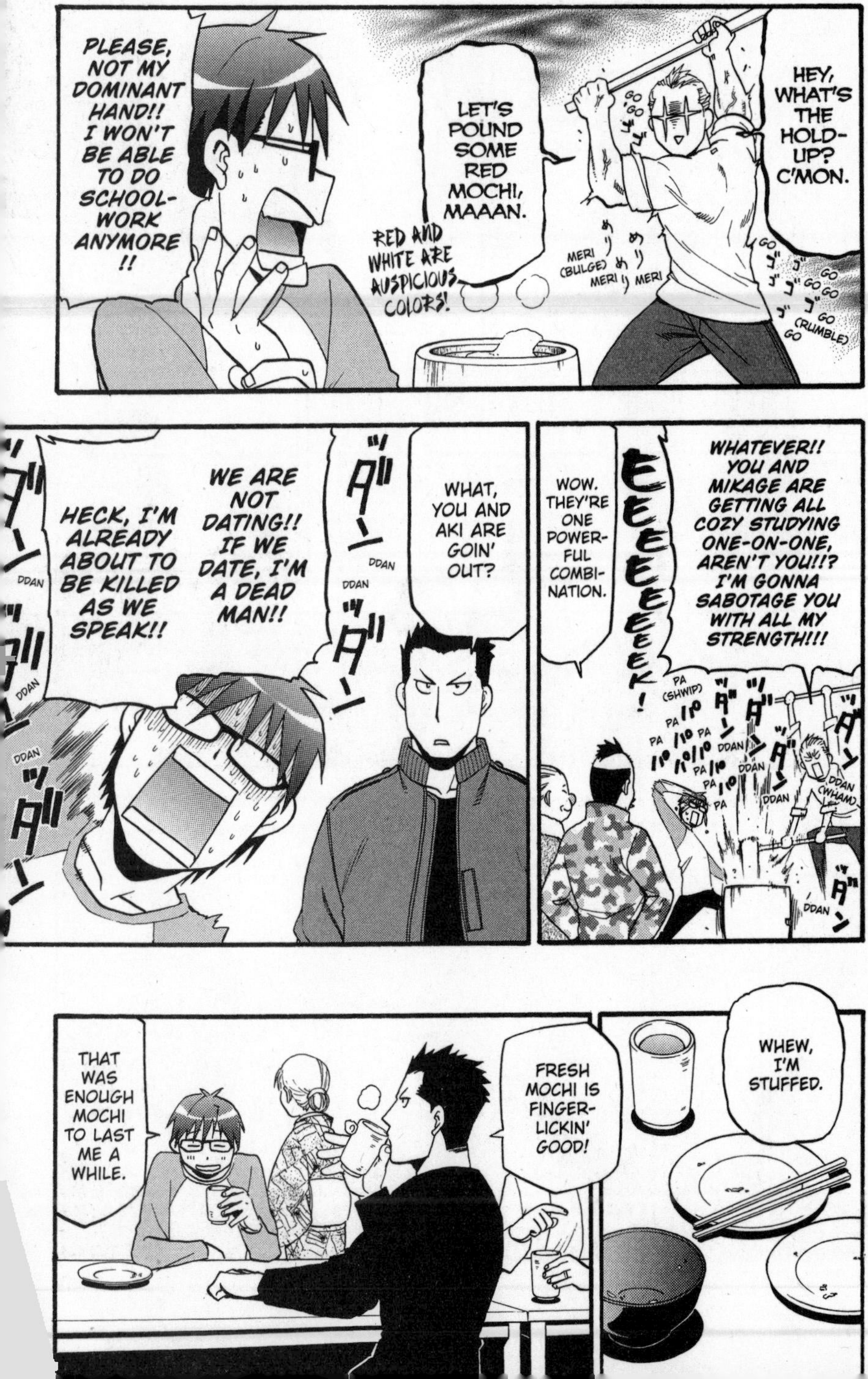
HEY, WHAT'S THE HOLD-UP? C'MON.
GO GO
LET'S POUND SOME RED MOCHI, MAAAN.
MERI (BULGE) MERI MERI MERI
GO GO GO GO GO GO (RUMBLE)
RED AND WHITE ARE AUSPICIOUS COLORS!
PLEASE, NOT MY DOMINANT HAND!! I WON'T BE ABLE TO DO SCHOOL-WORK ANYMORE!!
WHATEVER!! YOU AND MIKAGE ARE GETTING ALL COZY STUDYING ONE-ON-ONE, AREN'T YOU!!? I'M GONNA SABOTAGE YOU WITH ALL MY STRENGTH!!!
EEEEEEEEEK!
WOW. THEY'RE ONE POWERFUL COMBINATION.
PA (SHWIP) PA PA PA PA PA PA PA PA
DDAN DDAN DDAN DDAN (WHAM) DDAN
WHAT, YOU AND AKI ARE GOIN' OUT?
DDAN DDAN
WE ARE NOT DATING!! IF WE DATE, I'M A DEAD MAN!!
HECK, I'M ALREADY ABOUT TO BE KILLED AS WE SPEAK!!
DDAN DDAN DDAN
WHEW, I'M STUFFED.
FRESH MOCHI IS FINGER-LICKIN' GOOD!
THAT WAS ENOUGH MOCHI TO LAST ME A WHILE.

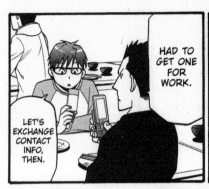

I'VE GOT SOME TIME UNTIL THE EVENING MILKING.
WHAT TO DO?
HUH? HEY, YOU HAVE A CELL PHONE!
HAD TO GET ONE FOR WORK.
LET'S EXCHANGE CONTACT INFO, THEN.
THAT'S A WASTE OF STOR-AGE SPACE.
WHY!?
IF YOU BOYS HAVE TIME, WHY DON'T YOU GO ON YOUR NEW YEAR'S SHRINE VISIT?
HO!
HO!
HO!

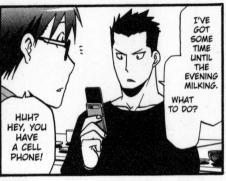

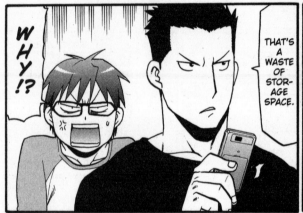

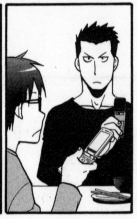

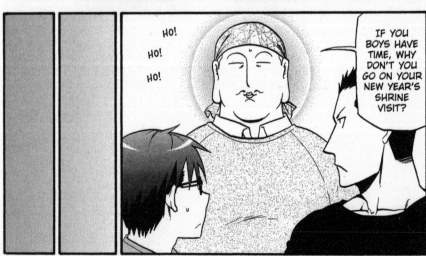

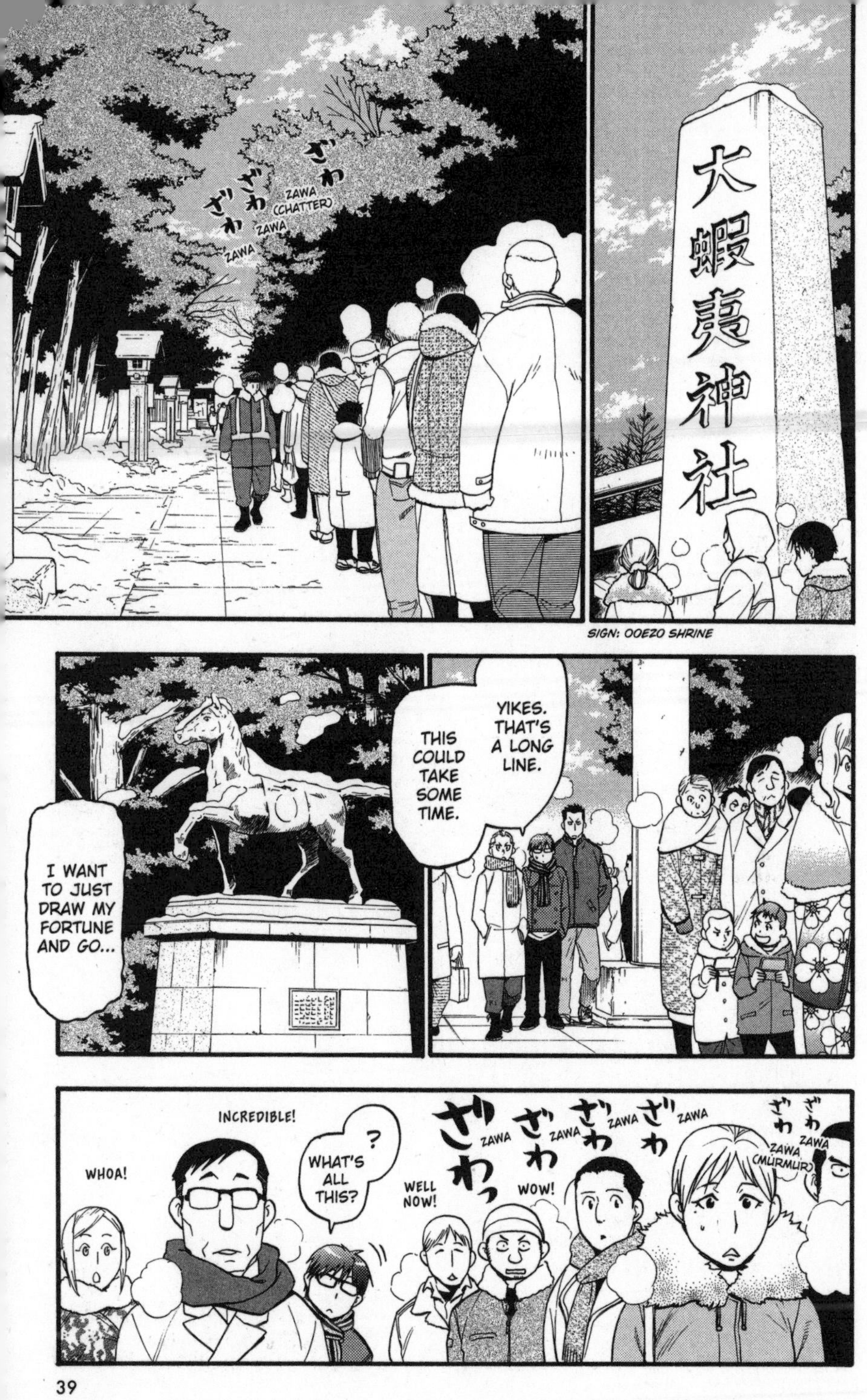
大蝦夷神社
SIGN: OOEZO SHRINE
ざわ ざわ ざわ
ZAWA (CHATTER)
ZAWA
ZAWA
YIKES. THAT'S A LONG LINE.
THIS COULD TAKE SOME TIME.
I WANT TO JUST DRAW MY FORTUNE AND GO...
ざわ ざわ
ZAWA
ZAWA (MURMUR)
ざわ
ZAWA
ざわ
ZAWA
ざわ
ZAWA
ざわっ
ZAWA
WOW!
WELL NOW!
?
WHAT'S ALL THIS?
INCREDIBLE!
WHOA!

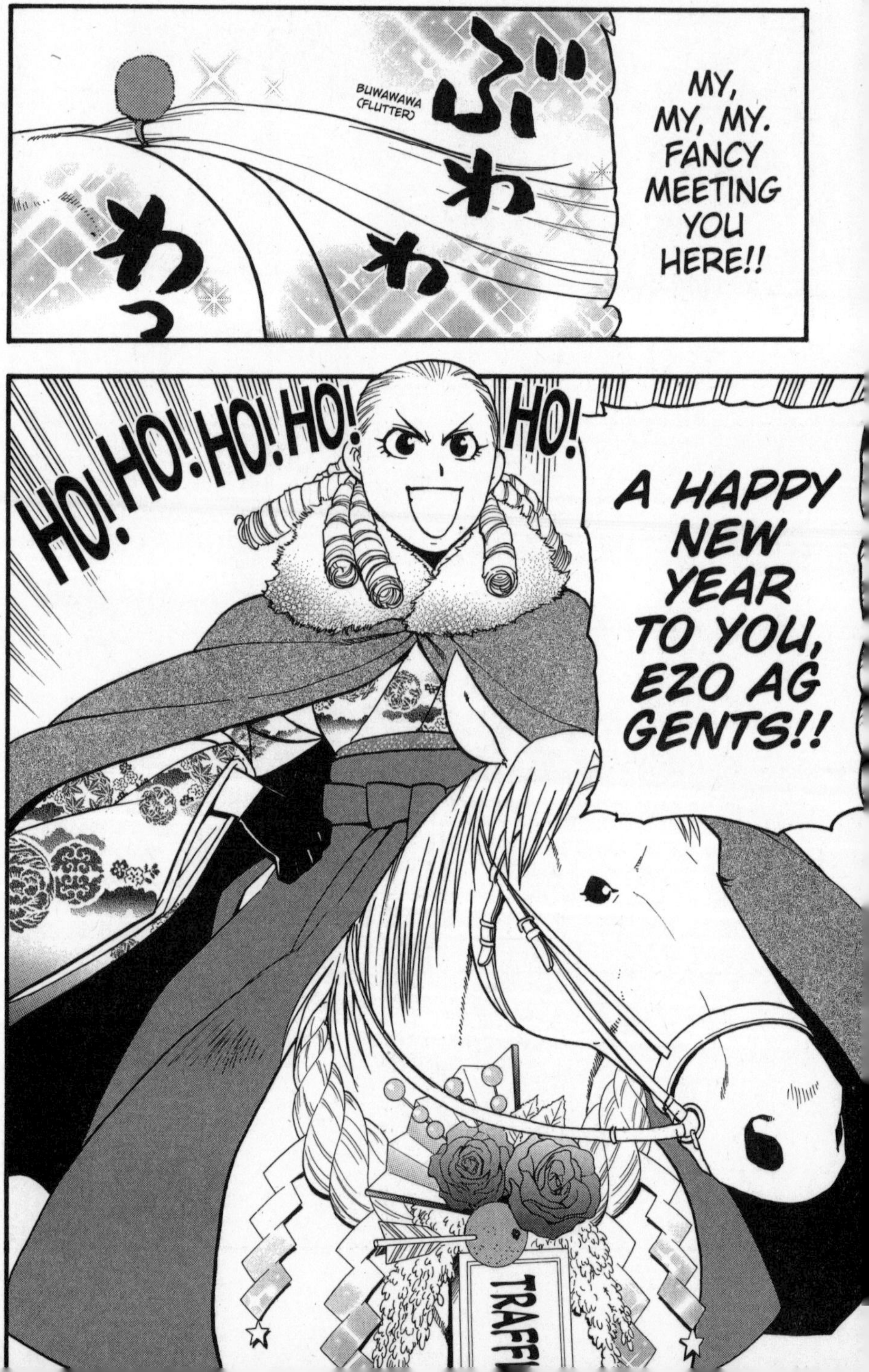
MY, MY, MY. FANCY MEETING YOU HERE!!
ぶわわわっ
BUWAWAWA (FLUTTER)
A HAPPY NEW YEAR TO YOU, EZO AG GENTS!!
HO! HO! HO! HO! HO!
TRAFFI

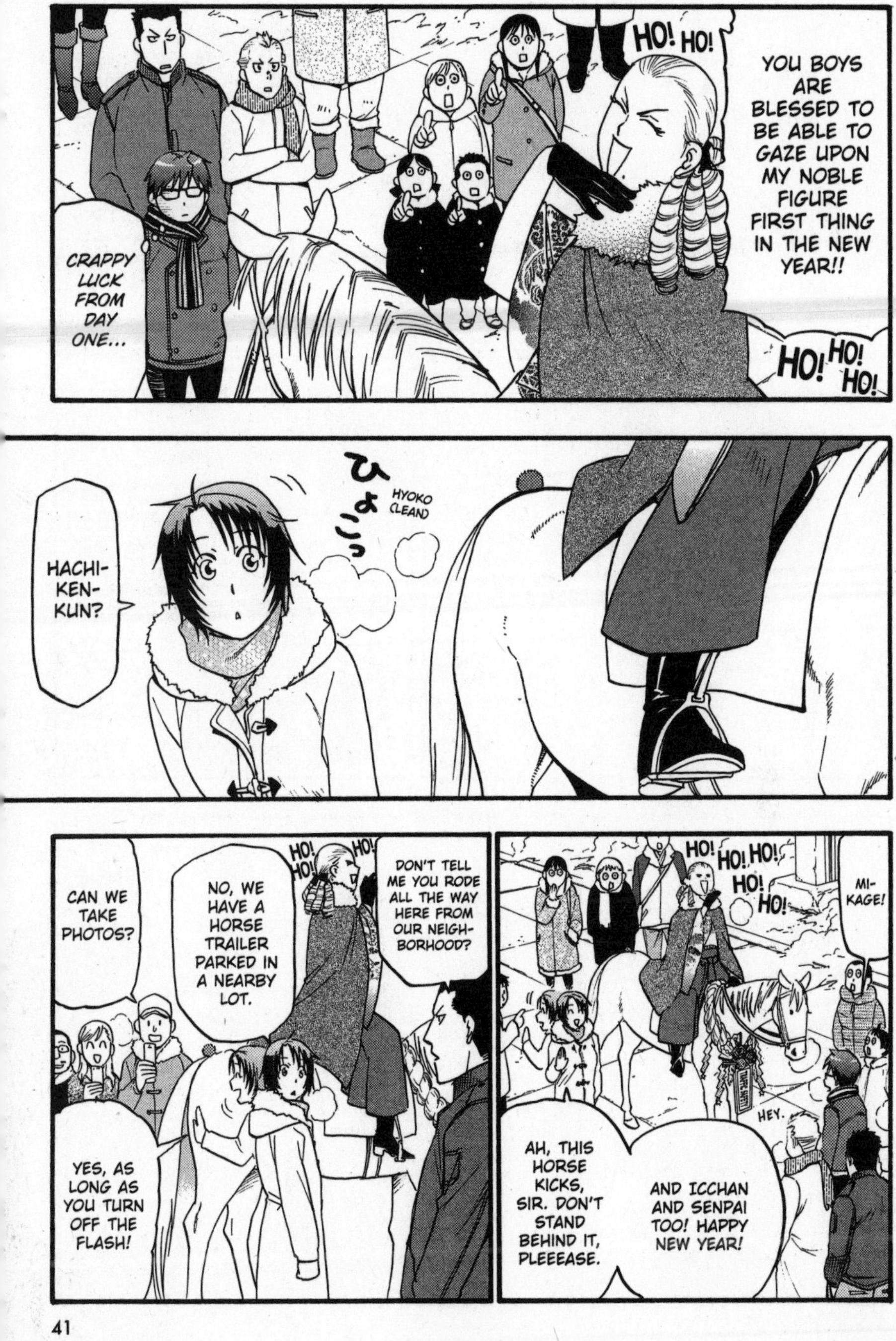
HO! HO!
YOU BOYS ARE BLESSED TO BE ABLE TO GAZE UPON MY NOBLE FIGURE FIRST THING IN THE NEW YEAR!!
HO! HO! HO!
CRAPPY LUCK FROM DAY ONE...
ひょこっ
HYOKO (LEAN)
HACHI-KEN-KUN?
HO! HO! HO! HO! HO!
MI-KAGE!
AND ICCHAN AND SENPAI TOO! HAPPY NEW YEAR!
HEY.
AH, THIS HORSE KICKS, SIR. DON'T STAND BEHIND IT, PLEEEASE.
HO! HO! HO!
DON'T TELL ME YOU RODE ALL THE WAY HERE FROM OUR NEIGH-BORHOOD?
NO, WE HAVE A HORSE TRAILER PARKED IN A NEARBY LOT.
CAN WE TAKE PHOTOS?
YES, AS LONG AS YOU TURN OFF THE FLASH!

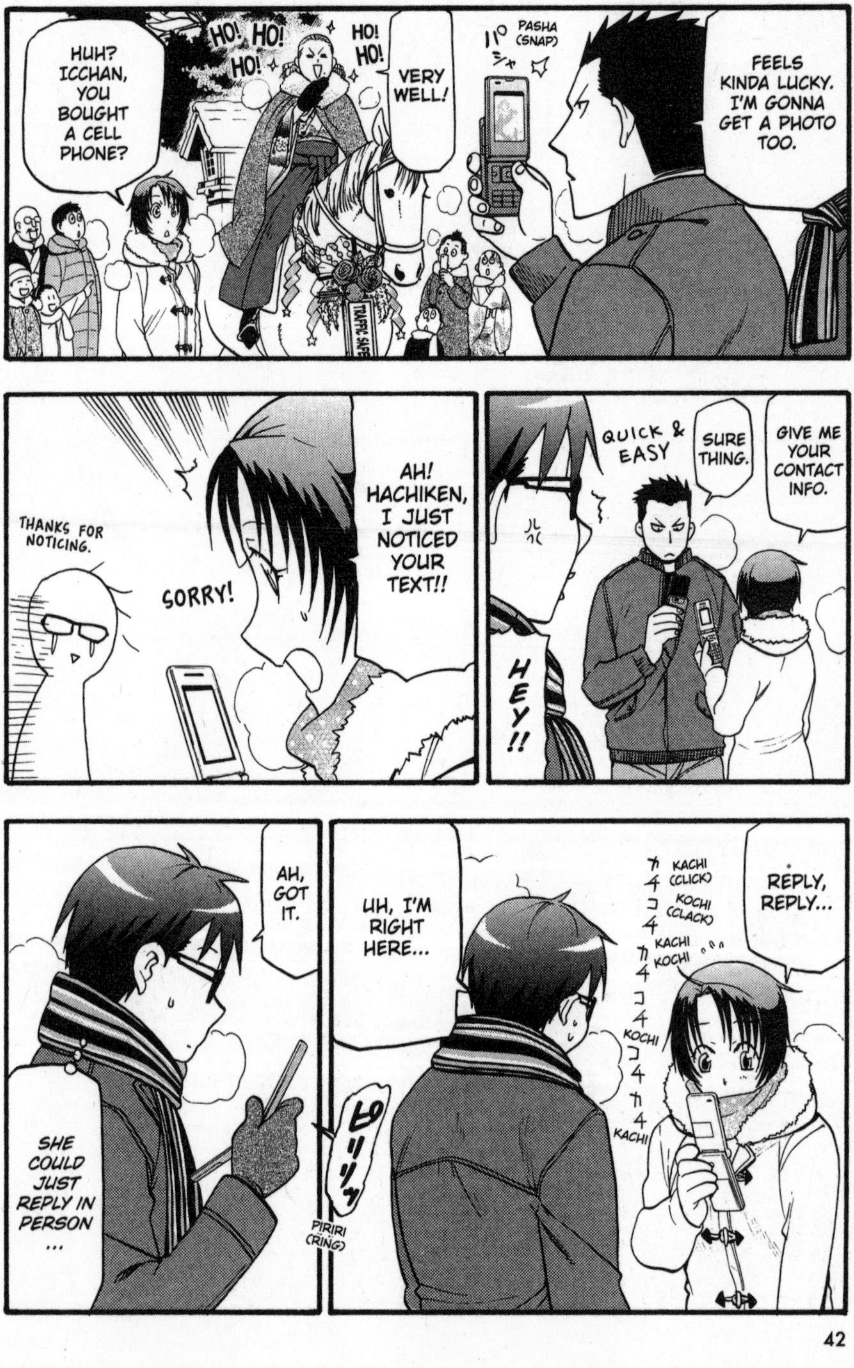

FEELS KINDA LUCKY. I'M GONNA GET A PHOTO TOO.
パシャ
PASHA (SNAP)
VERY WELL!
HO! HO!
HO! HO! HO!
HUH? ICCHAN, YOU BOUGHT A CELL PHONE?
GIVE ME YOUR CONTACT INFO.
SURE THING.
QUICK & EASY
HEY!!
AH! HACHIKEN, I JUST NOTICED YOUR TEXT!!
SORRY!
THANKS FOR NOTICING.
REPLY, REPLY...
KACHI (CLICK)
KOCHI (CLACK)
KACHI KOCHI
KOCHI
KACHI
UH, I'M RIGHT HERE...
AH, GOT IT.
PIRIRI (RING)
SHE COULD JUST REPLY IN PERSON ...

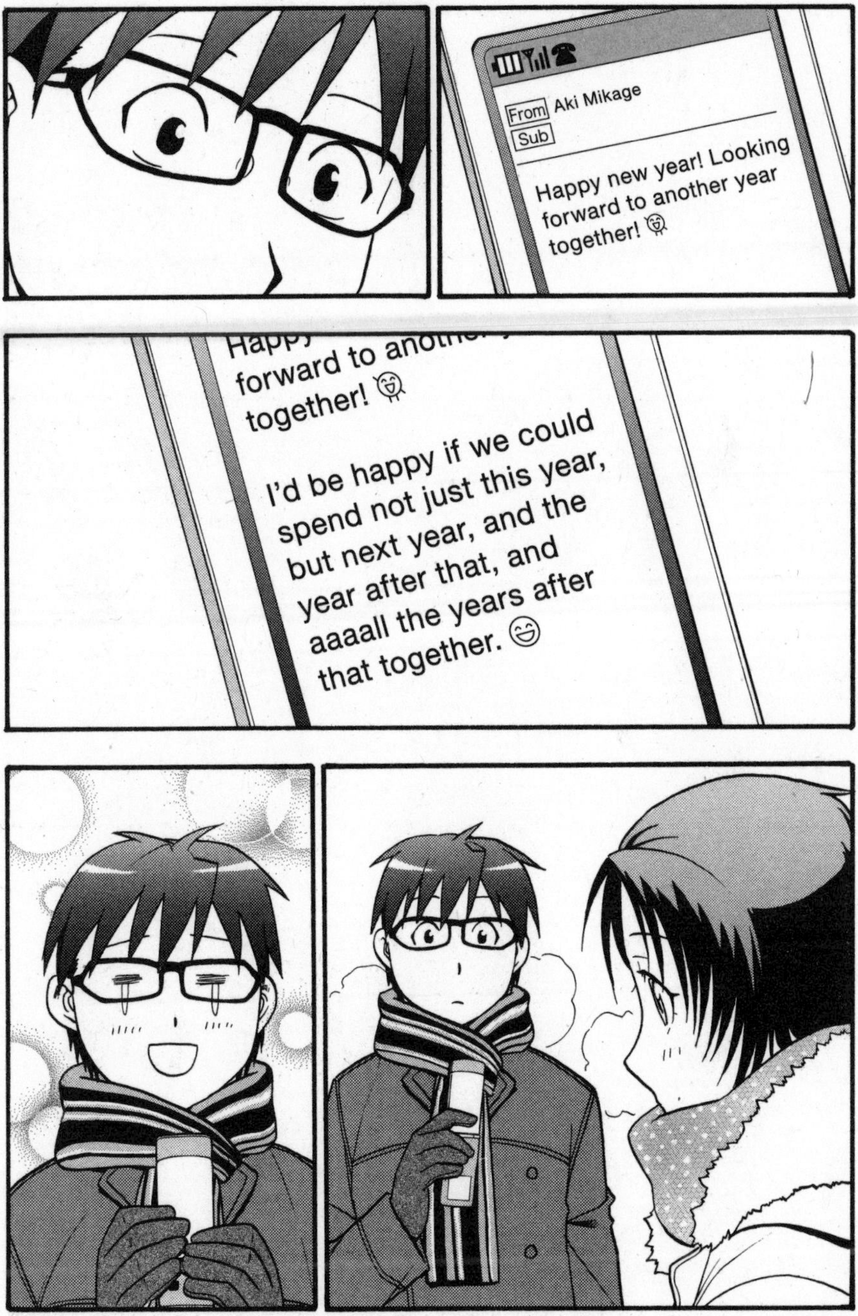
From Aki Mikage
Sub
Happy new year! Looking forward to another year together!
together!
I'd be happy if we could spend not just this year, but next year, and the year after that, and aaaall the years after that together.

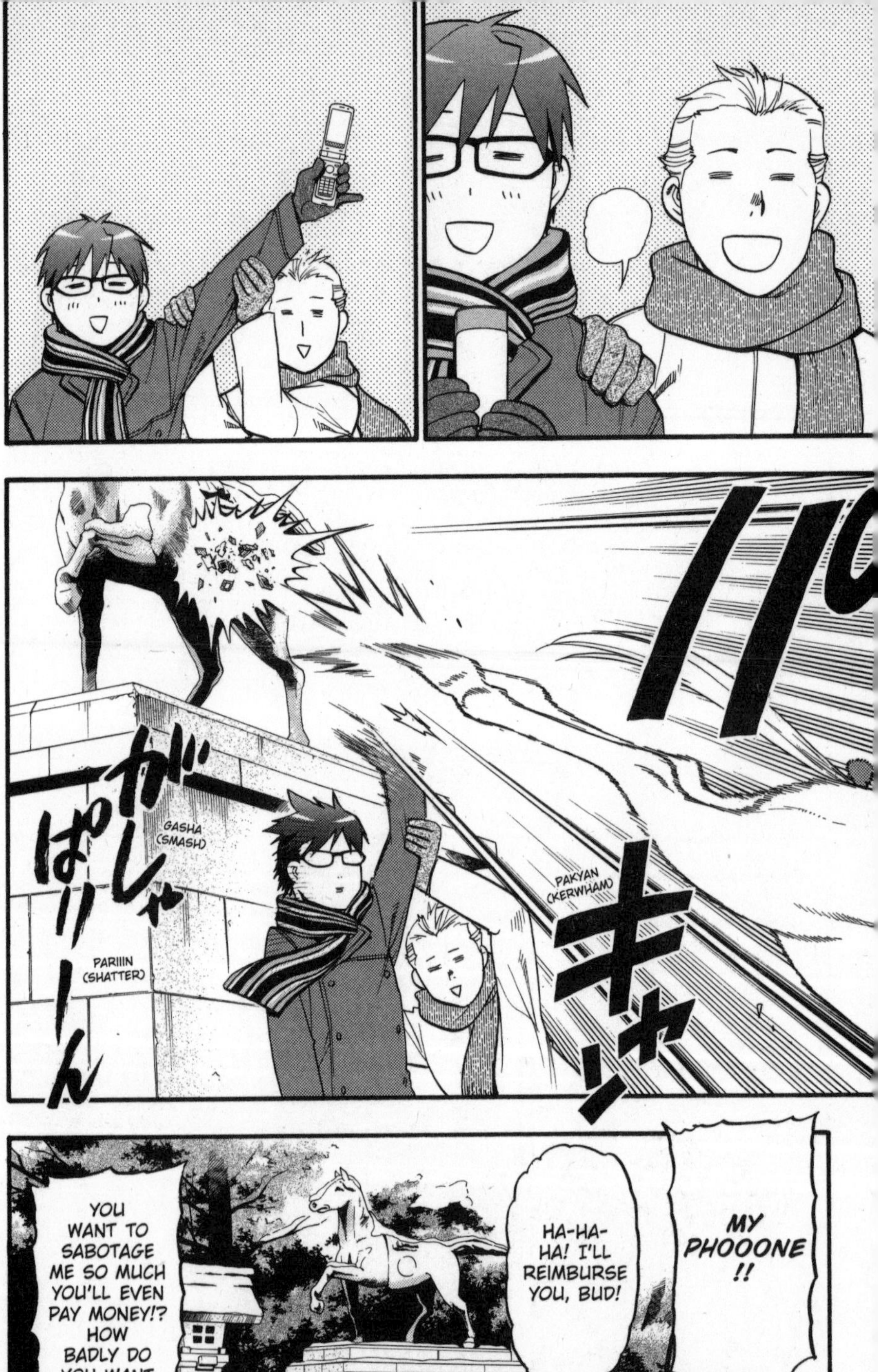

キャン
PAKYAN (KERWHAM)
がしゃ
GASHA (SMASH)
ぱりーん
PARIIN (SHATTER)
MY PHOOONE!!
HA-HA-HA! I'LL REIMBURSE YOU, BUD!
YOU WANT TO SABOTAGE ME SO MUCH YOU'LL EVEN PAY MONEY!? HOW BADLY DO YOU WANT THIS!?

Silver Spoon

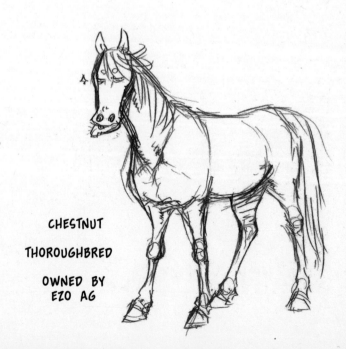

CHESTNUT

THOROUGHBRED

OWNED BY
EZO AG

Chapter 82:
Tale of Winter ⑲

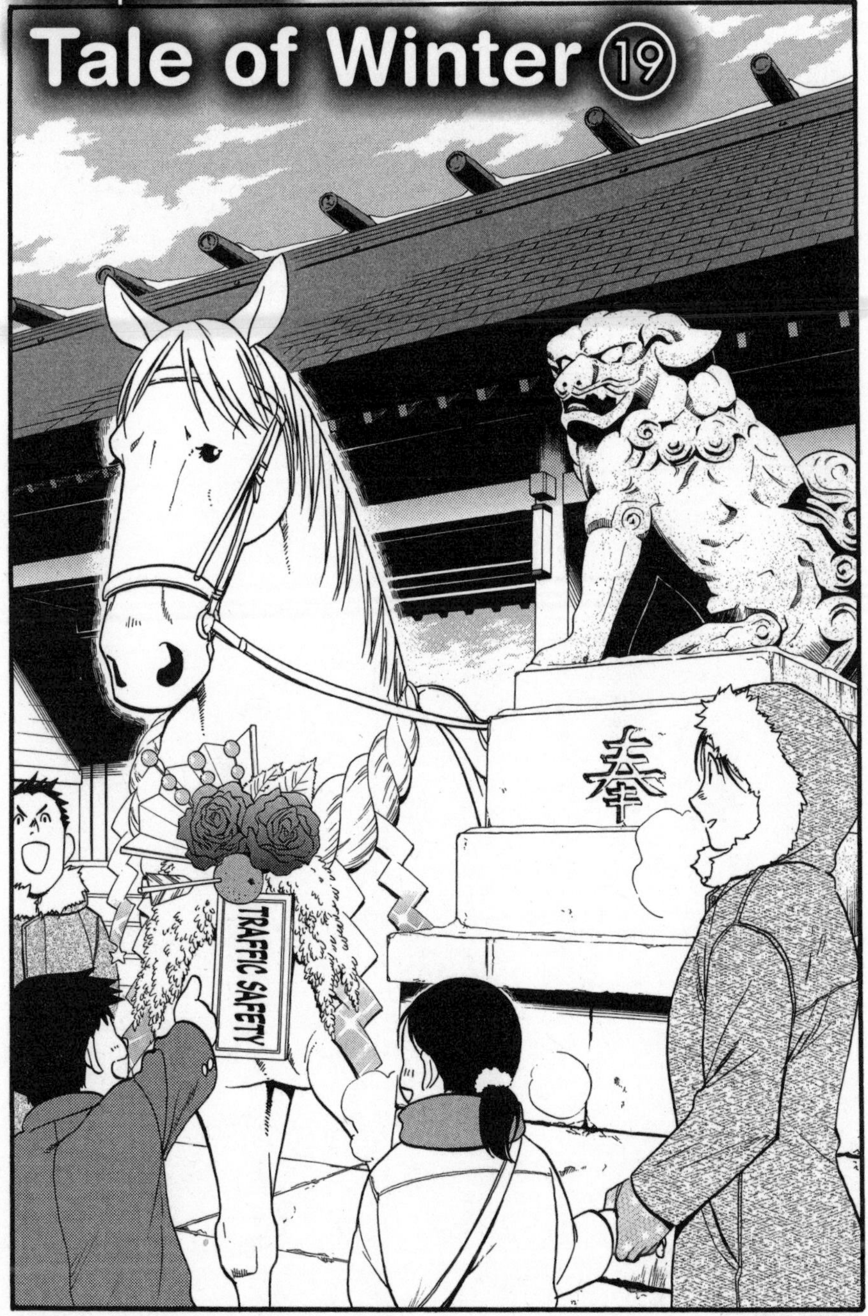

奉
TRAFFIC SAFETY

STONE: OFFERING

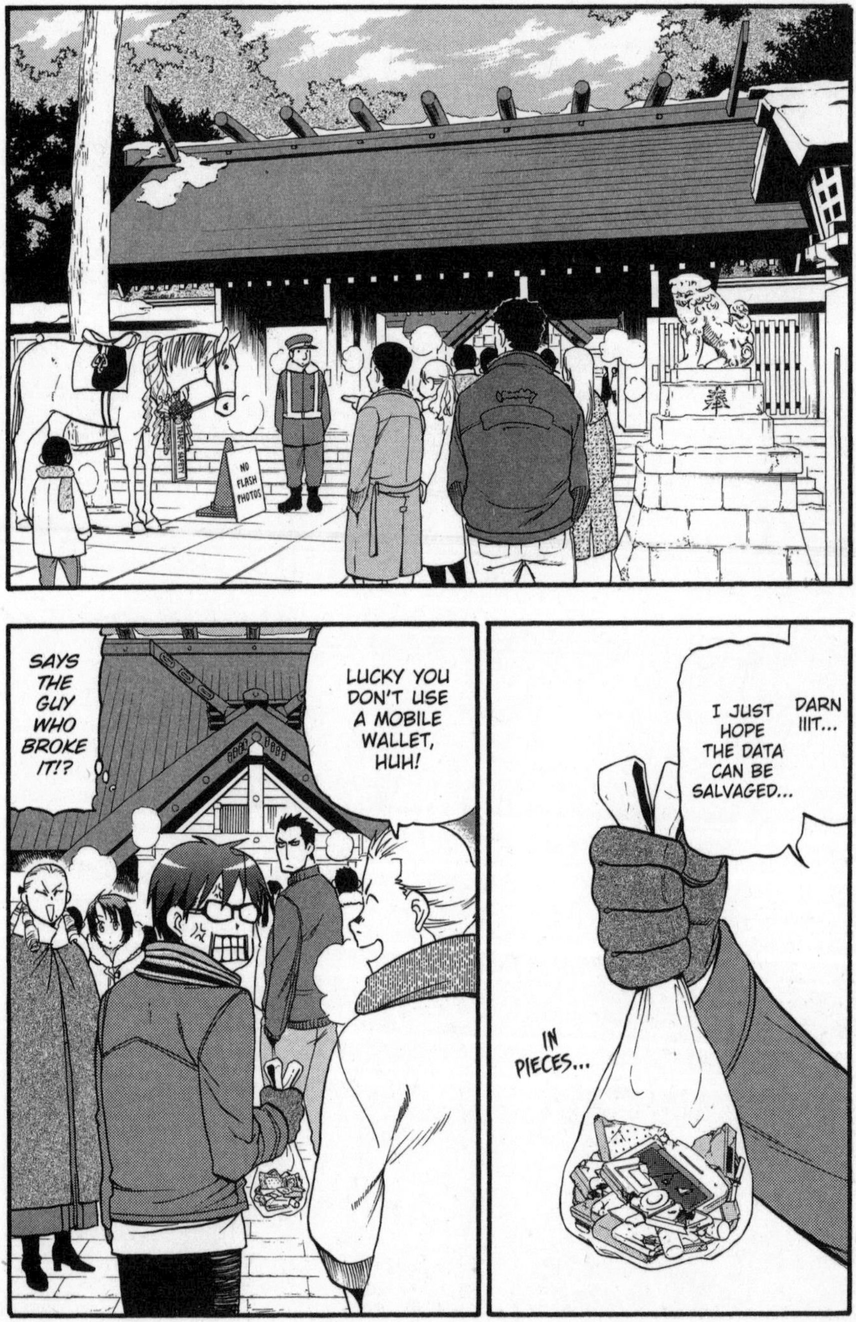
TRAFFIC SAFETY
NO FLASH PHOTOS
DARN IIIT...
I JUST HOPE THE DATA CAN BE SALVAGED...
IN PIECES...
LUCKY YOU DON'T USE A MOBILE WALLET, HUH!
SAYS THE GUY WHO BROKE IT!?

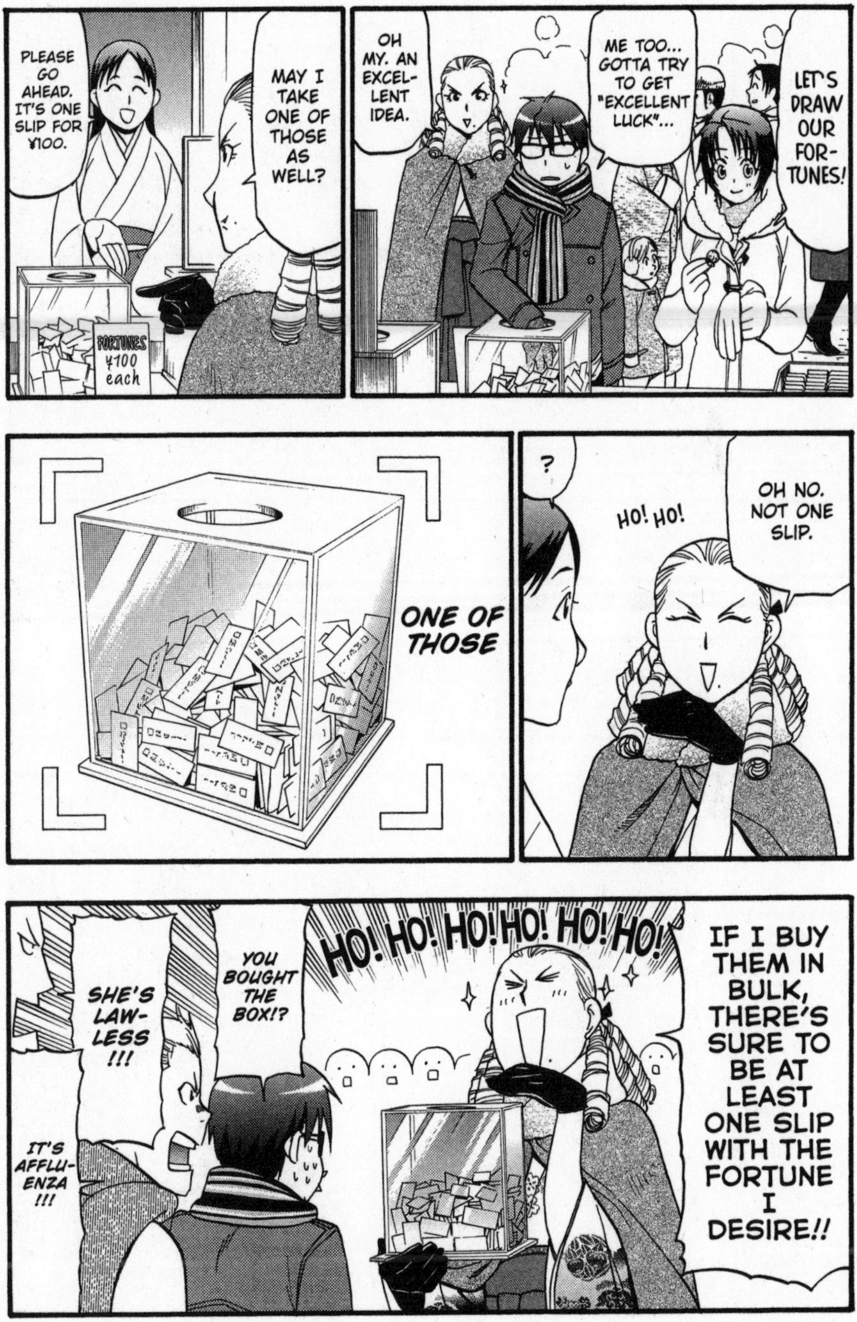
LET'S DRAW OUR FORTUNES!
ME TOO... GOTTA TRY TO GET "EXCELLENT LUCK"...
OH MY. AN EXCELLENT IDEA.
MAY I TAKE ONE OF THOSE AS WELL?
PLEASE GO AHEAD. IT'S ONE SLIP FOR ¥100.
FORTUNES ¥100 each
OH NO. NOT ONE SLIP.
HO! HO!
?
ONE OF THOSE
IF I BUY THEM IN BULK, THERE'S SURE TO BE AT LEAST ONE SLIP WITH THE FORTUNE I DESIRE!!
HO! HO! HO! HO! HO! HO!
YOU BOUGHT THE BOX!?
SHE'S LAWLESS!!!
IT'S AFFLUENZA!!!

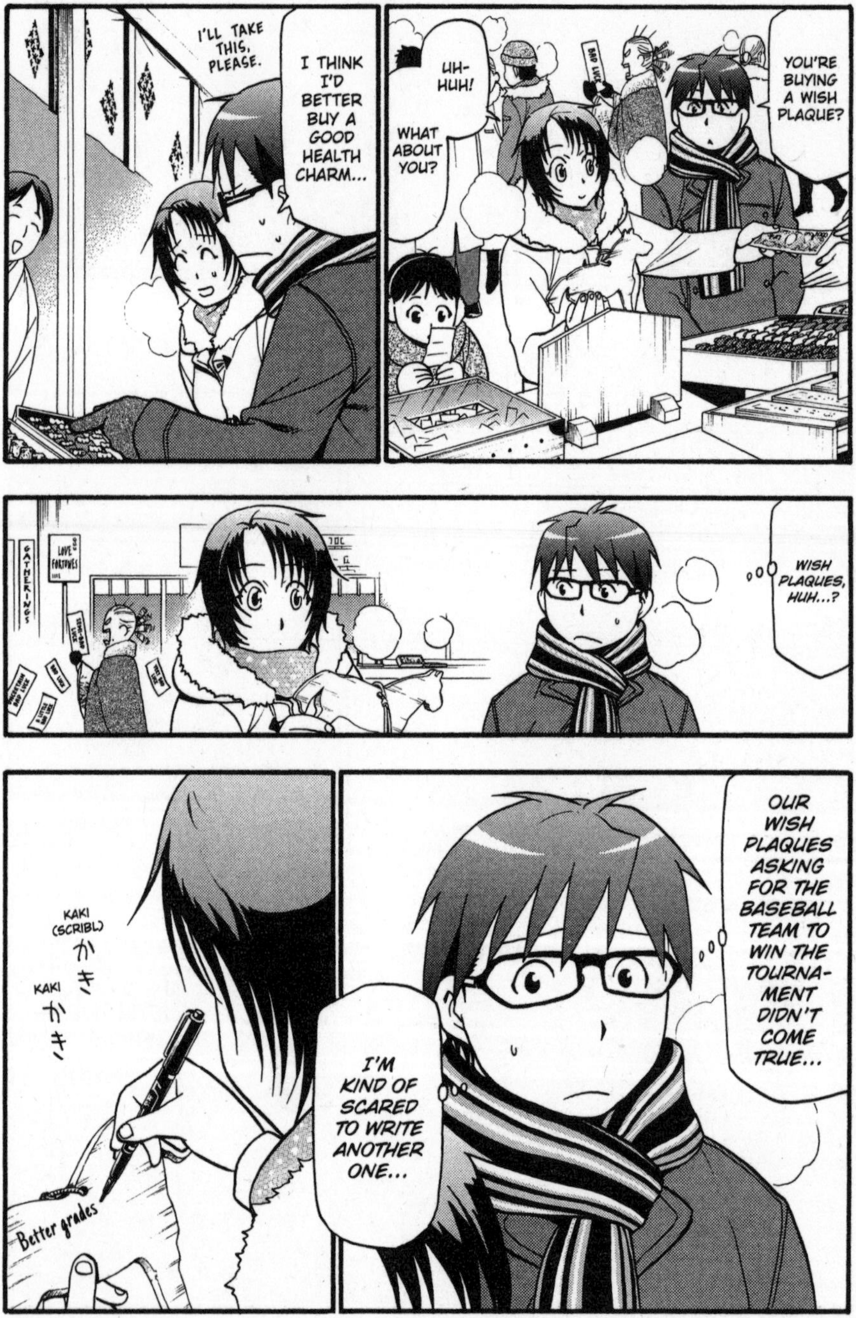
YOU'RE BUYING A WISH PLAQUE?
UH-HUH!
WHAT ABOUT YOU?
BAD LUCK
I THINK I'D BETTER BUY A GOOD HEALTH CHARM...
I'LL TAKE THIS, PLEASE.
WISH PLAQUES, HUH...?
LOVE FORTUNES
GATHERINGS
BAD LUCK
OUR WISH PLAQUES ASKING FOR THE BASEBALL TEAM TO WIN THE TOURNAMENT DIDN'T COME TRUE...
I'M KIND OF SCARED TO WRITE ANOTHER ONE...
KAKI (SCRIBL) かき
KAKI かき
Better grades

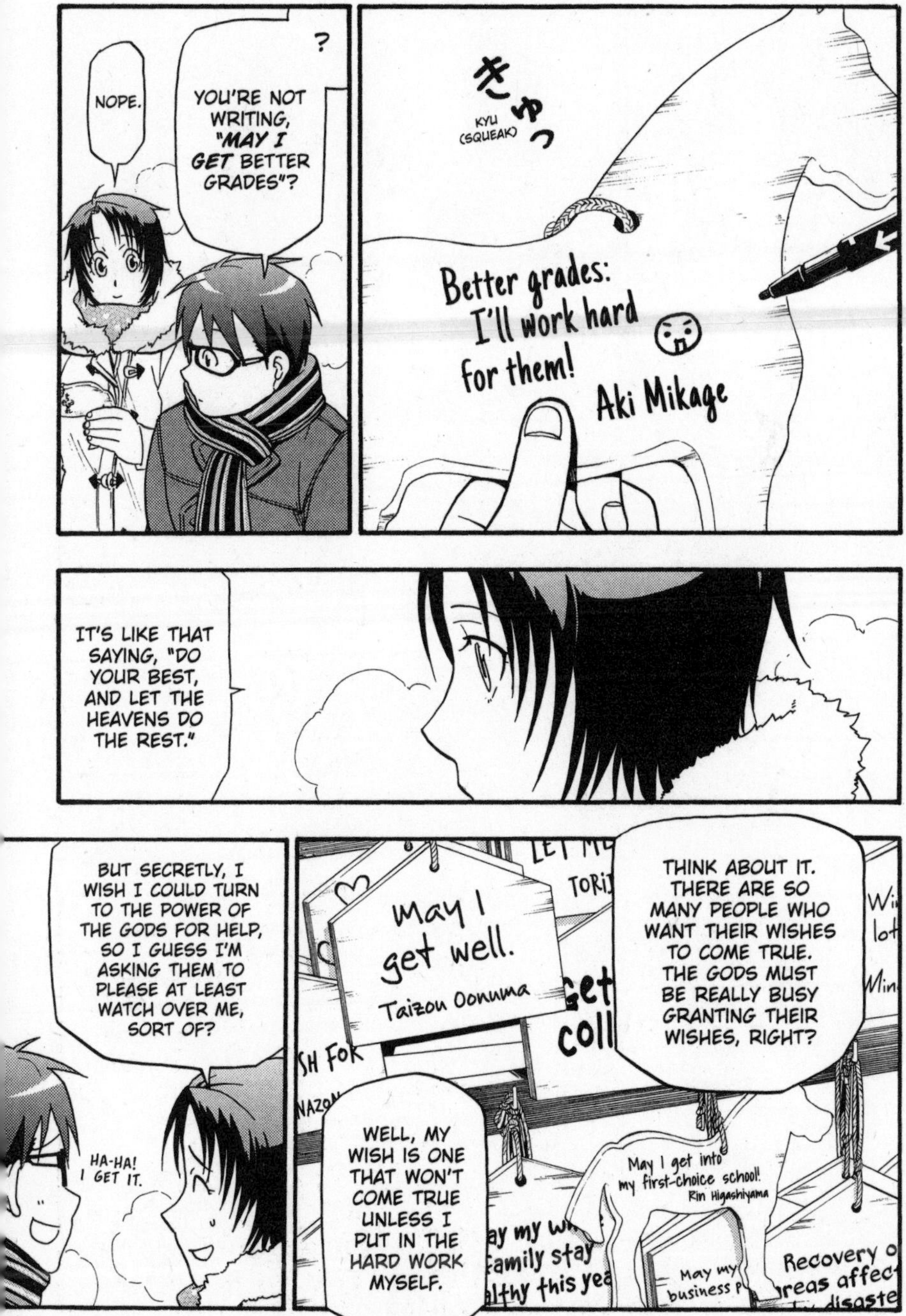
きゅっ
KYU (SQUEAK)
Better grades: I'll work hard for them!
Aki Mikage
?
YOU'RE NOT WRITING, "MAY I GET BETTER GRADES"?
NOPE.
IT'S LIKE THAT SAYING, "DO YOUR BEST, AND LET THE HEAVENS DO THE REST."
THINK ABOUT IT. THERE ARE SO MANY PEOPLE WHO WANT THEIR WISHES TO COME TRUE. THE GODS MUST BE REALLY BUSY GRANTING THEIR WISHES, RIGHT?
May I get well.
Taizou Oonuma
May I get into my first-choice school!
Rin Higashiyama
WELL, MY WISH IS ONE THAT WON'T COME TRUE UNLESS I PUT IN THE HARD WORK MYSELF.
BUT SECRETLY, I WISH I COULD TURN TO THE POWER OF THE GODS FOR HELP, SO I GUESS I'M ASKING THEM TO PLEASE AT LEAST WATCH OVER ME, SORT OF?
HA-HA! I GET IT.

SHOULD I BUY ONE TOO, AND WRITE, "I'LL BRING MIKAGE'S GRADES UP"?
YOU USE YOUR WISH ON YOURSELF!
ON MYSELF, HUH...
A WISH FOR MYSELF, OTHER THAN FOR HEALTH ......
"MAY I FIND A GOAL"?
"PORK FUND SUCCESS"?
"MAY OUR CHEESE TURN OUT WELL"?
May I pass my high school entrance exams.
GET INTO MY TOP SCHOOL!
I want to get a job please.
May I be healthy this year too.
I WANT TO STUDY ABROAD!
May business take off
May Dad get better.
May I go on my trip.
STEADY PROGRESS
I want to be happy.
May I do well in school.
WHAT DID THE OTHERS WRITE...?
May I get Valentine's Day chocolate Shinei ookawa
Cosmic Peace Ayame Minamikujou
OOKAWA-SENPAI, YOU'RE GONNA ASK THE JAPANESE GODS FOR A WESTERN HOLIDAY WISH!?
MINAMI-KUJOU... THAT'S AN ENORMOUS WISH!!
KOMABA, YOU'RE NOT BUYING A WISH PLAQUE?
NOPE.

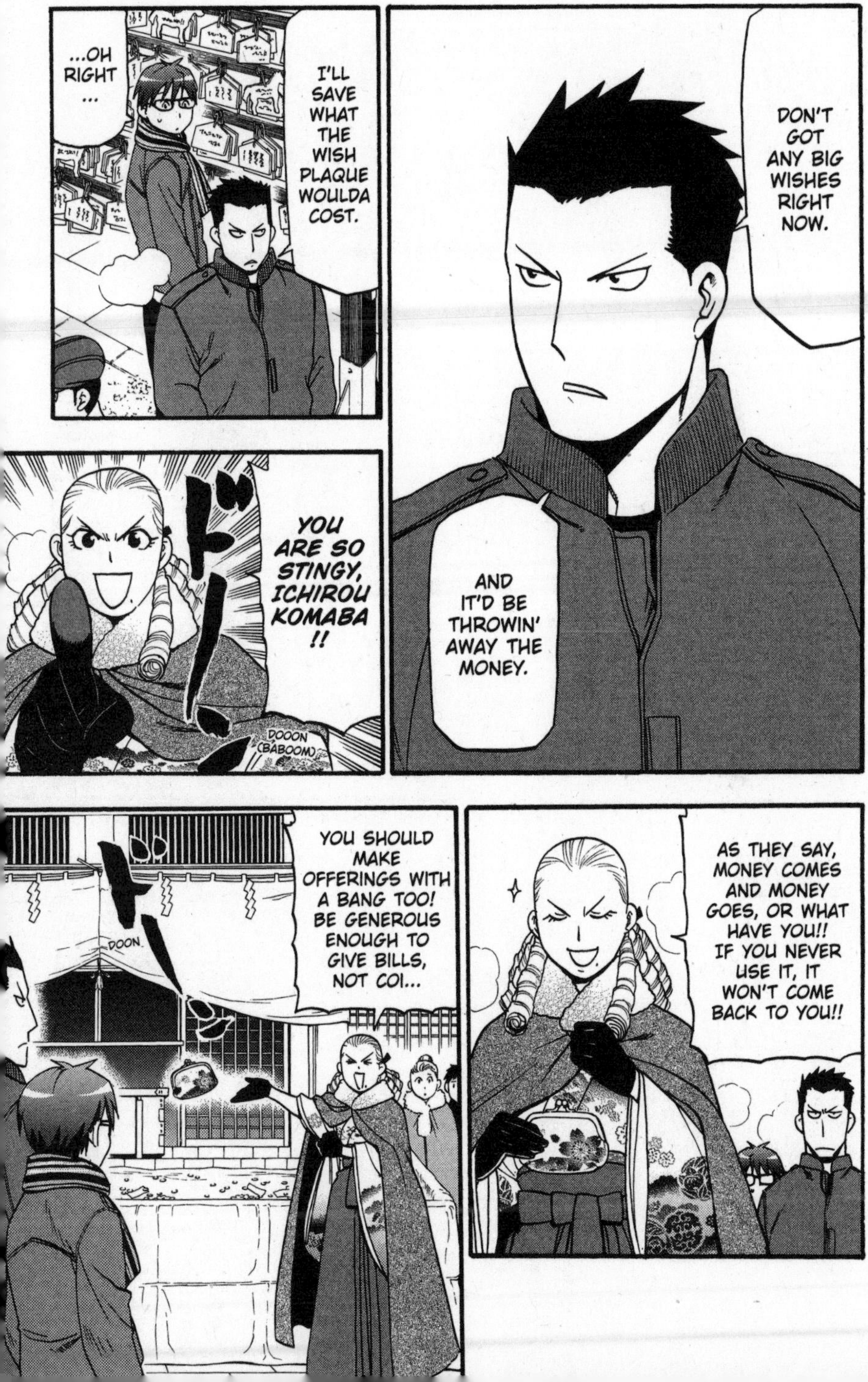
DON'T GOT ANY BIG WISHES RIGHT NOW.
AND IT'D BE THROWIN' AWAY THE MONEY.
I'LL SAVE WHAT THE WISH PLAQUE WOULDA COST.
...OH RIGHT...
YOU ARE SO STINGY, ICHIROU KOMABA!!
DOOON (BABOOM)
AS THEY SAY, MONEY COMES AND MONEY GOES, OR WHAT HAVE YOU!! IF YOU NEVER USE IT, IT WON'T COME BACK TO YOU!!
YOU SHOULD MAKE OFFERINGS WITH A BANG TOO! BE GENEROUS ENOUGH TO GIVE BILLS, NOT COI...
DOON

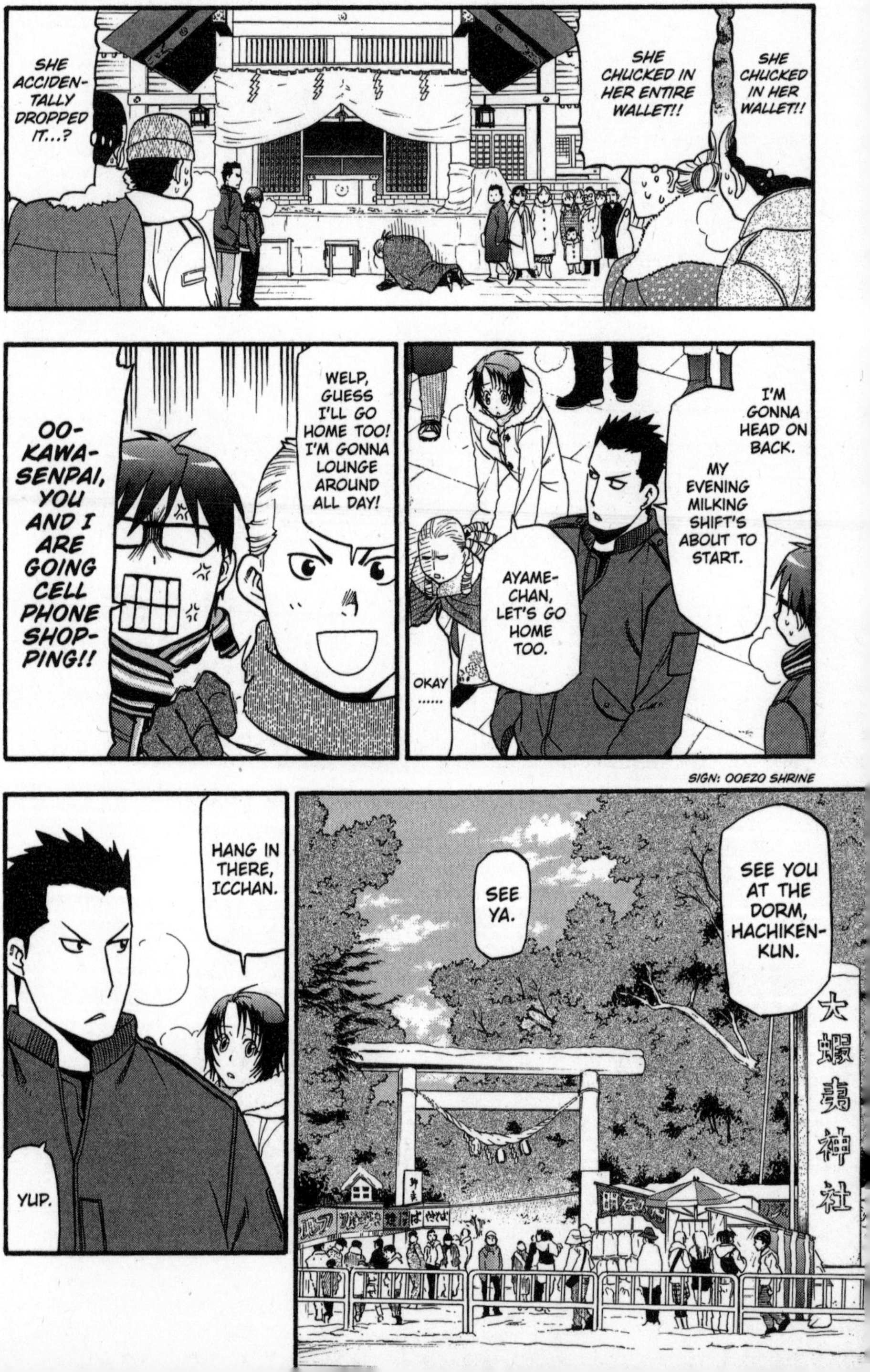
SHE CHUCKED IN HER WALLET!!
SHE CHUCKED IN HER ENTIRE WALLET!!
SHE ACCIDENTALLY DROPPED IT...?
I'M GONNA HEAD ON BACK.
MY EVENING MILKING SHIFT'S ABOUT TO START.
AYAME-CHAN, LET'S GO HOME TOO.
OKAY ......
WELP, GUESS I'LL GO HOME TOO! I'M GONNA LOUNGE AROUND ALL DAY!
OOKAWA-SENPAI, YOU AND I ARE GOING CELL PHONE SHOPPING!!
SIGN: OOEZO SHRINE
SEE YOU AT THE DORM, HACHIKEN-KUN.
SEE YA.
大蝦夷神社
HANG IN THERE, ICCHAN.
YUP.

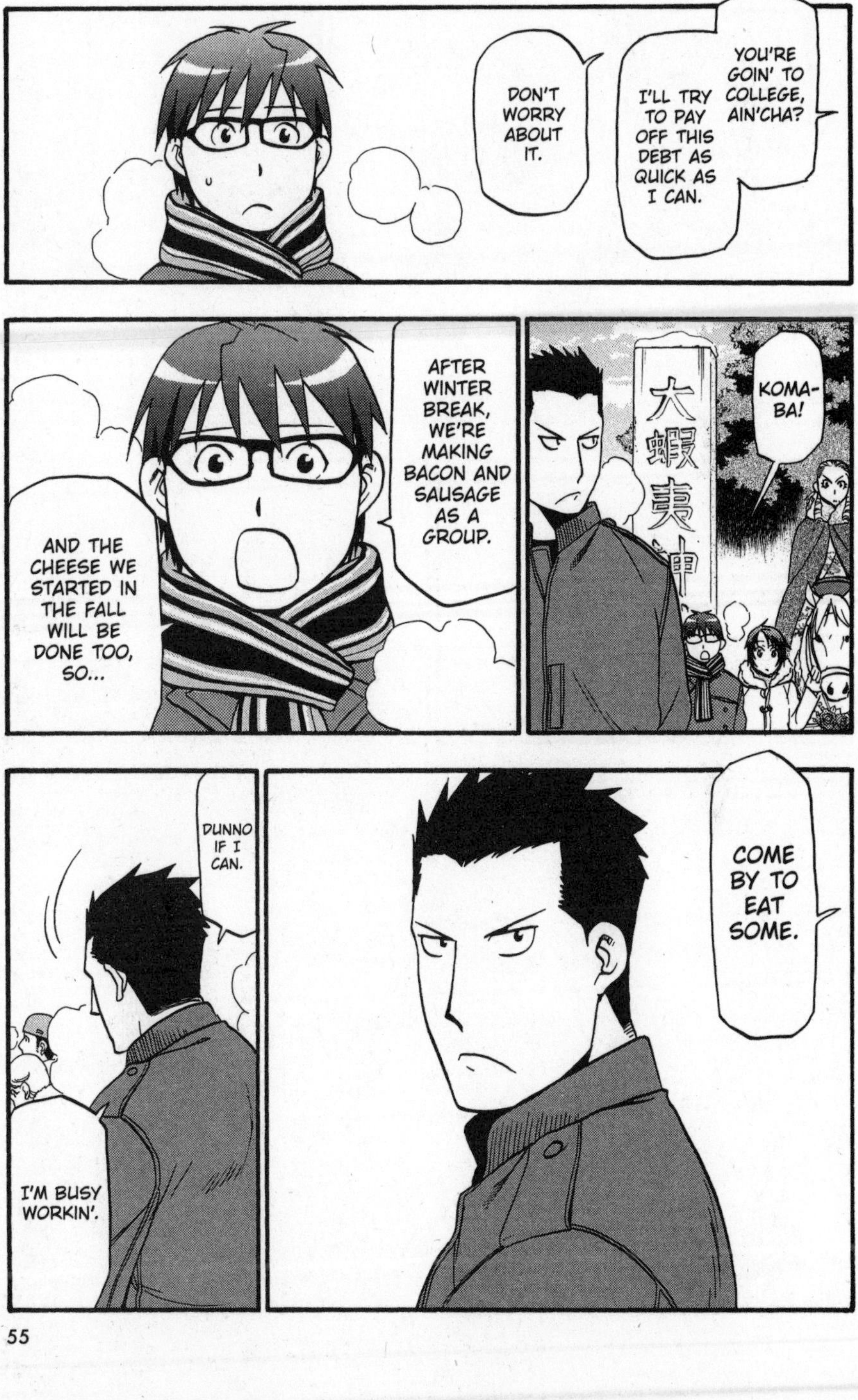
YOU'RE GOIN' TO COLLEGE, AIN'CHA?
I'LL TRY TO PAY OFF THIS DEBT AS QUICK AS I CAN.
DON'T WORRY ABOUT IT.
KOMA-BA!
大蝦夷
AFTER WINTER BREAK, WE'RE MAKING BACON AND SAUSAGE AS A GROUP.
AND THE CHEESE WE STARTED IN THE FALL WILL BE DONE TOO, SO...
COME BY TO EAT SOME.
DUNNO IF I CAN.
I'M BUSY WORKIN'.

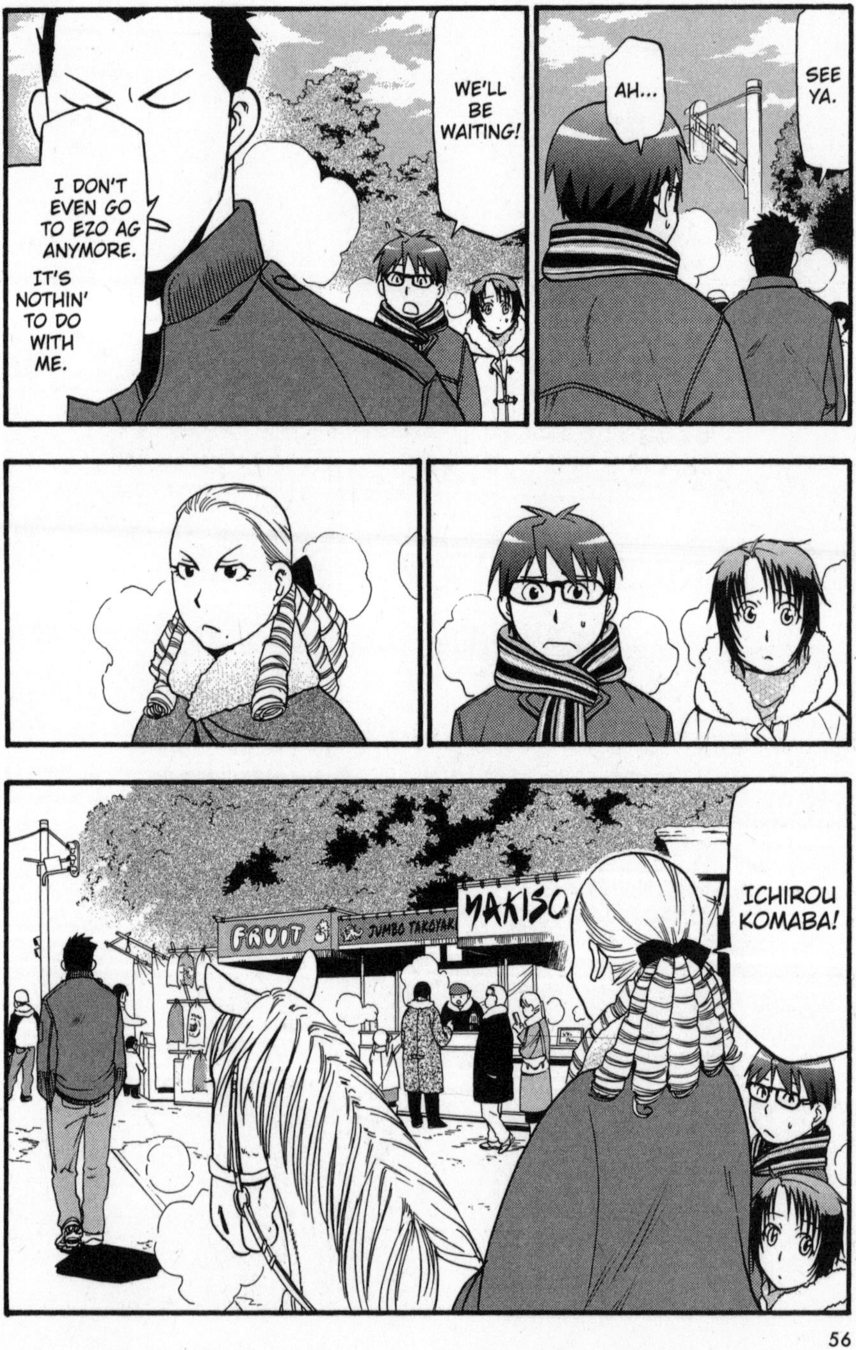
SEE YA.
AH...
WE'LL BE WAITING!
I DON'T EVEN GO TO EZO AG ANYMORE.
IT'S NOTHIN' TO DO WITH ME.
ICHIROU KOMABA!
YAKISO
JUMBO TAKOYAKI
FRUIT

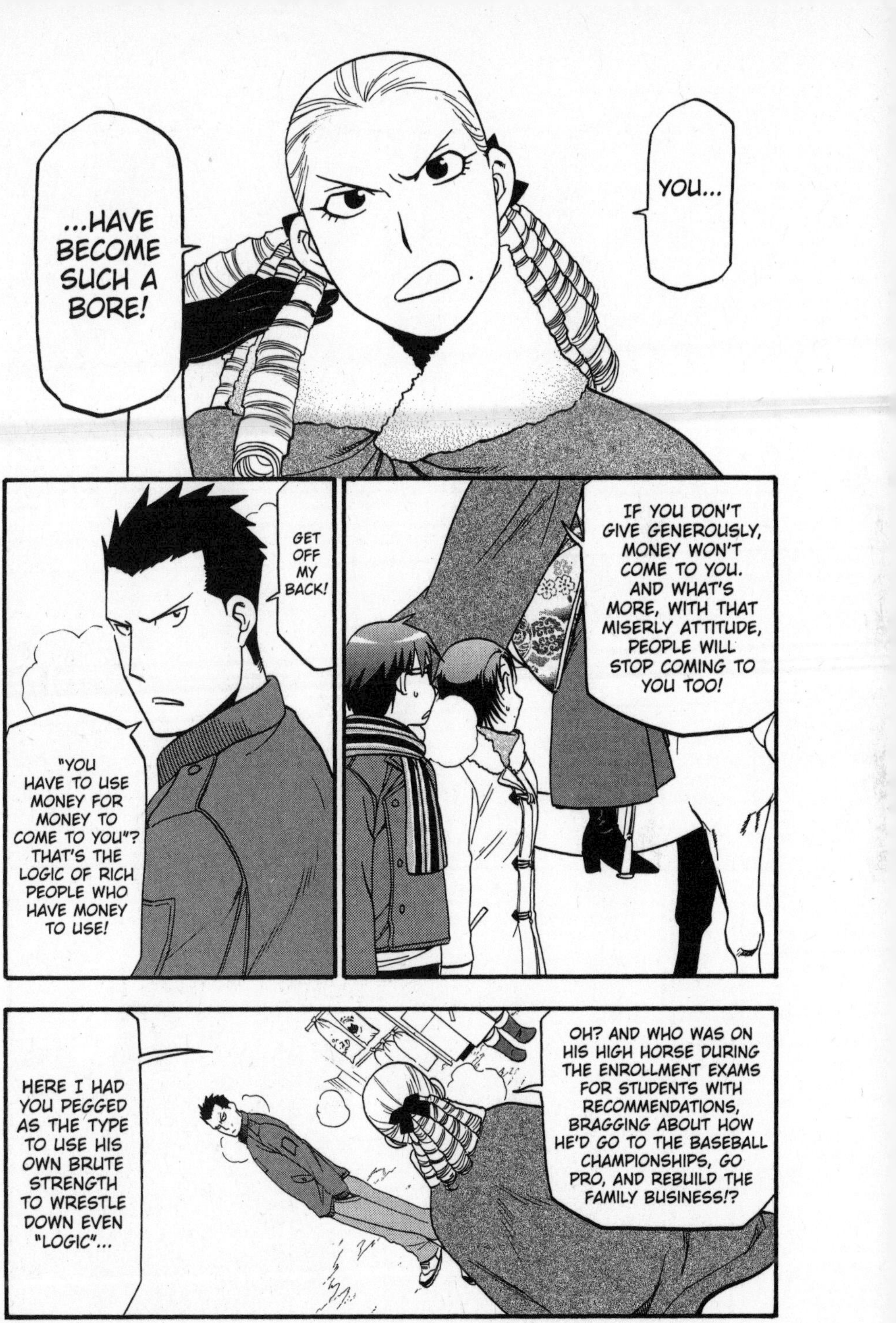
YOU...
...HAVE BECOME SUCH A BORE!
IF YOU DON'T GIVE GENEROUSLY, MONEY WON'T COME TO YOU. AND WHAT'S MORE, WITH THAT MISERLY ATTITUDE, PEOPLE WILL STOP COMING TO YOU TOO!
GET OFF MY BACK!
"YOU HAVE TO USE MONEY FOR MONEY TO COME TO YOU"? THAT'S THE LOGIC OF RICH PEOPLE WHO HAVE MONEY TO USE!
OH? AND WHO WAS ON HIS HIGH HORSE DURING THE ENROLLMENT EXAMS FOR STUDENTS WITH RECOMMENDATIONS, BRAGGING ABOUT HOW HE'D GO TO THE BASEBALL CHAMPIONSHIPS, GO PRO, AND REBUILD THE FAMILY BUSINESS!?
HERE I HAD YOU PEGGED AS THE TYPE TO USE HIS OWN BRUTE STRENGTH TO WRESTLE DOWN EVEN "LOGIC"...

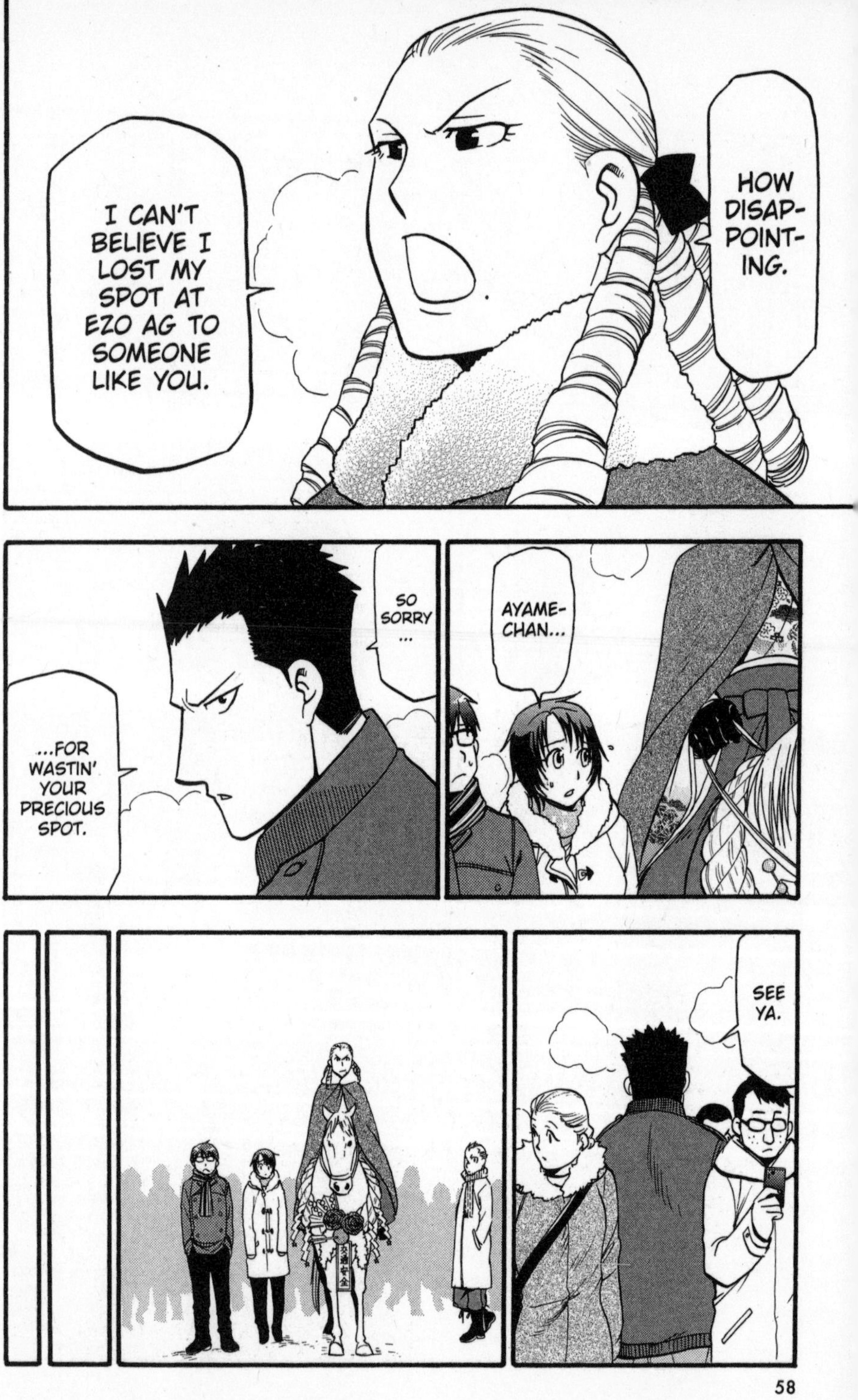
HOW DISAP-POINT-ING.
I CAN'T BELIEVE I LOST MY SPOT AT EZO AG TO SOMEONE LIKE YOU.
AYAME-CHAN...
SO SORRY ...
...FOR WASTIN' YOUR PRECIOUS SPOT.
SEE YA.

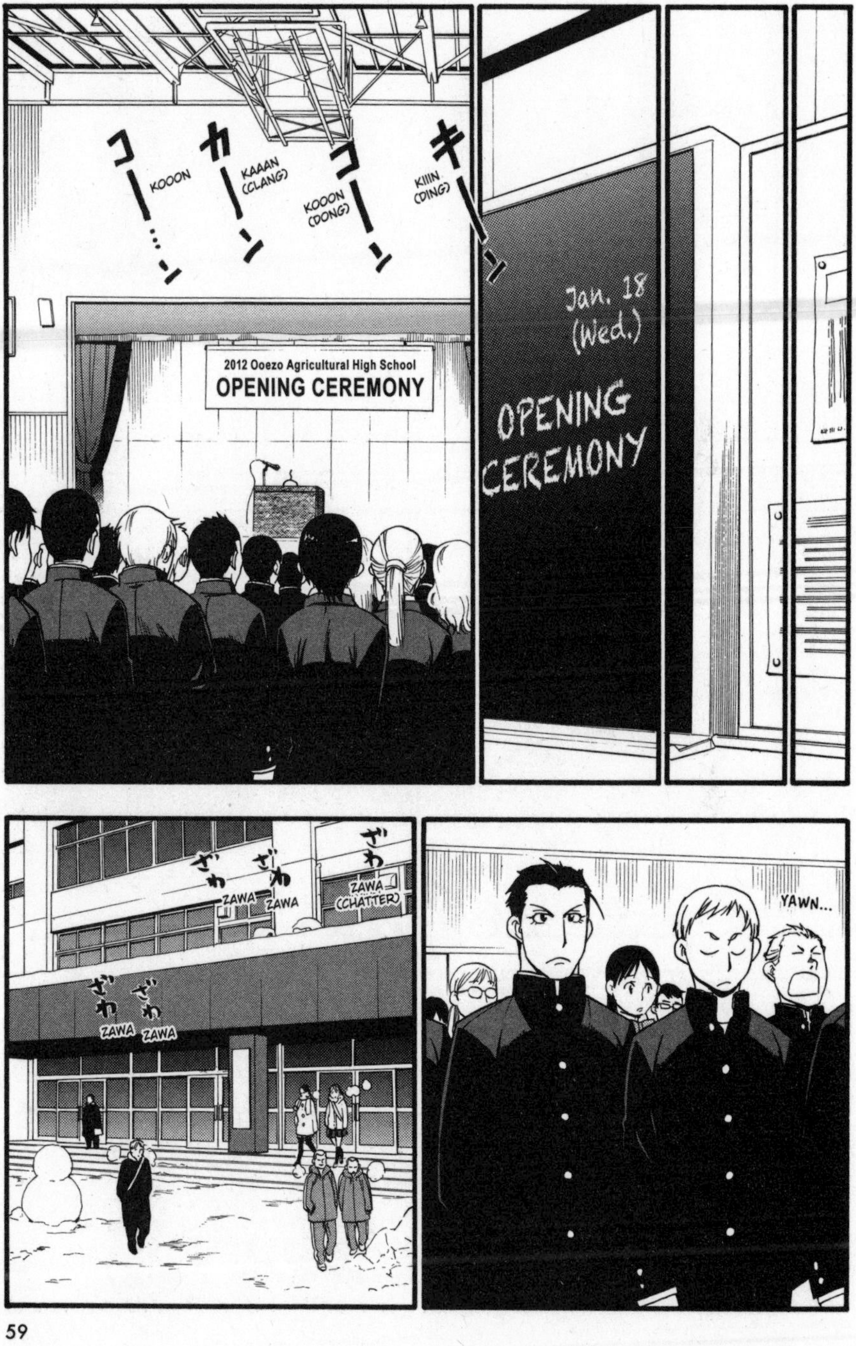
Jan. 18 (Wed.)
OPENING CEREMONY
キーン
KIIN (DING)
コーン
KOOON (DONG)
カーン
KAAAN (CLANG)
コーン…ン
KOOON
2012 Ooezo Agricultural High School
OPENING CEREMONY
YAWN...
ざわ
ZAWA (CHATTER)
ざわ ざわ
ZAWA ZAWA
ざわ ざわ
ZAWA ZAWA

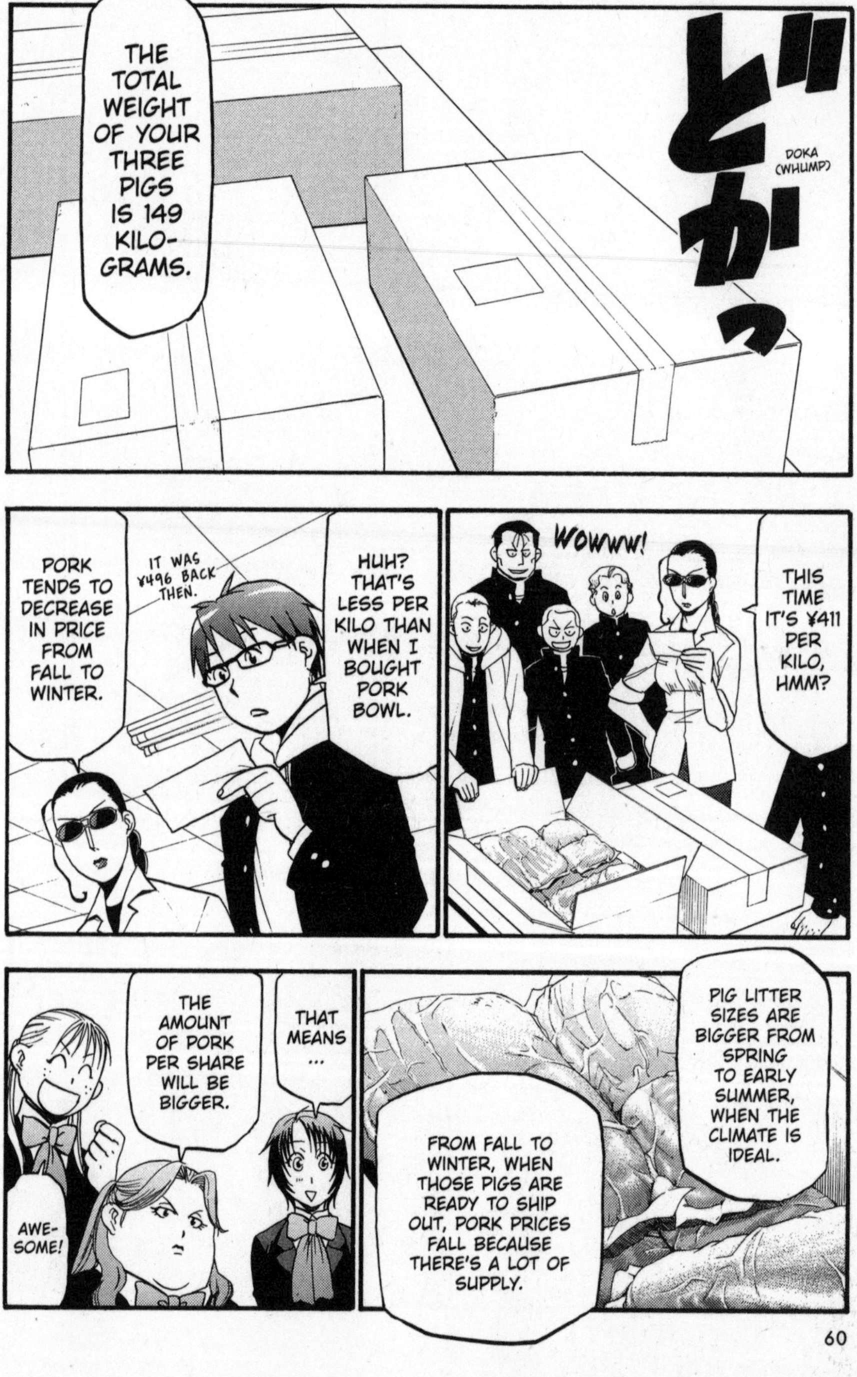
どかっ
DOKA (WHUMP)
THE TOTAL WEIGHT OF YOUR THREE PIGS IS 149 KILOGRAMS.
THIS TIME IT'S ¥411 PER KILO, HMM?
WOWWW!
HUH? THAT'S LESS PER KILO THAN WHEN I BOUGHT PORK BOWL.
IT WAS ¥496 BACK THEN.
PORK TENDS TO DECREASE IN PRICE FROM FALL TO WINTER.
PIG LITTER SIZES ARE BIGGER FROM SPRING TO EARLY SUMMER, WHEN THE CLIMATE IS IDEAL.
FROM FALL TO WINTER, WHEN THOSE PIGS ARE READY TO SHIP OUT, PORK PRICES FALL BECAUSE THERE'S A LOT OF SUPPLY.
THAT MEANS ...
THE AMOUNT OF PORK PER SHARE WILL BE BIGGER.
AWESOME!

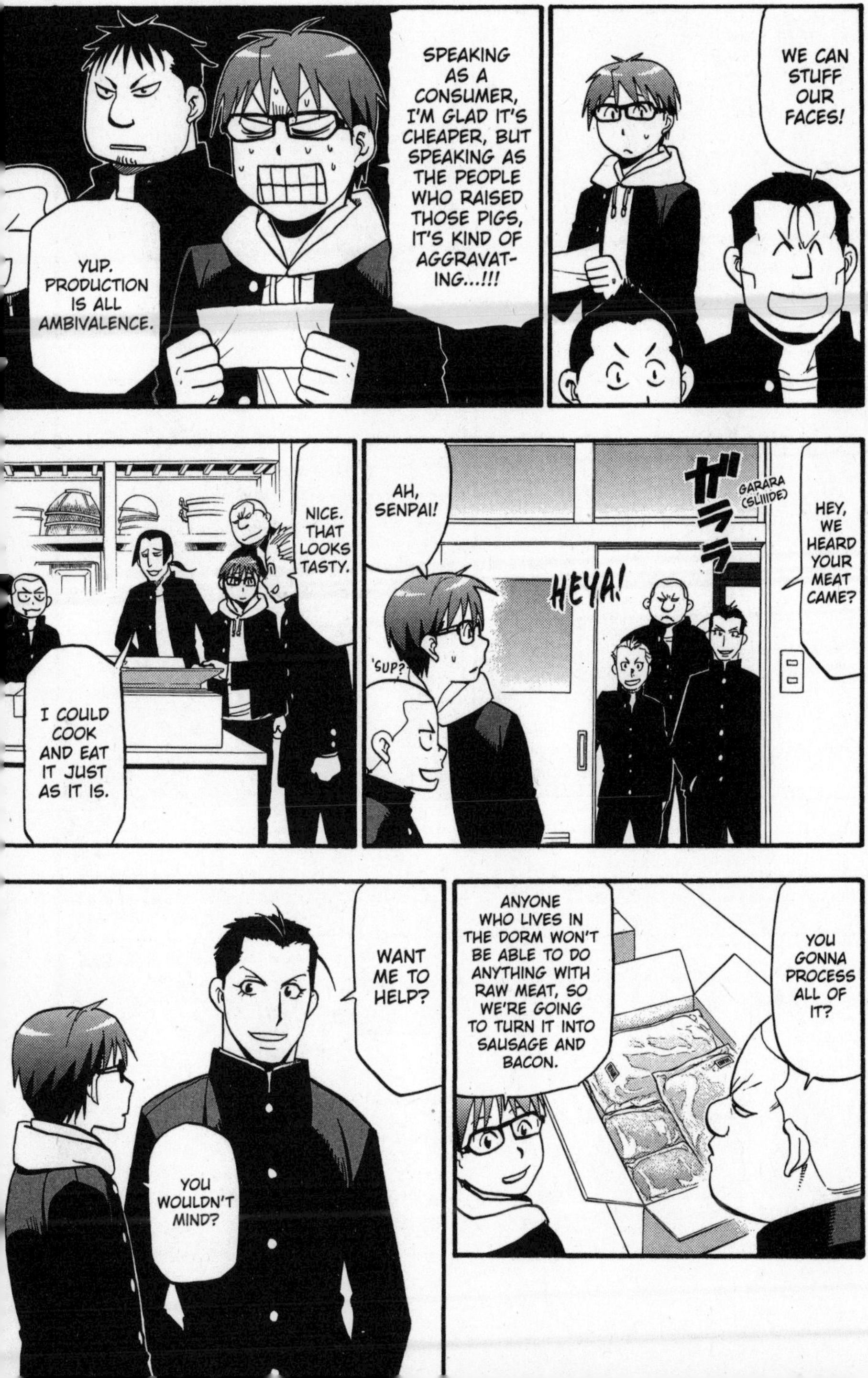
WE CAN STUFF OUR FACES!
SPEAKING AS A CONSUMER, I'M GLAD IT'S CHEAPER, BUT SPEAKING AS THE PEOPLE WHO RAISED THOSE PIGS, IT'S KIND OF AGGRAVATING...!!!
YUP. PRODUCTION IS ALL AMBIVALENCE.
HEY, WE HEARD YOUR MEAT CAME?
ガラ ラ
GARARA (SLIIIDE)
HEYA!
AH, SENPAI!
'SUP?
NICE. THAT LOOKS TASTY.
I COULD COOK AND EAT IT JUST AS IT IS.
YOU GONNA PROCESS ALL OF IT?
ANYONE WHO LIVES IN THE DORM WON'T BE ABLE TO DO ANYTHING WITH RAW MEAT, SO WE'RE GOING TO TURN IT INTO SAUSAGE AND BACON.
WANT ME TO HELP?
YOU WOULDN'T MIND?

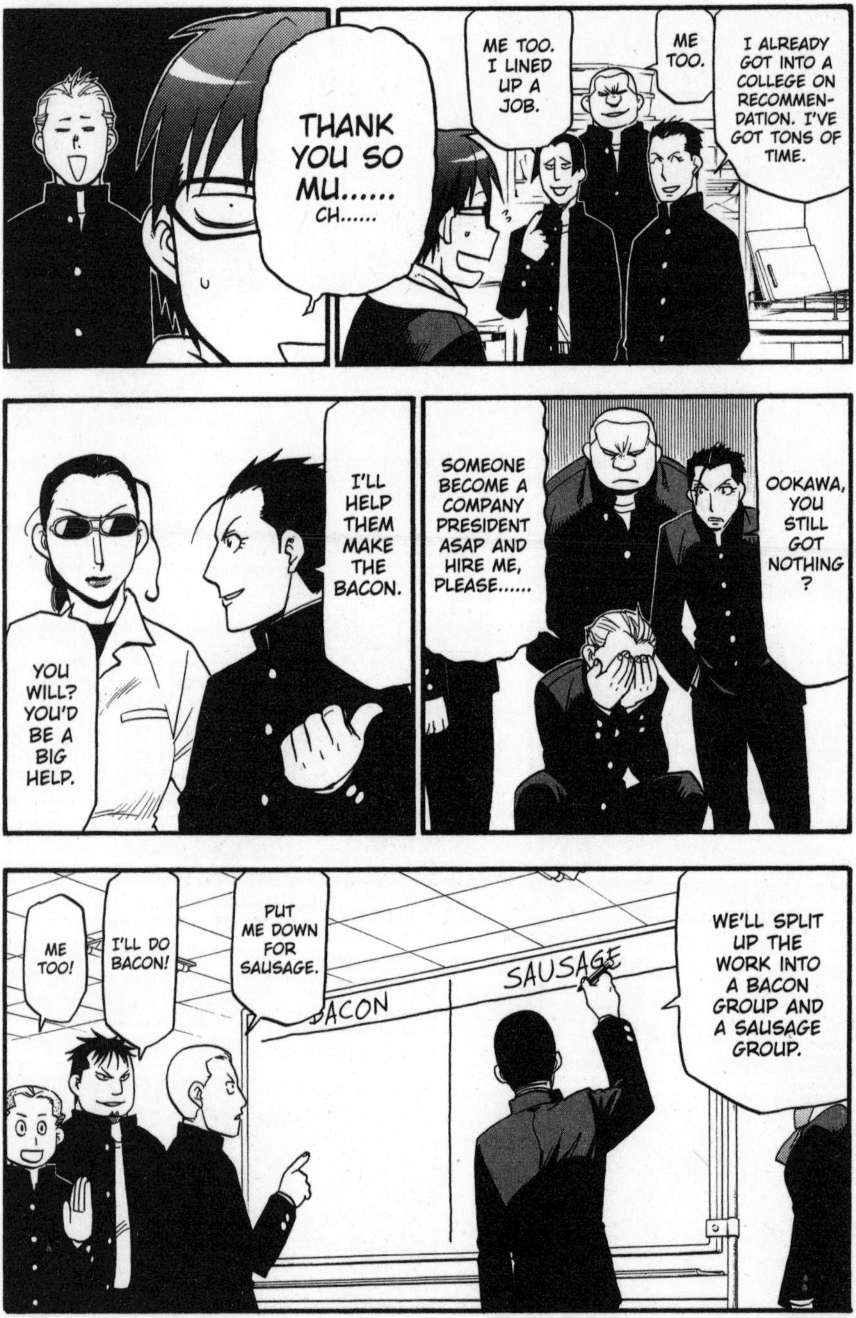
I ALREADY GOT INTO A COLLEGE ON RECOMMEN-DATION. I'VE GOT TONS OF TIME.
ME TOO.
ME TOO. I LINED UP A JOB.
THANK YOU SO MU...... CH......
OOKAWA, YOU STILL GOT NOTHING?
SOMEONE BECOME A COMPANY PRESIDENT ASAP AND HIRE ME, PLEASE......
I'LL HELP THEM MAKE THE BACON.
YOU WILL? YOU'D BE A BIG HELP.
WE'LL SPLIT UP THE WORK INTO A BACON GROUP AND A SAUSAGE GROUP.
SAUSAGE
PUT ME DOWN FOR SAUSAGE.
BACON
I'LL DO BACON!
ME TOO!

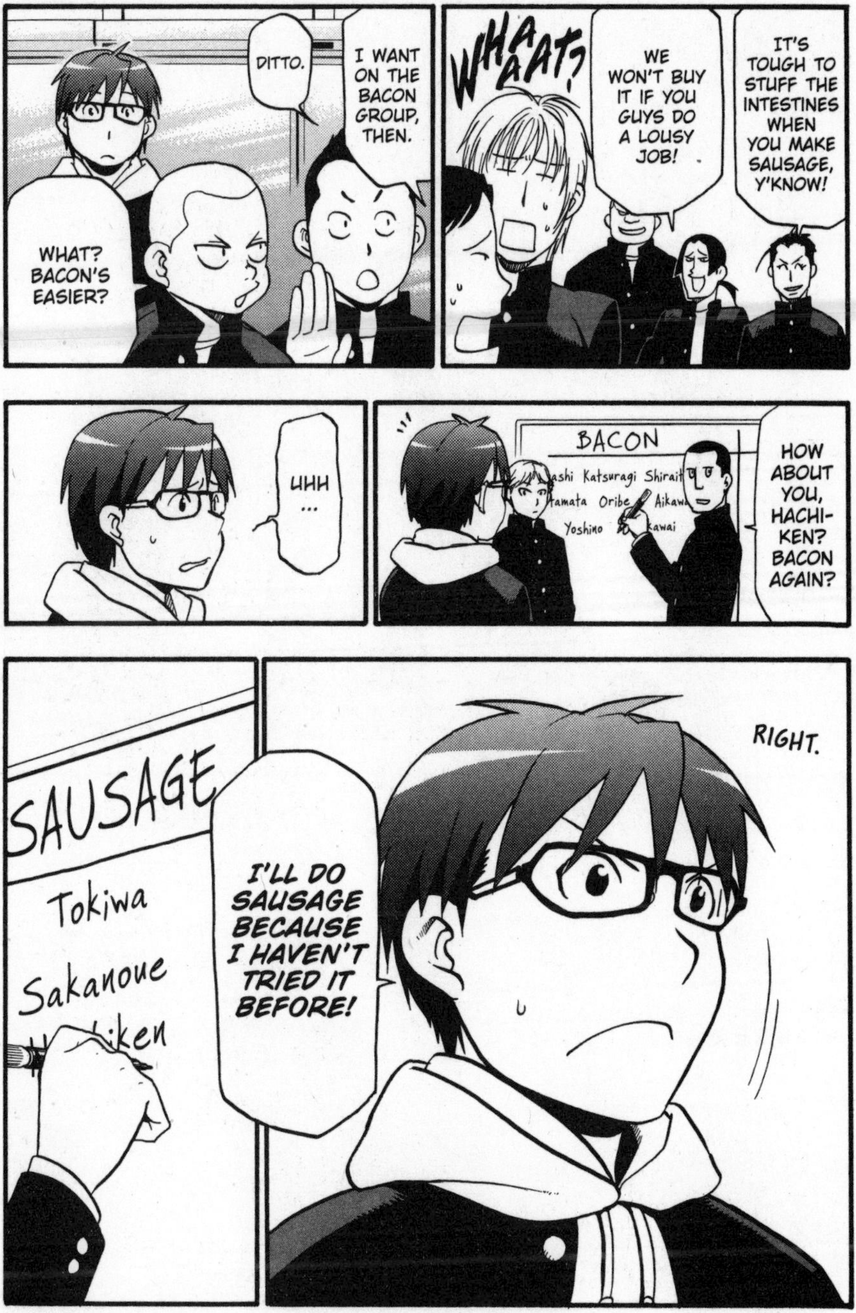
IT'S TOUGH TO STUFF THE INTESTINES WHEN YOU MAKE SAUSAGE, Y'KNOW!
WE WON'T BUY IT IF YOU GUYS DO A LOUSY JOB!
WHAAAT?
I WANT ON THE BACON GROUP, THEN.
DITTO.
WHAT? BACON'S EASIER?
HOW ABOUT YOU, HACHI-KEN? BACON AGAIN?
BACON
Katsuragi
Oribe
Yoshino
UHH ...
RIGHT.
I'LL DO SAUSAGE BECAUSE I HAVEN'T TRIED IT BEFORE!
SAUSAGE
Tokiwa
Sakanoue

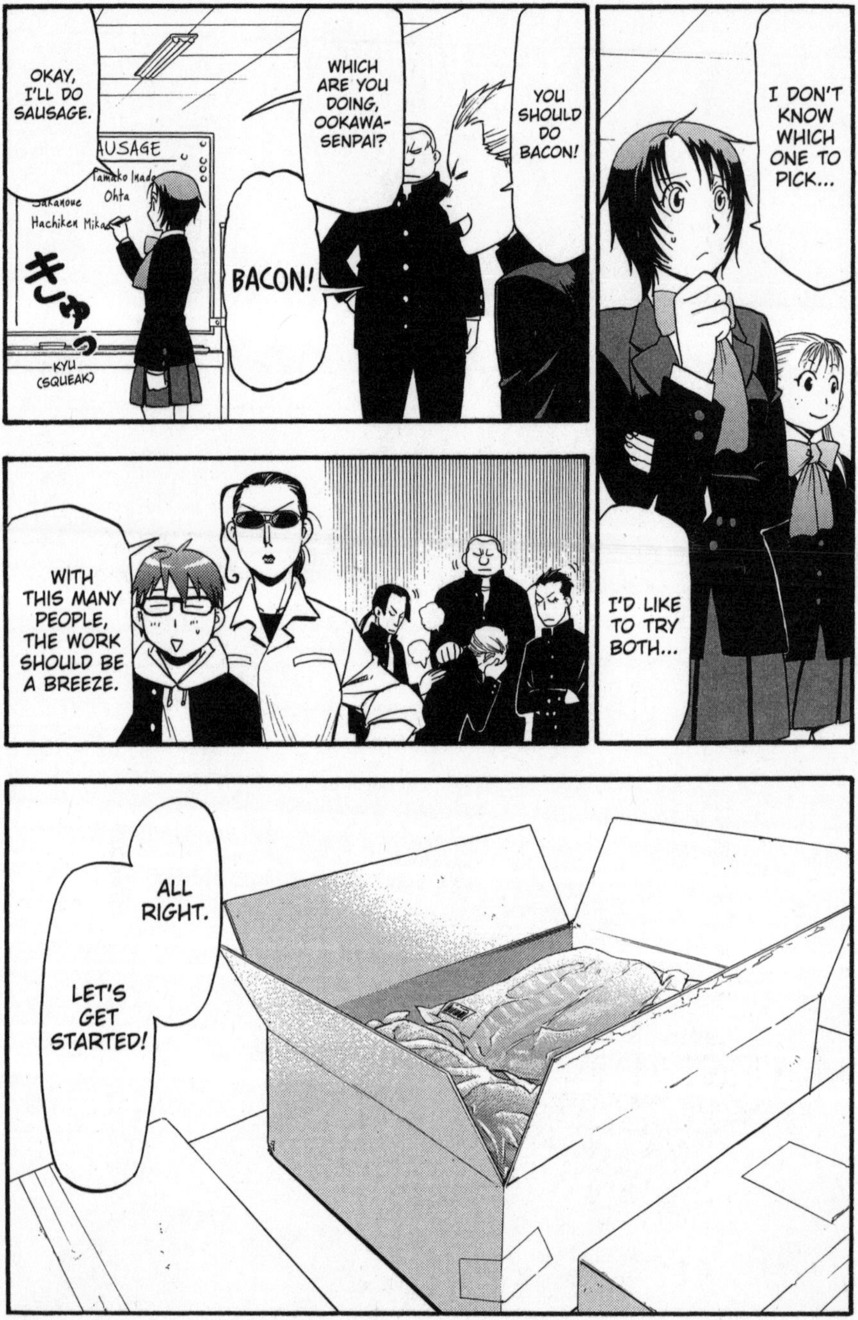
I DON'T KNOW WHICH ONE TO PICK...
I'D LIKE TO TRY BOTH...
YOU SHOULD DO BACON!
WHICH ARE YOU DOING, OOKAWA-SENPAI?
BACON!
OKAY, I'LL DO SAUSAGE.
AUSAGE
Tamako Inada
Ohta
Hachiken Mika
きゅっ
KYU (SQUEAK)
WITH THIS MANY PEOPLE, THE WORK SHOULD BE A BREEZE.
ALL RIGHT.
LET'S GET STARTED!

Silver Spoon

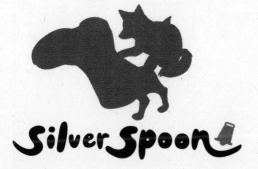

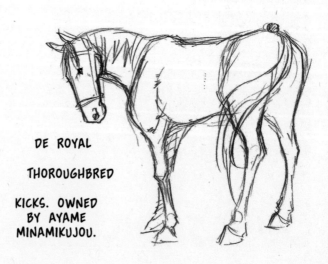

DE ROYAL

THOROUGHBRED

KICKS. OWNED
BY AYAME
MINAMIKUJOU.

Tale of Winter ⑳

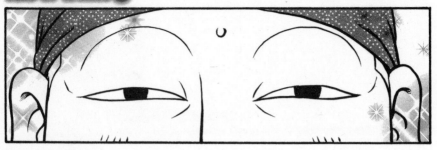

In Heaven...

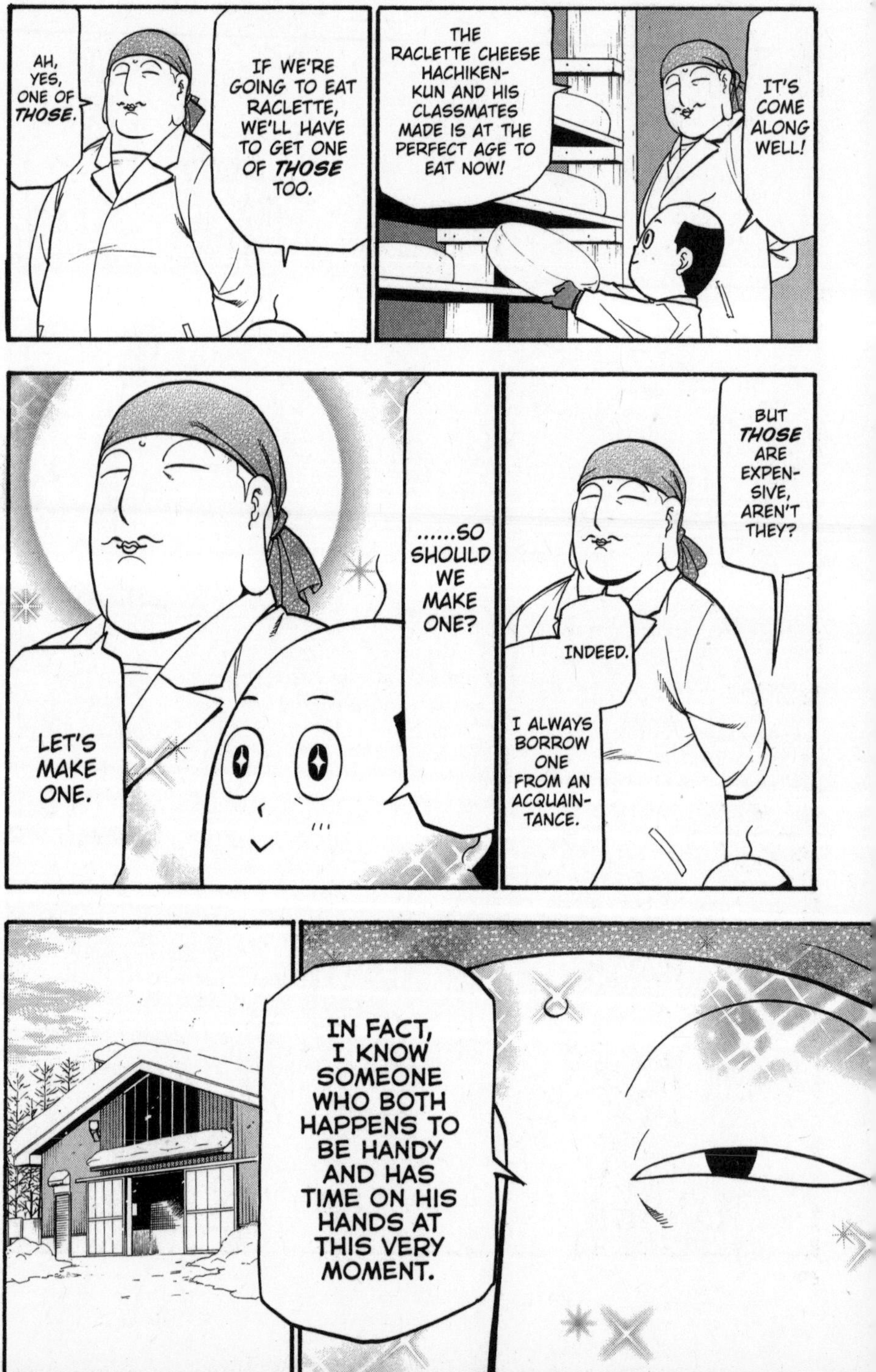
IT'S COME ALONG WELL!
THE RACLETTE CHEESE HACHIKEN-KUN AND HIS CLASSMATES MADE IS AT THE PERFECT AGE TO EAT NOW!
IF WE'RE GOING TO EAT RACLETTE, WE'LL HAVE TO GET ONE OF *THOSE* TOO.
AH, YES, ONE OF *THOSE*.
BUT *THOSE* ARE EXPEN-SIVE, AREN'T THEY?
INDEED.
I ALWAYS BORROW ONE FROM AN ACQUAIN-TANCE.
......SO SHOULD WE MAKE ONE?
LET'S MAKE ONE.
IN FACT, I KNOW SOMEONE WHO BOTH HAPPENS TO BE HANDY AND HAS TIME ON HIS HANDS AT THIS VERY MOMENT.

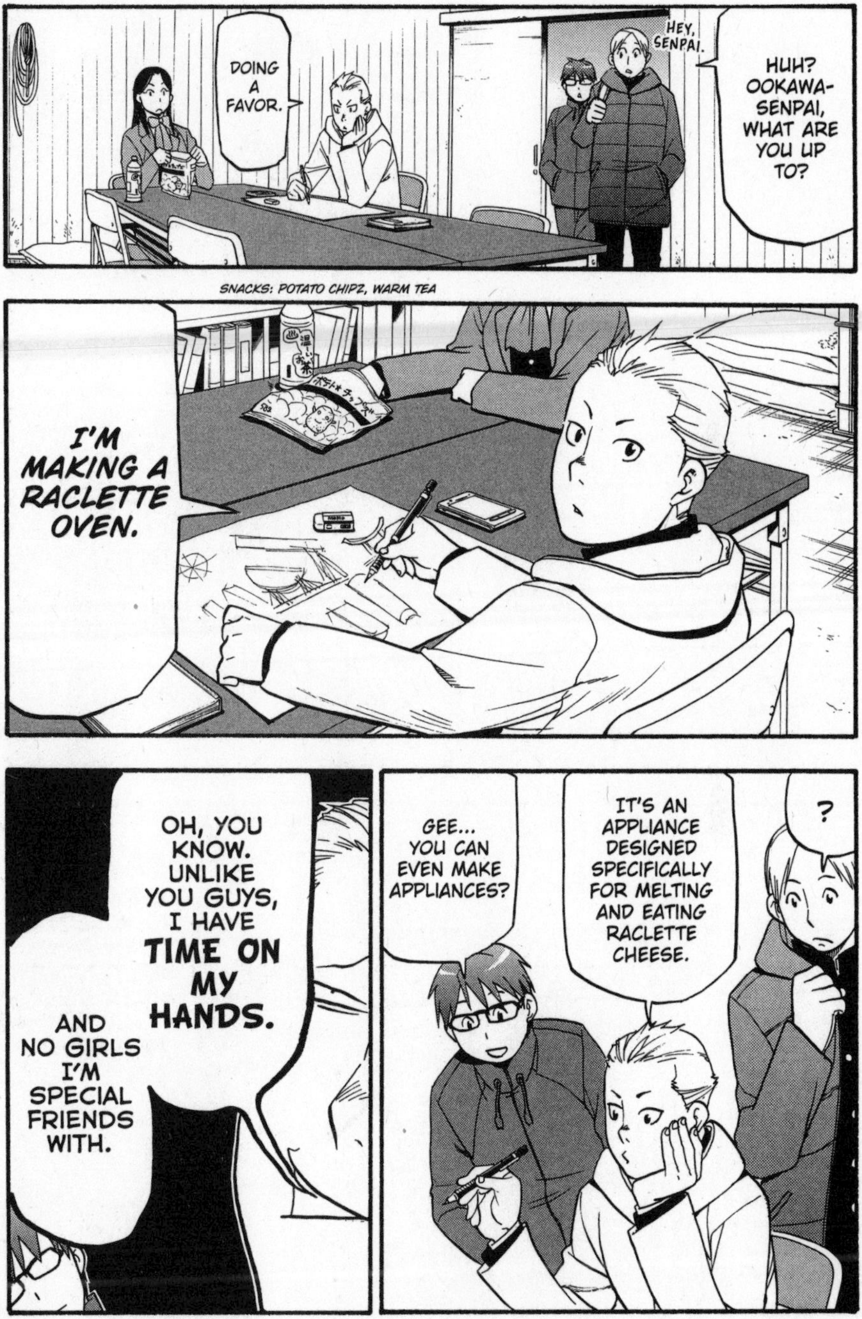
HEY, SENPAI.
HUH? OOKAWA-SENPAI, WHAT ARE YOU UP TO?
DOING A FAVOR.
SNACKS: POTATO CHIPZ, WARM TEA
I'M MAKING A RACLETTE OVEN.
?
IT'S AN APPLIANCE DESIGNED SPECIFICALLY FOR MELTING AND EATING RACLETTE CHEESE.
GEE... YOU CAN EVEN MAKE APPLIANCES?
OH, YOU KNOW. UNLIKE YOU GUYS, I HAVE TIME ON MY HANDS.
AND NO GIRLS I'M SPECIAL FRIENDS WITH.

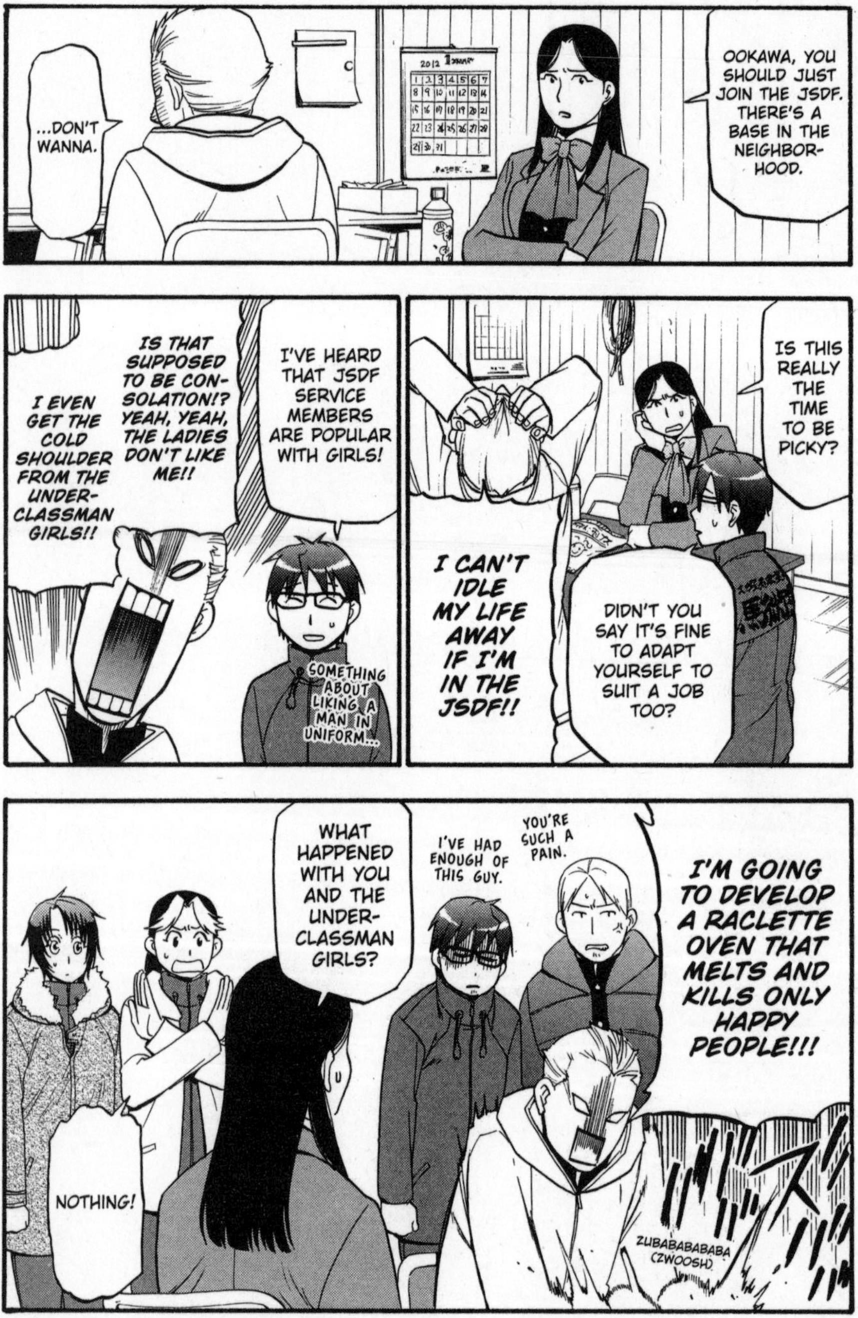
OOKAWA, YOU SHOULD JUST JOIN THE JSDF. THERE'S A BASE IN THE NEIGHBORHOOD.
...DON'T WANNA.
IS THIS REALLY THE TIME TO BE PICKY?
DIDN'T YOU SAY IT'S FINE TO ADAPT YOURSELF TO SUIT A JOB TOO?
I CAN'T IDLE MY LIFE AWAY IF I'M IN THE JSDF!!
I'VE HEARD THAT JSDF SERVICE MEMBERS ARE POPULAR WITH GIRLS!
SOMETHING ABOUT LIKING A MAN IN UNIFORM...
IS THAT SUPPOSED TO BE CONSOLATION!? YEAH, YEAH, THE LADIES DON'T LIKE ME!!
I EVEN GET THE COLD SHOULDER FROM THE UNDERCLASSMAN GIRLS!!
I'M GOING TO DEVELOP A RACLETTE OVEN THAT MELTS AND KILLS ONLY HAPPY PEOPLE!!!
ZUBABABABABA (ZWOOSH)
YOU'RE SUCH A PAIN.
I'VE HAD ENOUGH OF THIS GUY.
WHAT HAPPENED WITH YOU AND THE UNDERCLASSMAN GIRLS?
NOTHING!

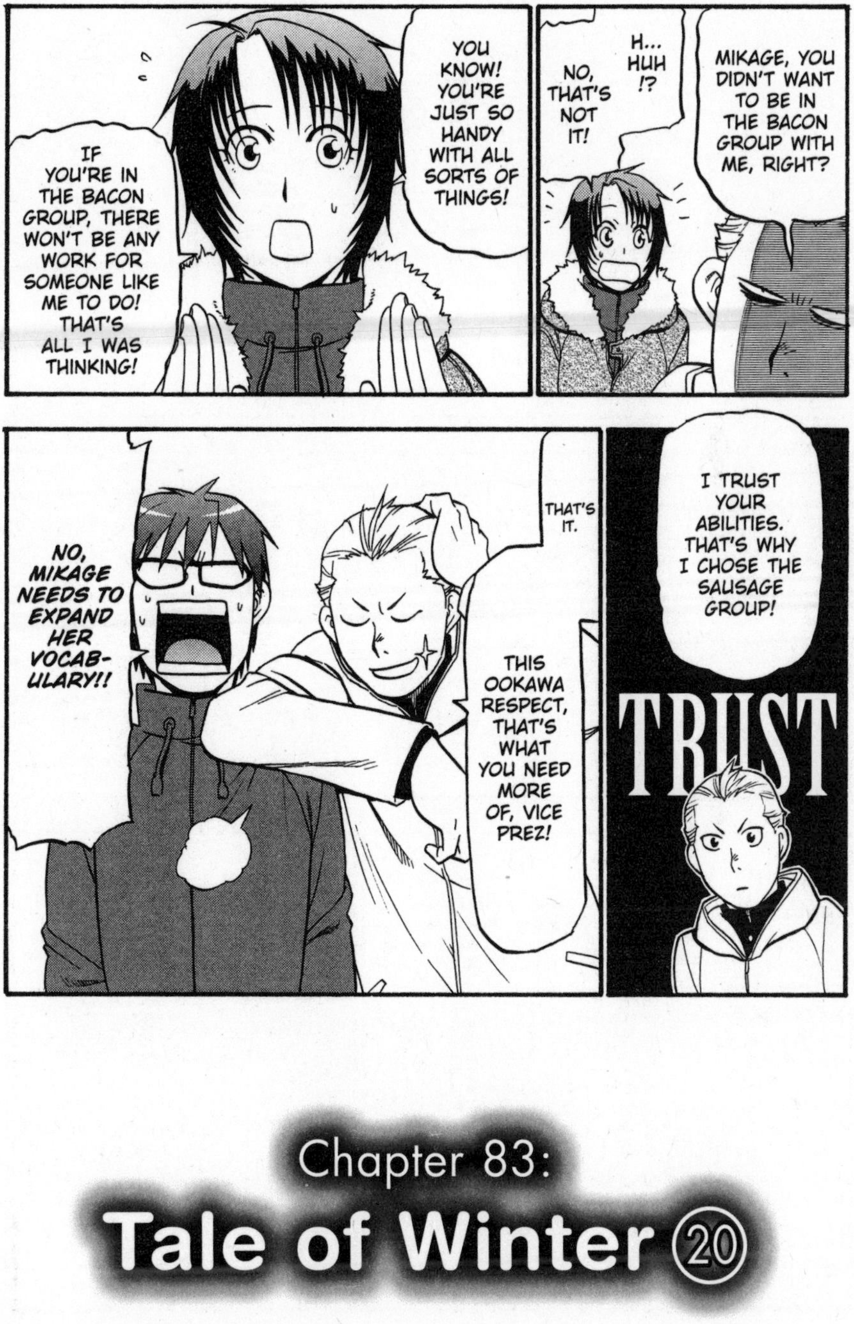
MIKAGE, YOU DIDN'T WANT TO BE IN THE BACON GROUP WITH ME, RIGHT?
H... HUH!?
NO, THAT'S NOT IT!
YOU KNOW! YOU'RE JUST SO HANDY WITH ALL SORTS OF THINGS!
IF YOU'RE IN THE BACON GROUP, THERE WON'T BE ANY WORK FOR SOMEONE LIKE ME TO DO! THAT'S ALL I WAS THINKING!
I TRUST YOUR ABILITIES. THAT'S WHY I CHOSE THE SAUSAGE GROUP!
TRUST
THAT'S IT.
THIS OOKAWA RESPECT, THAT'S WHAT YOU NEED MORE OF, VICE PREZ!
NO, MIKAGE NEEDS TO EXPAND HER VOCAB-ULARY!!

Chapter 83: Tale of Winter ⑳

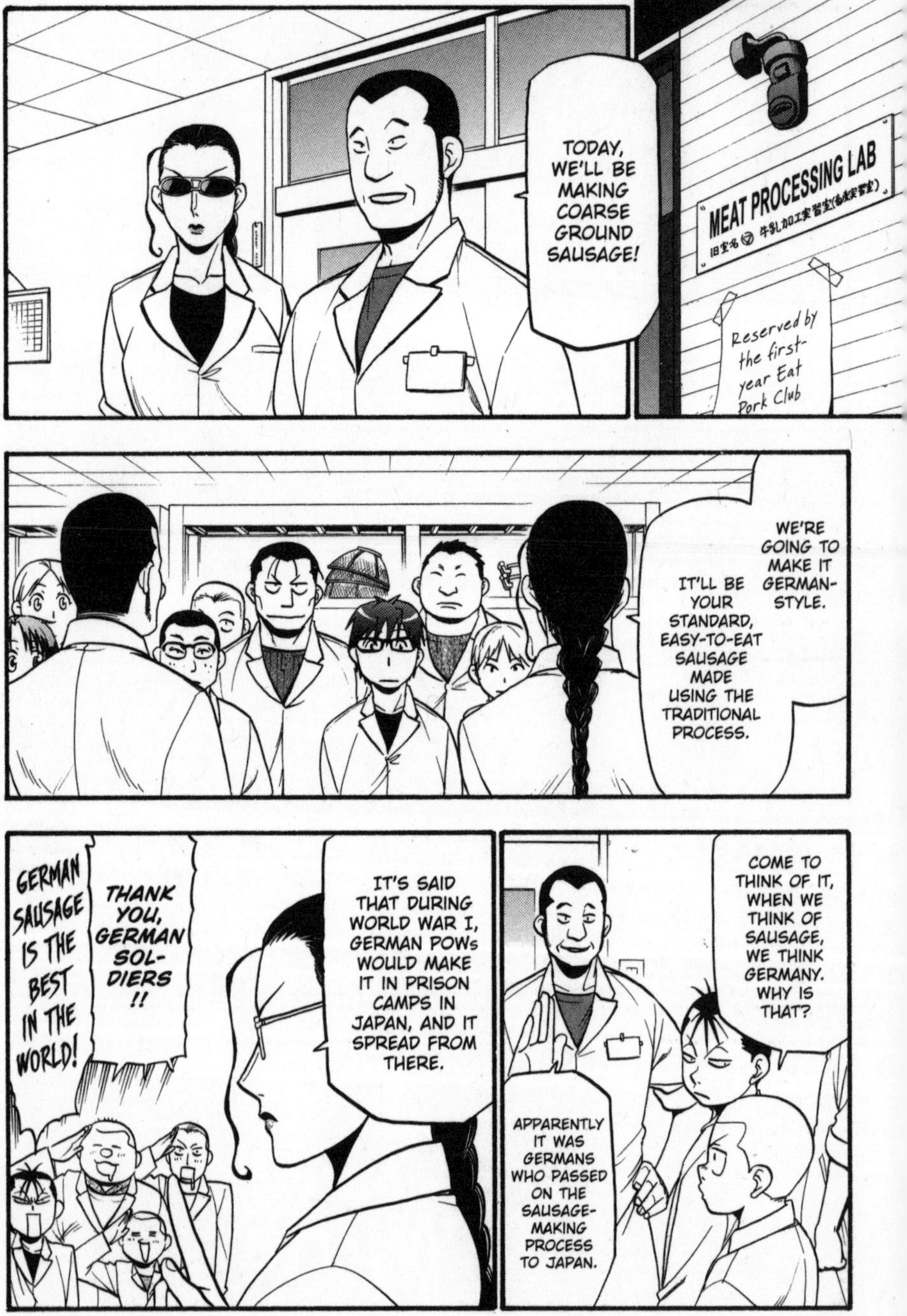
MEAT PROCESSING LAB
Reserved by the first-year Eat Pork Club
TODAY, WE'LL BE MAKING COARSE GROUND SAUSAGE!
WE'RE GOING TO MAKE IT GERMAN-STYLE.
IT'LL BE YOUR STANDARD, EASY-TO-EAT SAUSAGE MADE USING THE TRADITIONAL PROCESS.
COME TO THINK OF IT, WHEN WE THINK OF SAUSAGE, WE THINK GERMANY. WHY IS THAT?
APPARENTLY IT WAS GERMANS WHO PASSED ON THE SAUSAGE-MAKING PROCESS TO JAPAN.
IT'S SAID THAT DURING WORLD WAR I, GERMAN POWs WOULD MAKE IT IN PRISON CAMPS IN JAPAN, AND IT SPREAD FROM THERE.
THANK YOU, GERMAN SOLDIERS!!
GERMAN SAUSAGE IS THE BEST IN THE WORLD!

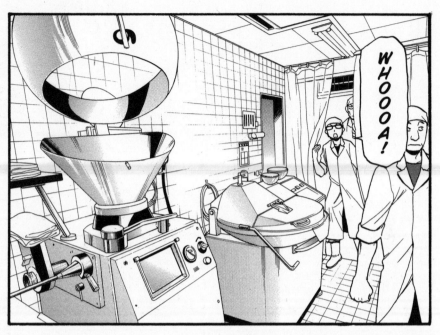

WHOOOA!
THIS SCHOOL SERIOUSLY HAS EVERYTHING.
WHAT'S GOING ON WITH THE SCHOOL BUDGET?
WE GOT IT ALL FOR CHEAP FROM A MANUFACTURER THAT WENT BANKRUPT.
THESE MACHINES ARE GERMAN TOO.
A BANKRUPT BUSINESS...

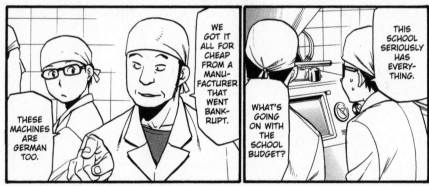

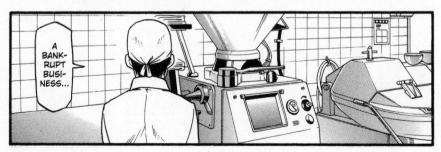

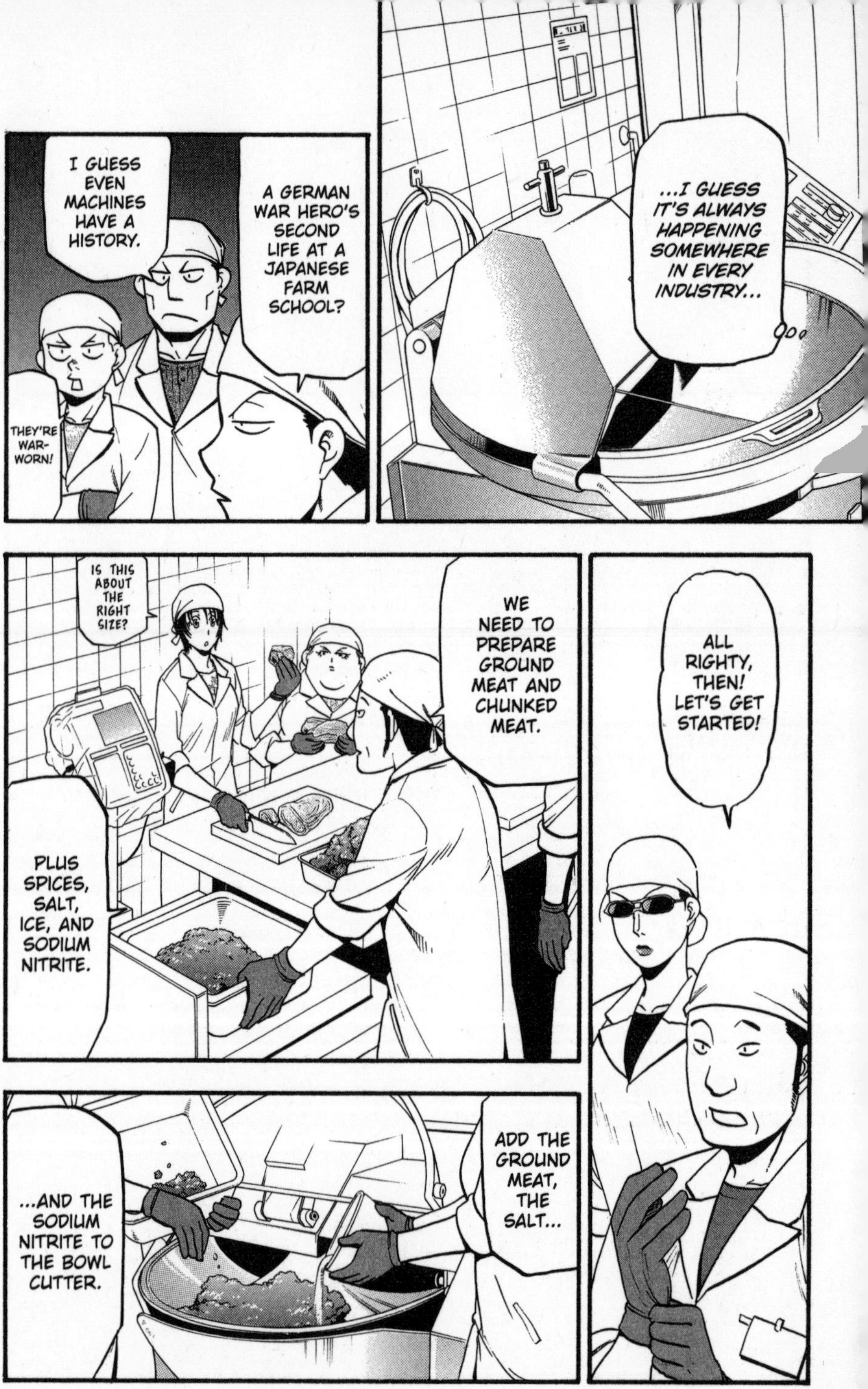
...I GUESS IT'S ALWAYS HAPPENING SOMEWHERE IN EVERY INDUSTRY...
A GERMAN WAR HERO'S SECOND LIFE AT A JAPANESE FARM SCHOOL?
I GUESS EVEN MACHINES HAVE A HISTORY.
THEY'RE WAR-WORN!
ALL RIGHTY, THEN! LET'S GET STARTED!
WE NEED TO PREPARE GROUND MEAT AND CHUNKED MEAT.
IS THIS ABOUT THE RIGHT SIZE?
PLUS SPICES, SALT, ICE, AND SODIUM NITRITE.
ADD THE GROUND MEAT, THE SALT...
...AND THE SODIUM NITRITE TO THE BOWL CUTTER.

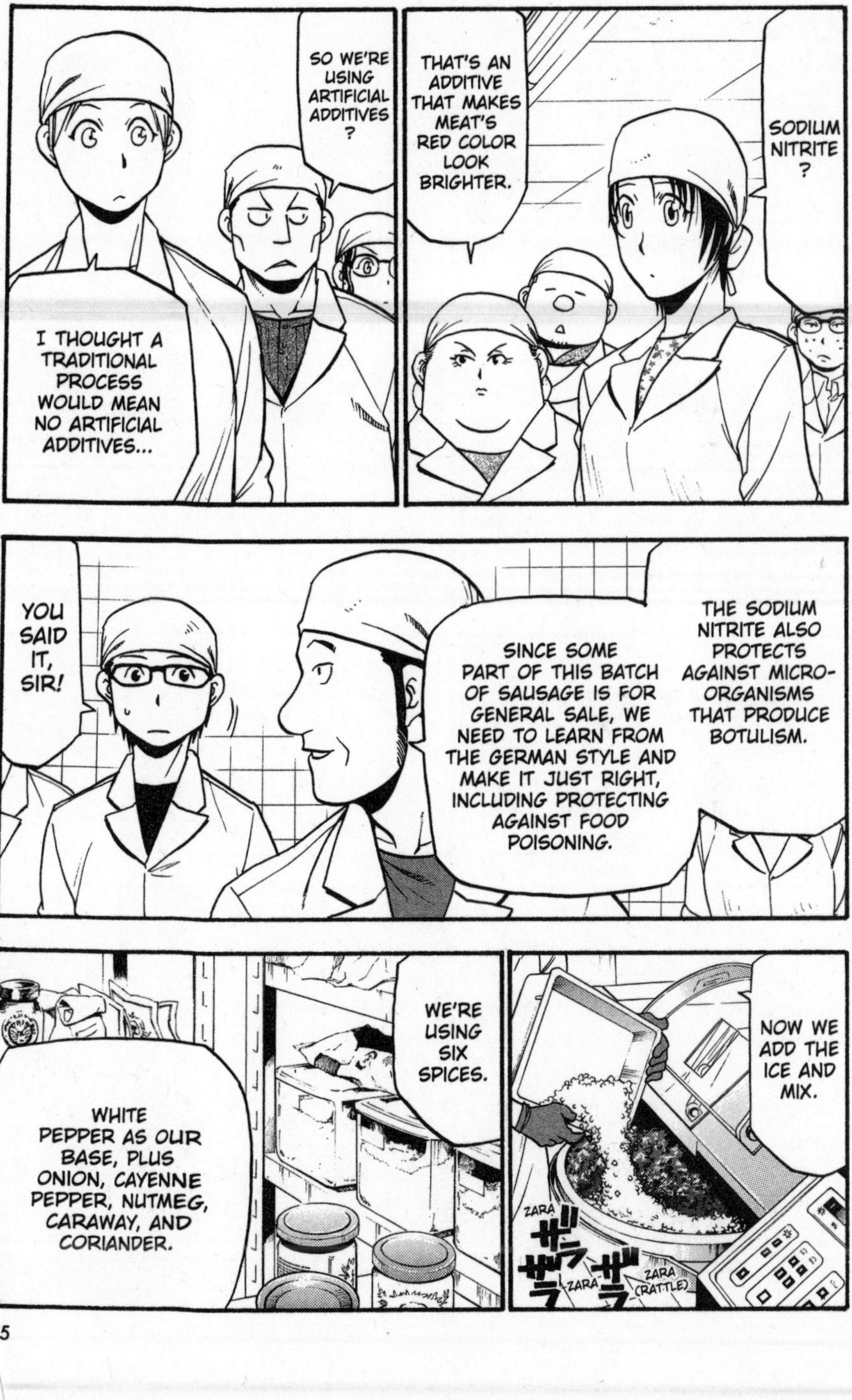
SODIUM NITRITE ?
THAT'S AN ADDITIVE THAT MAKES MEAT'S RED COLOR LOOK BRIGHTER.
SO WE'RE USING ARTIFICIAL ADDITIVES ?
I THOUGHT A TRADITIONAL PROCESS WOULD MEAN NO ARTIFICIAL ADDITIVES...
THE SODIUM NITRITE ALSO PROTECTS AGAINST MICRO-ORGANISMS THAT PRODUCE BOTULISM.
SINCE SOME PART OF THIS BATCH OF SAUSAGE IS FOR GENERAL SALE, WE NEED TO LEARN FROM THE GERMAN STYLE AND MAKE IT JUST RIGHT, INCLUDING PROTECTING AGAINST FOOD POISONING.
YOU SAID IT, SIR!
NOW WE ADD THE ICE AND MIX.
ZARA
ZARA
ZARA (RATTLE)
WE'RE USING SIX SPICES.
WHITE PEPPER AS OUR BASE, PLUS ONION, CAYENNE PEPPER, NUTMEG, CARAWAY, AND CORIANDER.

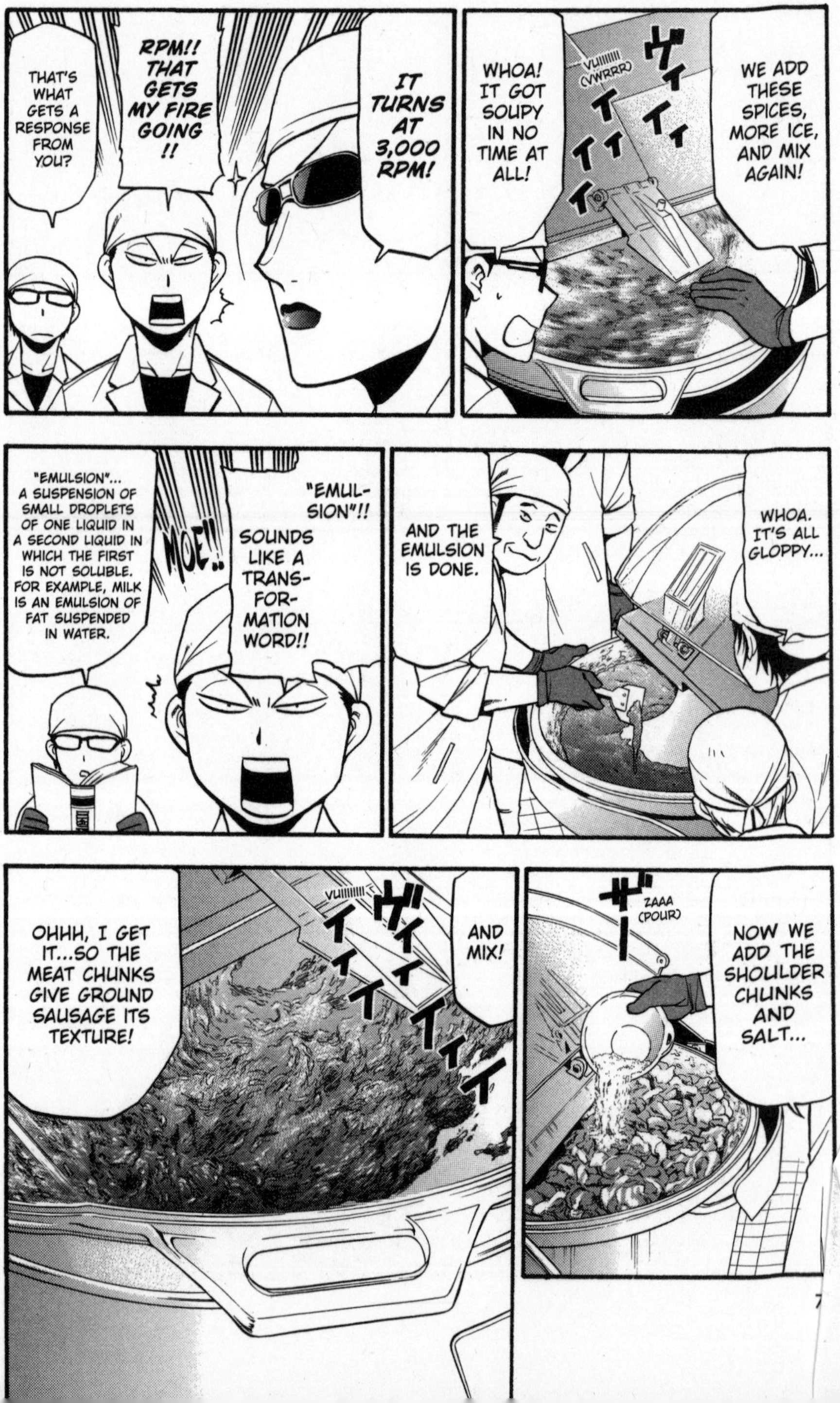
WE ADD THESE SPICES, MORE ICE, AND MIX AGAIN!
VUIIIIIII (VWRRR)
WHOA! IT GOT SOUPY IN NO TIME AT ALL!
IT TURNS AT 3,000 RPM!
RPM!! THAT GETS MY FIRE GOING!!
THAT'S WHAT GETS A RESPONSE FROM YOU?
WHOA. IT'S ALL GLOPPY...
AND THE EMULSION IS DONE.
"EMULSION"!!
SOUNDS LIKE A TRANSFORMATION WORD!!
MOE!!
"EMULSION"... A SUSPENSION OF SMALL DROPLETS OF ONE LIQUID IN A SECOND LIQUID IN WHICH THE FIRST IS NOT SOLUBLE. FOR EXAMPLE, MILK IS AN EMULSION OF FAT SUSPENDED IN WATER.
ZAAA (POUR)
NOW WE ADD THE SHOULDER CHUNKS AND SALT...
AND MIX!
VUIIIIIII
OHHH, I GET IT...SO THE MEAT CHUNKS GIVE GROUND SAUSAGE ITS TEXTURE!

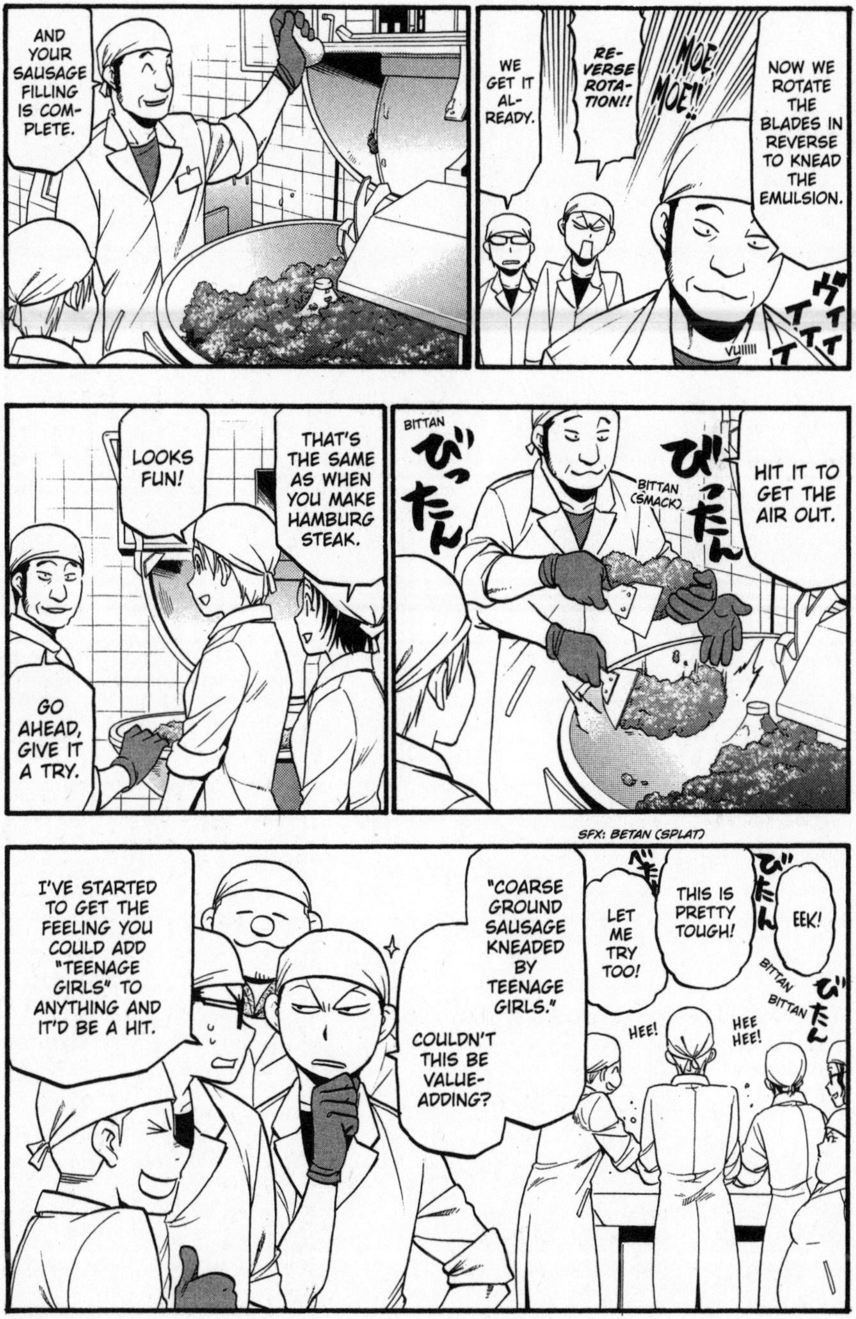
NOW WE ROTATE THE BLADES IN REVERSE TO KNEAD THE EMULSION.
MOE MOE!!
REVERSE ROTATION!!
WE GET IT ALREADY.
VUIIIII
AND YOUR SAUSAGE FILLING IS COMPLETE.
HIT IT TO GET THE AIR OUT.
びったん
BITTAN (SMACK)
びったん
BITTAN
THAT'S THE SAME AS WHEN YOU MAKE HAMBURG STEAK.
LOOKS FUN!
GO AHEAD, GIVE IT A TRY.
SFX: BETAN (SPLAT)
EEK!
BITTAN BITTAN
THIS IS PRETTY TOUGH!
LET ME TRY TOO!
HEE HEE!
HEE!
"COARSE GROUND SAUSAGE KNEADED BY TEENAGE GIRLS."
COULDN'T THIS BE VALUE-ADDING?
I'VE STARTED TO GET THE FEELING YOU COULD ADD "TEENAGE GIRLS" TO ANYTHING AND IT'D BE A HIT.

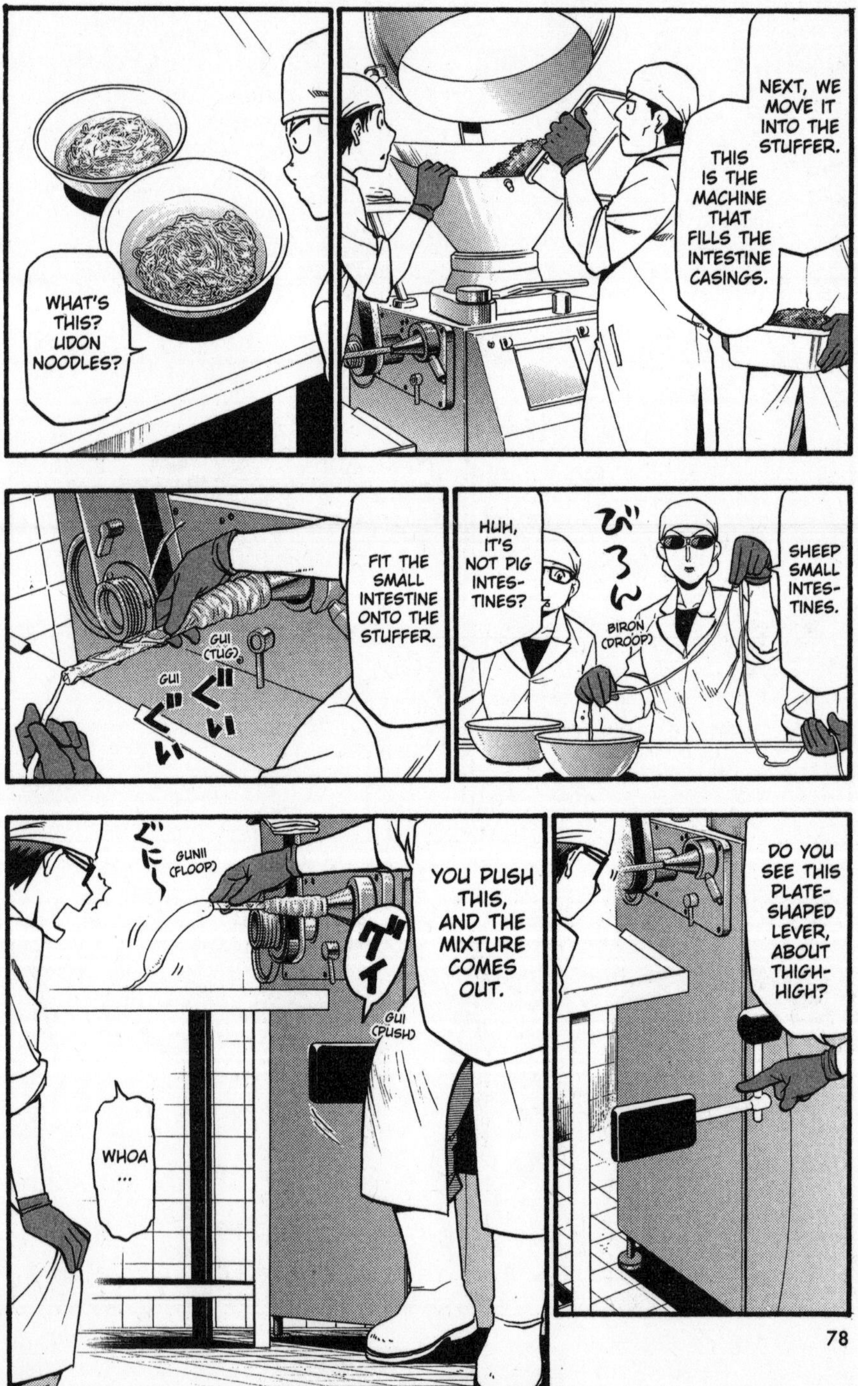
NEXT, WE MOVE IT INTO THE STUFFER.
THIS IS THE MACHINE THAT FILLS THE INTESTINE CASINGS.
WHAT'S THIS? UDON NOODLES?
SHEEP SMALL INTES-TINES.
HUH, IT'S NOT PIG INTES-TINES?
びろん
BIRON (DROOP)
FIT THE SMALL INTESTINE ONTO THE STUFFER.
GUI (TUG)
GUI
ぐい ぐい ぐい
DO YOU SEE THIS PLATE-SHAPED LEVER, ABOUT THIGH-HIGH?
YOU PUSH THIS, AND THE MIXTURE COMES OUT.
グイ
GUI (PUSH)
ぐに~
GUNII (FLOOP)
WHOA ...

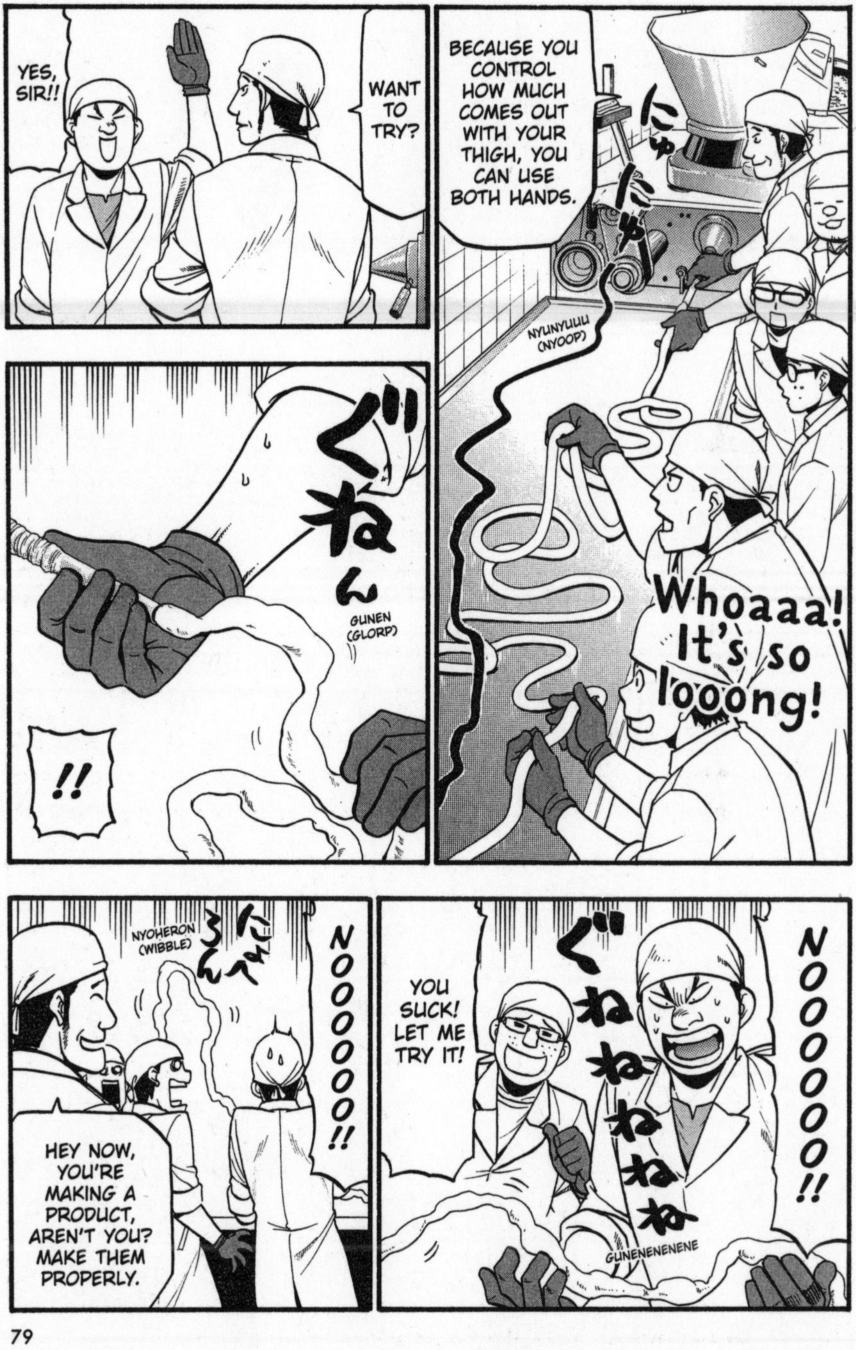
BECAUSE YOU CONTROL HOW MUCH COMES OUT WITH YOUR THIGH, YOU CAN USE BOTH HANDS.
NYUNYUUU (NYOOP)
Whoaaa! It's so looong!
WANT TO TRY?
YES, SIR!!
ぐねん
GUNEN (GLORP)
!!
NOOOOOOOO!!
ぐねねねね
GUNENENENENE
YOU SUCK! LET ME TRY IT!
NOOOOOOOO!!
NYOHERON (WIBBLE)
HEY NOW, YOU'RE MAKING A PRODUCT, AREN'T YOU? MAKE THEM PROPERLY.

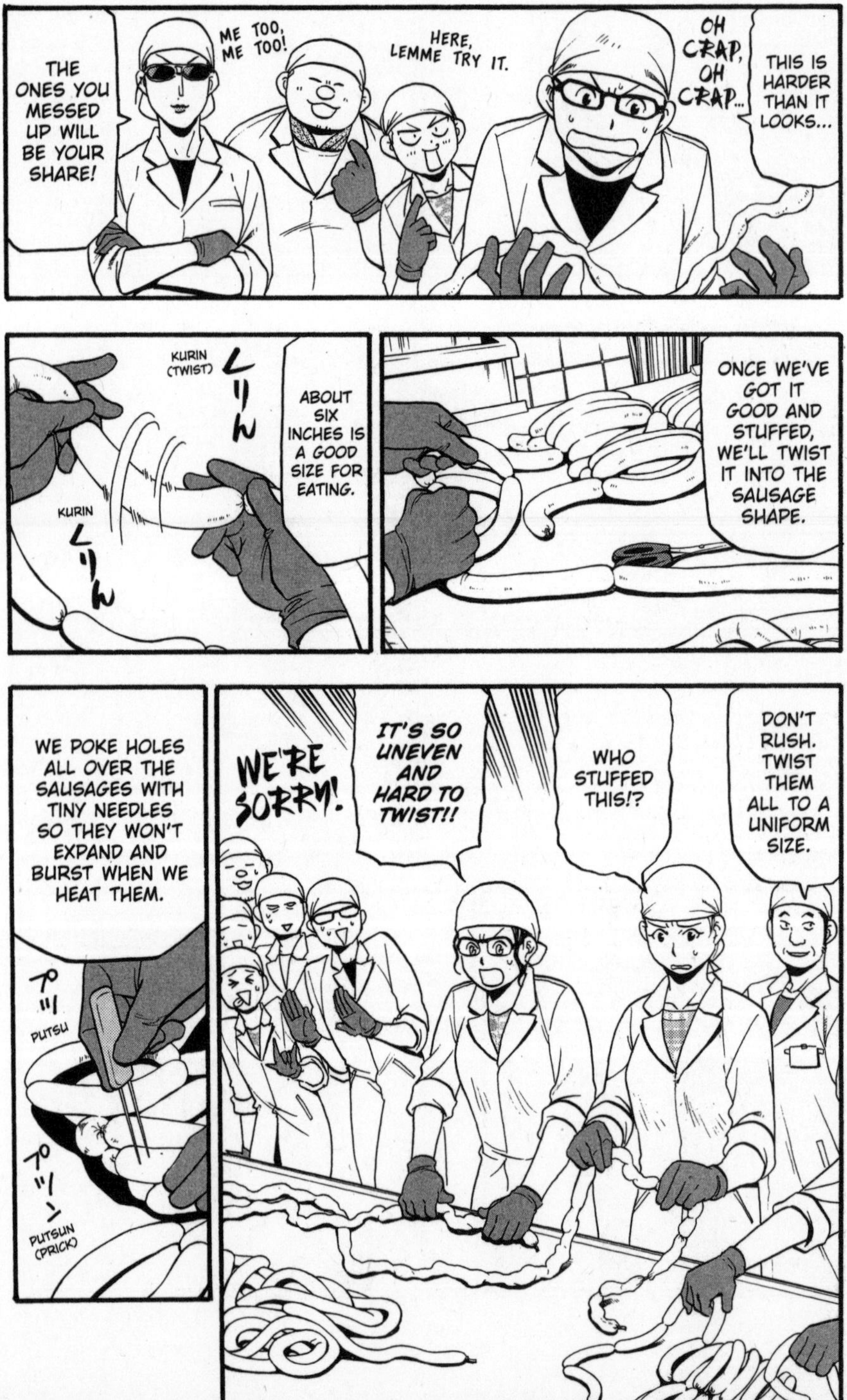
THIS IS HARDER THAN IT LOOKS...
OH CRAP, OH CRAP...
HERE, LEMME TRY IT.
ME TOO, ME TOO!
THE ONES YOU MESSED UP WILL BE YOUR SHARE!
ONCE WE'VE GOT IT GOOD AND STUFFED, WE'LL TWIST IT INTO THE SAUSAGE SHAPE.
ABOUT SIX INCHES IS A GOOD SIZE FOR EATING.
くりん KURIN (TWIST)
くりん KURIN
DON'T RUSH. TWIST THEM ALL TO A UNIFORM SIZE.
WHO STUFFED THIS!?
IT'S SO UNEVEN AND HARD TO TWIST!!
WE'RE SORRY!
WE POKE HOLES ALL OVER THE SAUSAGES WITH TINY NEEDLES SO THEY WON'T EXPAND AND BURST WHEN WE HEAT THEM.
プツ PUTSU
プツン PUTSUN (PRICK)

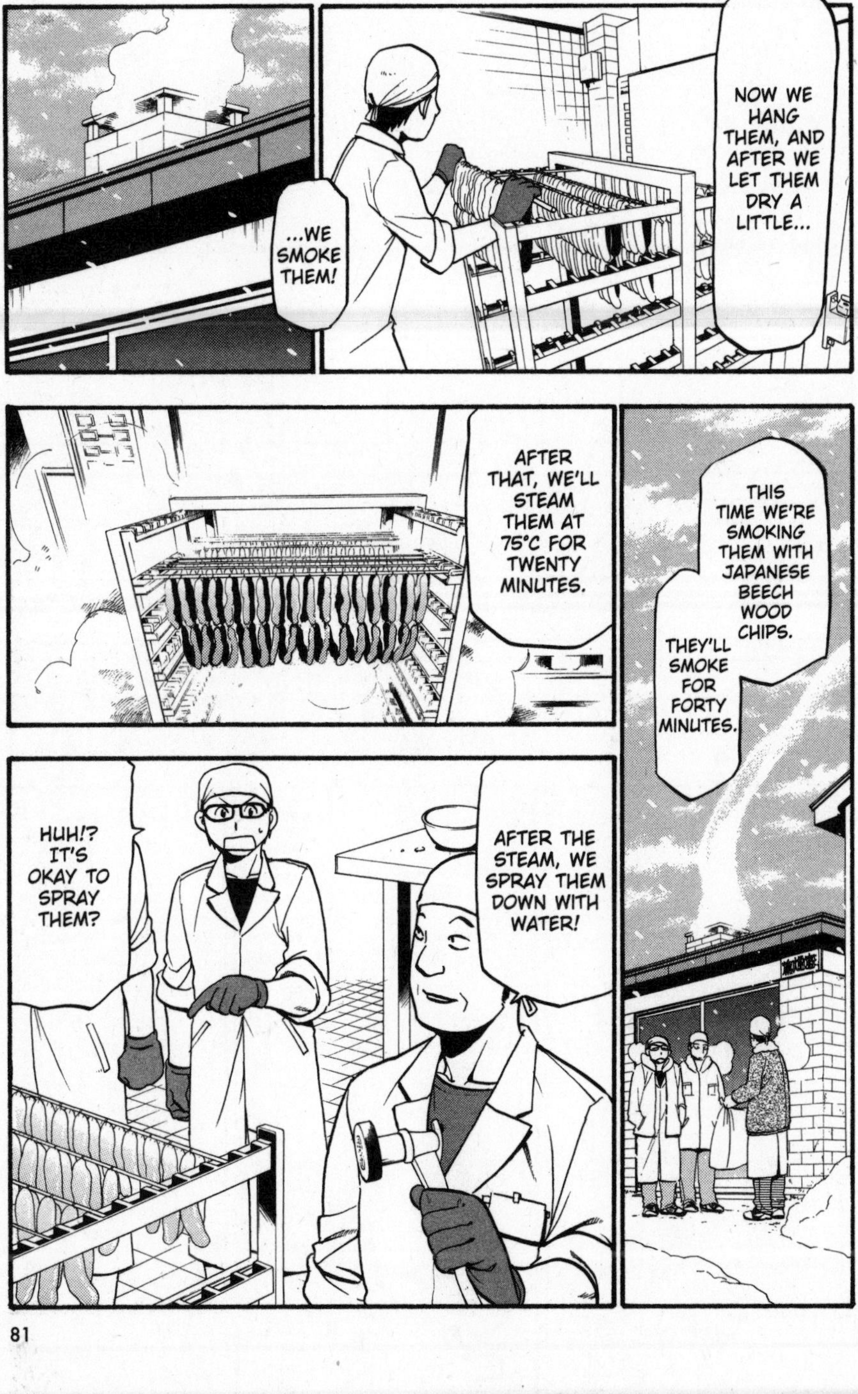
NOW WE HANG THEM, AND AFTER WE LET THEM DRY A LITTLE...
...WE SMOKE THEM!
THIS TIME WE'RE SMOKING THEM WITH JAPANESE BEECH WOOD CHIPS.
THEY'LL SMOKE FOR FORTY MINUTES.
AFTER THAT, WE'LL STEAM THEM AT 75°C FOR TWENTY MINUTES.
AFTER THE STEAM, WE SPRAY THEM DOWN WITH WATER!
HUH!? IT'S OKAY TO SPRAY THEM?

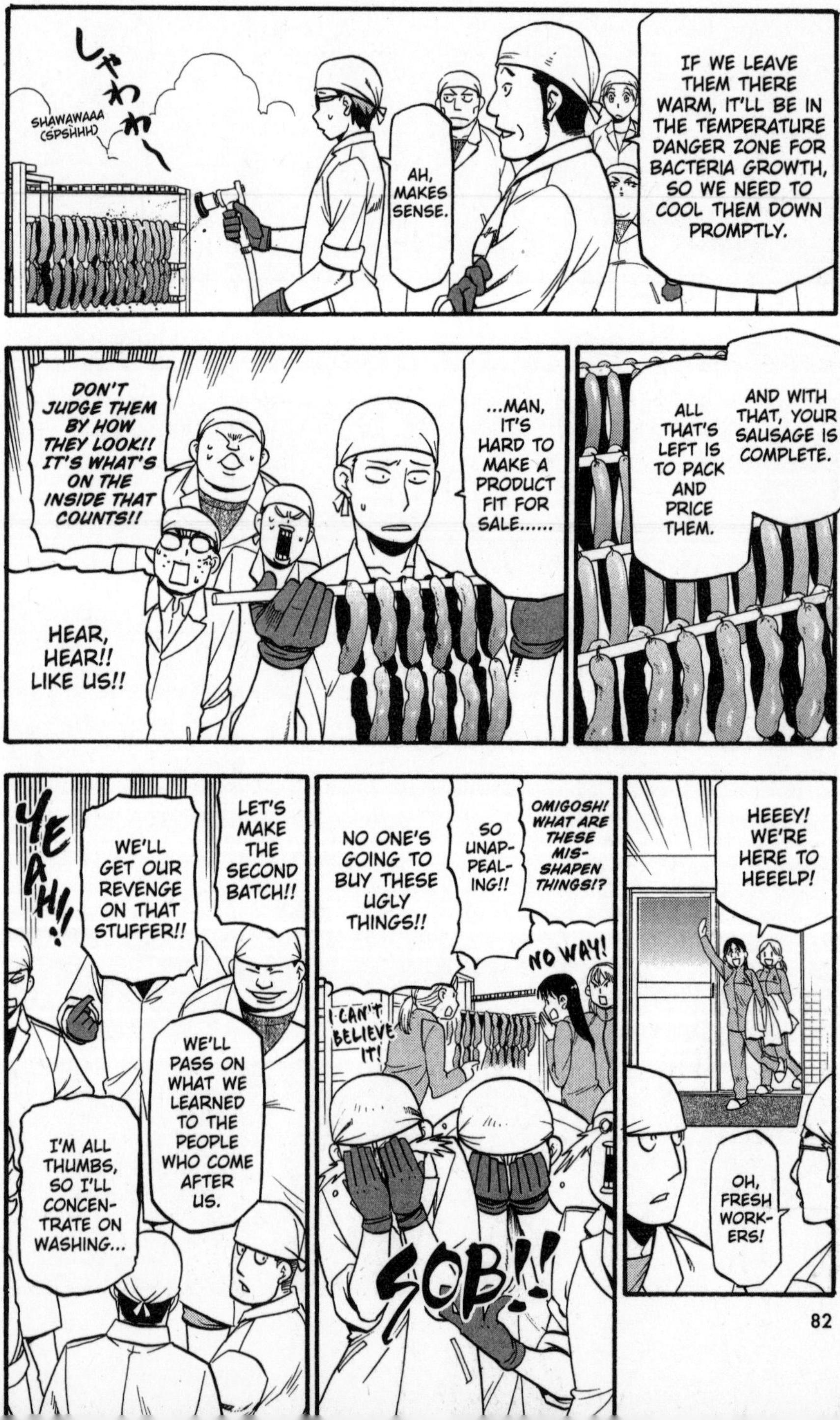
IF WE LEAVE THEM THERE WARM, IT'LL BE IN THE TEMPERATURE DANGER ZONE FOR BACTERIA GROWTH, SO WE NEED TO COOL THEM DOWN PROMPTLY.
AH, MAKES SENSE.
しゃわわ〜
SHAWAWAAA (SPSHHH)
AND WITH THAT, YOUR SAUSAGE IS COMPLETE.
ALL THAT'S LEFT IS TO PACK AND PRICE THEM.
...MAN, IT'S HARD TO MAKE A PRODUCT FIT FOR SALE......
DON'T JUDGE THEM BY HOW THEY LOOK!! IT'S WHAT'S ON THE INSIDE THAT COUNTS!!
HEAR, HEAR!! LIKE US!!
HEEEY! WE'RE HERE TO HEEELP!
OH, FRESH WORKERS!
OMIGOSH! WHAT ARE THESE MIS-SHAPEN THINGS!?
SO UNAP-PEAL-ING!!
NO ONE'S GOING TO BUY THESE UGLY THINGS!!
NO WAY!
I CAN'T BELIEVE IT!
SOB!!
LET'S MAKE THE SECOND BATCH!!
WE'LL GET OUR REVENGE ON THAT STUFFER!!
YEAH!!
WE'LL PASS ON WHAT WE LEARNED TO THE PEOPLE WHO COME AFTER US.
I'M ALL THUMBS, SO I'LL CONCEN-TRATE ON WASHING...

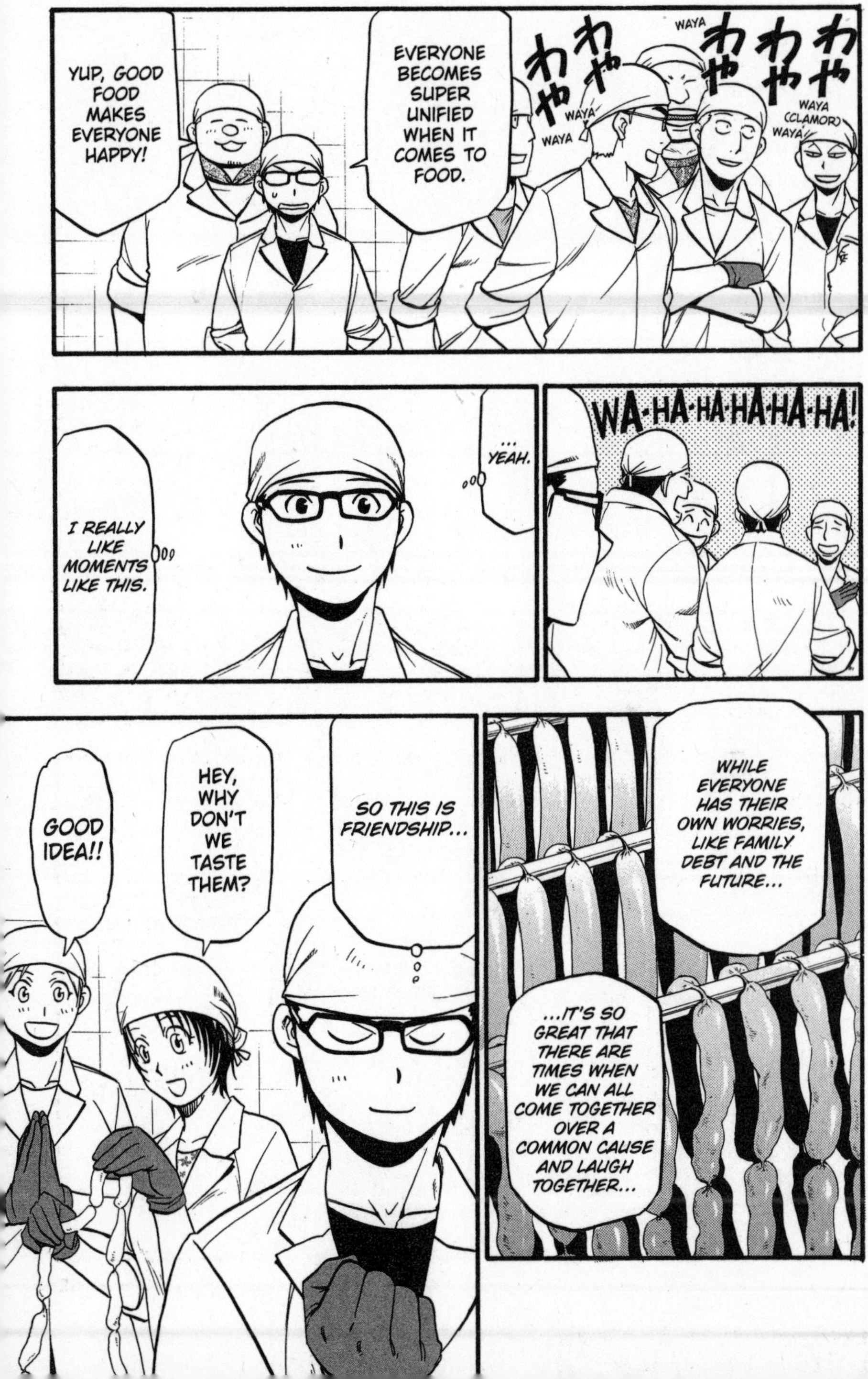
わや
WAYA
わや
WAYA (CLAMOR)
わや
WAYA
わや
WAYA
わや
EVERYONE BECOMES SUPER UNIFIED WHEN IT COMES TO FOOD.
YUP, GOOD FOOD MAKES EVERYONE HAPPY!
WA-HA-HA-HA-HA-HA!
...YEAH.
I REALLY LIKE MOMENTS LIKE THIS.
WHILE EVERYONE HAS THEIR OWN WORRIES, LIKE FAMILY DEBT AND THE FUTURE...
...IT'S SO GREAT THAT THERE ARE TIMES WHEN WE CAN ALL COME TOGETHER OVER A COMMON CAUSE AND LAUGH TOGETHER...
SO THIS IS FRIENDSHIP...
HEY, WHY DON'T WE TASTE THEM?
GOOD IDEA!!

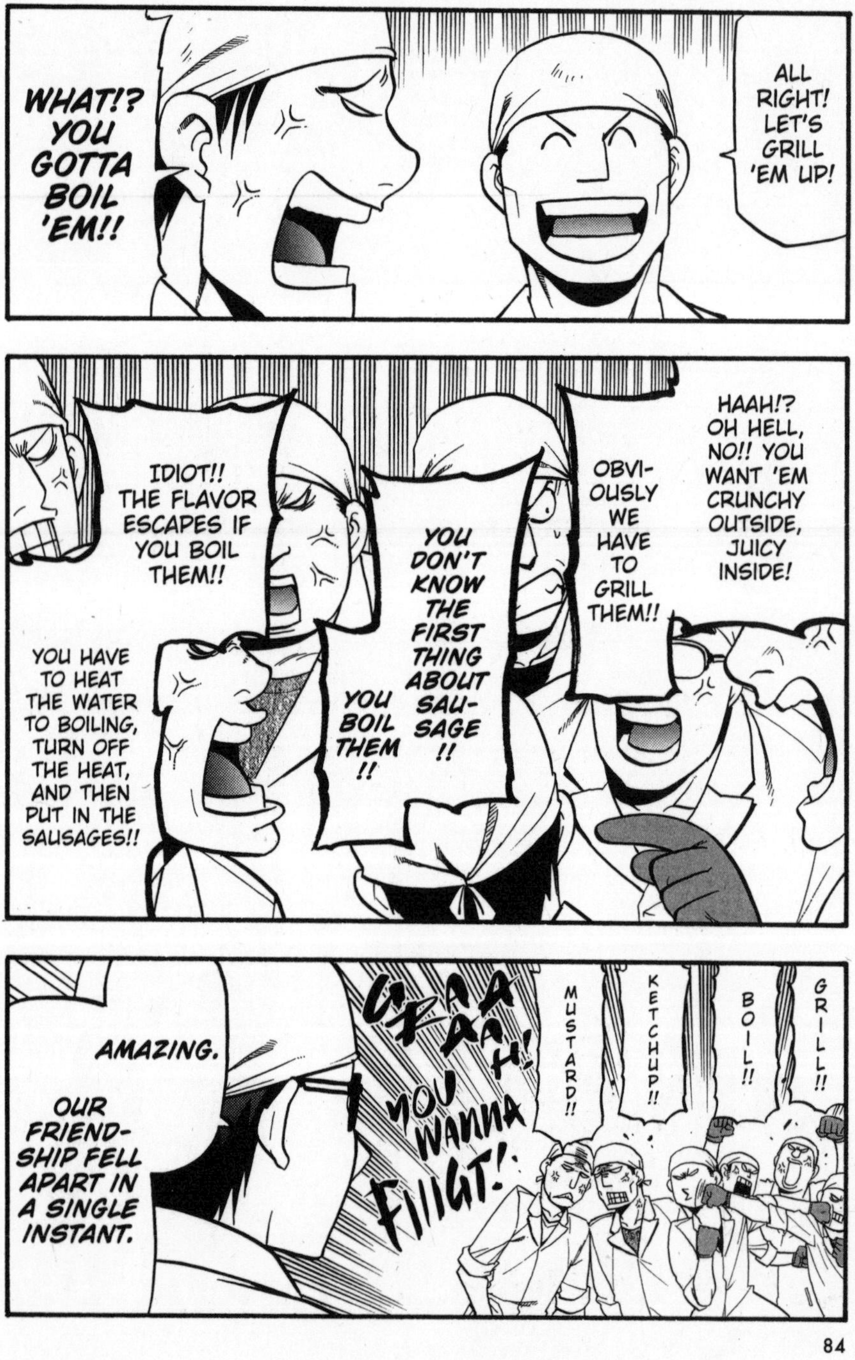
ALL RIGHT! LET'S GRILL 'EM UP!
WHAT!? YOU GOTTA BOIL 'EM!!
HAAH!? OH HELL, NO!! YOU WANT 'EM CRUNCHY OUTSIDE, JUICY INSIDE!
OBVIOUSLY WE HAVE TO GRILL THEM!!
YOU DON'T KNOW THE FIRST THING ABOUT SAUSAGE!!
YOU BOIL THEM!!
IDIOT!! THE FLAVOR ESCAPES IF YOU BOIL THEM!!
YOU HAVE TO HEAT THE WATER TO BOILING, TURN OFF THE HEAT, AND THEN PUT IN THE SAUSAGES!!
GRILL!!
BOIL!!
KETCHUP!!
MUSTARD!!
UZAAAAH! YOU WANNA FIIIGT!
AMAZING.
OUR FRIENDSHIP FELL APART IN A SINGLE INSTANT.

Silver Spoon

PORK BOWL

SANGENTON HOG
(CROSSBREED OF THREE
PIG BREEDS)

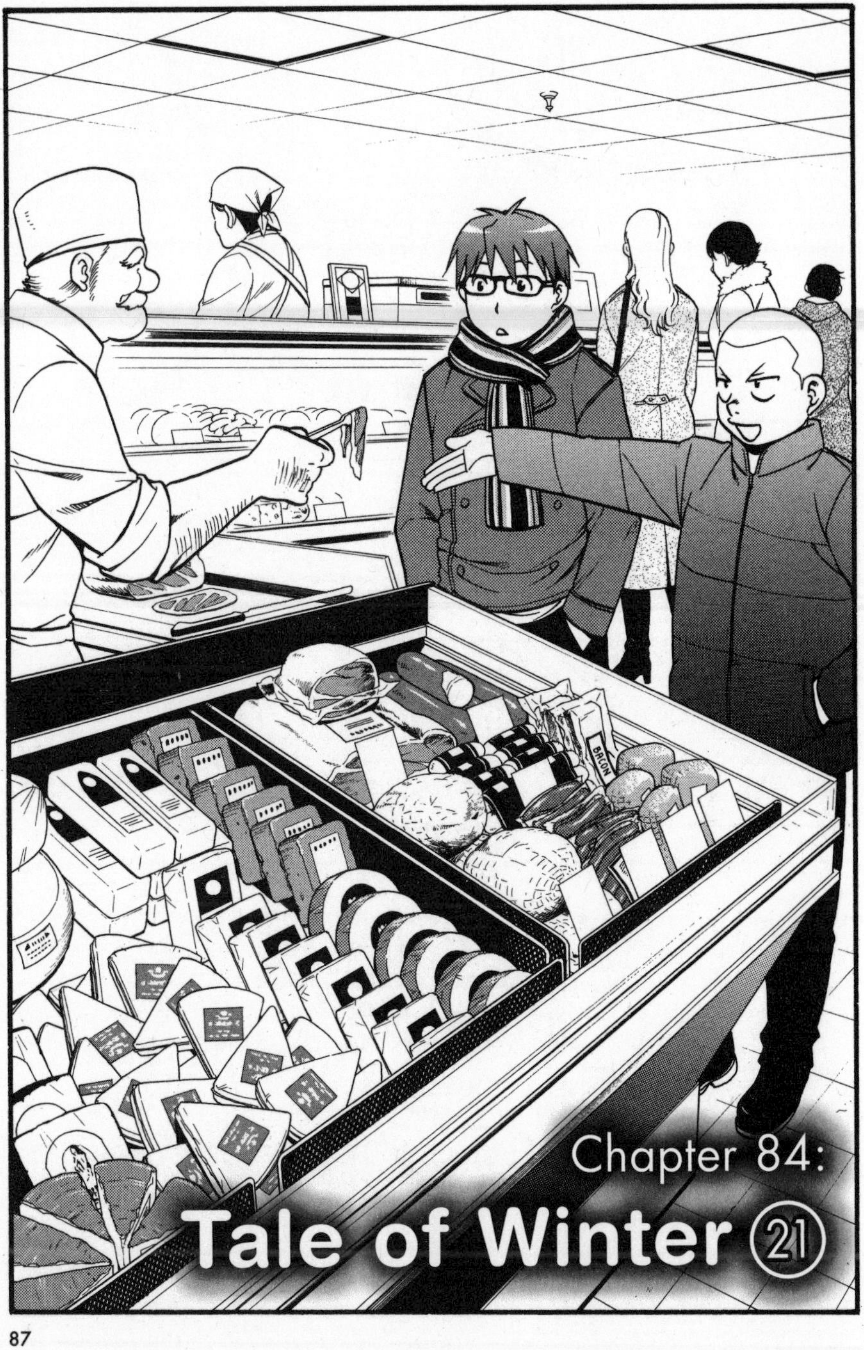
BACON
Chapter 84:
Tale of Winter ㉑

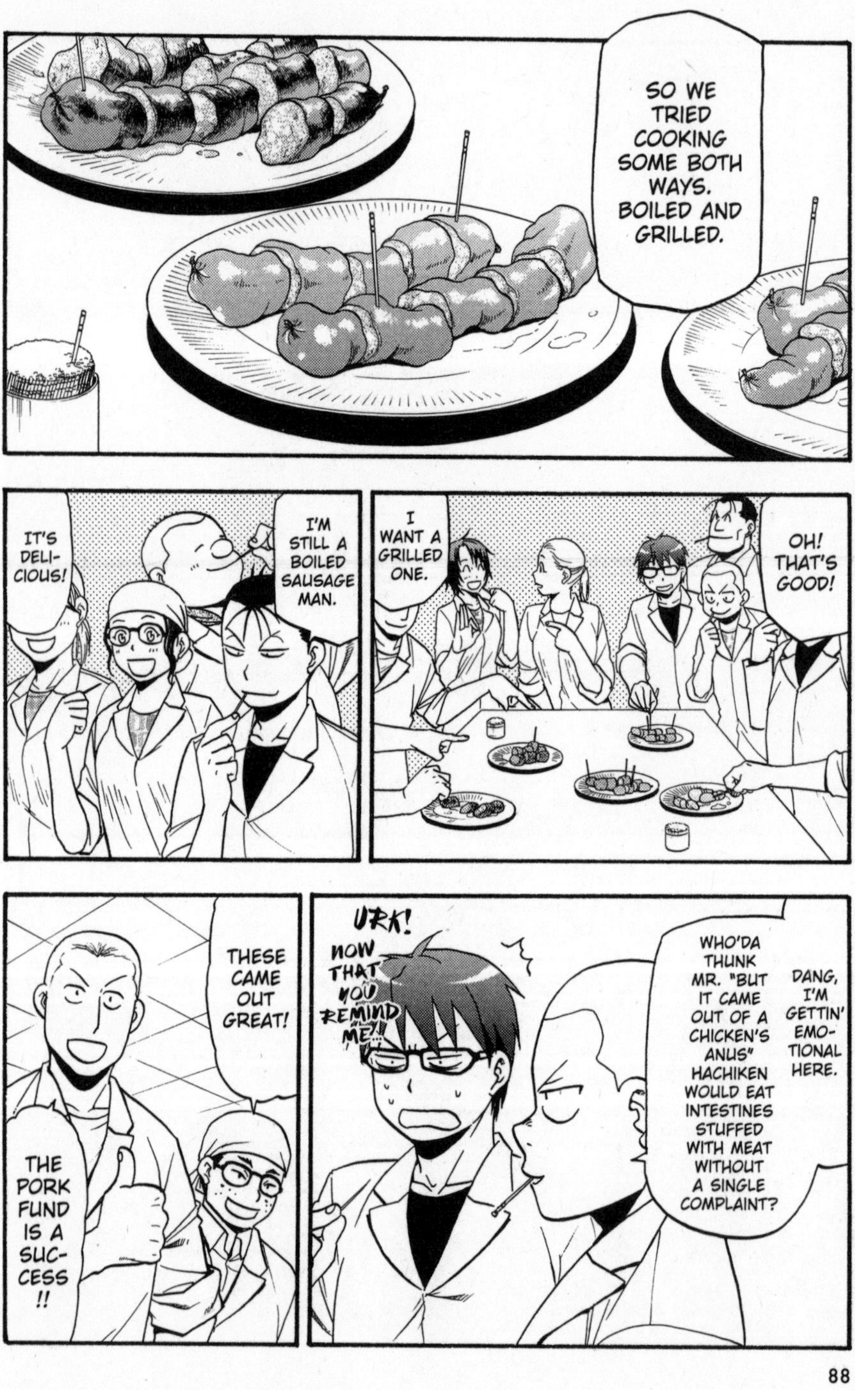
SO WE TRIED COOKING SOME BOTH WAYS. BOILED AND GRILLED.
OH! THAT'S GOOD!
I WANT A GRILLED ONE.
I'M STILL A BOILED SAUSAGE MAN.
IT'S DELICIOUS!
DANG, I'M GETTIN' EMOTIONAL HERE.
WHO'DA THUNK MR. "BUT IT CAME OUT OF A CHICKEN'S ANUS" HACHIKEN WOULD EAT INTESTINES STUFFED WITH MEAT WITHOUT A SINGLE COMPLAINT?
URK!
NOW THAT YOU REMIND ME...
THESE CAME OUT GREAT!
THE PORK FUND IS A SUCCESS!!

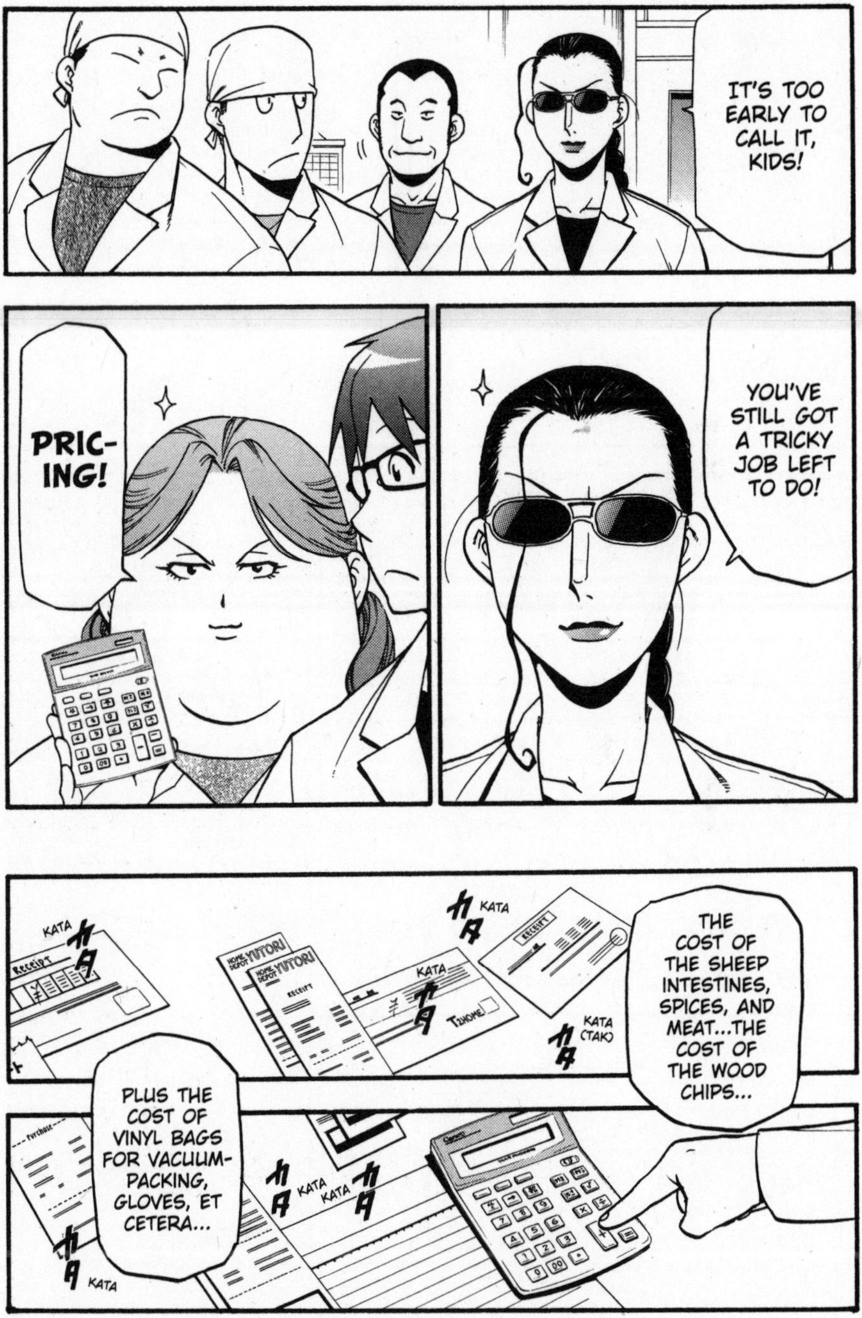
IT'S TOO EARLY TO CALL IT, KIDS!
YOU'VE STILL GOT A TRICKY JOB LEFT TO DO!
PRIC-ING!
KATA
THE COST OF THE SHEEP INTESTINES, SPICES, AND MEAT...THE COST OF THE WOOD CHIPS...
KATA (TAK)
KATA
KATA
KATA
KATA
PLUS THE COST OF VINYL BAGS FOR VACUUM-PACKING, GLOVES, ET CETERA...
KATA

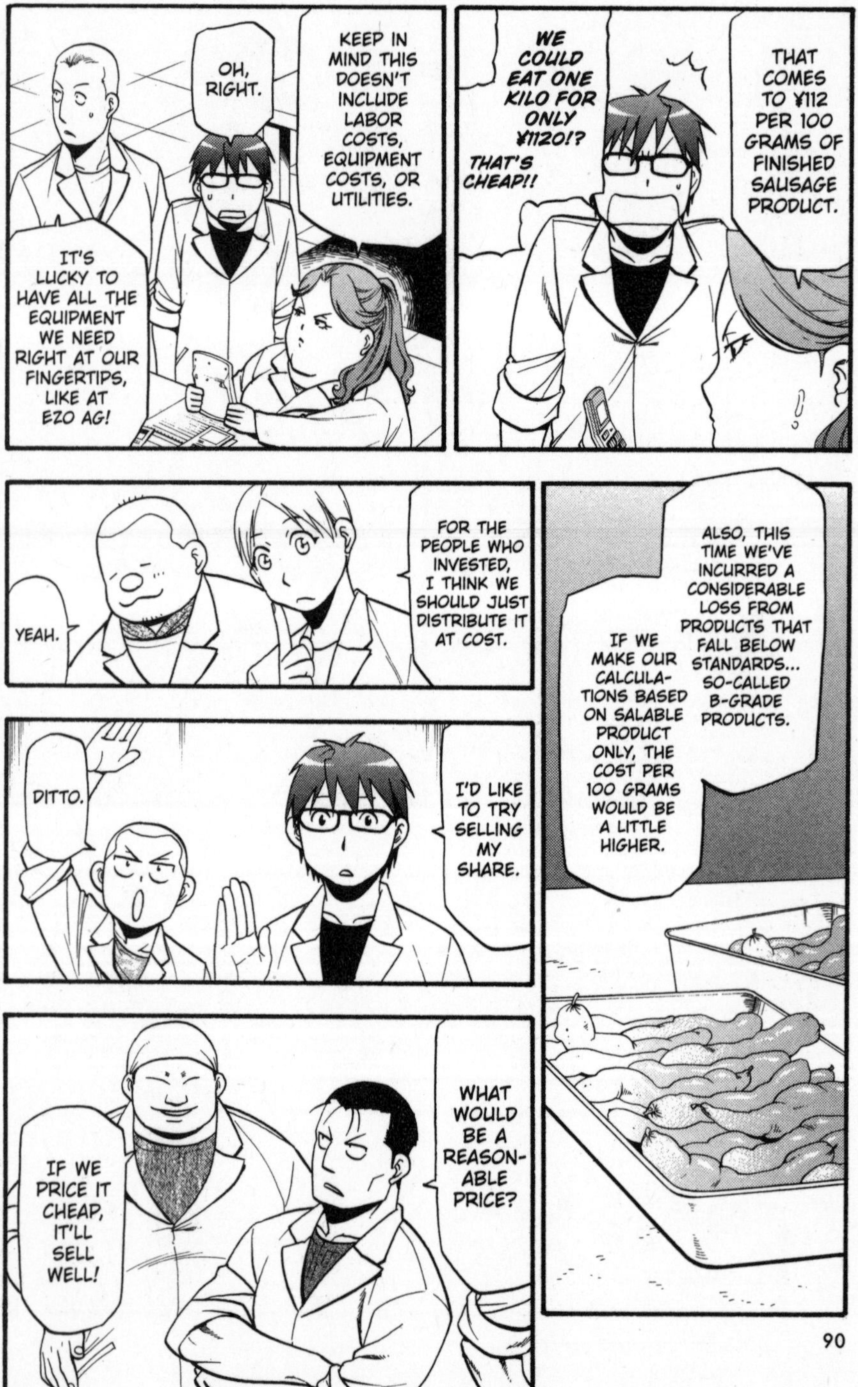
THAT COMES TO ¥112 PER 100 GRAMS OF FINISHED SAUSAGE PRODUCT.
WE COULD EAT ONE KILO FOR ONLY ¥1120!?
THAT'S CHEAP!!
KEEP IN MIND THIS DOESN'T INCLUDE LABOR COSTS, EQUIPMENT COSTS, OR UTILITIES.
OH, RIGHT.
IT'S LUCKY TO HAVE ALL THE EQUIPMENT WE NEED RIGHT AT OUR FINGERTIPS, LIKE AT EZO AG!
ALSO, THIS TIME WE'VE INCURRED A CONSIDERABLE LOSS FROM PRODUCTS THAT FALL BELOW STANDARDS... SO-CALLED B-GRADE PRODUCTS.
IF WE MAKE OUR CALCULATIONS BASED ON SALABLE PRODUCT ONLY, THE COST PER 100 GRAMS WOULD BE A LITTLE HIGHER.
FOR THE PEOPLE WHO INVESTED, I THINK WE SHOULD JUST DISTRIBUTE IT AT COST.
YEAH.
I'D LIKE TO TRY SELLING MY SHARE.
DITTO.
WHAT WOULD BE A REASONABLE PRICE?
IF WE PRICE IT CHEAP, IT'LL SELL WELL!

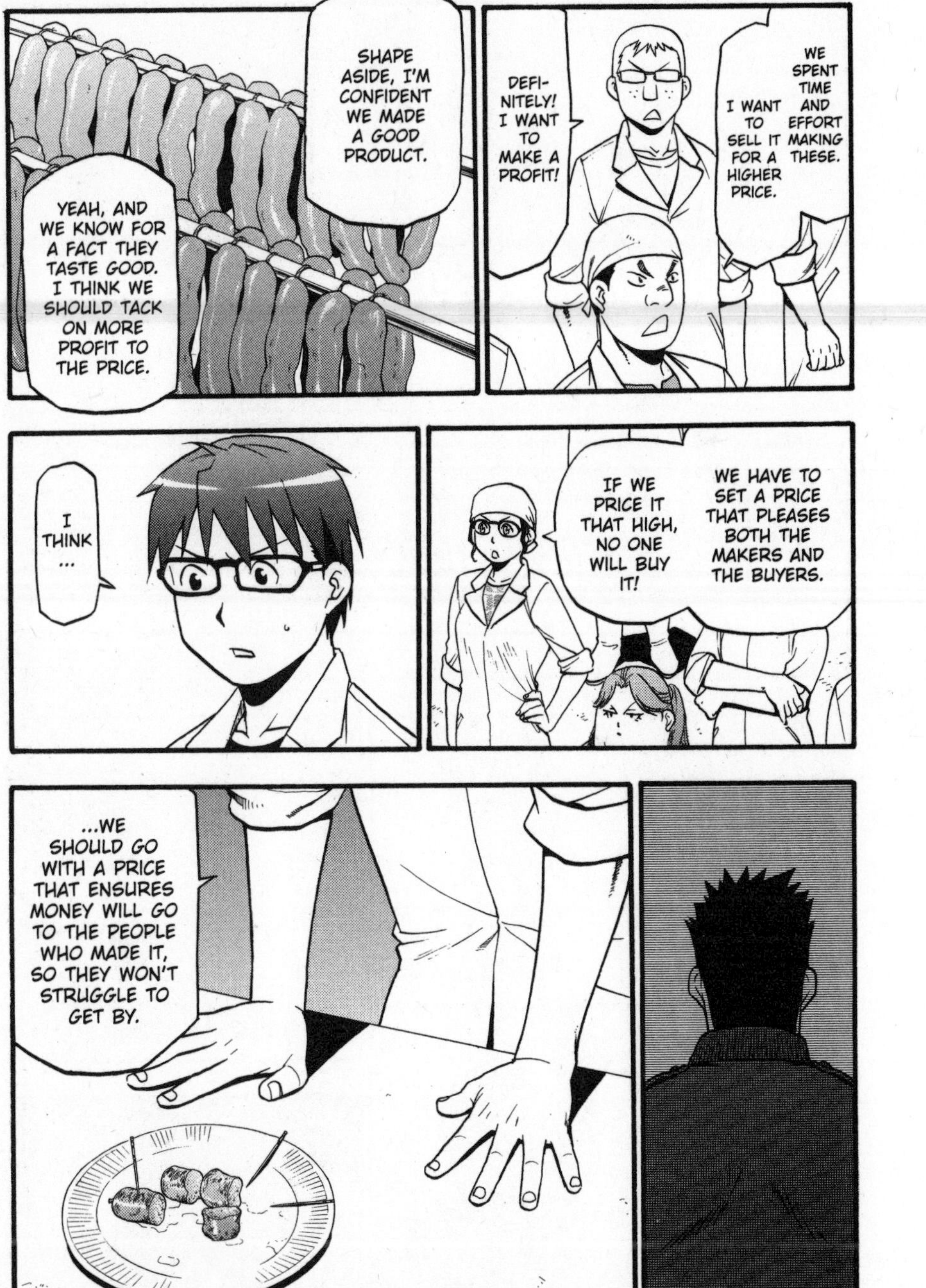
WE SPENT TIME AND EFFORT MAKING THESE.
I WANT TO SELL IT FOR A HIGHER PRICE.
DEFI-NITELY! I WANT TO MAKE A PROFIT!
SHAPE ASIDE, I'M CONFIDENT WE MADE A GOOD PRODUCT.
YEAH, AND WE KNOW FOR A FACT THEY TASTE GOOD. I THINK WE SHOULD TACK ON MORE PROFIT TO THE PRICE.
WE HAVE TO SET A PRICE THAT PLEASES BOTH THE MAKERS AND THE BUYERS.
IF WE PRICE IT THAT HIGH, NO ONE WILL BUY IT!
I THINK ...
...WE SHOULD GO WITH A PRICE THAT ENSURES MONEY WILL GO TO THE PEOPLE WHO MADE IT, SO THEY WON'T STRUGGLE TO GET BY.

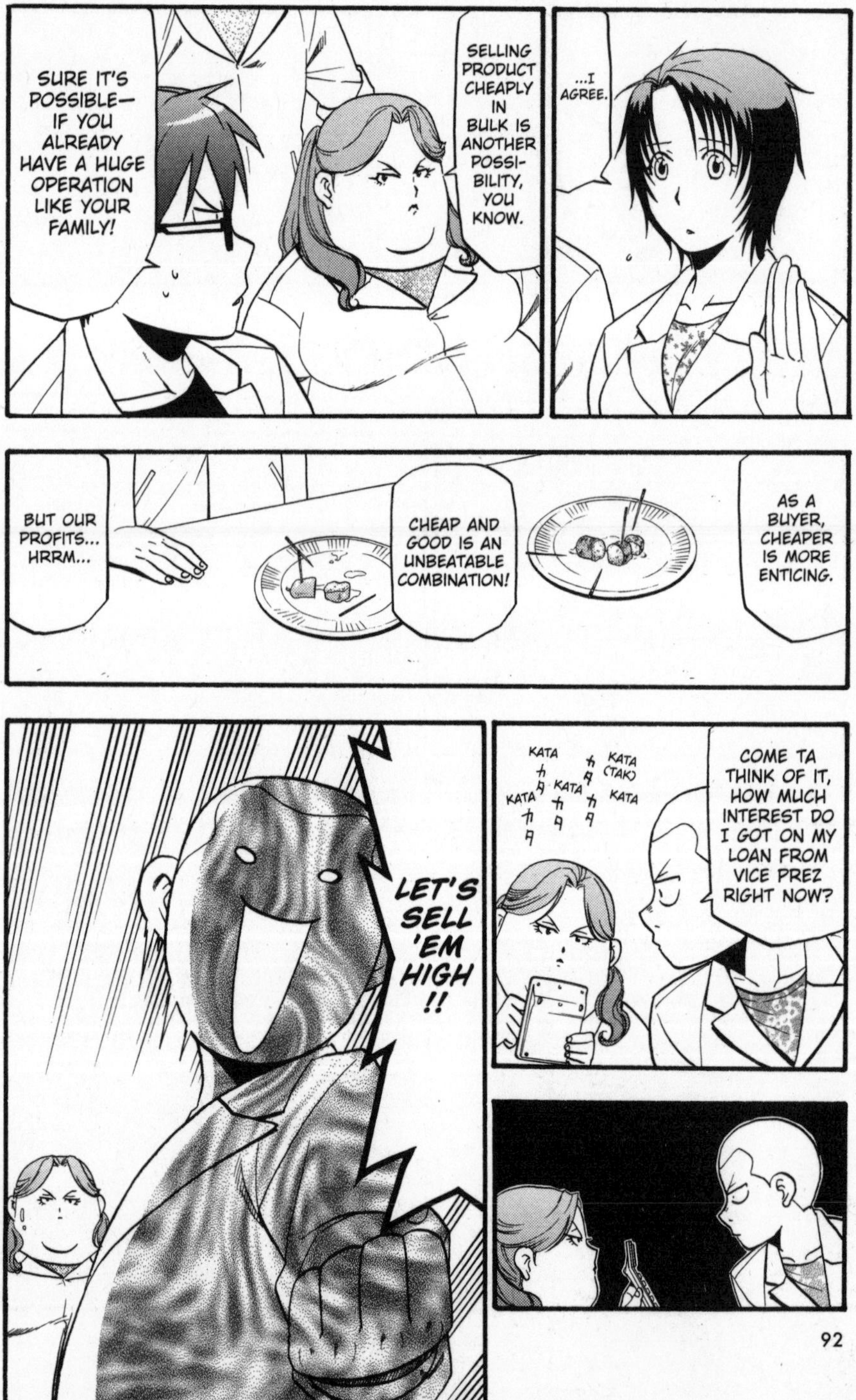
...I AGREE.
SELLING PRODUCT CHEAPLY IN BULK IS ANOTHER POSSIBILITY, YOU KNOW.
SURE IT'S POSSIBLE—IF YOU ALREADY HAVE A HUGE OPERATION LIKE YOUR FAMILY!
AS A BUYER, CHEAPER IS MORE ENTICING.
CHEAP AND GOOD IS AN UNBEATABLE COMBINATION!
BUT OUR PROFITS... HRRM...
COME TA THINK OF IT, HOW MUCH INTEREST DO I GOT ON MY LOAN FROM VICE PREZ RIGHT NOW?
KATA (TAK) KATA
カタ カタ
KATA KATA
カタ カタ
KATA
LET'S SELL 'EM HIGH!!

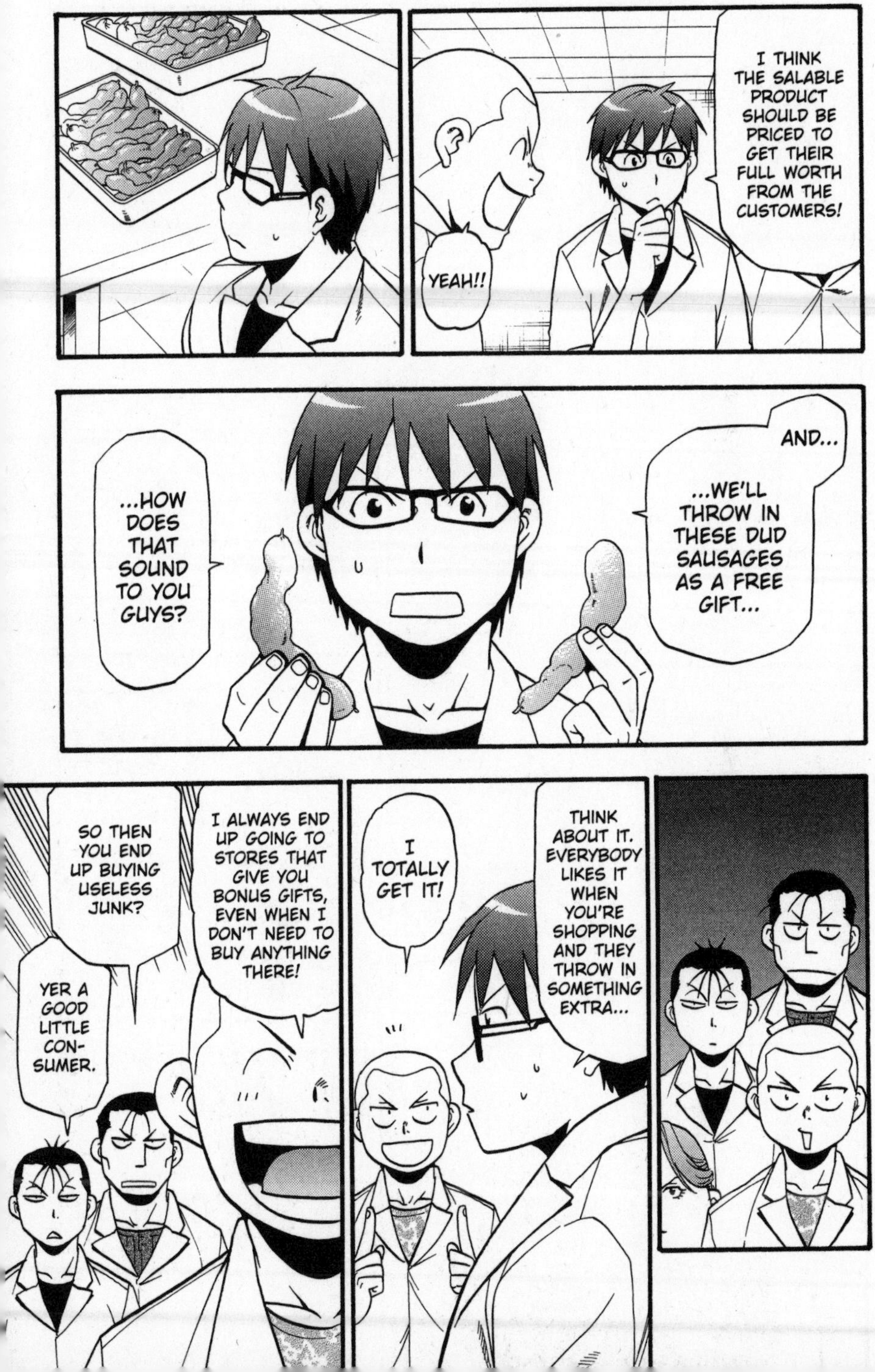
I THINK THE SALABLE PRODUCT SHOULD BE PRICED TO GET THEIR FULL WORTH FROM THE CUSTOMERS!
YEAH!!
AND...
...WE'LL THROW IN THESE DUD SAUSAGES AS A FREE GIFT...
...HOW DOES THAT SOUND TO YOU GUYS?
THINK ABOUT IT. EVERYBODY LIKES IT WHEN YOU'RE SHOPPING AND THEY THROW IN SOMETHING EXTRA...
I TOTALLY GET IT!
I ALWAYS END UP GOING TO STORES THAT GIVE YOU BONUS GIFTS, EVEN WHEN I DON'T NEED TO BUY ANYTHING THERE!
SO THEN YOU END UP BUYING USELESS JUNK?
YER A GOOD LITTLE CON-SUMER.

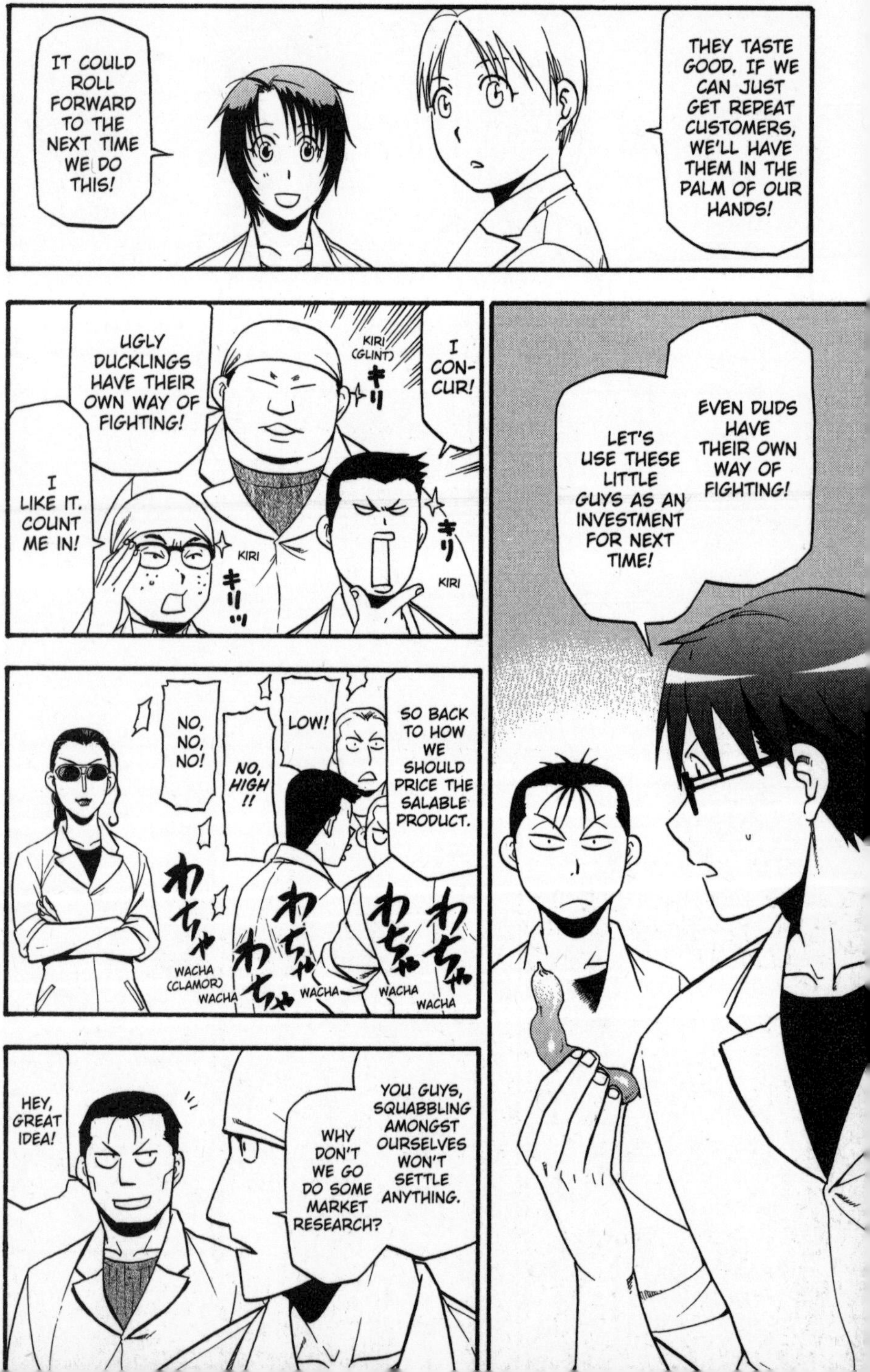

THEY TASTE GOOD. IF WE CAN JUST GET REPEAT CUSTOMERS, WE'LL HAVE THEM IN THE PALM OF OUR HANDS!
IT COULD ROLL FORWARD TO THE NEXT TIME WE DO THIS!
EVEN DUDS HAVE THEIR OWN WAY OF FIGHTING!
LET'S USE THESE LITTLE GUYS AS AN INVESTMENT FOR NEXT TIME!
I CON-CUR!
KIRI (GLINT)
キリ
UGLY DUCKLINGS HAVE THEIR OWN WAY OF FIGHTING!
キリ
KIRI
I LIKE IT. COUNT ME IN!
KIRI
キリッ
SO BACK TO HOW WE SHOULD PRICE THE SALABLE PRODUCT.
LOW!
NO, HIGH!!
NO, NO, NO!
わちゃ
WACHA
わちゃ
WACHA
わちゃ
WACHA
わちゃ
WACHA
わちゃ
WACHA
わちゃ
WACHA (CLAMOR)
YOU GUYS, SQUABBLING AMONGST OURSELVES WON'T SETTLE ANYTHING.
WHY DON'T WE GO DO SOME MARKET RESEARCH?
HEY, GREAT IDEA!

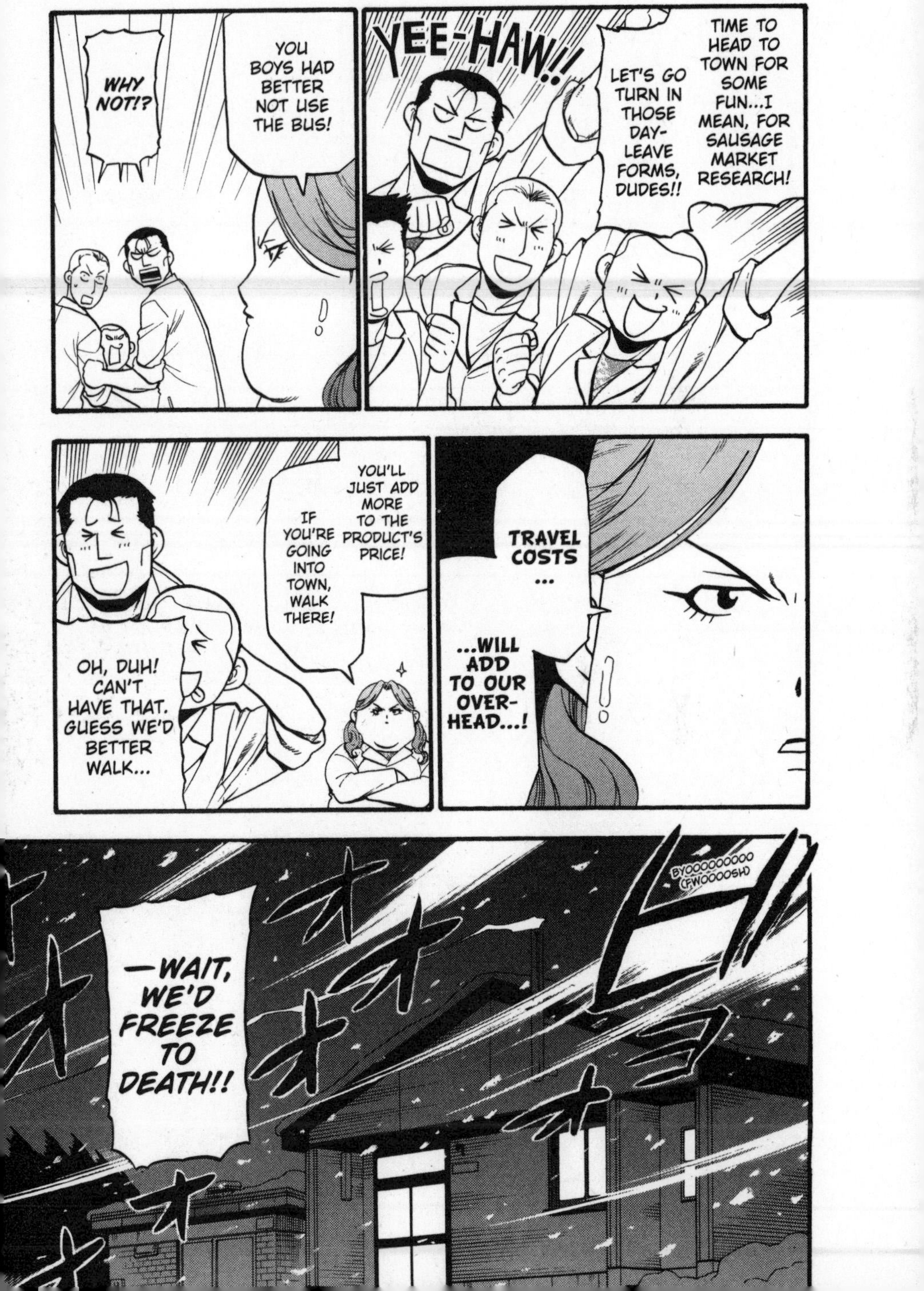

TIME TO HEAD TO TOWN FOR SOME FUN...I MEAN, FOR SAUSAGE MARKET RESEARCH!
LET'S GO TURN IN THOSE DAY-LEAVE FORMS, DUDES!!
YEE-HAW!!
YOU BOYS HAD BETTER NOT USE THE BUS!
WHY NOT!?
TRAVEL COSTS ...
...WILL ADD TO OUR OVER-HEAD...!
YOU'LL JUST ADD MORE TO THE PRODUCT'S PRICE!
IF YOU'RE GOING INTO TOWN, WALK THERE!
OH, DUH! CAN'T HAVE THAT. GUESS WE'D BETTER WALK...
BYOOOOOOOOO (FWOOOOSH)
—WAIT, WE'D FREEZE TO DEATH!!

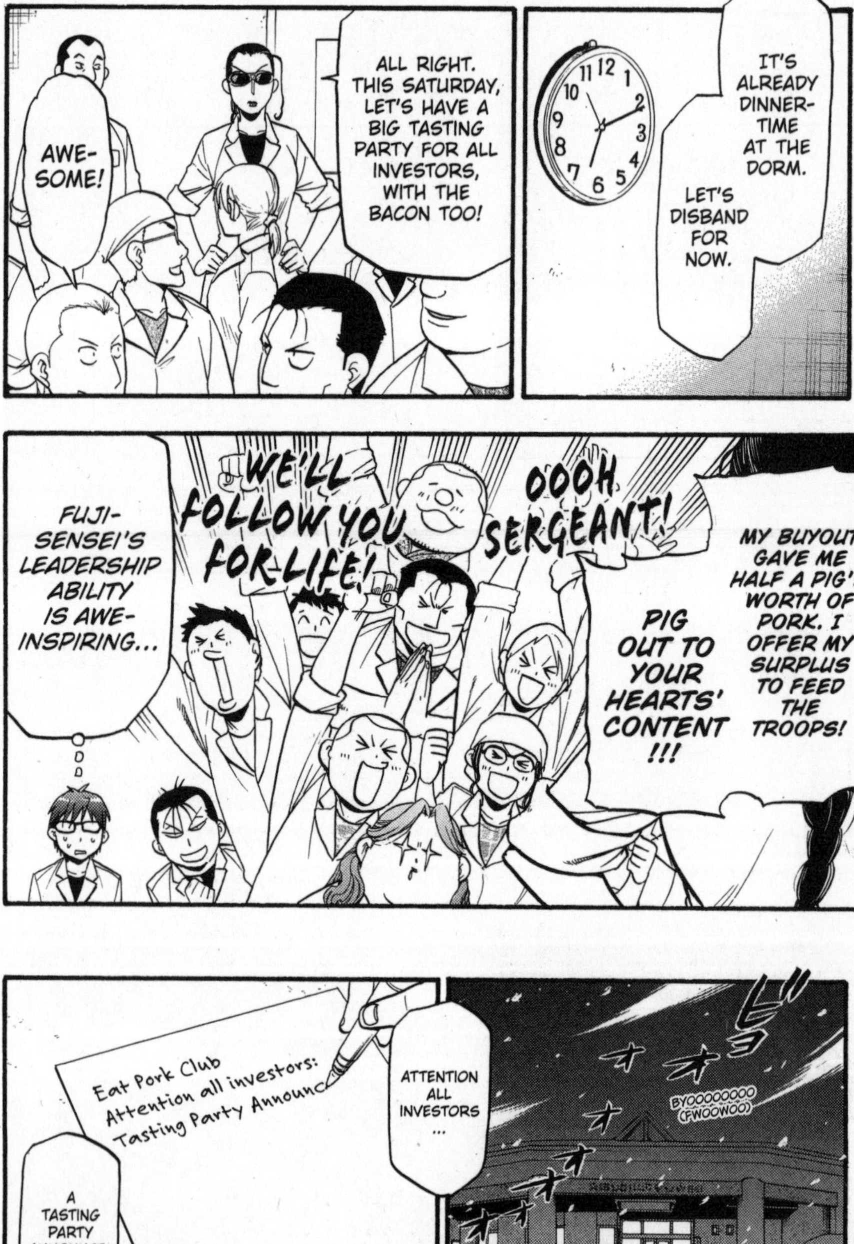
IT'S ALREADY DINNER-TIME AT THE DORM.
LET'S DISBAND FOR NOW.
ALL RIGHT. THIS SATURDAY, LET'S HAVE A BIG TASTING PARTY FOR ALL INVESTORS, WITH THE BACON TOO!
AWE-SOME!
MY BUYOUT GAVE ME HALF A PIG'S WORTH OF PORK. I OFFER MY SURPLUS TO FEED THE TROOPS!
PIG OUT TO YOUR HEARTS' CONTENT!!!
OOOH SERGEANT!
WE'LL FOLLOW YOU FOR LIFE!
FUJI-SENSEI'S LEADERSHIP ABILITY IS AWE-INSPIRING...
BYOOOOOOOO (FWOOWOO)
ATTENTION ALL INVESTORS...
Eat Pork Club
Attention all investors:
Tasting Party Announc
A TASTING PARTY ANNOUNCEMENT...

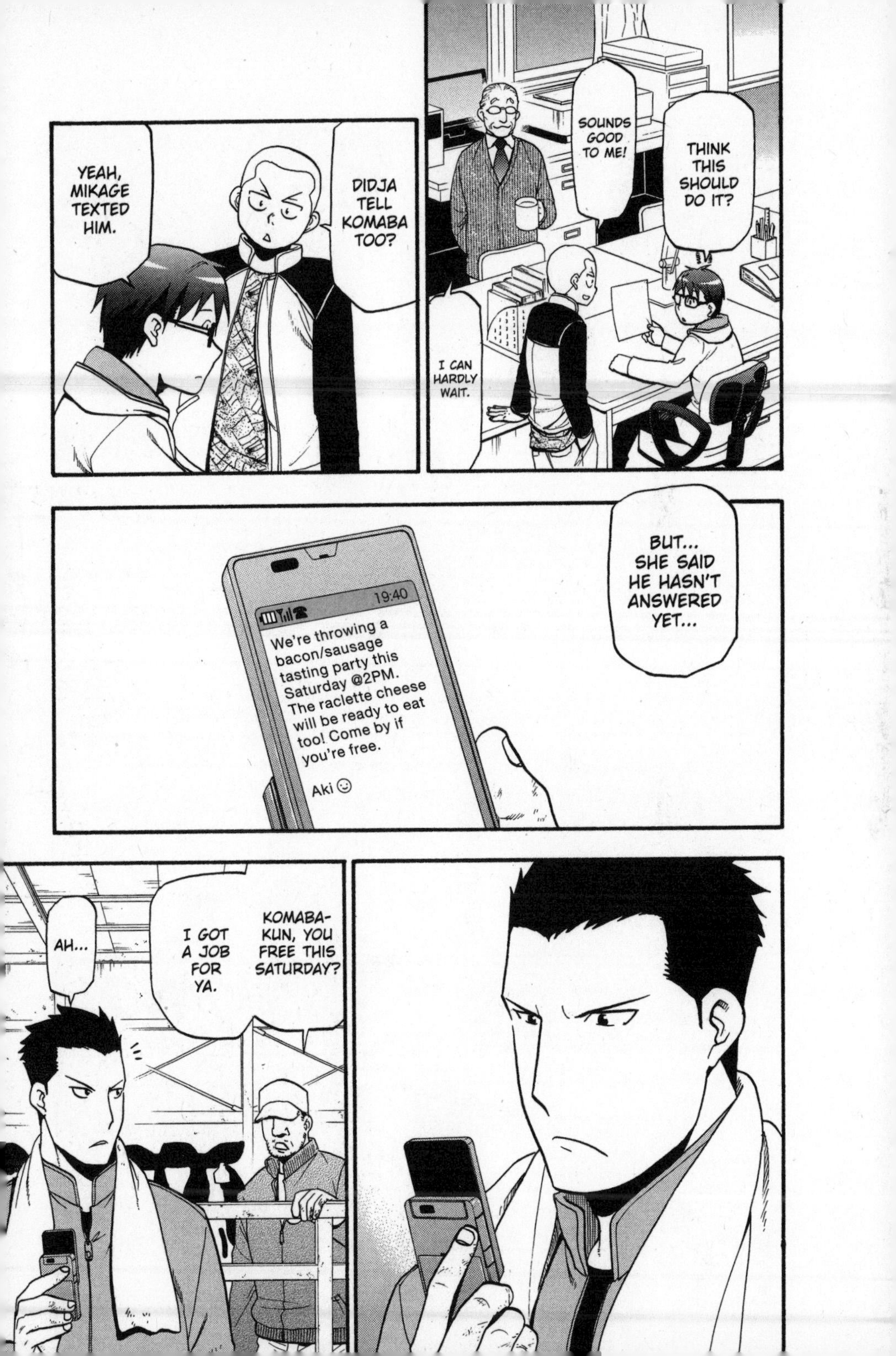
THINK THIS SHOULD DO IT?
SOUNDS GOOD TO ME!
I CAN HARDLY WAIT.
DIDJA TELL KOMABA TOO?
YEAH, MIKAGE TEXTED HIM.
BUT... SHE SAID HE HASN'T ANSWERED YET...
19:40
We're throwing a bacon/sausage tasting party this Saturday @2PM. The raclette cheese will be ready to eat too! Come by if you're free.
Aki ☺
KOMABA-KUN, YOU FREE THIS SATURDAY?
I GOT A JOB FOR YA.
AH...

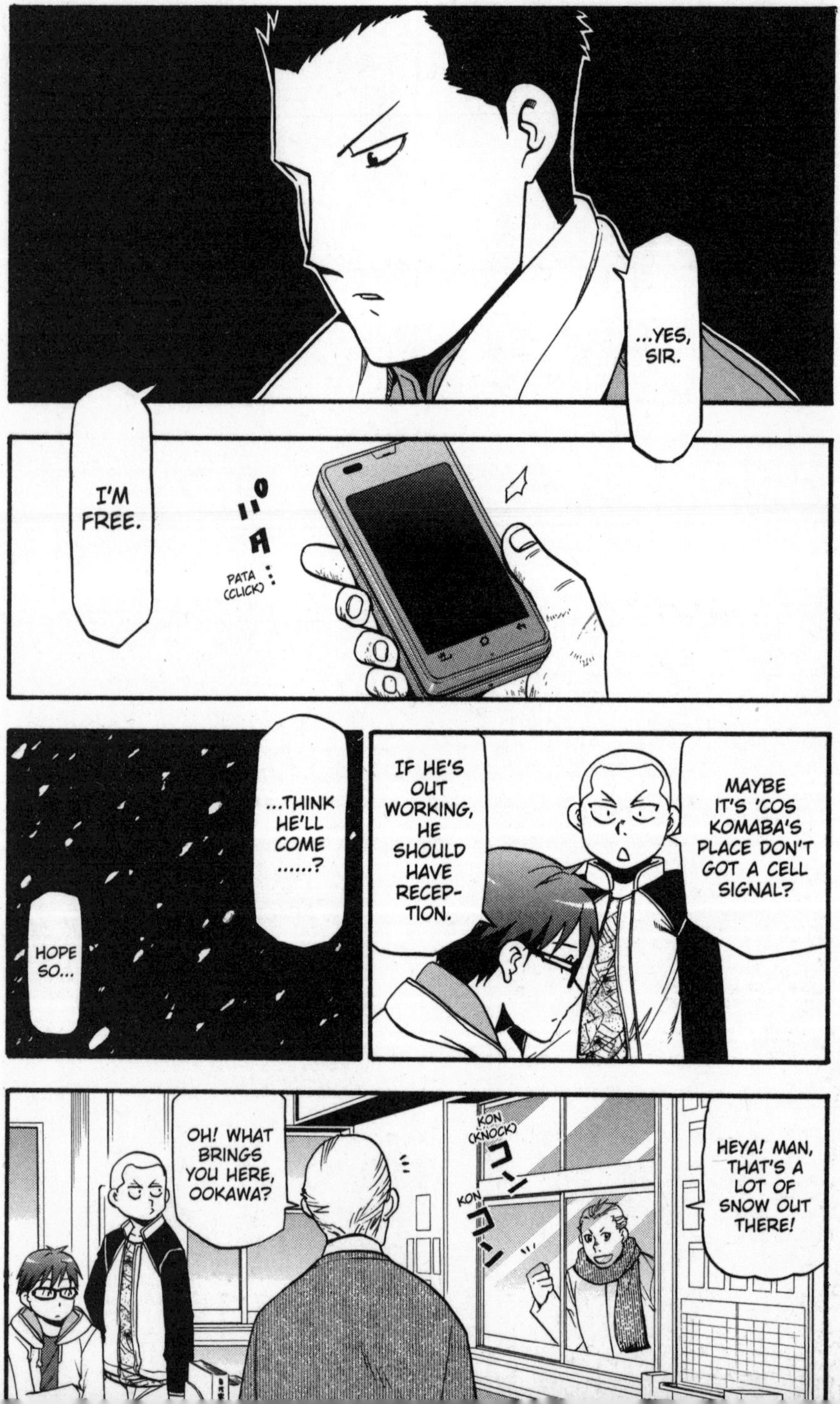
...YES, SIR.
I'M FREE.
PATA (CLICK)
MAYBE IT'S 'COS KOMABA'S PLACE DON'T GOT A CELL SIGNAL?
IF HE'S OUT WORKING, HE SHOULD HAVE RECEPTION.
...THINK HE'LL COME ......?
HOPE SO...
HEYA! MAN, THAT'S A LOT OF SNOW OUT THERE!
KON (KNOCK)
KON
OH! WHAT BRINGS YOU HERE, OOKAWA?

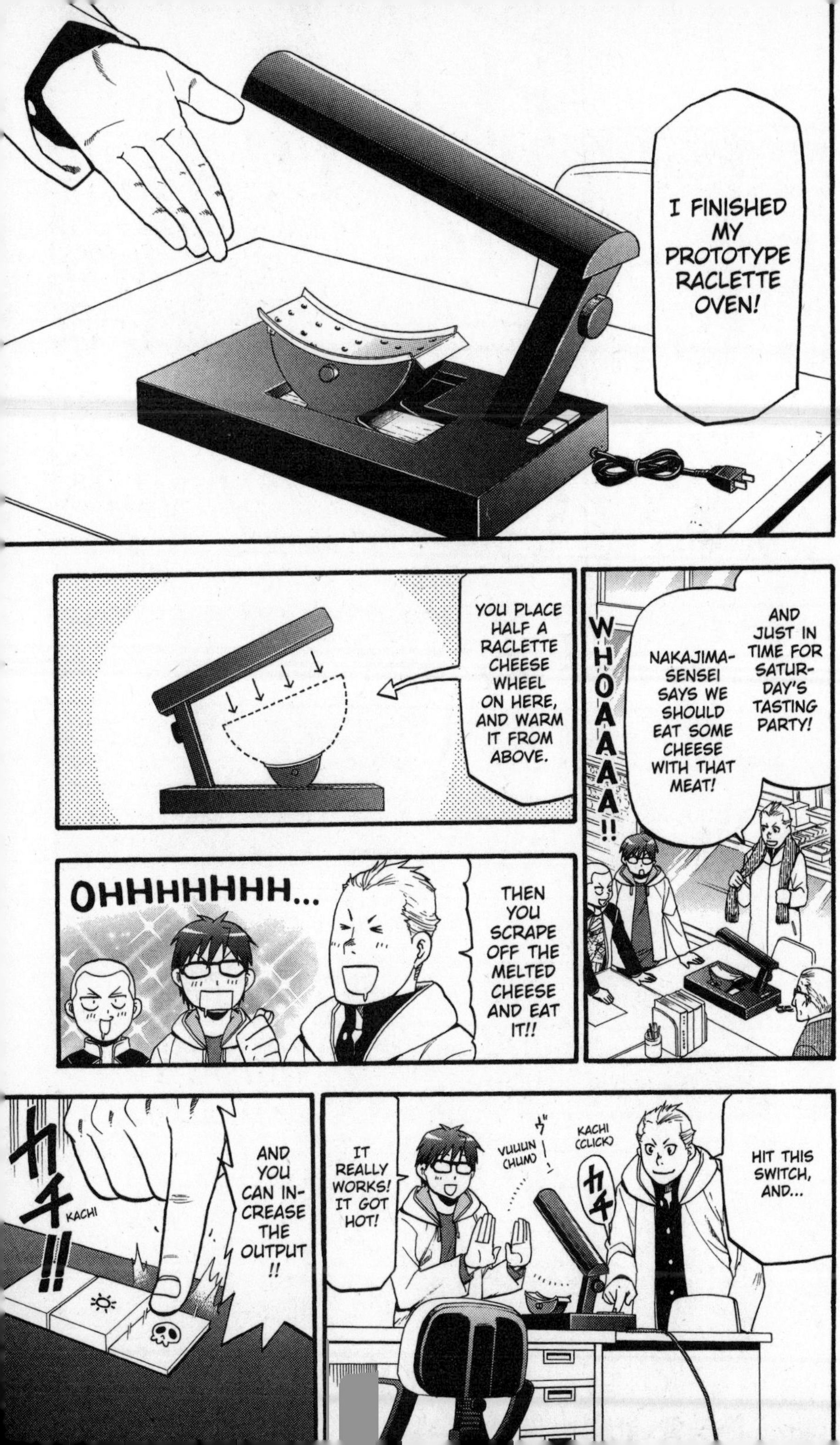
I FINISHED MY PROTOTYPE RACLETTE OVEN!
AND JUST IN TIME FOR SATURDAY'S TASTING PARTY!
NAKAJIMA-SENSEI SAYS WE SHOULD EAT SOME CHEESE WITH THAT MEAT!
WHOAAAAA!!
YOU PLACE HALF A RACLETTE CHEESE WHEEL ON HERE, AND WARM IT FROM ABOVE.
THEN YOU SCRAPE OFF THE MELTED CHEESE AND EAT IT!!
OHHHHHHH...
HIT THIS SWITCH, AND...
KACHI (CLICK)
カチ
ヴ
VUUUN (HUM)
IT REALLY WORKS! IT GOT HOT!
AND YOU CAN INCREASE THE OUTPUT!!
カチ!!
KACHI

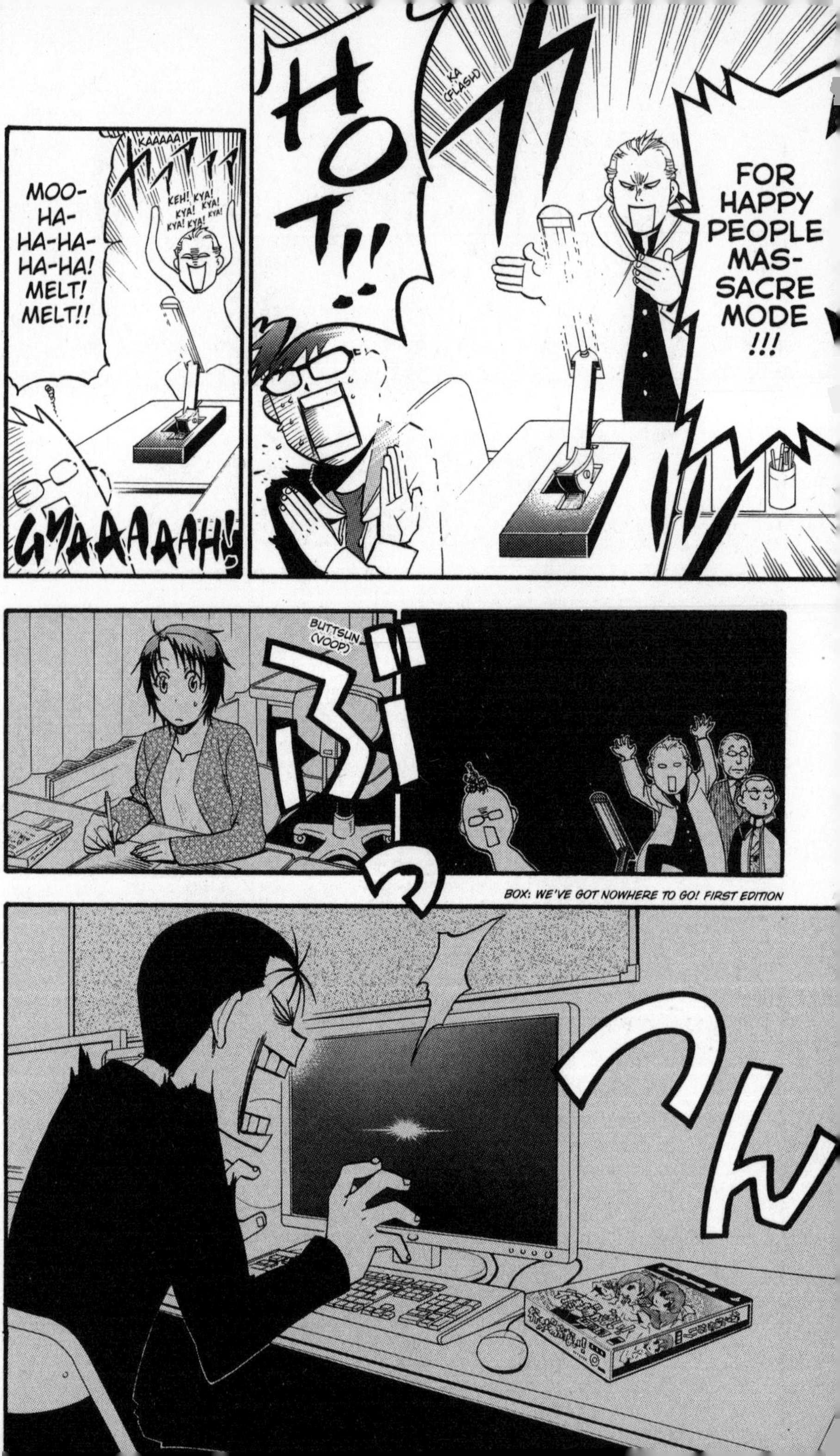
KA (FLASH)
HOT!!
FOR HAPPY PEOPLE MAS-SACRE MODE!!!
KAAAAA
KEH! KYA! KYA! KYA! KYA! KYA!
MOO-HA-HA-HA-HA-HA! MELT! MELT!!
GYAAAAAAH!
BUTTSUN (VOOP)
BOX: WE'VE GOT NOWHERE TO GO! FIRST EDITION

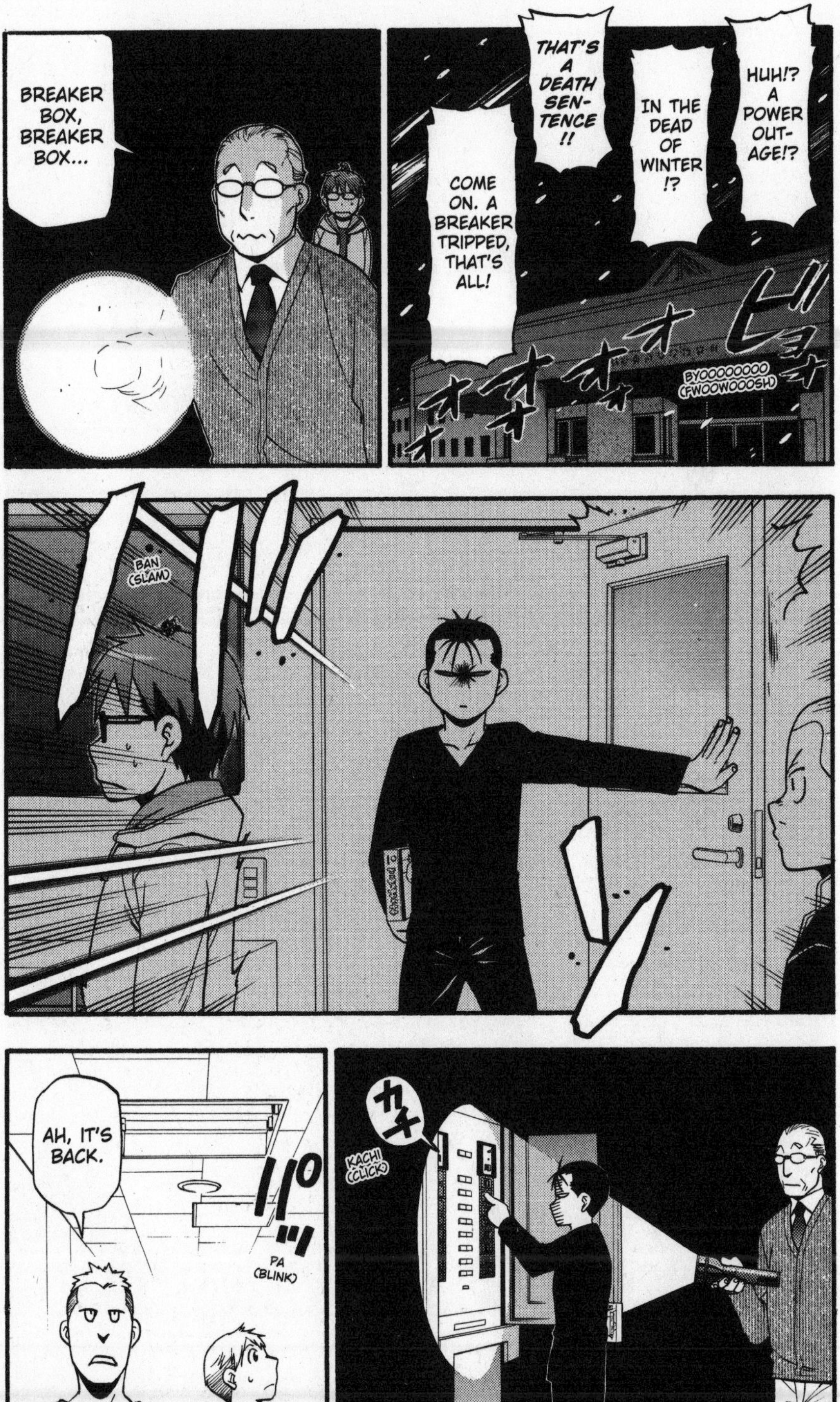
HUH!? A POWER OUT-AGE!?
IN THE DEAD OF WINTER !?
THAT'S A DEATH SEN-TENCE !!
COME ON. A BREAKER TRIPPED, THAT'S ALL!
BYOOOOOOOO (FWOOWOOOSH)
BREAKER BOX, BREAKER BOX...
BAN (SLAM)
カチ
KACHI (CLICK)
AH, IT'S BACK.
パッ
PA (BLINK)

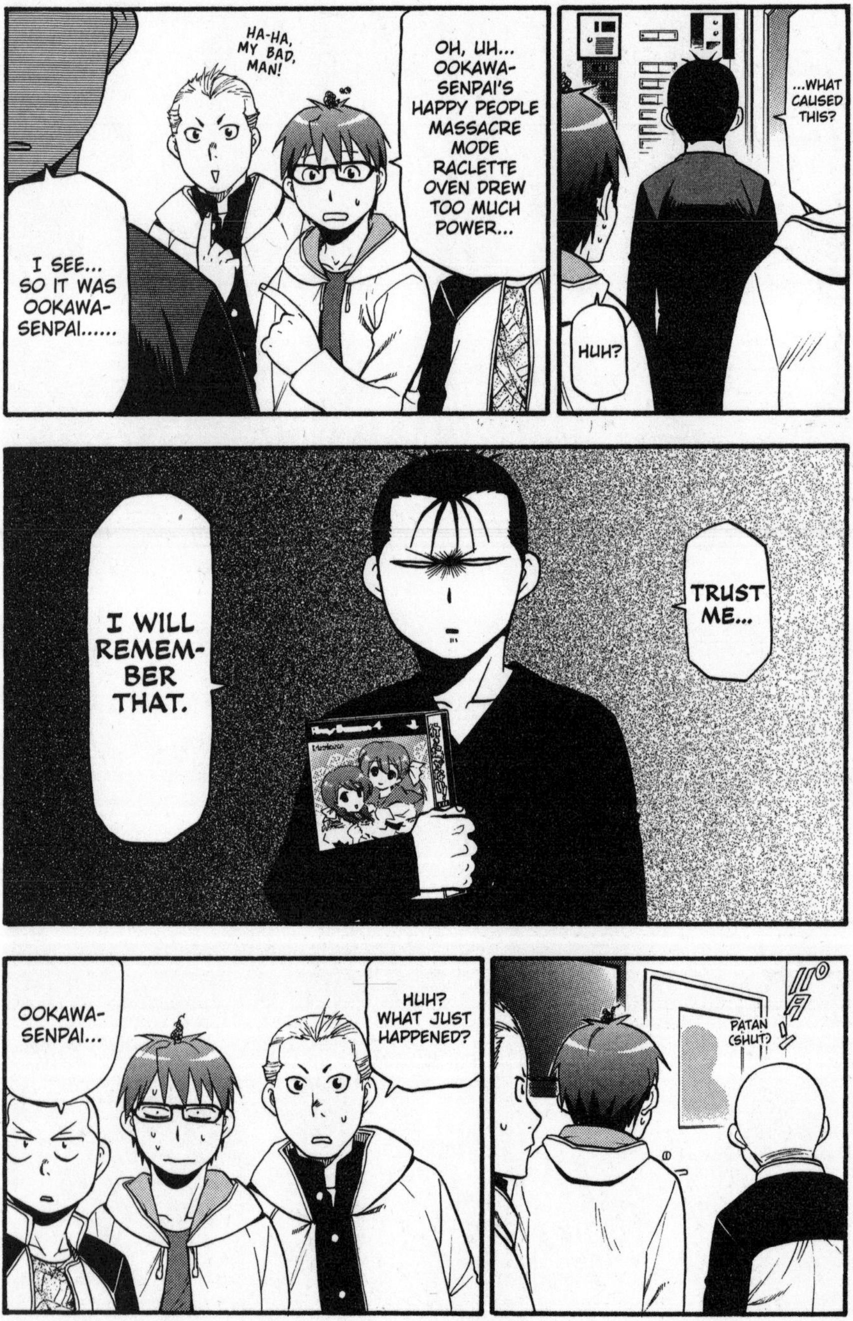
...WHAT CAUSED THIS?
HUH?
OH, UH... OOKAWA-SENPAI'S HAPPY PEOPLE MASSACRE MODE RACLETTE OVEN DREW TOO MUCH POWER...
HA-HA, MY BAD, MAN!
I SEE... SO IT WAS OOKAWA-SENPAI......
TRUST ME...
I WILL REMEMBER THAT.
PATAN (SHUT)
HUH? WHAT JUST HAPPENED?
OOKAWA-SENPAI...

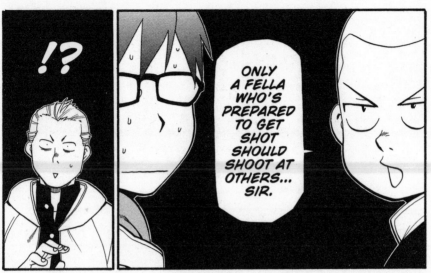

ONLY A FELLA WHO'S PREPARED TO GET SHOT SHOULD SHOOT AT OTHERS... SIR.
!?
OH, A TASTING PARTY? SOUNDS GREAT!
THIS SATUR-DAY?
YEAH.
FOOD SCIENCE 3-C
COULD I ASK YOU TO DISTRIBUTE THESE TO OUR THIRD-YEAR INVESTORS?
SURE THING.
THANKS. I APPRECIATE IT!

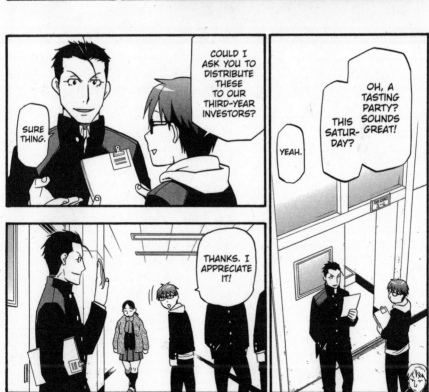

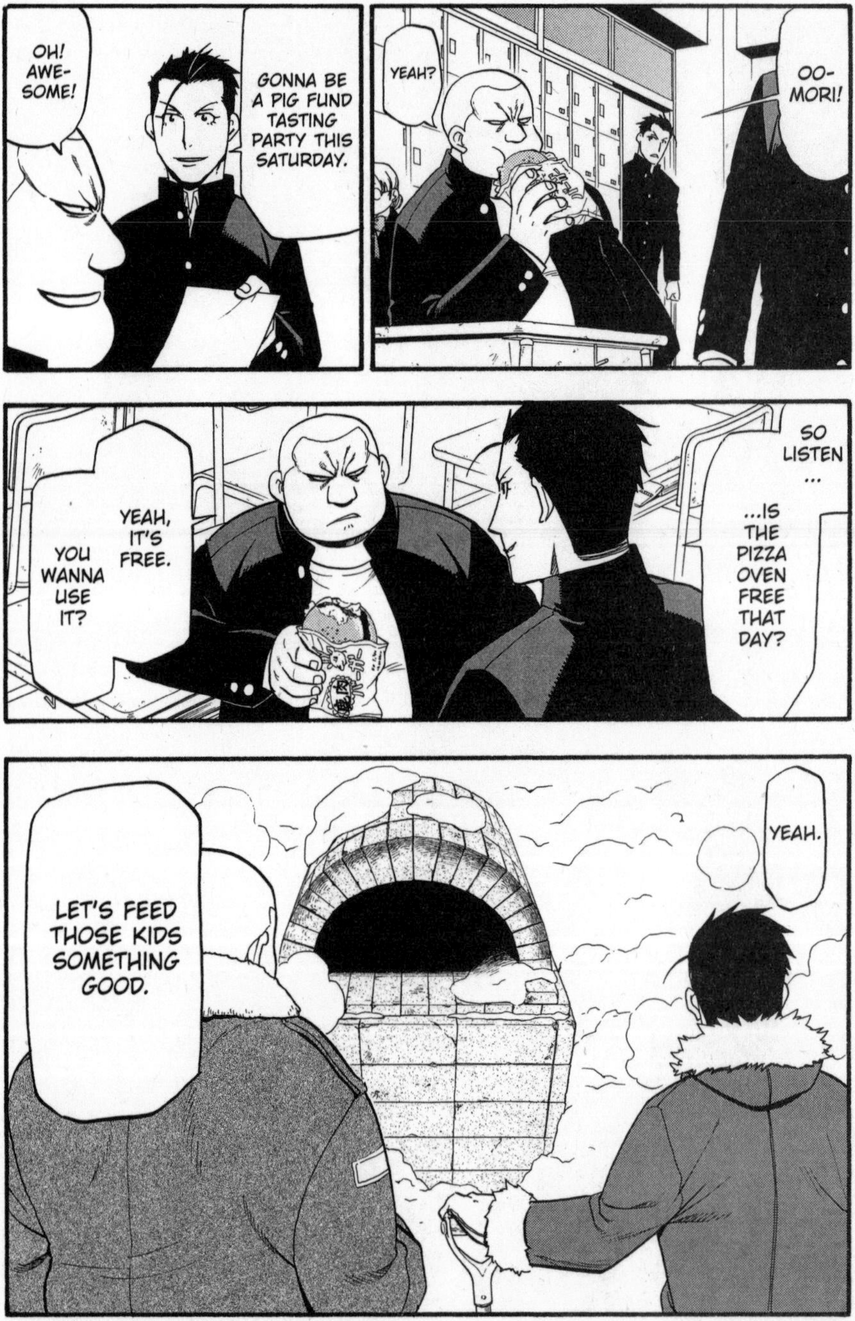
OO-MORI!
YEAH?
GONNA BE A PIG FUND TASTING PARTY THIS SATURDAY.
OH! AWE-SOME!
SO LISTEN...
...IS THE PIZZA OVEN FREE THAT DAY?
YEAH, IT'S FREE.
YOU WANNA USE IT?
YEAH.
LET'S FEED THOSE KIDS SOMETHING GOOD.

Silver Spoon

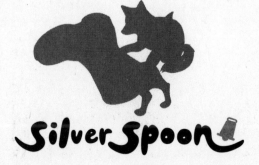

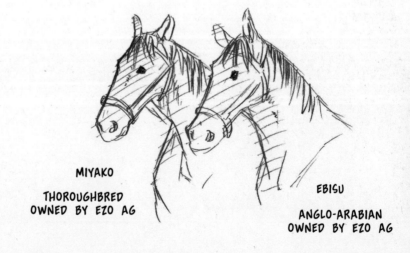

MIYAKO

THOROUGHBRED
OWNED BY EZO AG

EBISU

ANGLO-ARABIAN
OWNED BY EZO AG

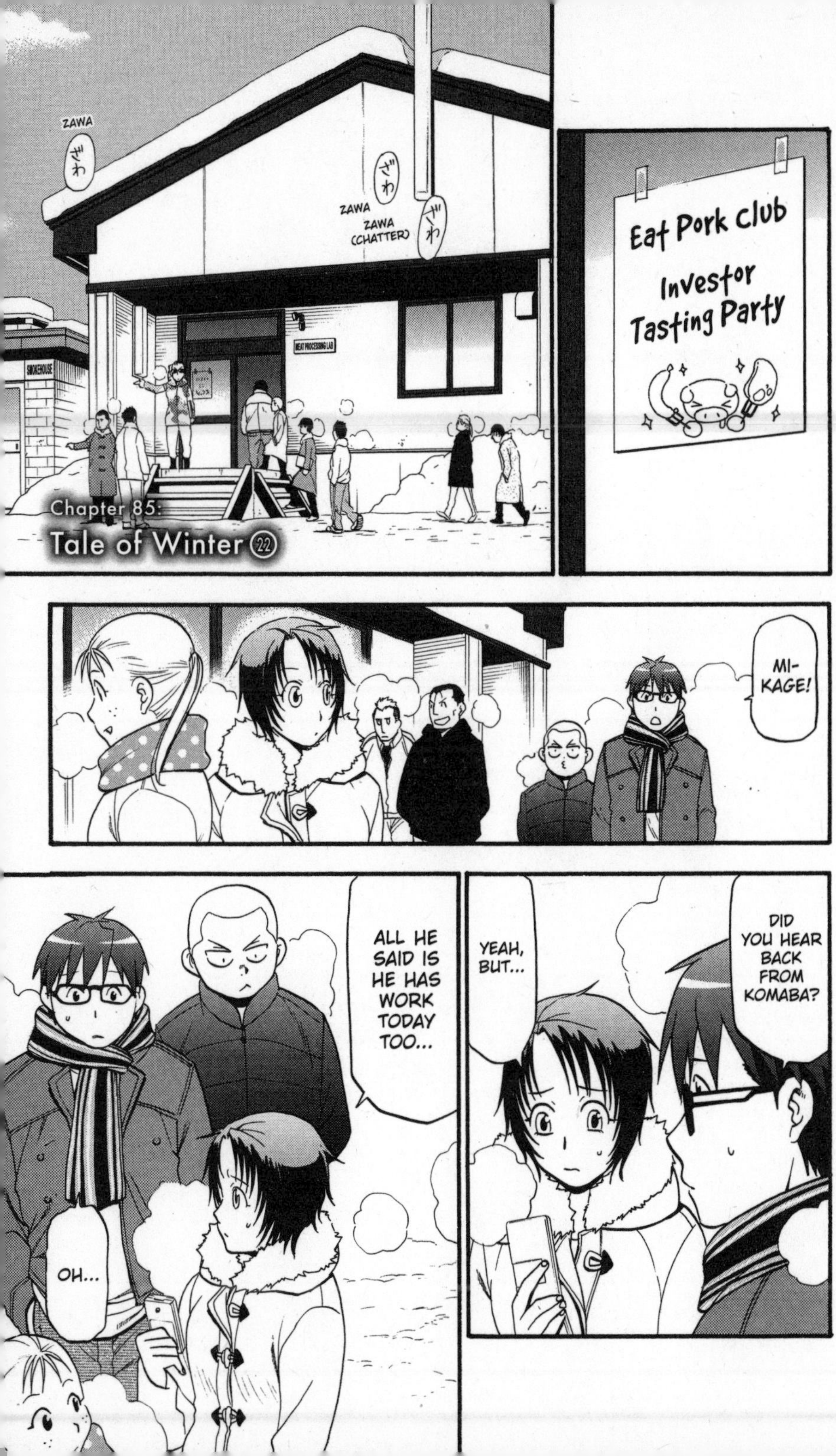

Eat Pork Club
Investor Tasting Party
ZAWA
ざわ
ざわ
ざわ
ZAWA
ZAWA (CHATTER)
SMOKEHOUSE
MEAT PROCESSING LAB
Chapter 85:
Tale of Winter ㉒
MI-KAGE!
DID YOU HEAR BACK FROM KOMABA?
YEAH, BUT...
ALL HE SAID IS HE HAS WORK TODAY TOO...
OH...

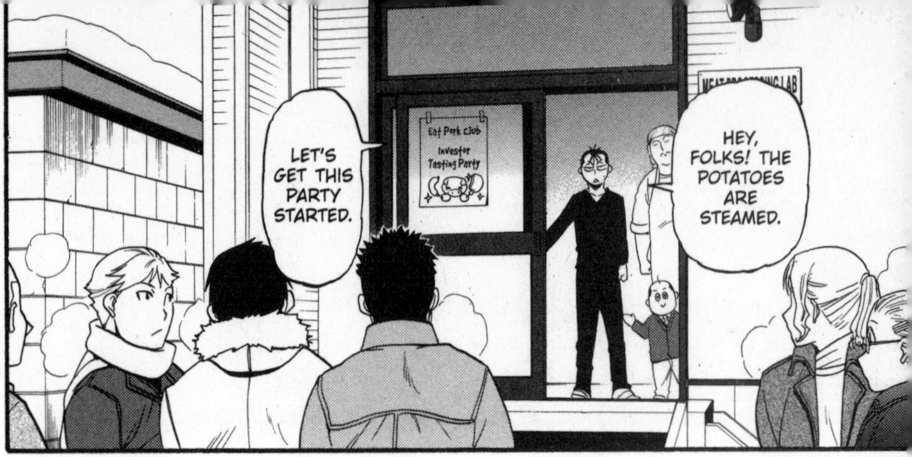
Eat Pork Club
Investor Tasting Party
HEY, FOLKS! THE POTATOES ARE STEAMED.
LET'S GET THIS PARTY STARTED.

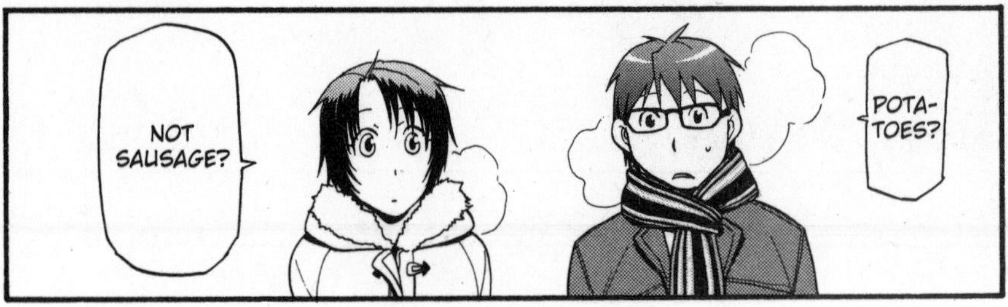
POTA-TOES?
NOT SAUSAGE?

Chapter 85:
Tale of Winter ㉒

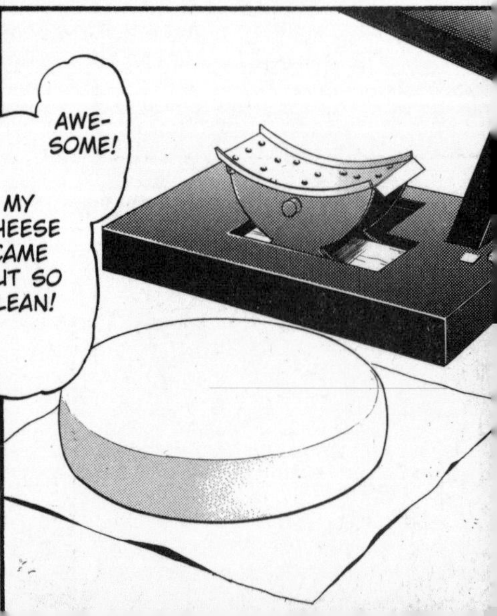
AWE-SOME!
MY CHEESE CAME OUT SO CLEAN!

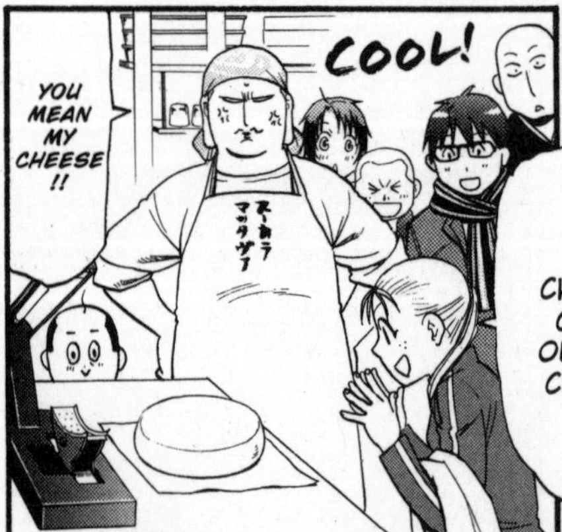
COOL!
YOU MEAN MY CHEESE !!

APRON: SUKARA MADDAVA

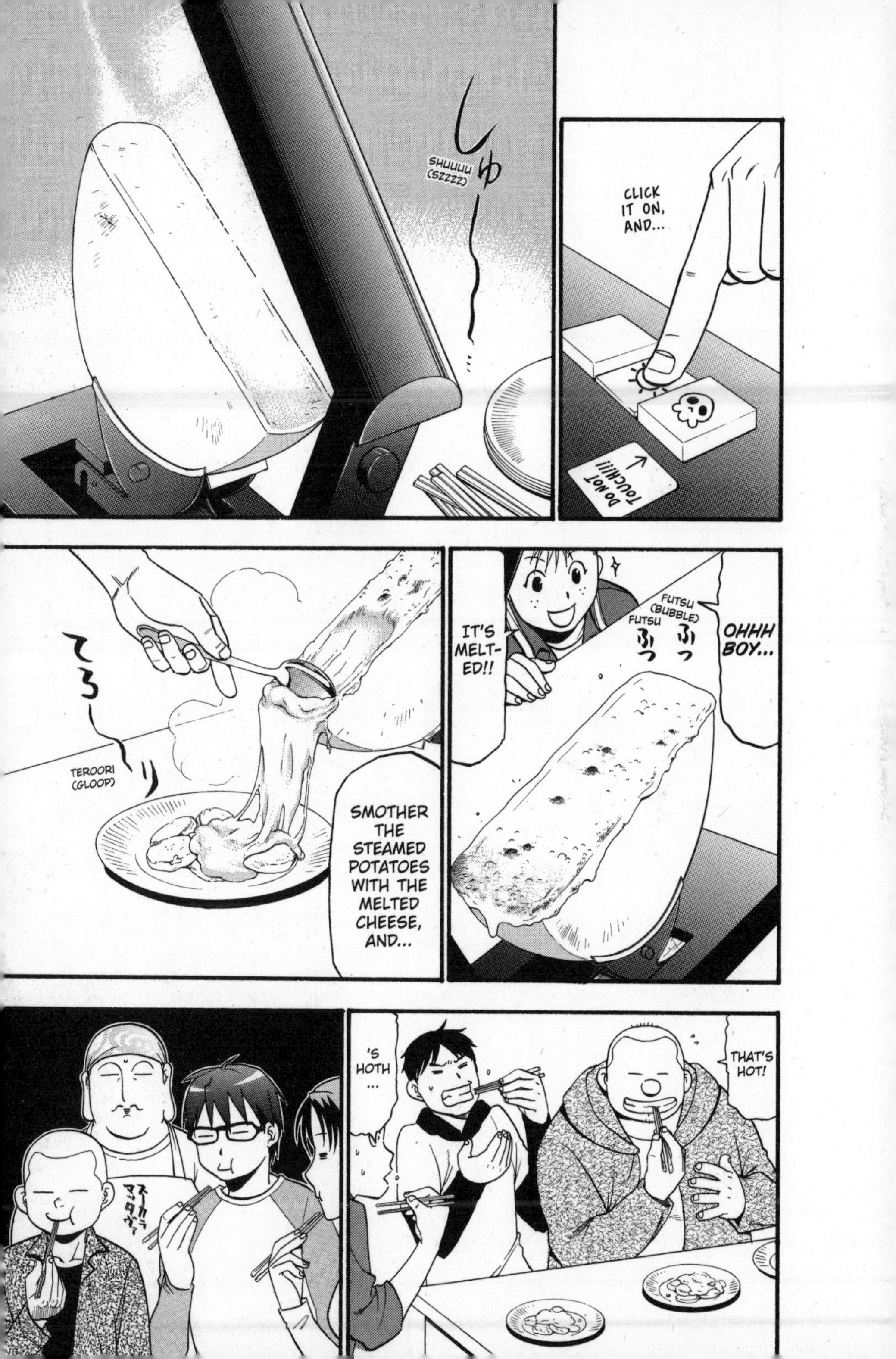
CLICK IT ON, AND...
DO NOT TOUCH!!!
しゅー
SHUUUU (SZZZZ)
FUTSU (BUBBLE)
ふっ
FUTSU
ふっ
OHHH BOY...
IT'S MELT-ED!!
SMOTHER THE STEAMED POTATOES WITH THE MELTED CHEESE, AND...
てろーり
TEROORI (GLOOP)
THAT'S HOT!
'S HOTH...

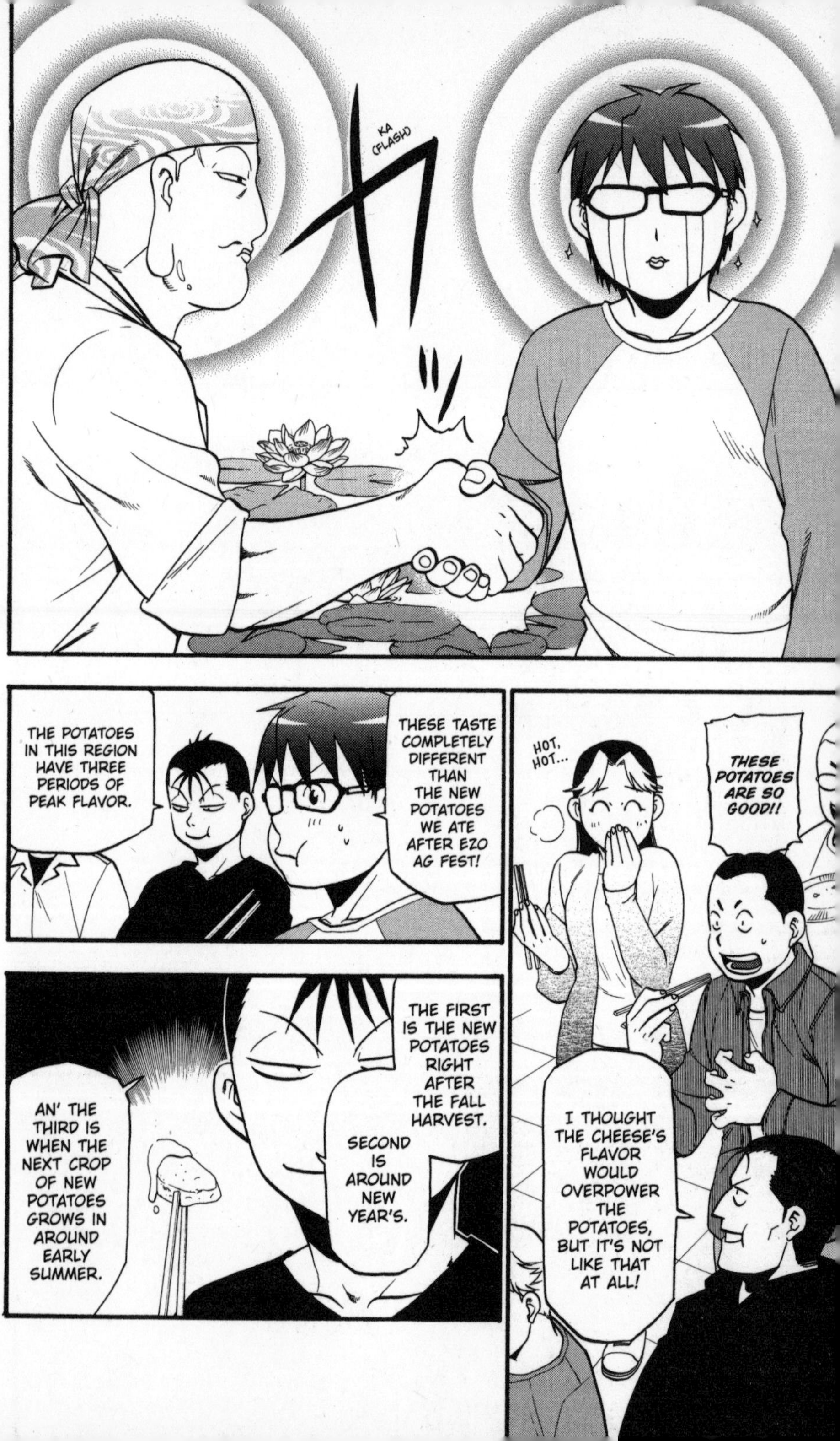
KA (FLASH)
THESE POTATOES ARE SO GOOD!!
HOT, HOT...
I THOUGHT THE CHEESE'S FLAVOR WOULD OVERPOWER THE POTATOES, BUT IT'S NOT LIKE THAT AT ALL!
THESE TASTE COMPLETELY DIFFERENT THAN THE NEW POTATOES WE ATE AFTER EZO AG FEST!
THE POTATOES IN THIS REGION HAVE THREE PERIODS OF PEAK FLAVOR.
THE FIRST IS THE NEW POTATOES RIGHT AFTER THE FALL HARVEST.
SECOND IS AROUND NEW YEAR'S.
AN' THE THIRD IS WHEN THE NEXT CROP OF NEW POTATOES GROWS IN AROUND EARLY SUMMER.

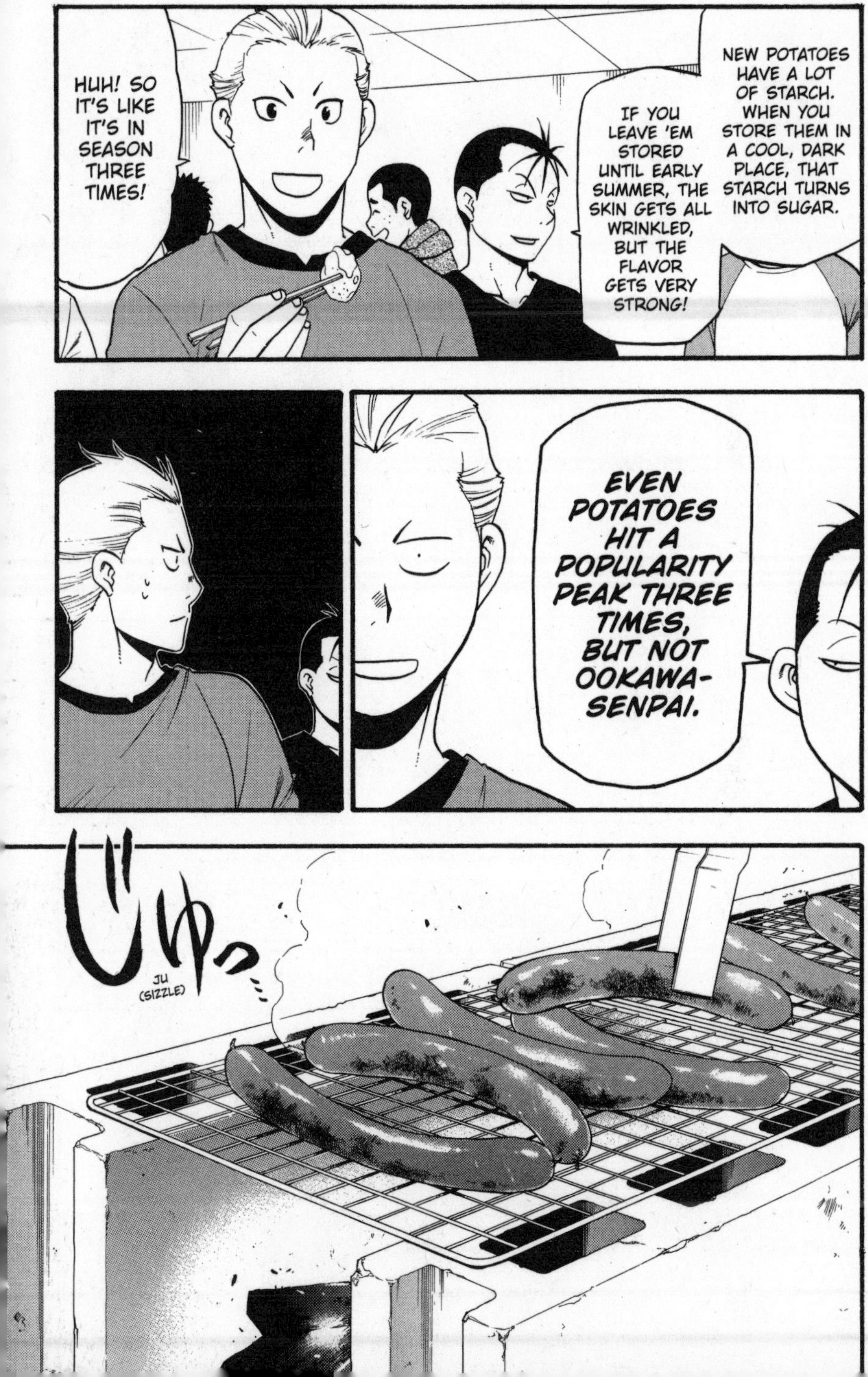
NEW POTATOES HAVE A LOT OF STARCH. WHEN YOU STORE THEM IN A COOL, DARK PLACE, THAT STARCH TURNS INTO SUGAR.
IF YOU LEAVE 'EM STORED UNTIL EARLY SUMMER, THE SKIN GETS ALL WRINKLED, BUT THE FLAVOR GETS VERY STRONG!
HUH! SO IT'S LIKE IT'S IN SEASON THREE TIMES!
EVEN POTATOES HIT A POPULARITY PEAK THREE TIMES, BUT NOT OOKAWA-SENPAI.
じゅっ…
JU (SIZZLE)

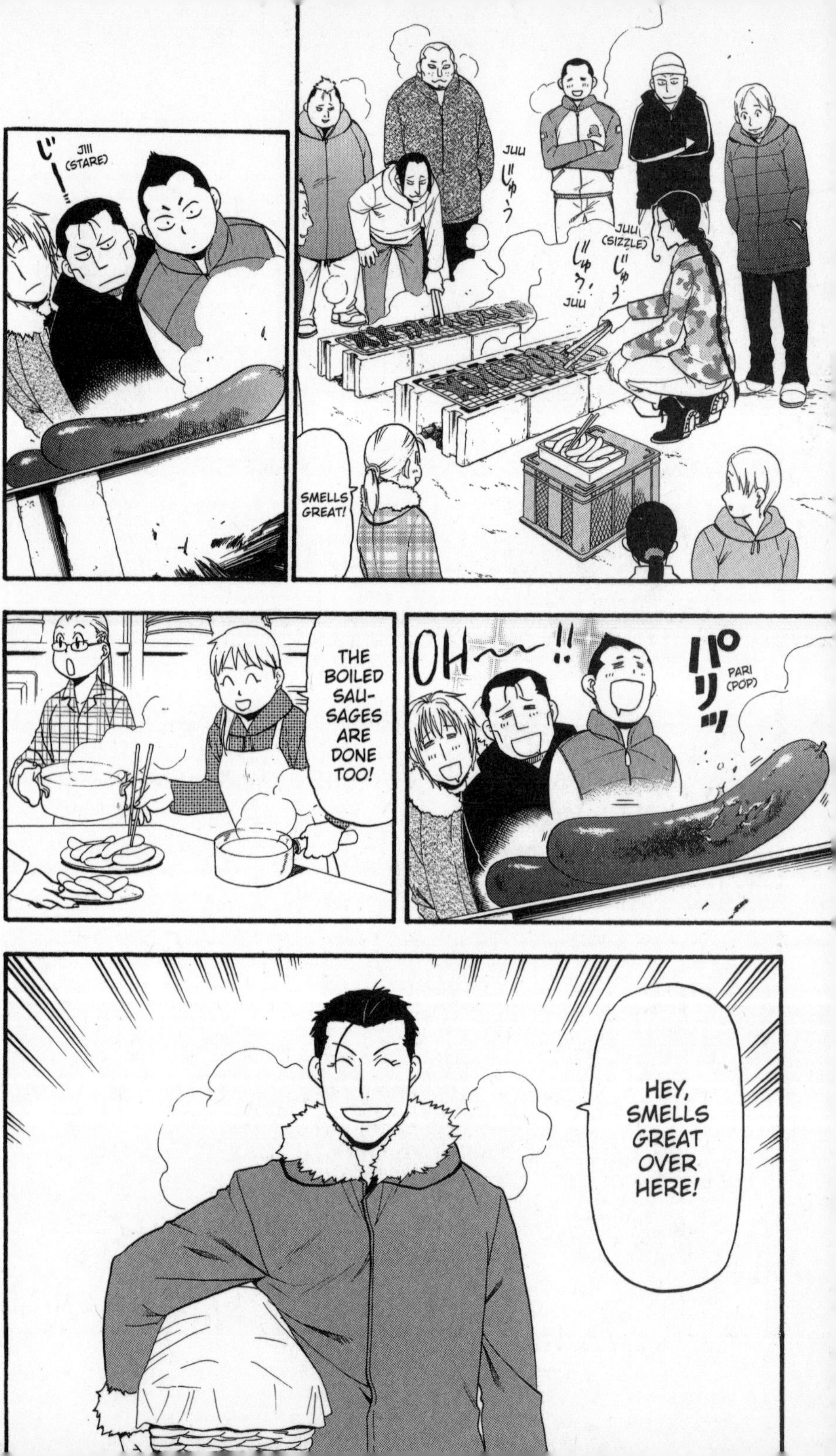

JUU
じゅう
JUU (SIZZLE)
じゅう
じゅう
JUU
SMELLS GREAT!
じー!!
JIII (STARE)
OH~~!!
パリッ
PARI (POP)
THE BOILED SAU-SAGES ARE DONE TOO!
HEY, SMELLS GREAT OVER HERE!

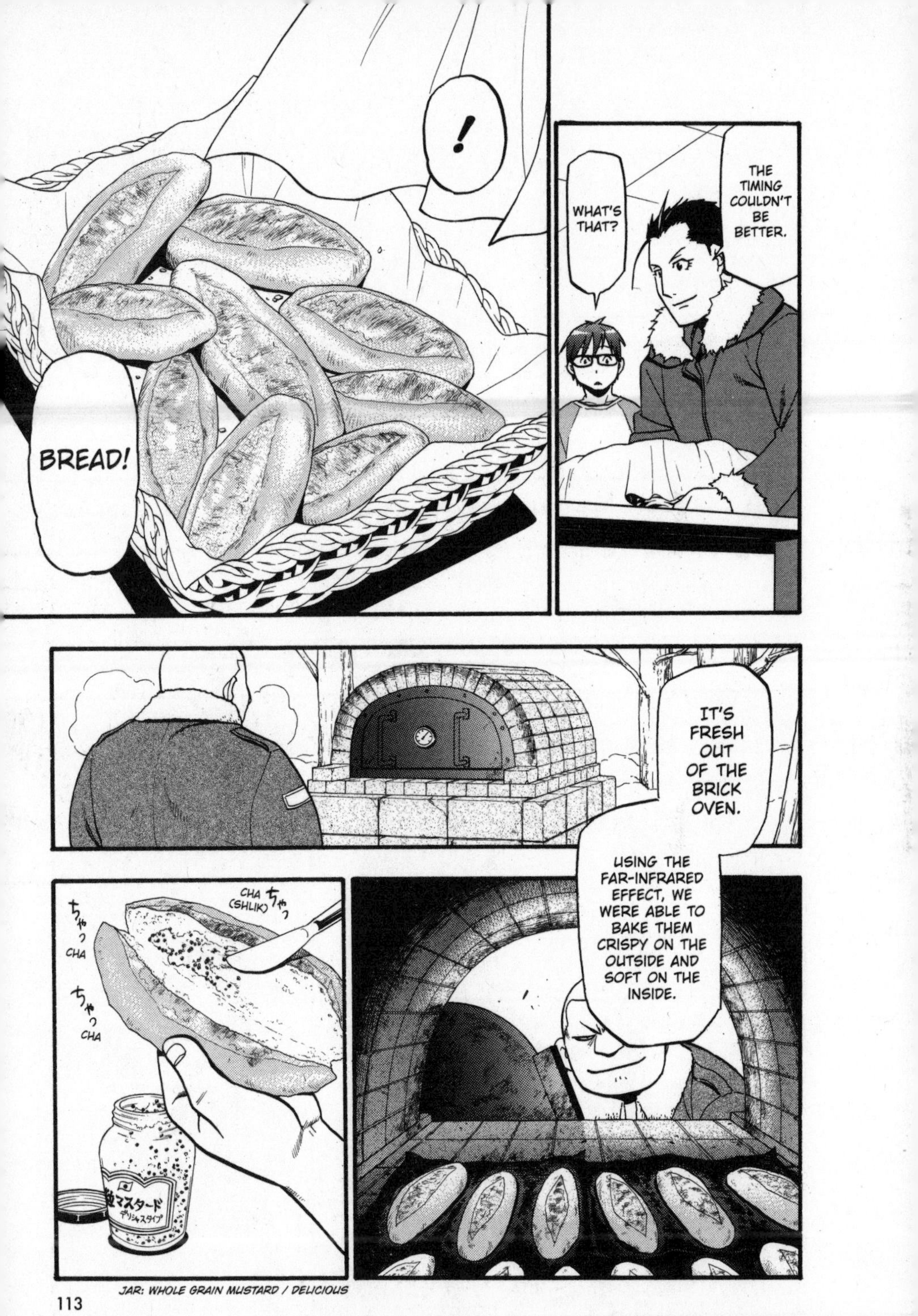
THE TIMING COULDN'T BE BETTER.
WHAT'S THAT?
!
BREAD!
IT'S FRESH OUT OF THE BRICK OVEN.
USING THE FAR-INFRARED EFFECT, WE WERE ABLE TO BAKE THEM CRISPY ON THE OUTSIDE AND SOFT ON THE INSIDE.
ちゃっ CHA (SHLIK)
ちゃっ CHA
ちゃっ CHA
JAR: WHOLE GRAIN MUSTARD / DELICIOUS

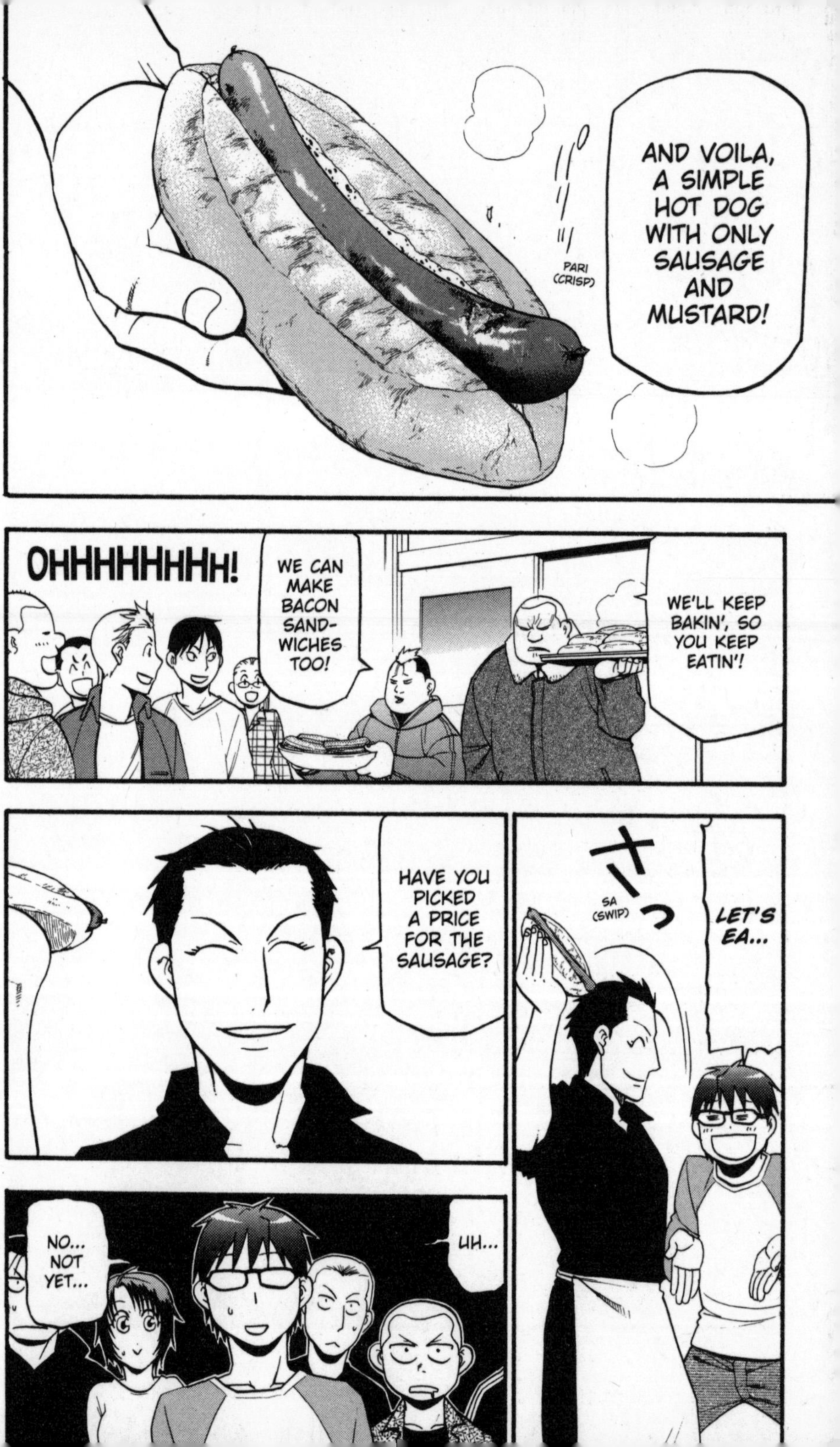
AND VOILA, A SIMPLE HOT DOG WITH ONLY SAUSAGE AND MUSTARD!
PARI (CRISP)
WE'LL KEEP BAKIN', SO YOU KEEP EATIN'!
WE CAN MAKE BACON SAND-WICHES TOO!
OHHHHHHHH!
LET'S EA...
SA (SWIP)
HAVE YOU PICKED A PRICE FOR THE SAUSAGE?
UH...
NO... NOT YET...

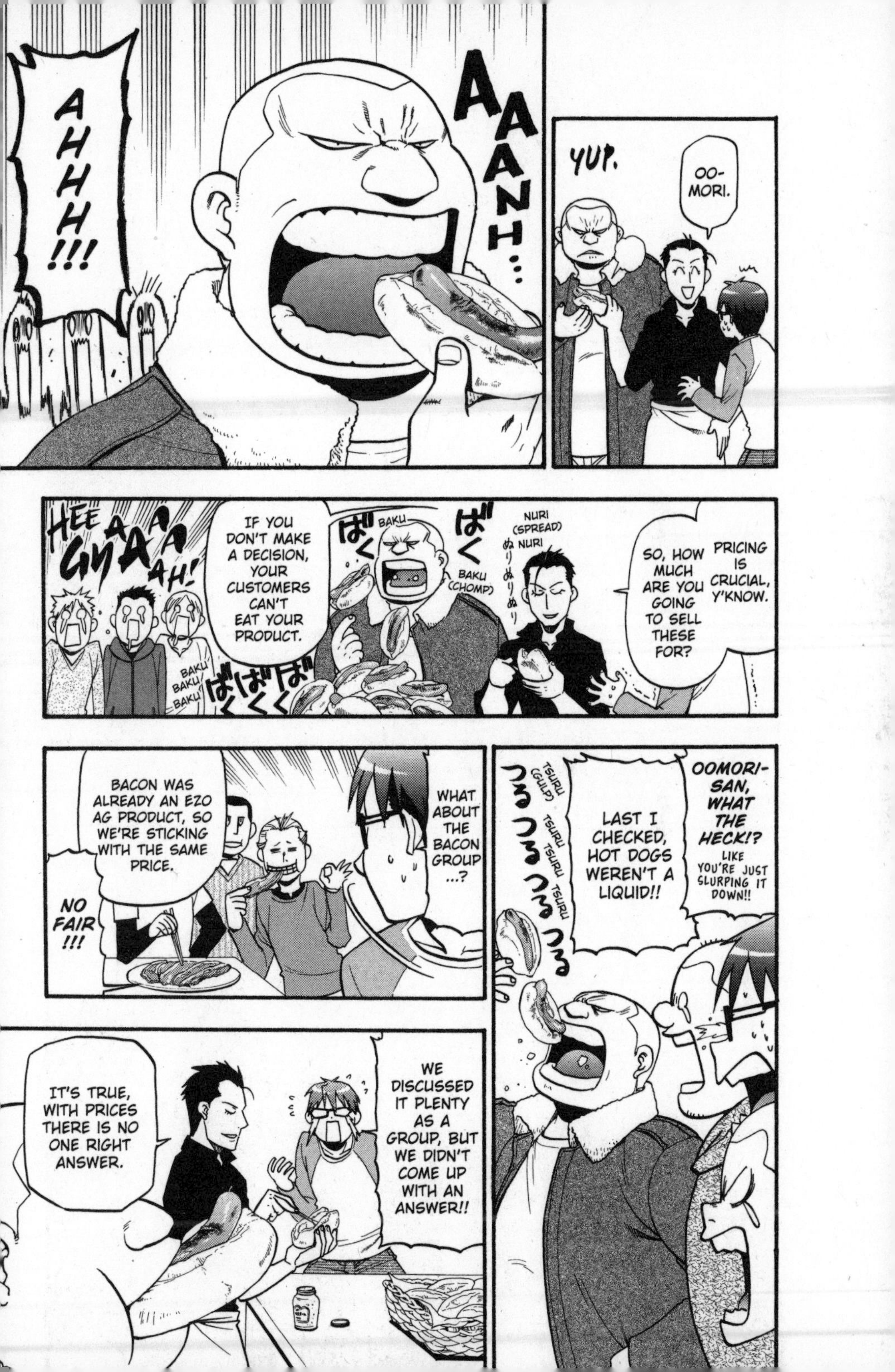
OO-MORI.
YUP.
AAANH...
AHHHH!!!
PRICING IS CRUCIAL, Y'KNOW.
SO, HOW MUCH ARE YOU GOING TO SELL THESE FOR?
NURI (SPREAD) ぬりぬりぬり NURI
ばく BAKU (CHOMP)
ばく BAKU
IF YOU DON'T MAKE A DECISION, YOUR CUSTOMERS CAN'T EAT YOUR PRODUCT.
ばばばくくく BAKU BAKU BAKU
HEE GYAAAAAH!
OOMORI-SAN, WHAT THE HECK!?
LIKE YOU'RE JUST SLURPING IT DOWN!!
LAST I CHECKED, HOT DOGS WEREN'T A LIQUID!!
つるつるつるつる TSURU (GULP) TSURU TSURU TSURU
WHAT ABOUT THE BACON GROUP...?
BACON WAS ALREADY AN EZO AG PRODUCT, SO WE'RE STICKING WITH THE SAME PRICE.
NO FAIR!!!
WE DISCUSSED IT PLENTY AS A GROUP, BUT WE DIDN'T COME UP WITH AN ANSWER!!
IT'S TRUE, WITH PRICES THERE IS NO ONE RIGHT ANSWER.

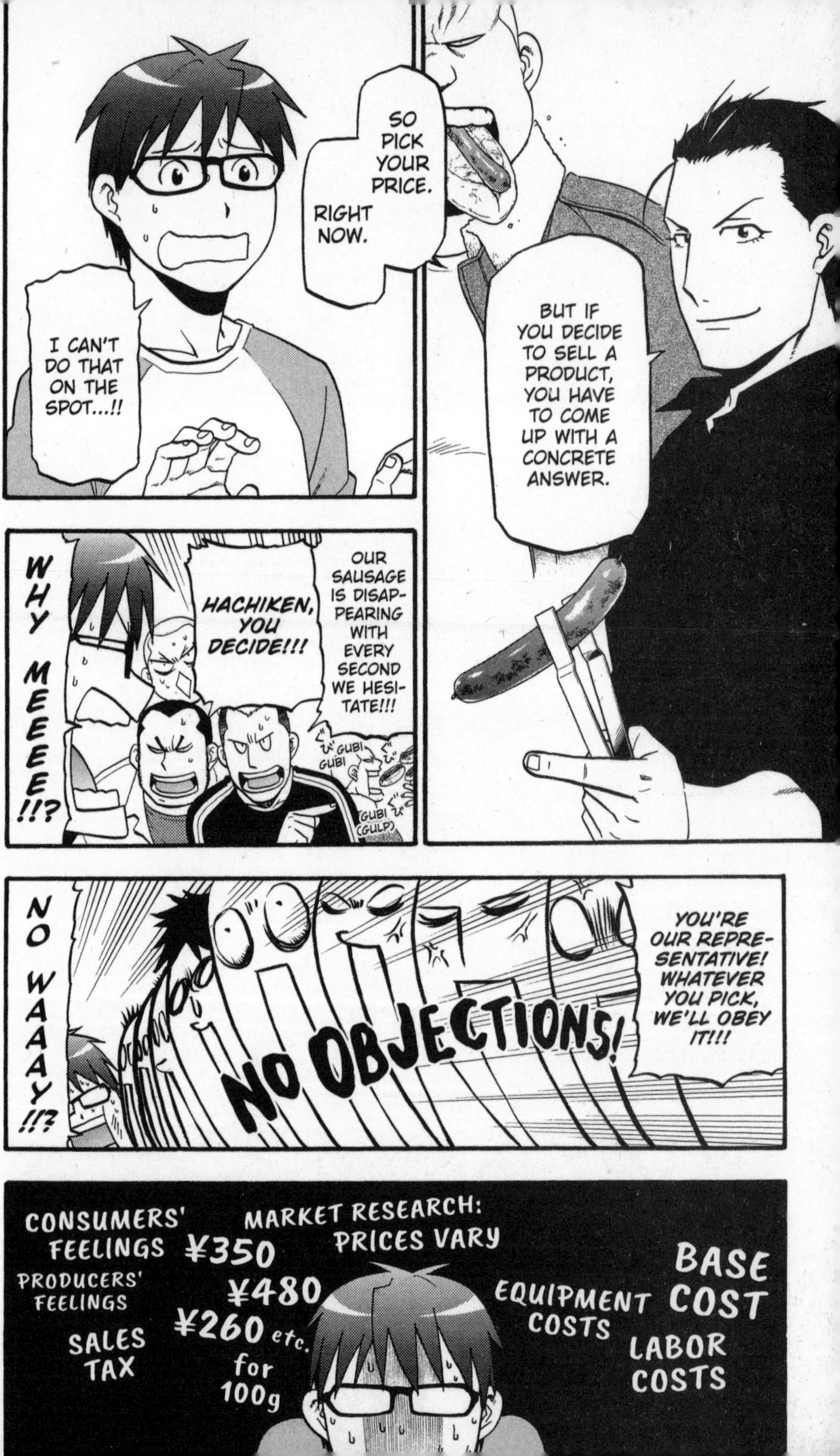
SO PICK YOUR PRICE.
RIGHT NOW.
BUT IF YOU DECIDE TO SELL A PRODUCT, YOU HAVE TO COME UP WITH A CONCRETE ANSWER.
I CAN'T DO THAT ON THE SPOT...!!
OUR SAUSAGE IS DISAPPEARING WITH EVERY SECOND WE HESITATE!!!
HACHIKEN, YOU DECIDE!!!
GUBI GUBI
GUBI (GULP)
WHY MEEEEE!!?
YOU'RE OUR REPRESENTATIVE! WHATEVER YOU PICK, WE'LL OBEY IT!!!
NO OBJECTIONS!
NO WAAAAY!!?
CONSUMERS' FEELINGS
MARKET RESEARCH: PRICES VARY
¥350
¥480
¥260 etc. for 100g
PRODUCERS' FEELINGS
SALES TAX
BASE COST
EQUIPMENT COSTS
LABOR COSTS

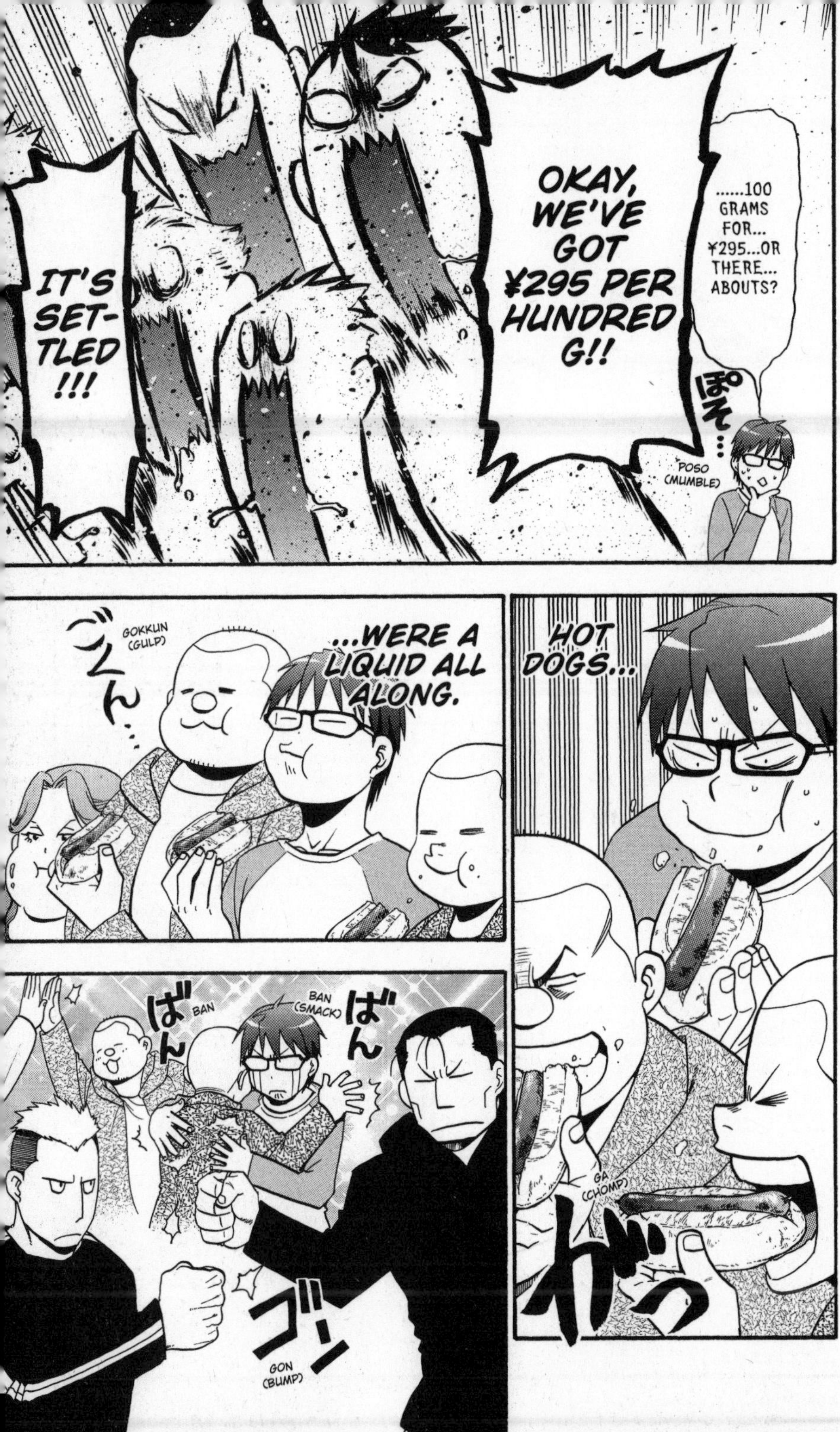
......100 GRAMS FOR... ¥295...OR THERE... ABOUTS?
ぽそ…
POSO (MUMBLE)
OKAY, WE'VE GOT ¥295 PER HUNDRED G!!
IT'S SET-TLED!!!
HOT DOGS...
がっ
GA (CHOMP)
...WERE A LIQUID ALL ALONG.
ごっくん…
GOKKUN (GULP)
ばん
BAN (SMACK)
ばん
BAN
ゴン
GON (BUMP)

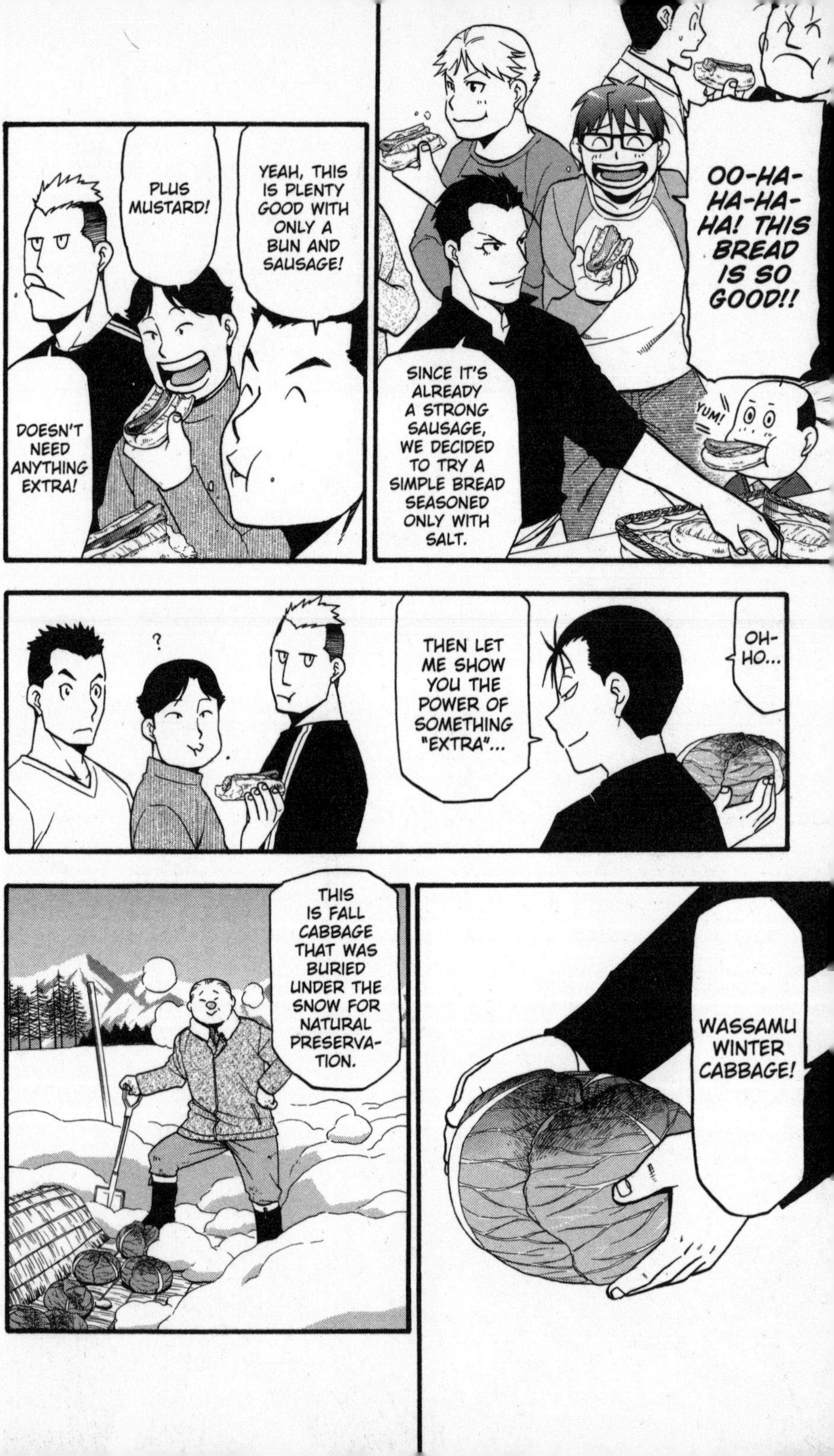
OO-HA-HA-HA! THIS BREAD IS SO GOOD!!
YUM!
SINCE IT'S ALREADY A STRONG SAUSAGE, WE DECIDED TO TRY A SIMPLE BREAD SEASONED ONLY WITH SALT.
YEAH, THIS IS PLENTY GOOD WITH ONLY A BUN AND SAUSAGE!
PLUS MUSTARD!
DOESN'T NEED ANYTHING EXTRA!
OH-HO...
THEN LET ME SHOW YOU THE POWER OF SOMETHING "EXTRA"...
?
WASSAMU WINTER CABBAGE!
THIS IS FALL CABBAGE THAT WAS BURIED UNDER THE SNOW FOR NATURAL PRESERVATION.

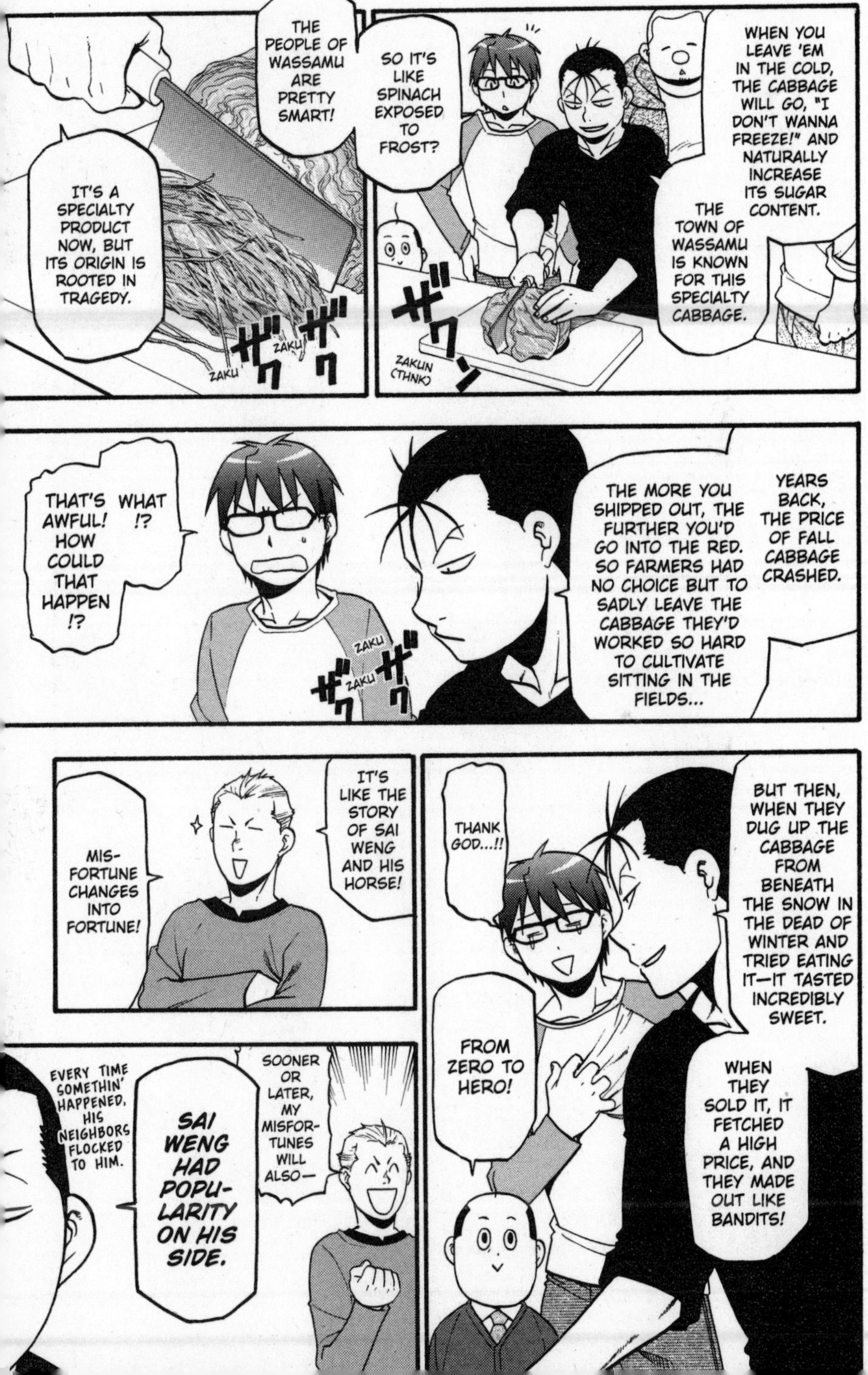
WHEN YOU LEAVE 'EM IN THE COLD, THE CABBAGE WILL GO, "I DON'T WANNA FREEZE!" AND NATURALLY INCREASE ITS SUGAR CONTENT.
THE TOWN OF WASSAMU IS KNOWN FOR THIS SPECIALTY CABBAGE.
SO IT'S LIKE SPINACH EXPOSED TO FROST?
ZAKUN (THNK)
THE PEOPLE OF WASSAMU ARE PRETTY SMART!
IT'S A SPECIALTY PRODUCT NOW, BUT ITS ORIGIN IS ROOTED IN TRAGEDY.
ZAKU
ZAKU
YEARS BACK, THE PRICE OF FALL CABBAGE CRASHED.
THE MORE YOU SHIPPED OUT, THE FURTHER YOU'D GO INTO THE RED. SO FARMERS HAD NO CHOICE BUT TO SADLY LEAVE THE CABBAGE THEY'D WORKED SO HARD TO CULTIVATE SITTING IN THE FIELDS...
WHAT !?
THAT'S AWFUL! HOW COULD THAT HAPPEN !?
ZAKU
ZAKU
BUT THEN, WHEN THEY DUG UP THE CABBAGE FROM BENEATH THE SNOW IN THE DEAD OF WINTER AND TRIED EATING IT—IT TASTED INCREDIBLY SWEET.
THANK GOD...!!
WHEN THEY SOLD IT, IT FETCHED A HIGH PRICE, AND THEY MADE OUT LIKE BANDITS!
FROM ZERO TO HERO!
IT'S LIKE THE STORY OF SAI WENG AND HIS HORSE!
MIS-FORTUNE CHANGES INTO FORTUNE!
SOONER OR LATER, MY MISFOR-TUNES WILL ALSO—
SAI WENG HAD POPU-LARITY ON HIS SIDE.
EVERY TIME SOMETHIN' HAPPENED, HIS NEIGHBORS FLOCKED TO HIM.

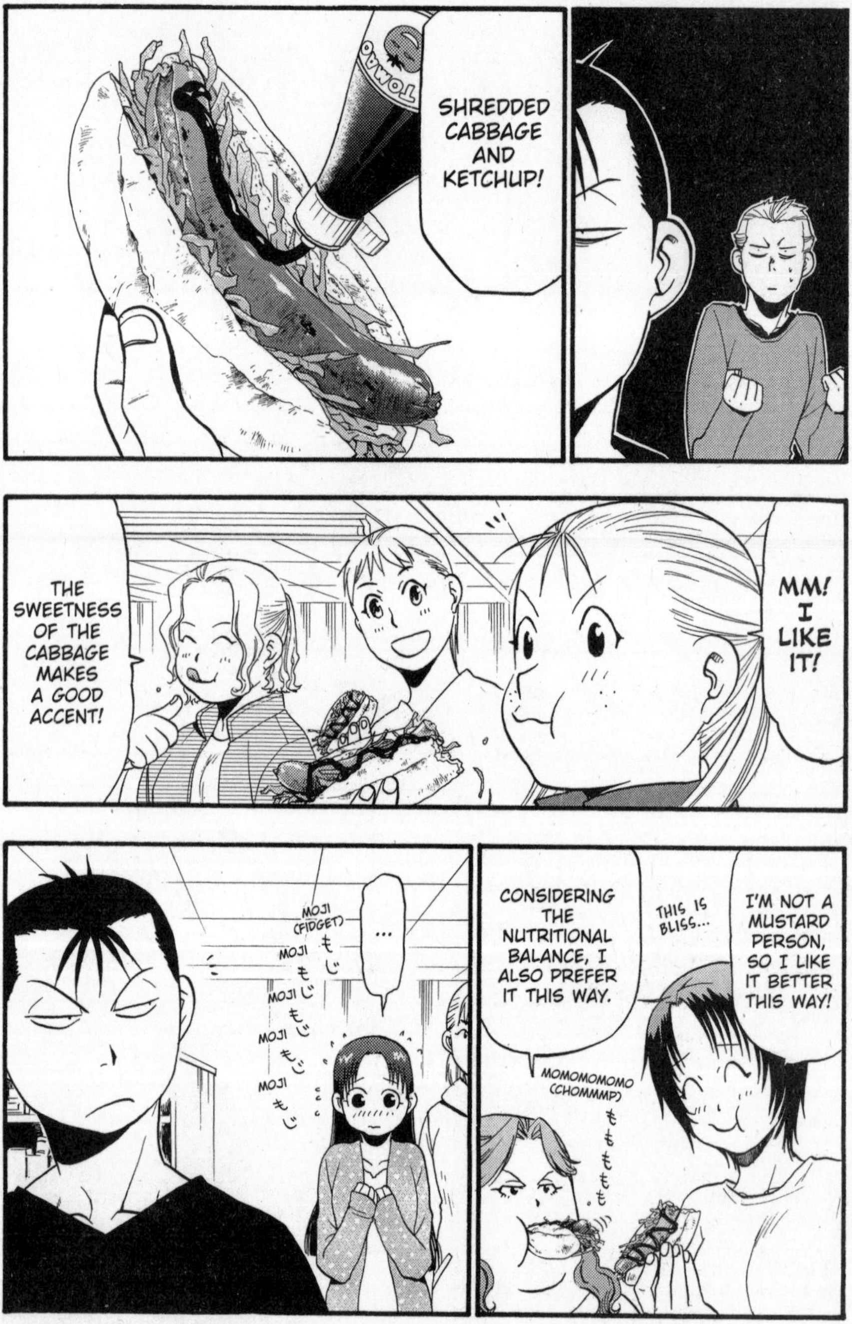

SHREDDED CABBAGE AND KETCHUP!
MM! I LIKE IT!
THE SWEETNESS OF THE CABBAGE MAKES A GOOD ACCENT!
I'M NOT A MUSTARD PERSON, SO I LIKE IT BETTER THIS WAY!
THIS IS BLISS...
CONSIDERING THE NUTRITIONAL BALANCE, I ALSO PREFER IT THIS WAY.
MOMOMOMOMO (CHOMMMP) ももももも
...
MOJI (FIDGET) もじ
MOJI もじ
MOJI もじ
MOJI もじ
MOJI もじ

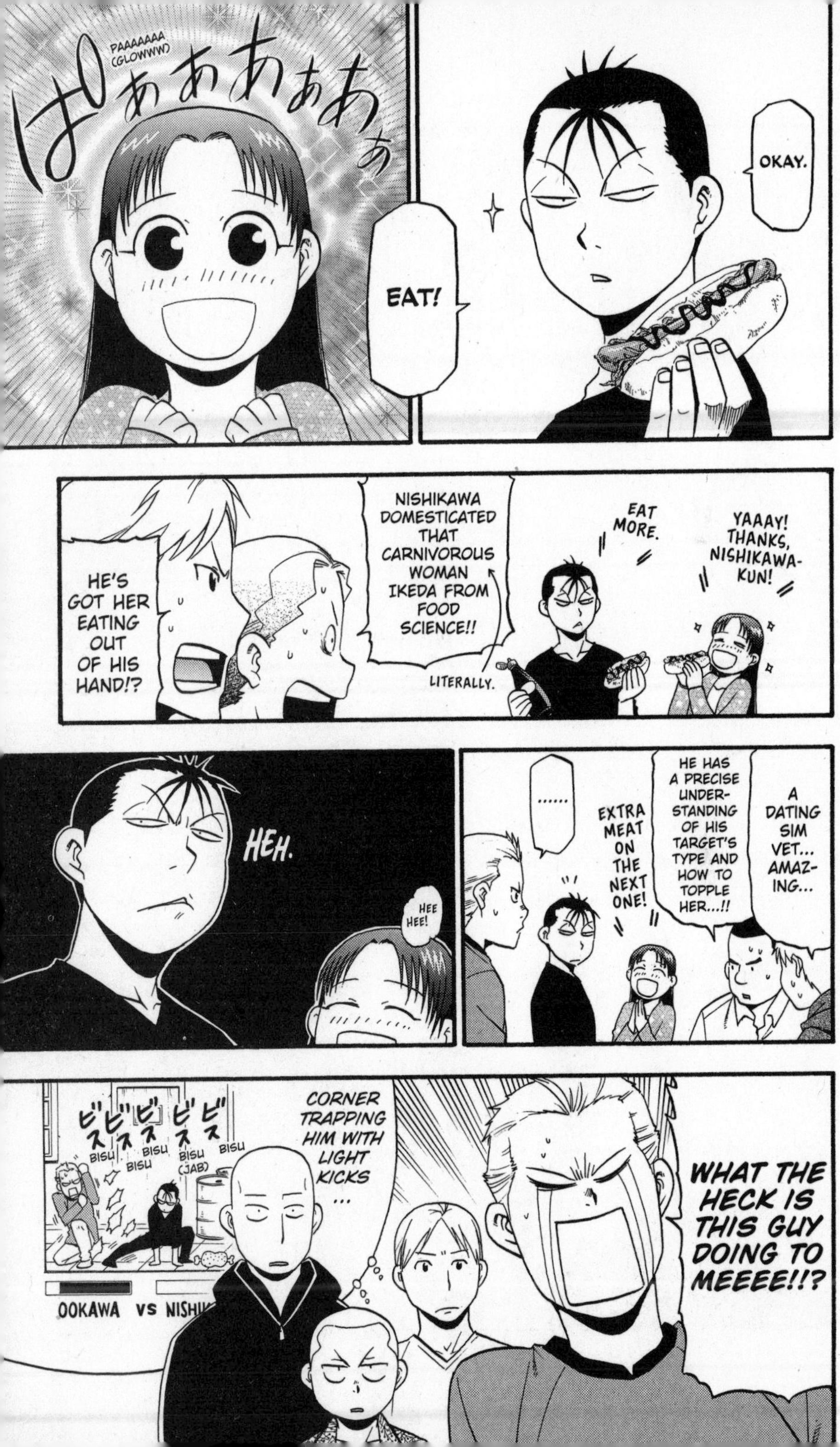
OKAY.
EAT!
ぱぁぁあぁぁぁ
PAAAAAAA (GLOWWW)
YAAAY! THANKS, NISHIKAWA-KUN!
EAT MORE.
NISHIKAWA DOMESTICATED THAT CARNIVOROUS WOMAN IKEDA FROM FOOD SCIENCE!!
LITERALLY.
HE'S GOT HER EATING OUT OF HIS HAND!?
A DATING SIM VET... AMAZING...
HE HAS A PRECISE UNDER-STANDING OF HIS TARGET'S TYPE AND HOW TO TOPPLE HER...!!
......
EXTRA MEAT ON THE NEXT ONE!
HEH.
HEE HEE!
WHAT THE HECK IS THIS GUY DOING TO MEEEE!!?
CORNER TRAPPING HIM WITH LIGHT KICKS ...
ビスビスビスビスビス
BISU BISU BISU BISU (JAB) BISU
OOKAWA VS NISHIK

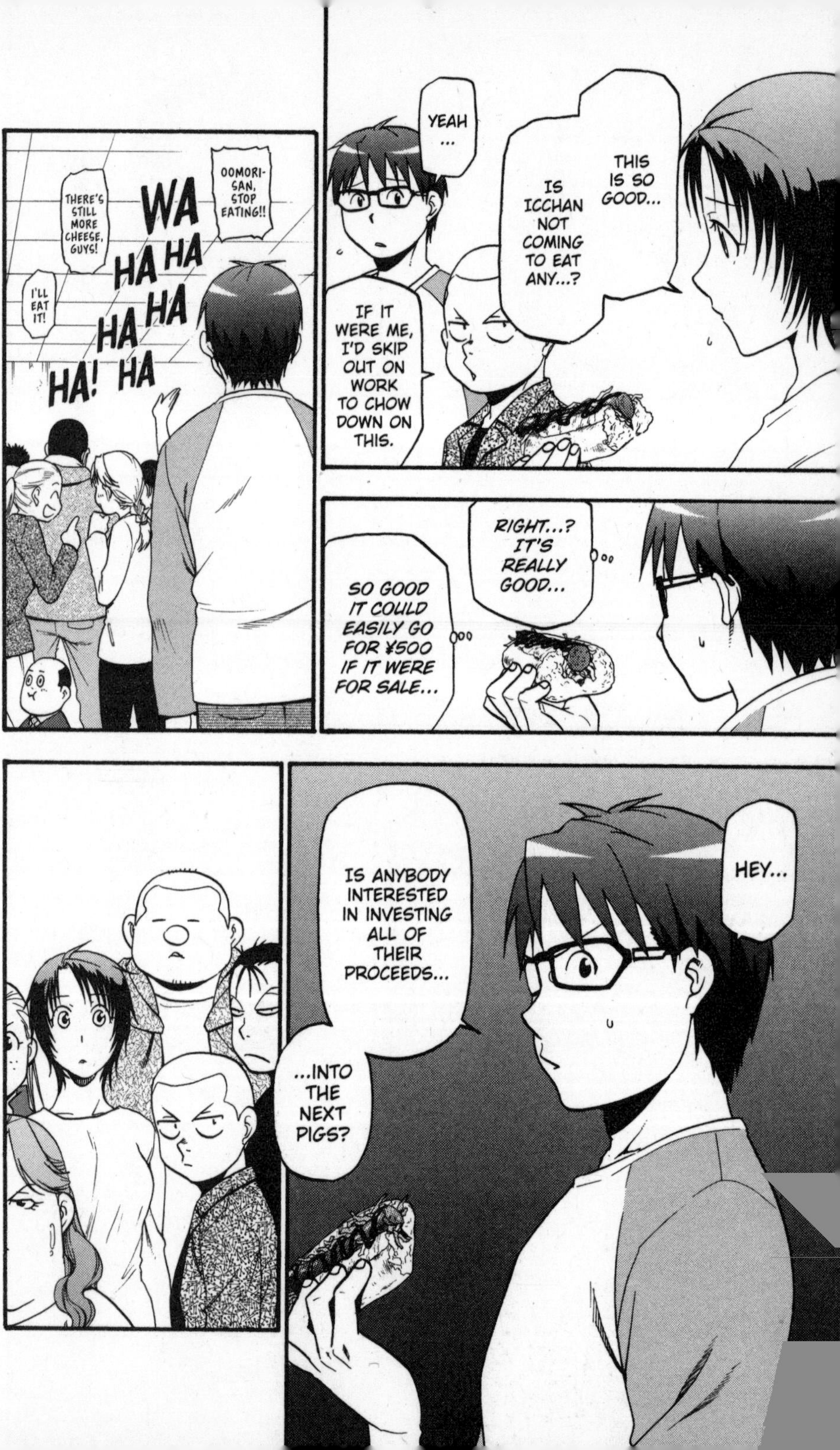
THIS IS SO GOOD...
IS ICCHAN NOT COMING TO EAT ANY...?
YEAH...
IF IT WERE ME, I'D SKIP OUT ON WORK TO CHOW DOWN ON THIS.
RIGHT...? IT'S REALLY GOOD...
SO GOOD IT COULD EASILY GO FOR ¥500 IF IT WERE FOR SALE...
OOMORI-SAN, STOP EATING!!
WA HA HA HA HA HA HA! HA
THERE'S STILL MORE CHEESE, GUYS!
I'LL EAT IT!
HEY...
IS ANYBODY INTERESTED IN INVESTING ALL OF THEIR PROCEEDS...
...INTO THE NEXT PIGS?

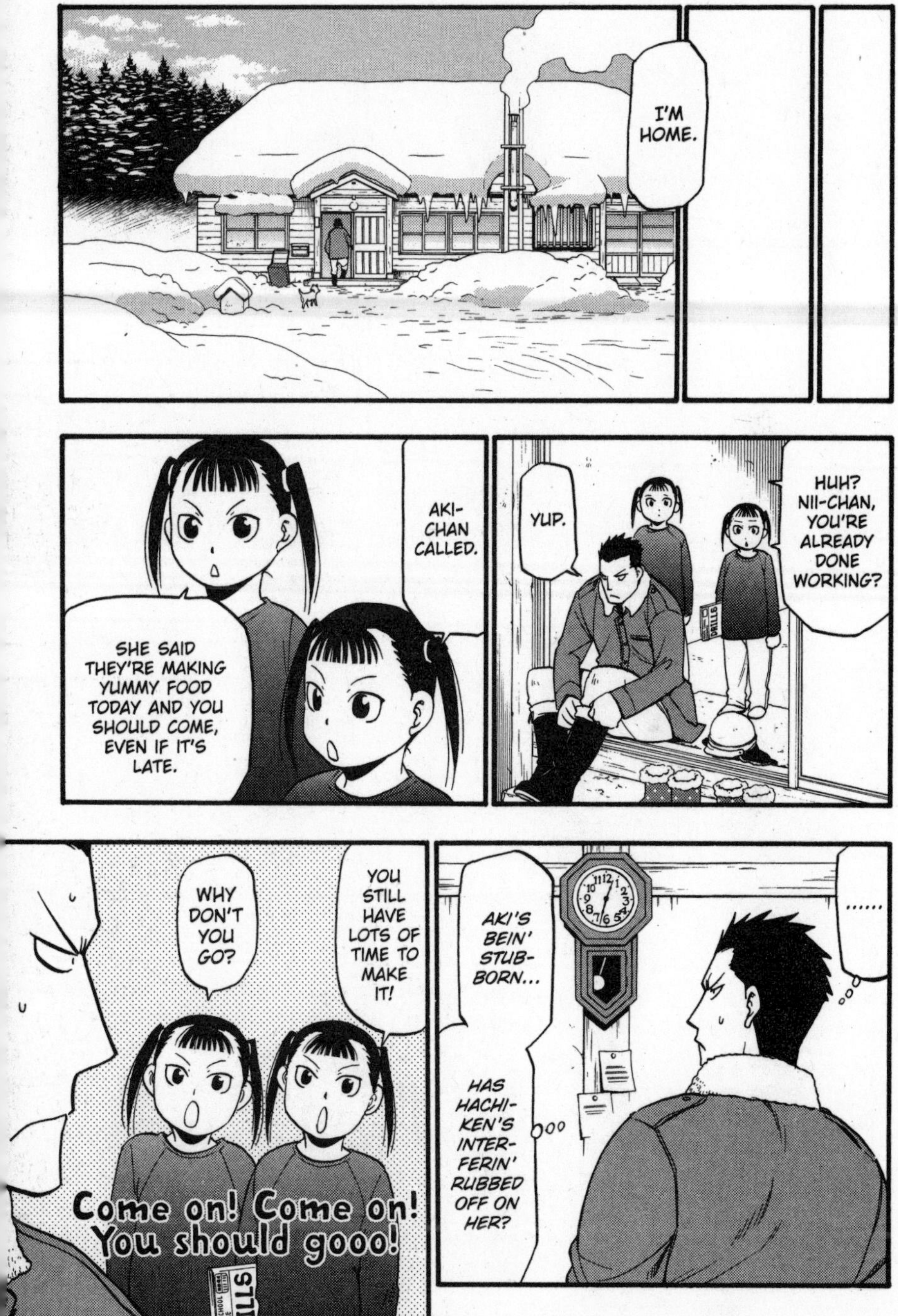
I'M HOME.
HUH? NII-CHAN, YOU'RE ALREADY DONE WORKING?
YUP.
AKI-CHAN CALLED.
SHE SAID THEY'RE MAKING YUMMY FOOD TODAY AND YOU SHOULD COME, EVEN IF IT'S LATE.
......
AKI'S BEIN' STUBBORN...
HAS HACHIKEN'S INTERFERIN' RUBBED OFF ON HER?
YOU STILL HAVE LOTS OF TIME TO MAKE IT!
WHY DON'T YOU GO?
Come on! Come on! You should gooo!
DRILLS

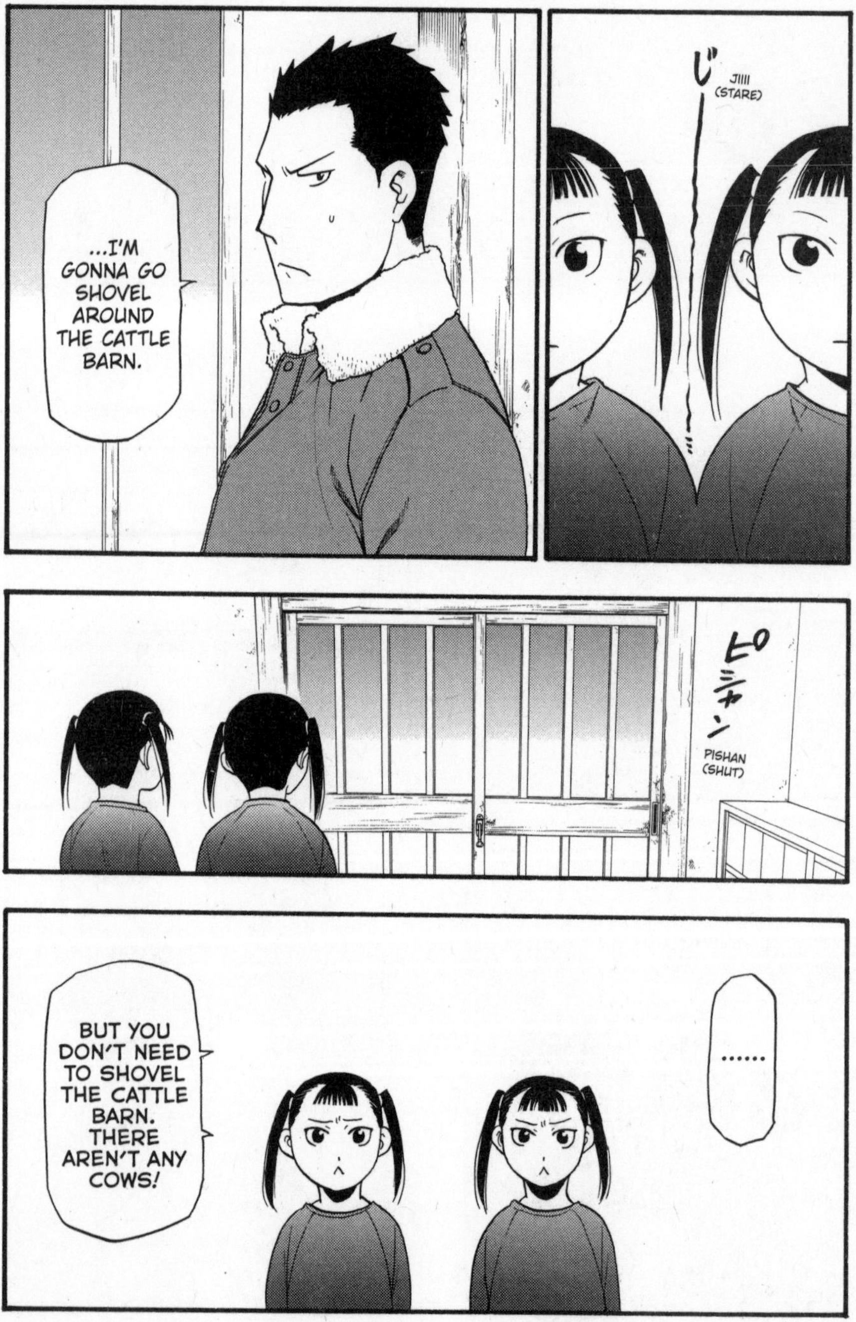
じ
JIIII (STARE)
...I'M GONNA GO SHOVEL AROUND THE CATTLE BARN.
ピシャン
PISHAN (SHUT)
......
BUT YOU DON'T NEED TO SHOVEL THE CATTLE BARN. THERE AREN'T ANY COWS!

Silver Spoon

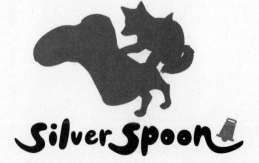

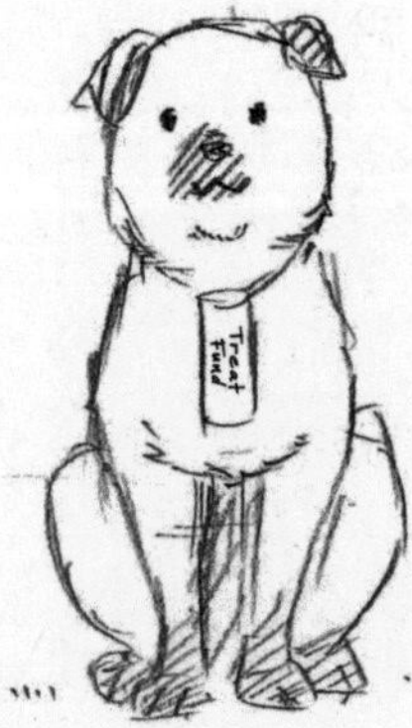
Treat Fund

VICE PREZ

MIXED BREED

Chapter 86: Tale of Winter ㉓

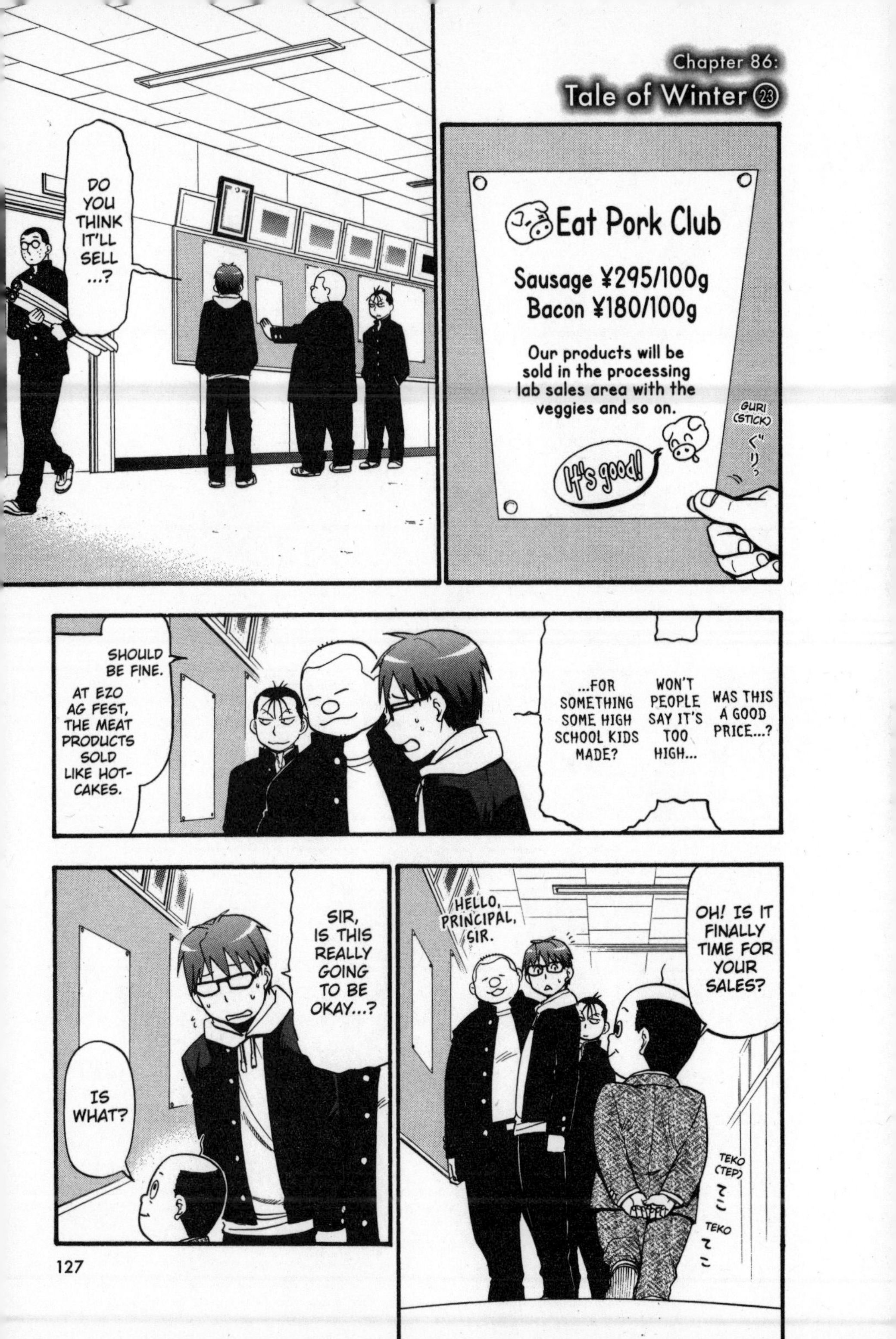

Eat Pork Club
Sausage ¥295/100g
Bacon ¥180/100g
Our products will be sold in the processing lab sales area with the veggies and so on.
It's good!
GURI (STICK)
ぐりっ
DO YOU THINK IT'LL SELL ...?
WAS THIS A GOOD PRICE...?
WON'T PEOPLE SAY IT'S TOO HIGH...
...FOR SOMETHING SOME HIGH SCHOOL KIDS MADE?
SHOULD BE FINE.
AT EZO AG FEST, THE MEAT PRODUCTS SOLD LIKE HOT-CAKES.
OH! IS IT FINALLY TIME FOR YOUR SALES?
HELLO, PRINCIPAL, SIR.
TEKO (TEP)
てこ
TEKO
てこ
SIR, IS THIS REALLY GOING TO BE OKAY...?
IS WHAT?

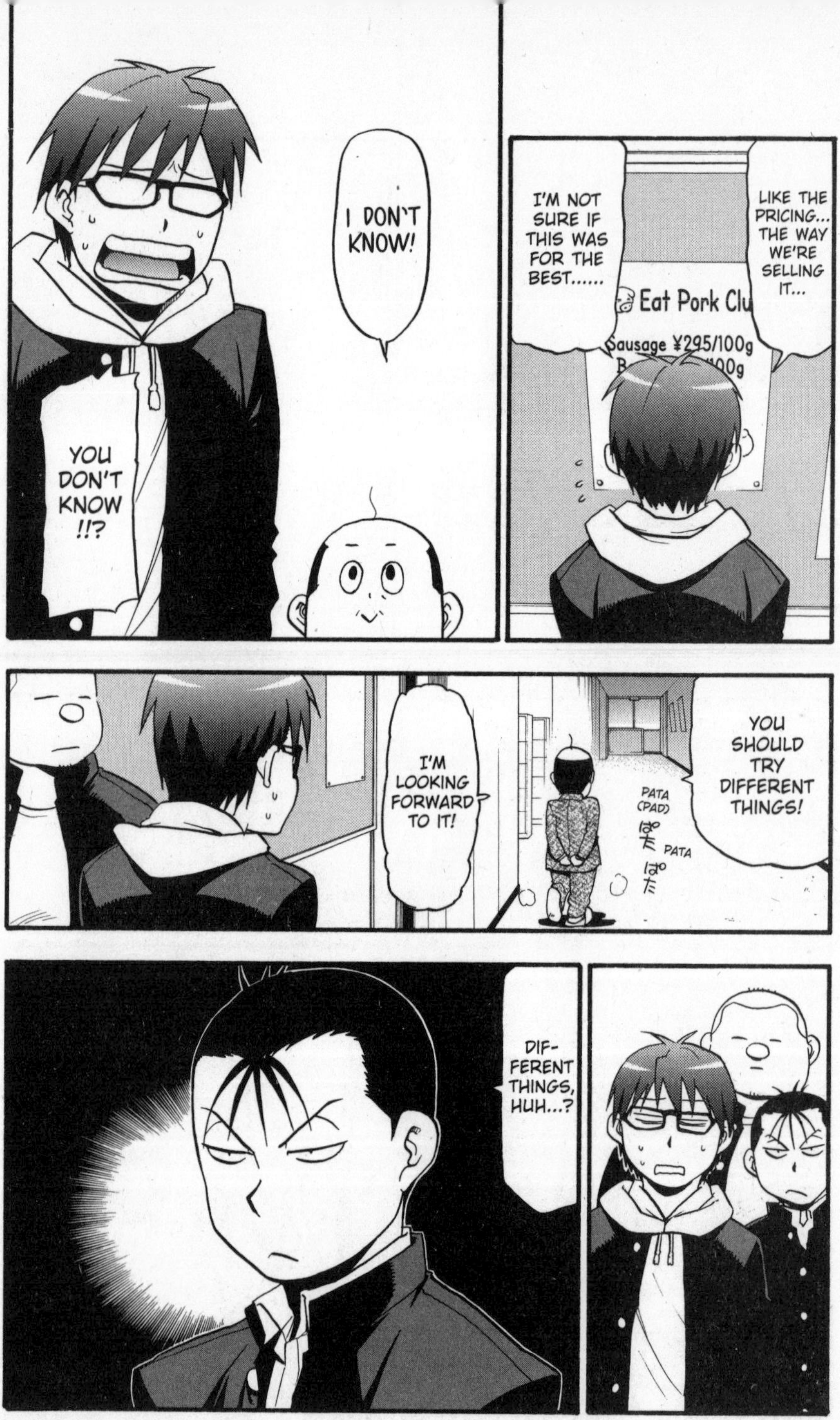
I'M NOT SURE IF THIS WAS FOR THE BEST......
LIKE THE PRICING... THE WAY WE'RE SELLING IT...
Eat Pork Clu
Sausage ¥295/100g
I DON'T KNOW!
YOU DON'T KNOW!!?
YOU SHOULD TRY DIFFERENT THINGS!
PATA (PAD)
ぱた
PATA
ぱた
I'M LOOKING FORWARD TO IT!
DIF-FERENT THINGS, HUH...?

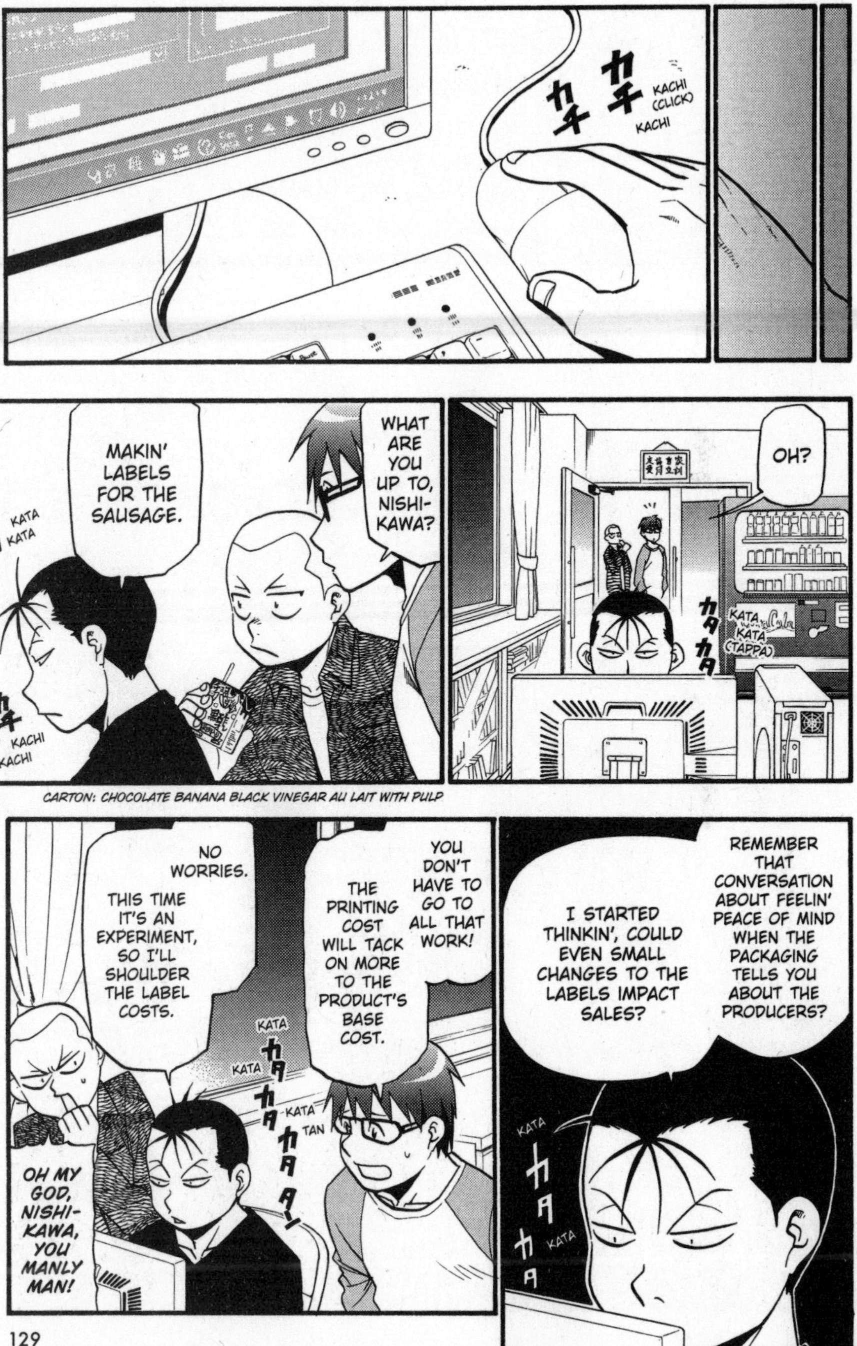
KACHI (CLICK)
KACHI
OH?
KATA KATA (TAPPA)
WHAT ARE YOU UP TO, NISHI-KAWA?
MAKIN' LABELS FOR THE SAUSAGE.
KATA KATA
KACHI KACHI
CARTON: CHOCOLATE BANANA BLACK VINEGAR AU LAIT WITH PULP
REMEMBER THAT CONVERSATION ABOUT FEELIN' PEACE OF MIND WHEN THE PACKAGING TELLS YOU ABOUT THE PRODUCERS?
I STARTED THINKIN', COULD EVEN SMALL CHANGES TO THE LABELS IMPACT SALES?
KATA
KATA
YOU DON'T HAVE TO GO TO ALL THAT WORK!
THE PRINTING COST WILL TACK ON MORE TO THE PRODUCT'S BASE COST.
NO WORRIES.
THIS TIME IT'S AN EXPERIMENT, SO I'LL SHOULDER THE LABEL COSTS.
KATA
KATA
KATA
TAN
OH MY GOD, NISHI-KAWA, YOU MANLY MAN!

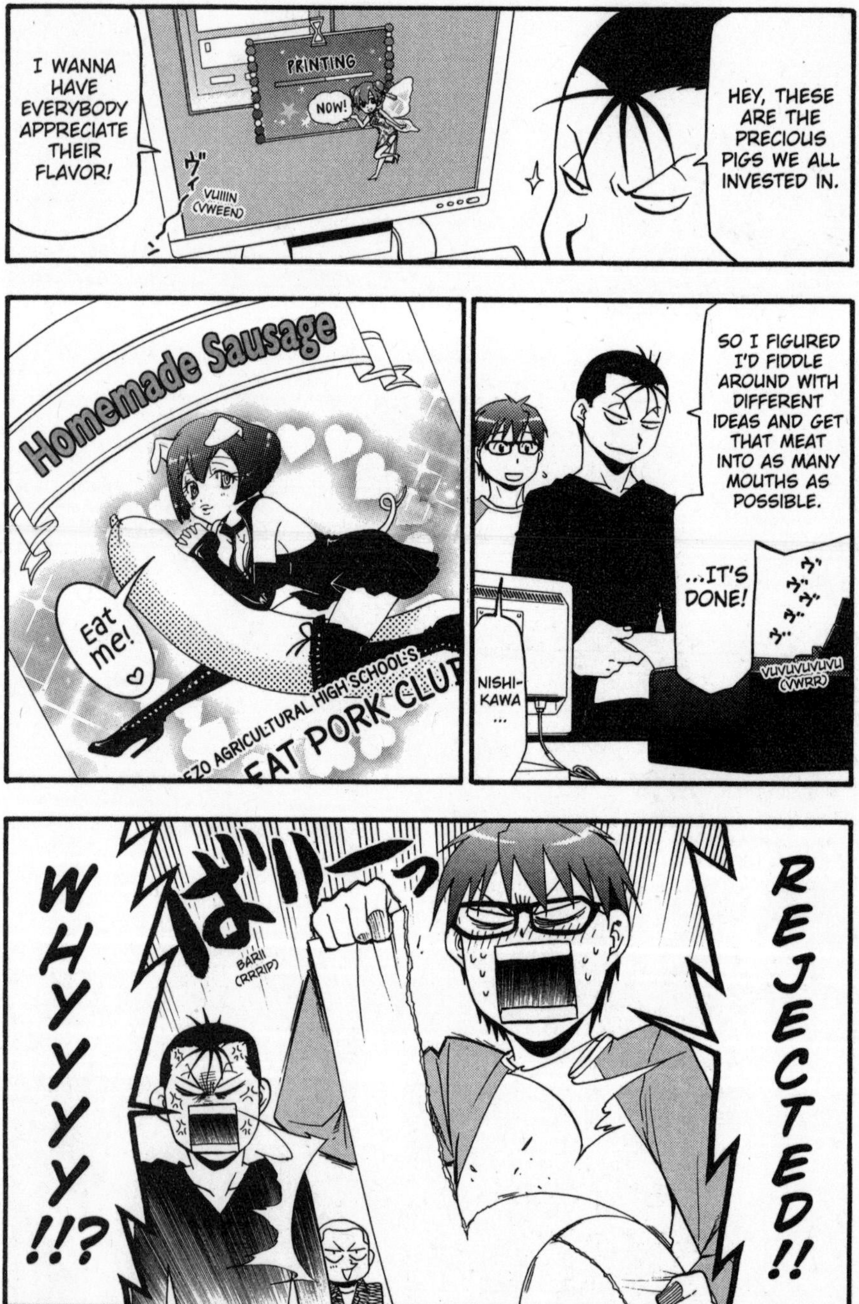
HEY, THESE ARE THE PRECIOUS PIGS WE ALL INVESTED IN.
PRINTING
NOW!
VUIIIN (VWEEN)
I WANNA HAVE EVERYBODY APPRECIATE THEIR FLAVOR!
SO I FIGURED I'D FIDDLE AROUND WITH DIFFERENT IDEAS AND GET THAT MEAT INTO AS MANY MOUTHS AS POSSIBLE.
VUVUVUVUVU (VWRR)
...IT'S DONE!
NISHIKAWA...
Homemade Sausage
Eat me! ♡
EZO AGRICULTURAL HIGH SCHOOL'S
EAT PORK CLUB
REJECTED!!
BARII (RRRIP)
WHYYYY!!?

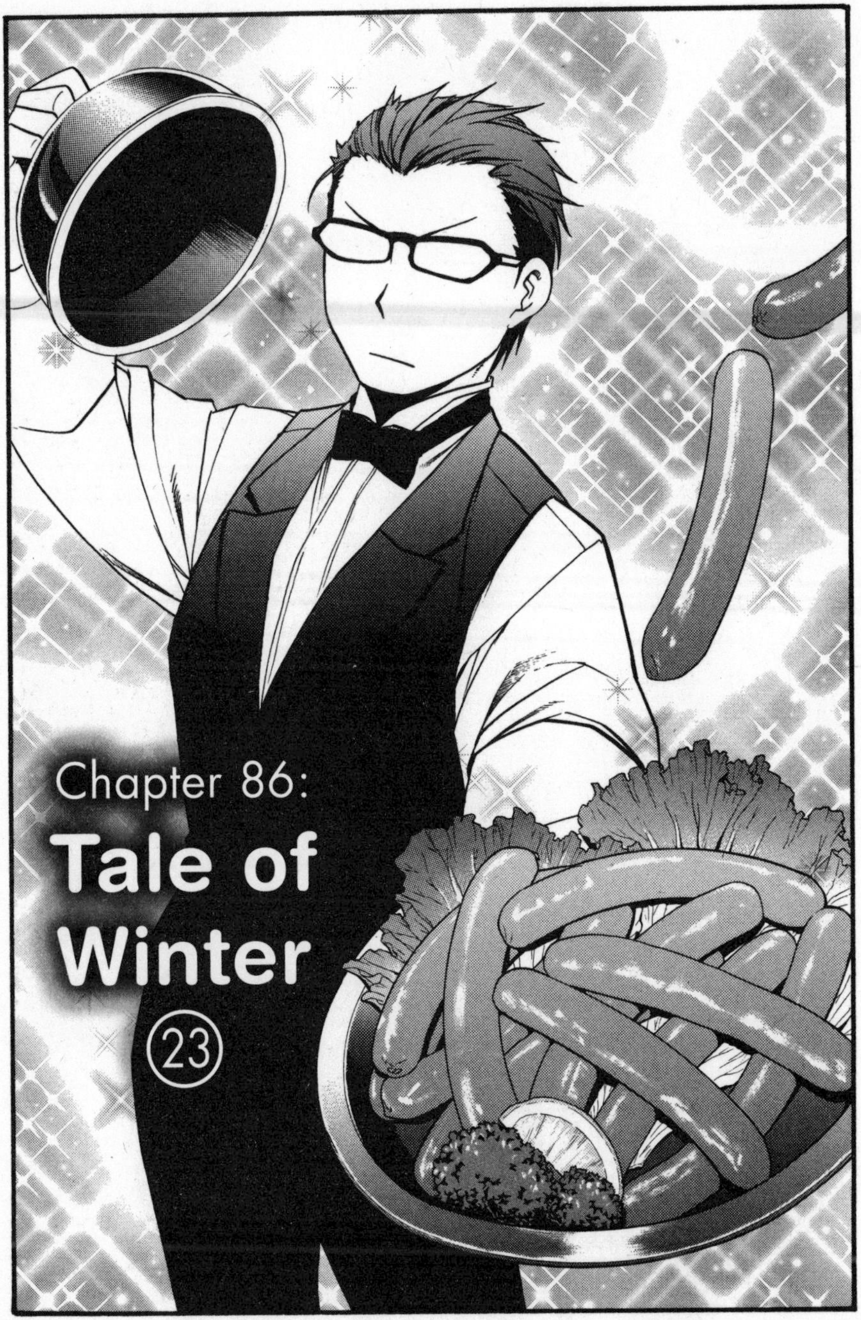
Chapter 86:
Tale of Winter
㉓

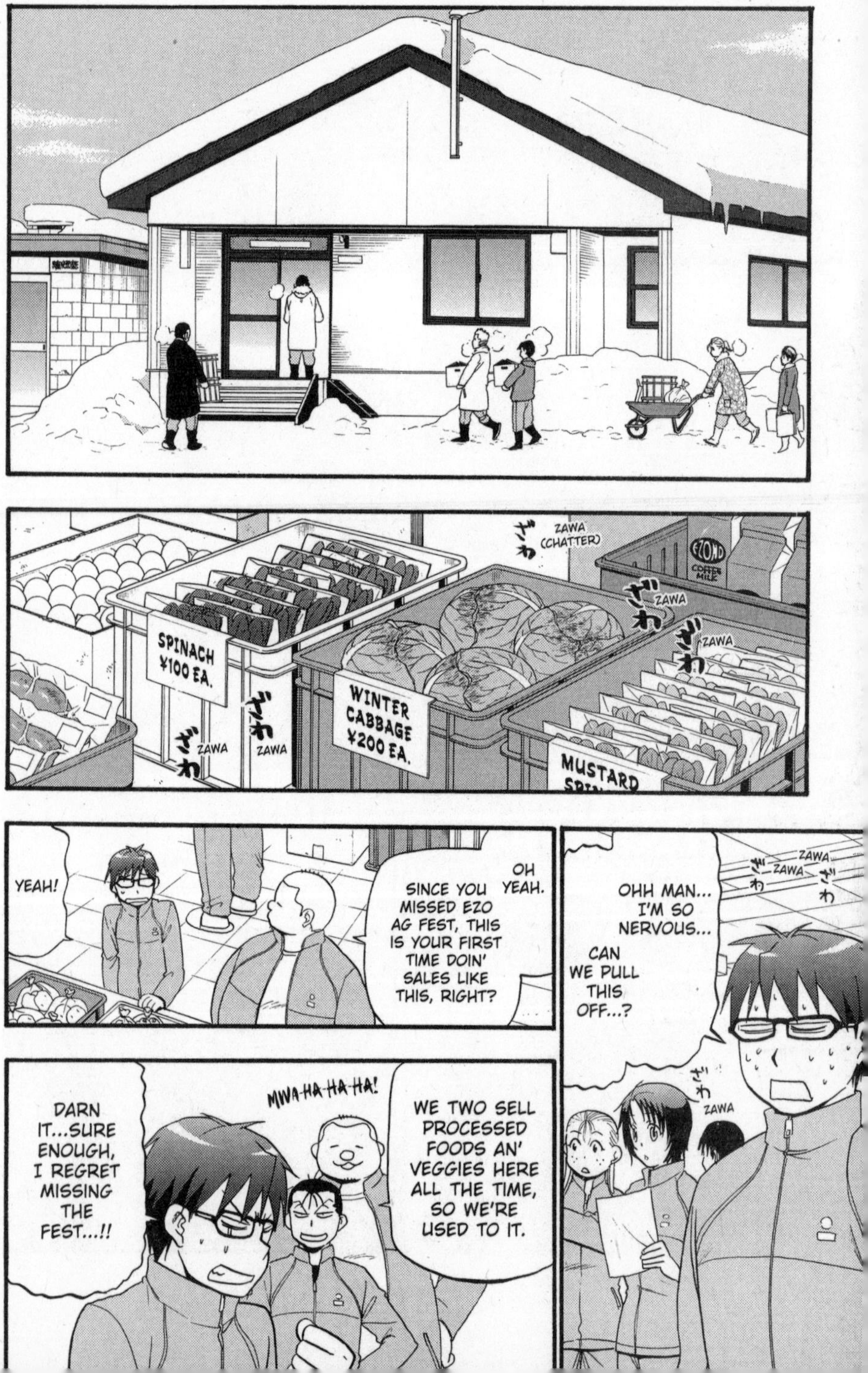
ZAWA (CHATTER)
ZAWA
ZAWA
SPINACH ¥100 EA.
WINTER CABBAGE ¥200 EA.
MUSTARD SPIN...
ZAWA
ZAWA
ZAWA ZAWA
OHH MAN... I'M SO NERVOUS...
CAN WE PULL THIS OFF...?
ZAWA
OH YEAH.
SINCE YOU MISSED EZO AG FEST, THIS IS YOUR FIRST TIME DOIN' SALES LIKE THIS, RIGHT?
YEAH!
WE TWO SELL PROCESSED FOODS AN' VEGGIES HERE ALL THE TIME, SO WE'RE USED TO IT.
MWA-HA-HA-HA!
DARN IT...SURE ENOUGH, I REGRET MISSING THE FEST...!!

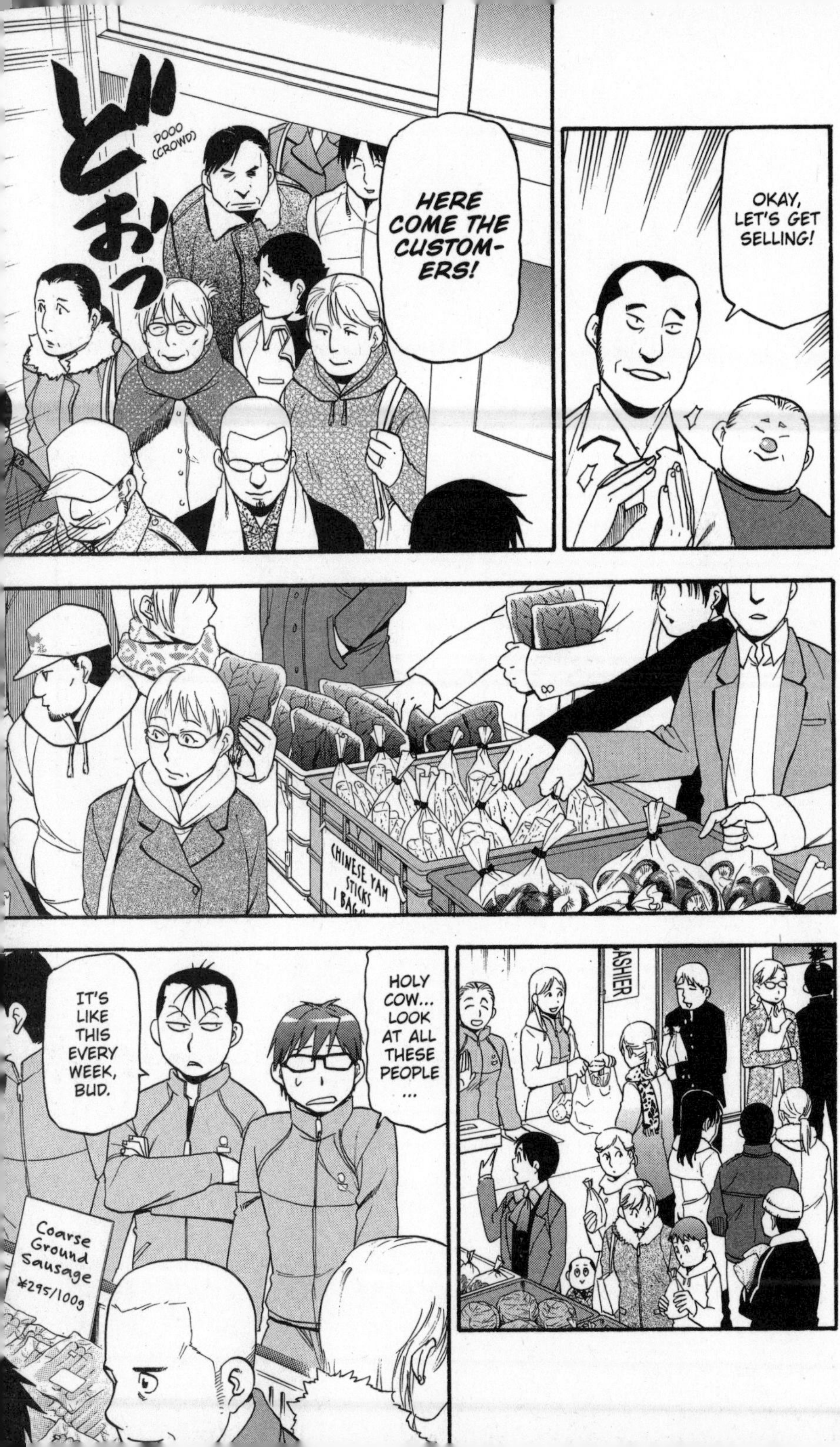
OKAY, LET'S GET SELLING!
HERE COME THE CUSTOM-ERS!
どおっ
DOOO (CROWD)
CHINESE YAM STICKS
HOLY COW... LOOK AT ALL THESE PEOPLE ...
IT'S LIKE THIS EVERY WEEK, BUD.
Coarse Ground Sausage
¥295/100g

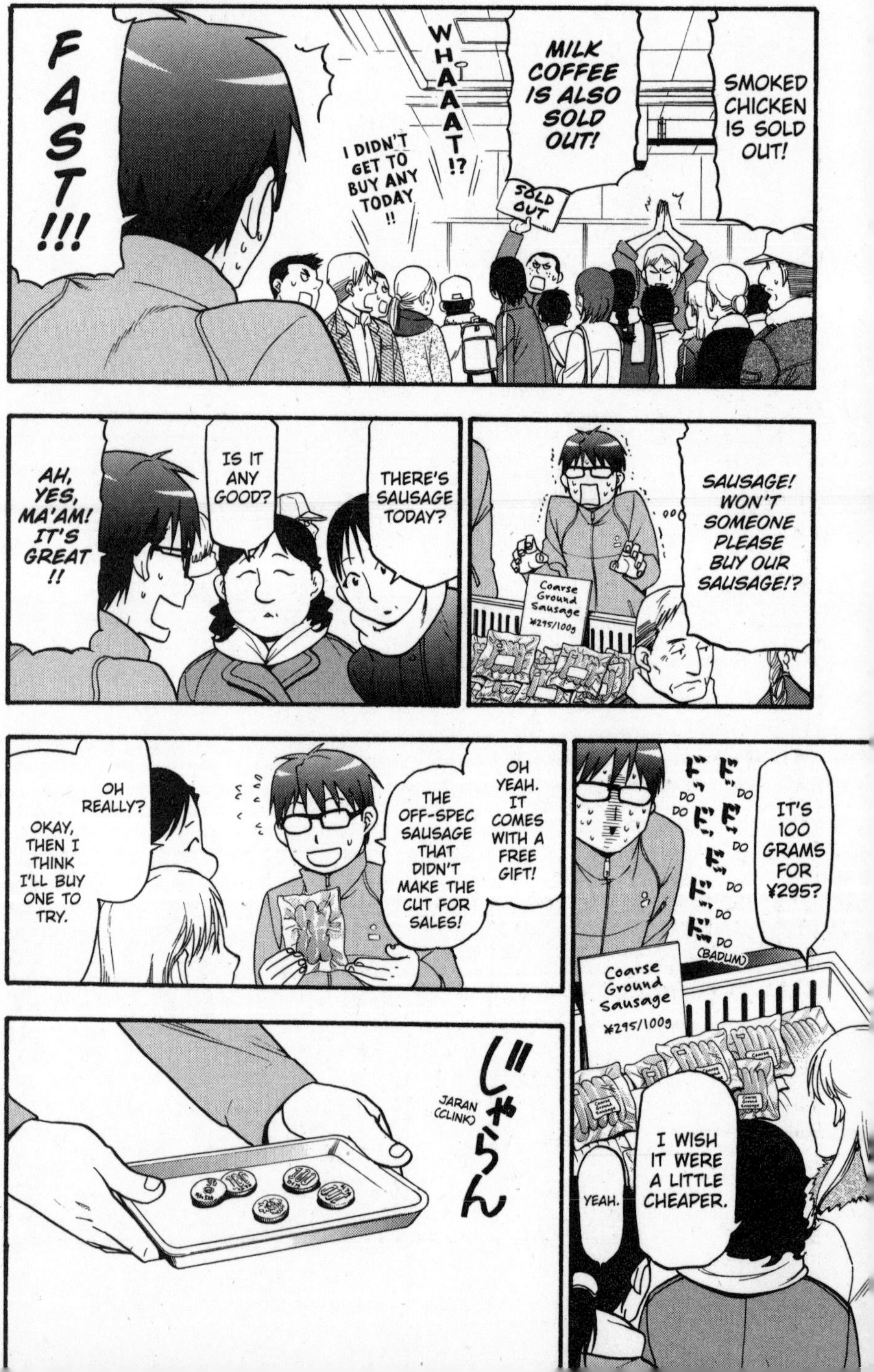
SMOKED CHICKEN IS SOLD OUT!
MILK COFFEE IS ALSO SOLD OUT!
SOLD OUT
WHAAAT!?
I DIDN'T GET TO BUY ANY TODAY!!
FAST!!!
SAUSAGE! WON'T SOMEONE PLEASE BUY OUR SAUSAGE!?
Coarse Ground Sausage ¥295/100g
THERE'S SAUSAGE TODAY?
IS IT ANY GOOD?
AH, YES, MA'AM! IT'S GREAT!!
IT'S 100 GRAMS FOR ¥295?
ドドドドドドドド
DO DO DO DO DO DO DO DO (BADUM)
Coarse Ground Sausage ¥295/100g
I WISH IT WERE A LITTLE CHEAPER.
YEAH.
OH YEAH. IT COMES WITH A FREE GIFT!
THE OFF-SPEC SAUSAGE THAT DIDN'T MAKE THE CUT FOR SALES!
OH REALLY?
OKAY, THEN I THINK I'LL BUY ONE TO TRY.
じゃらん
JARAN (CLINK)

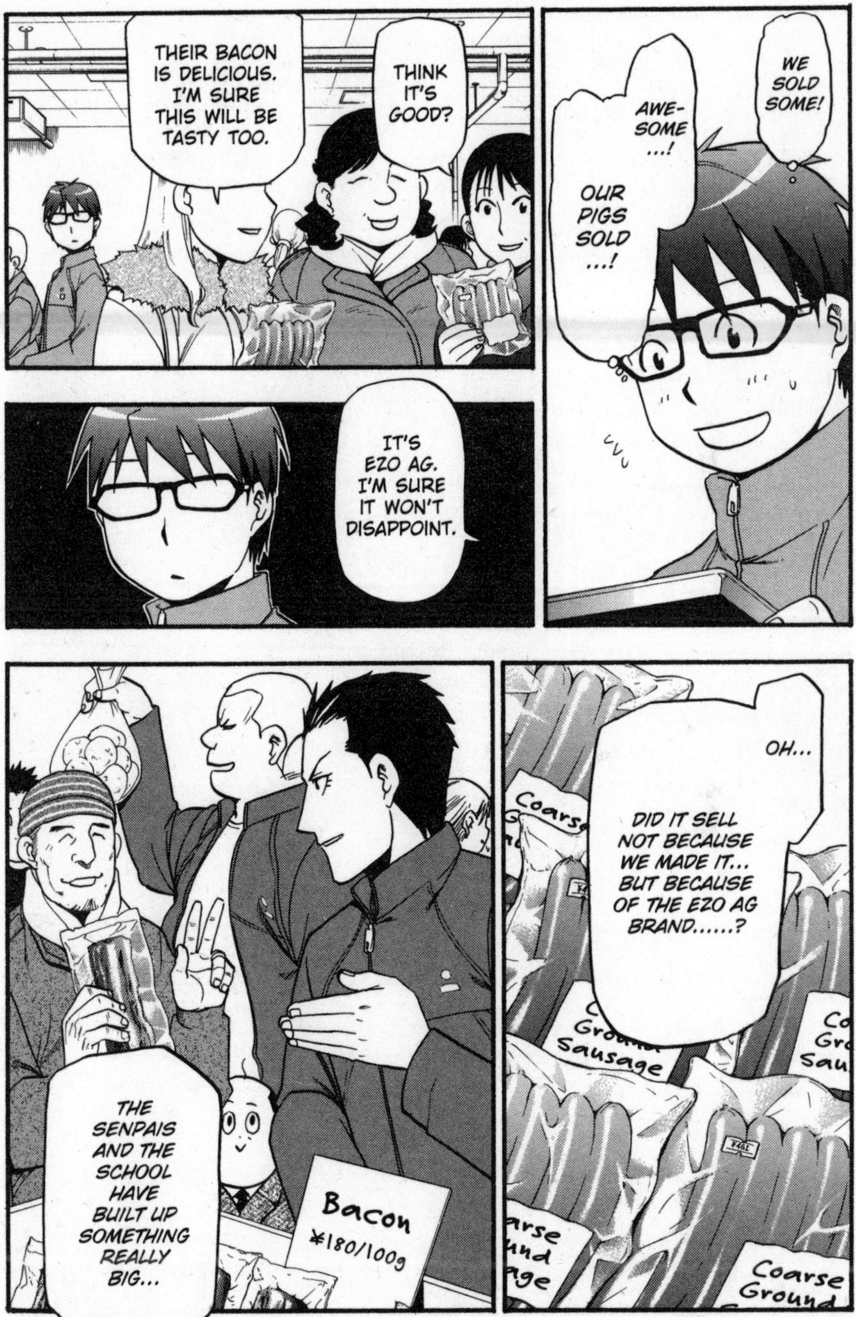
WE SOLD SOME!
AWE-SOME ...!
OUR PIGS SOLD ...!
THINK IT'S GOOD?
THEIR BACON IS DELICIOUS. I'M SURE THIS WILL BE TASTY TOO.
IT'S EZO AG. I'M SURE IT WON'T DISAPPOINT.
OH...
DID IT SELL NOT BECAUSE WE MADE IT... BUT BECAUSE OF THE EZO AG BRAND......?
Coarse Ground Sausage
Coarse Ground
THE SENPAIS AND THE SCHOOL HAVE BUILT UP SOMETHING REALLY BIG...
Bacon ¥180/100g

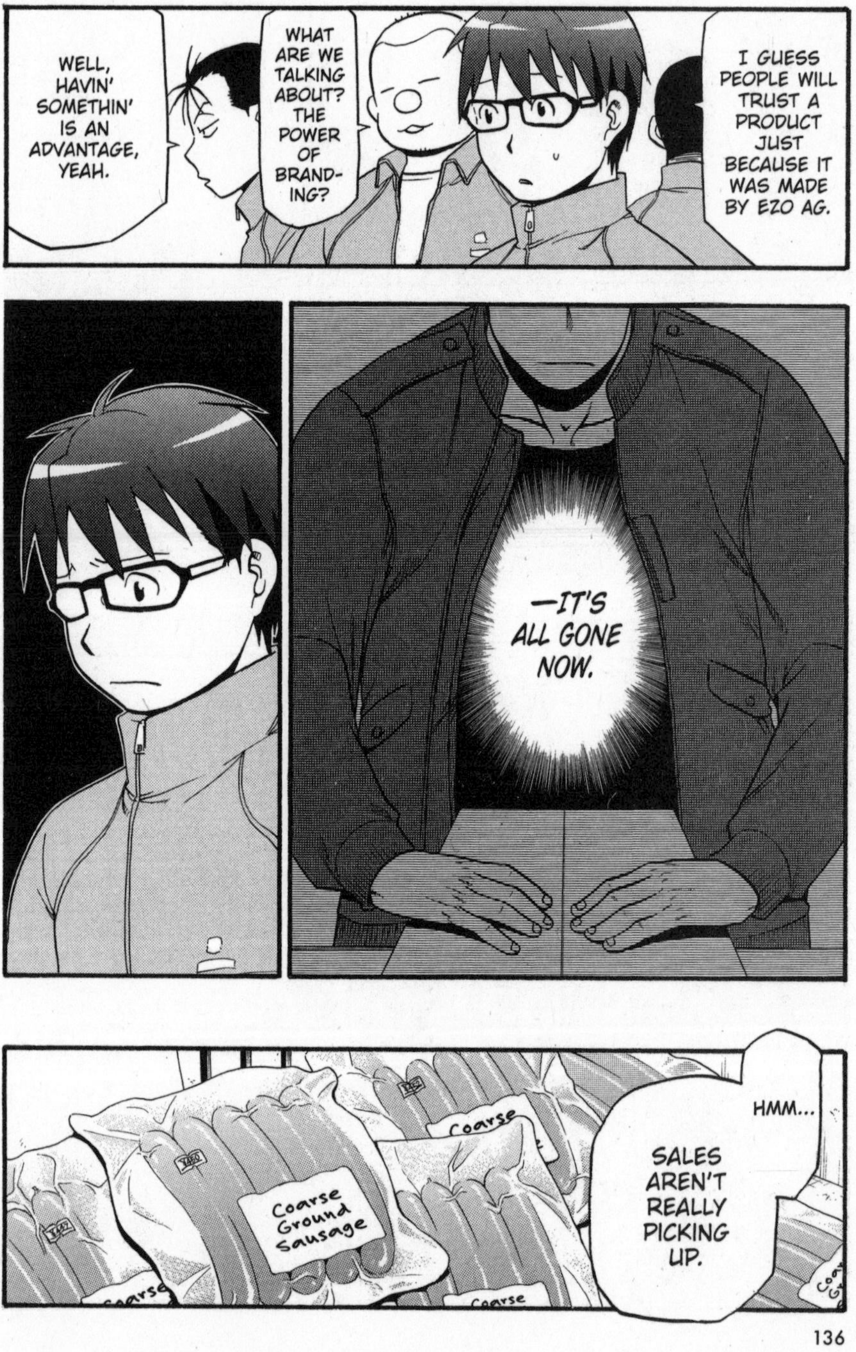
I GUESS PEOPLE WILL TRUST A PRODUCT JUST BECAUSE IT WAS MADE BY EZO AG.
WHAT ARE WE TALKING ABOUT? THE POWER OF BRANDING?
WELL, HAVIN' SOMETHIN' IS AN ADVANTAGE, YEAH.
—IT'S ALL GONE NOW.
HMM...
SALES AREN'T REALLY PICKING UP.
Coarse
Coarse Ground Sausage
Coarse
Coarse

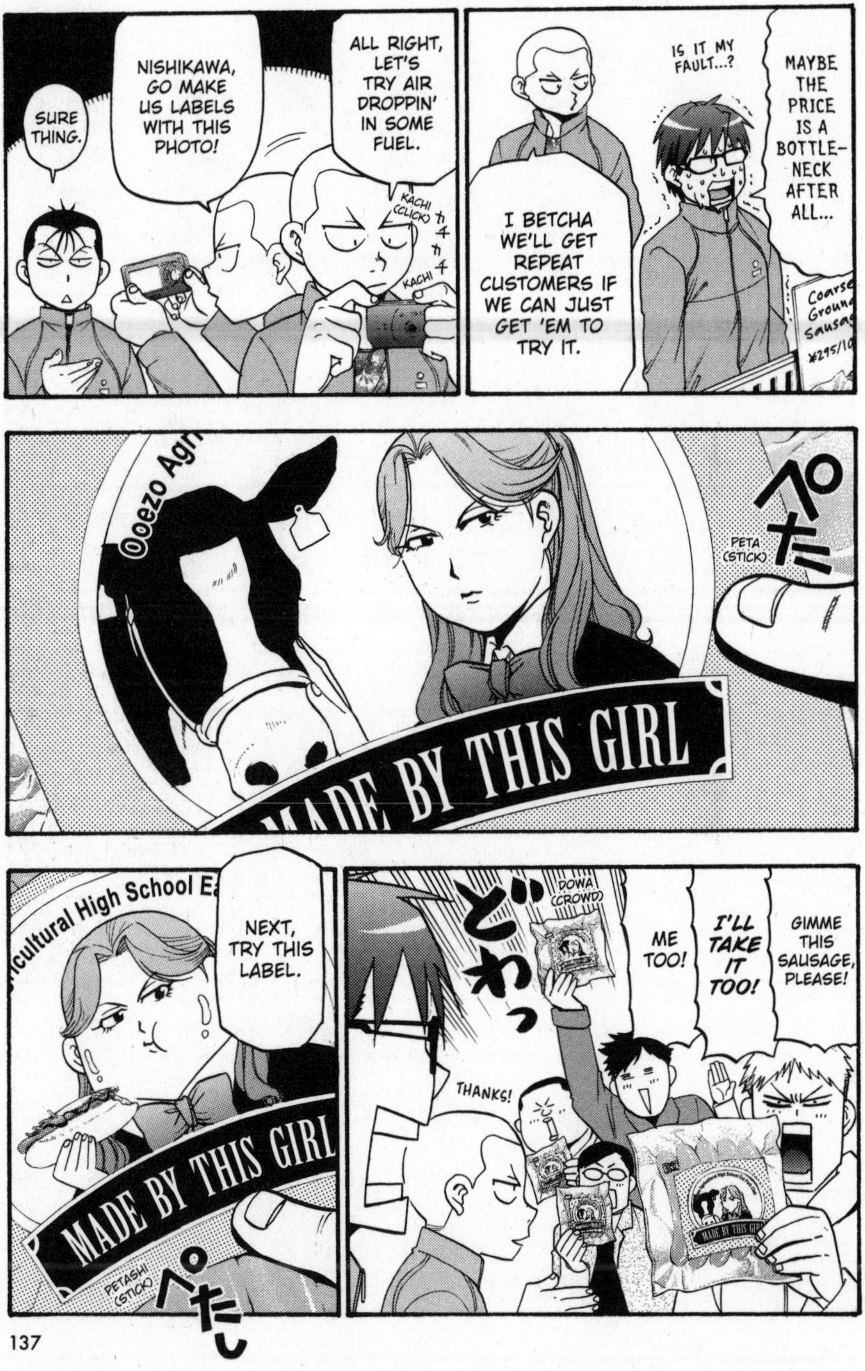
MAYBE THE PRICE IS A BOTTLENECK AFTER ALL...
IS IT MY FAULT...?
I BETCHA WE'LL GET REPEAT CUSTOMERS IF WE CAN JUST GET 'EM TO TRY IT.
ALL RIGHT, LET'S TRY AIR DROPPIN' IN SOME FUEL.
KACHI (CLICK)
KACHI
NISHIKAWA, GO MAKE US LABELS WITH THIS PHOTO!
SURE THING.
PETA (STICK)
MADE BY THIS GIRL
GIMME THIS SAUSAGE, PLEASE!
I'LL TAKE IT TOO!
ME TOO!
DOWA (CROWD)
THANKS!
NEXT, TRY THIS LABEL.
MADE BY THIS GIRL
PETASHI (STICK)

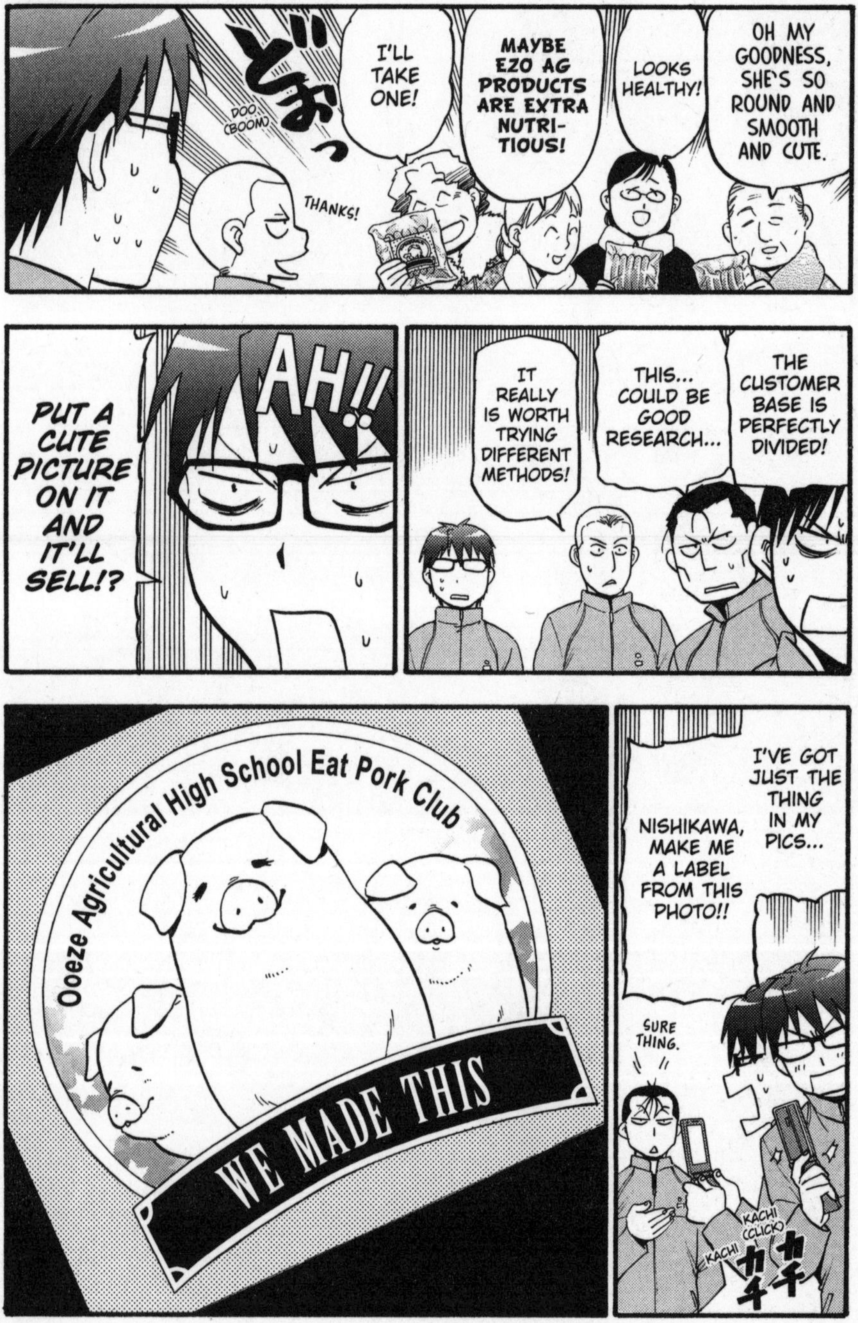
OH MY GOODNESS, SHE'S SO ROUND AND SMOOTH AND CUTE.
LOOKS HEALTHY!
MAYBE EZO AG PRODUCTS ARE EXTRA NUTRI-TIOUS!
I'LL TAKE ONE!
DOO (BOOM)
THANKS!
THE CUSTOMER BASE IS PERFECTLY DIVIDED!
THIS... COULD BE GOOD RESEARCH...
IT REALLY IS WORTH TRYING DIFFERENT METHODS!
AH!!
PUT A CUTE PICTURE ON IT AND IT'LL SELL!?
I'VE GOT JUST THE THING IN MY PICS...
NISHIKAWA, MAKE ME A LABEL FROM THIS PHOTO!!
SURE THING.
KACHI (CLICK)
KACHI
Ooeze Agricultural High School Eat Pork Club
WE MADE THIS

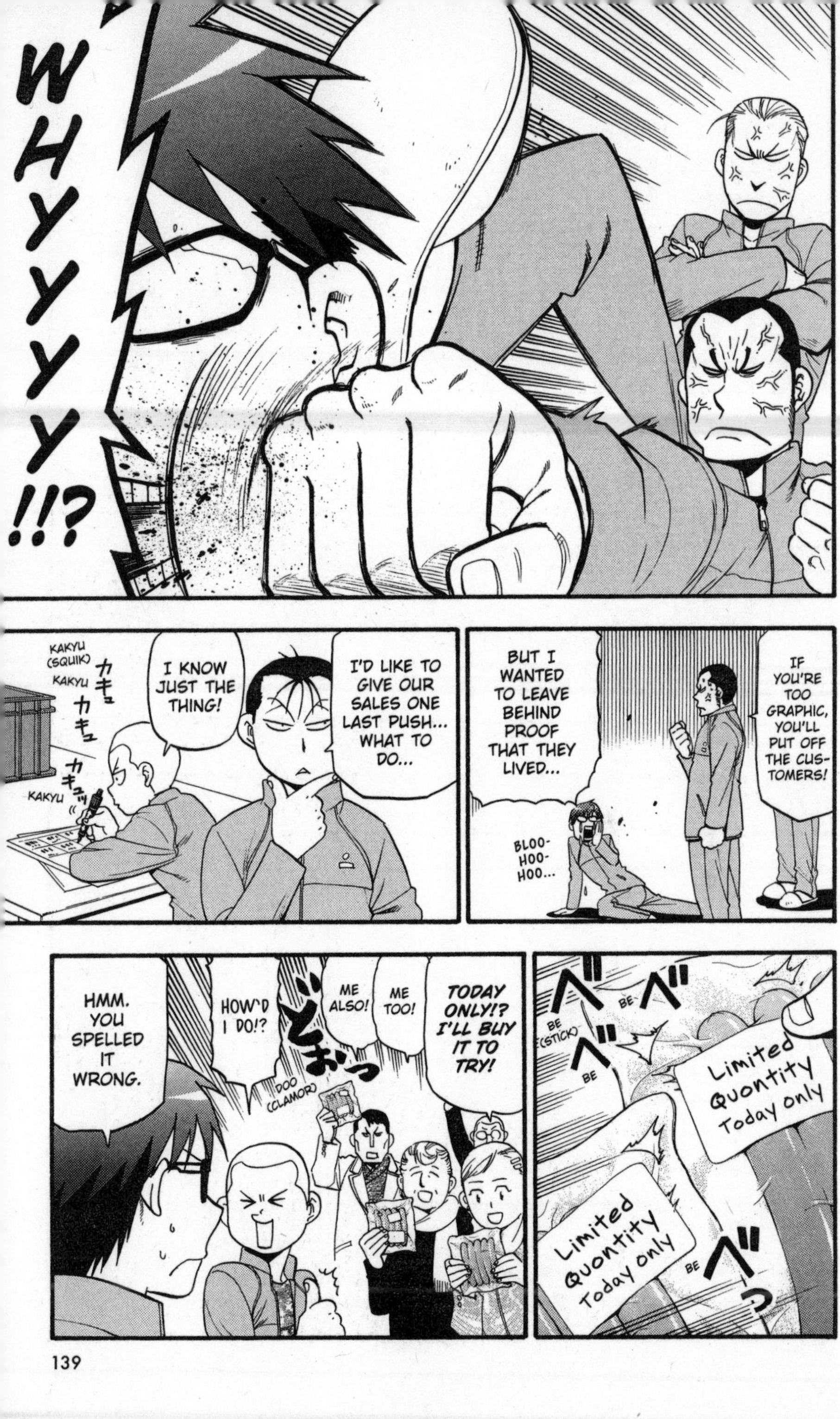
WHYYYYY!!!?
IF YOU'RE TOO GRAPHIC, YOU'LL PUT OFF THE CUSTOMERS!
BUT I WANTED TO LEAVE BEHIND PROOF THAT THEY LIVED...
BLOO-HOO-HOO...
I'D LIKE TO GIVE OUR SALES ONE LAST PUSH... WHAT TO DO...
I KNOW JUST THE THING!
KAKYU (SQUIK) カキュ
KAKYU カキュ
KAKYU カキュッ
BE べ
BE (STICK) べ
BE べ
Limited Quontity Today only
Limited Quontity Today only
BE べ
TODAY ONLY!? I'LL BUY IT TO TRY!
ME TOO!
ME ALSO!
DOO (CLAMOR) どぉっ
HOW'D I DO!?
HMM. YOU SPELLED IT WRONG.

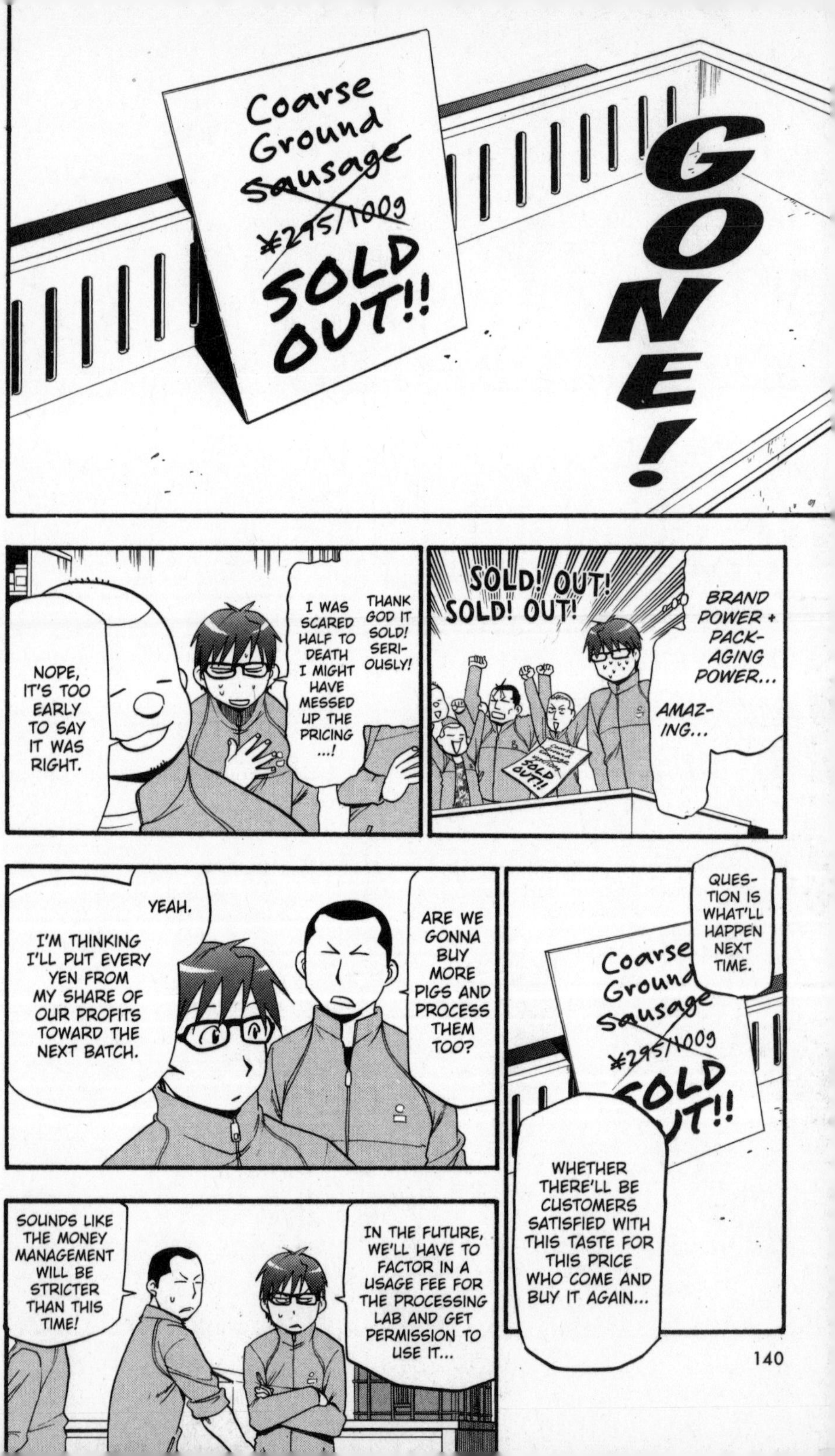
Coarse Ground Sausage ¥295/100g
SOLD OUT!!
GONE!
SOLD! OUT! SOLD! OUT!
BRAND POWER + PACKAGING POWER...
AMAZING...
Coarse Ground Sausage SOLD OUT!!
THANK GOD IT SOLD! SERIOUSLY!
I WAS SCARED HALF TO DEATH I MIGHT HAVE MESSED UP THE PRICING ...!
NOPE, IT'S TOO EARLY TO SAY IT WAS RIGHT.
QUESTION IS WHAT'LL HAPPEN NEXT TIME.
Coarse Ground Sausage ¥295/100g SOLD OUT!!
WHETHER THERE'LL BE CUSTOMERS SATISFIED WITH THIS TASTE FOR THIS PRICE WHO COME AND BUY IT AGAIN...
ARE WE GONNA BUY MORE PIGS AND PROCESS THEM TOO?
YEAH.
I'M THINKING I'LL PUT EVERY YEN FROM MY SHARE OF OUR PROFITS TOWARD THE NEXT BATCH.
IN THE FUTURE, WE'LL HAVE TO FACTOR IN A USAGE FEE FOR THE PROCESSING LAB AND GET PERMISSION TO USE IT...
SOUNDS LIKE THE MONEY MANAGEMENT WILL BE STRICTER THAN THIS TIME!

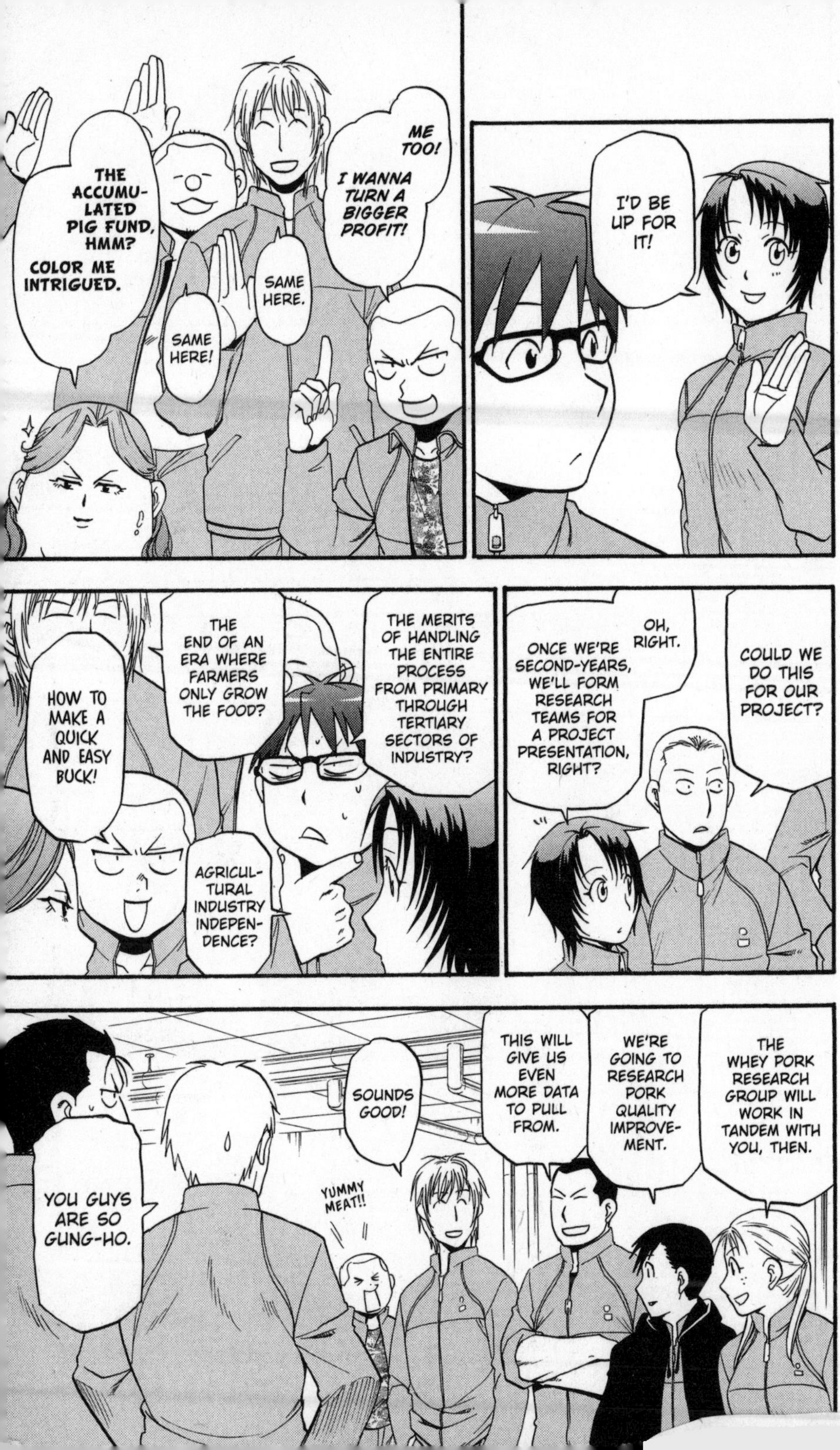
I'D BE UP FOR IT!
ME TOO! I WANNA TURN A BIGGER PROFIT!
THE ACCUMULATED PIG FUND, HMM? COLOR ME INTRIGUED.
SAME HERE.
SAME HERE!
COULD WE DO THIS FOR OUR PROJECT?
OH, RIGHT.
ONCE WE'RE SECOND-YEARS, WE'LL FORM RESEARCH TEAMS FOR A PROJECT PRESENTATION, RIGHT?
THE MERITS OF HANDLING THE ENTIRE PROCESS FROM PRIMARY THROUGH TERTIARY SECTORS OF INDUSTRY?
THE END OF AN ERA WHERE FARMERS ONLY GROW THE FOOD?
HOW TO MAKE A QUICK AND EASY BUCK!
AGRICULTURAL INDEPENDENCE?
THE WHEY PORK RESEARCH GROUP WILL WORK IN TANDEM WITH YOU, THEN.
WE'RE GOING TO RESEARCH PORK QUALITY IMPROVEMENT.
THIS WILL GIVE US EVEN MORE DATA TO PULL FROM.
SOUNDS GOOD!
YUMMY MEAT!!
YOU GUYS ARE SO GUNG-HO.

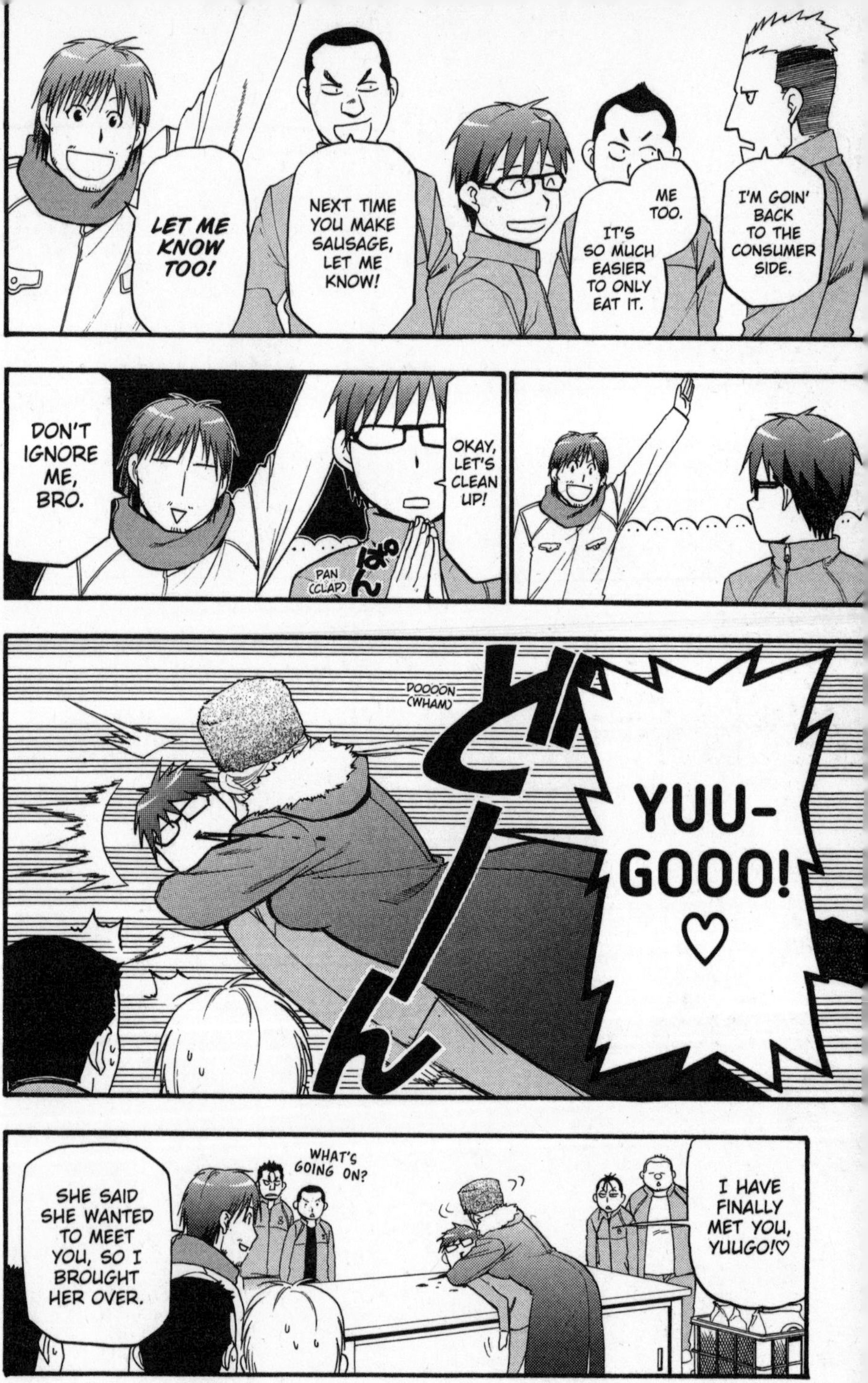
I'M GOIN' BACK TO THE CONSUMER SIDE.
ME TOO.
IT'S SO MUCH EASIER TO ONLY EAT IT.
NEXT TIME YOU MAKE SAUSAGE, LET ME KNOW!
LET ME KNOW TOO!
OKAY, LET'S CLEAN UP!
ぱん
PAN (CLAP)
DON'T IGNORE ME, BRO.
YUU-GOOO! ♡
どーん
DOOOON (WHAM)
I HAVE FINALLY MET YOU, YUUGO!♡
WHAT'S GOING ON?
SHE SAID SHE WANTED TO MEET YOU, SO I BROUGHT HER OVER.

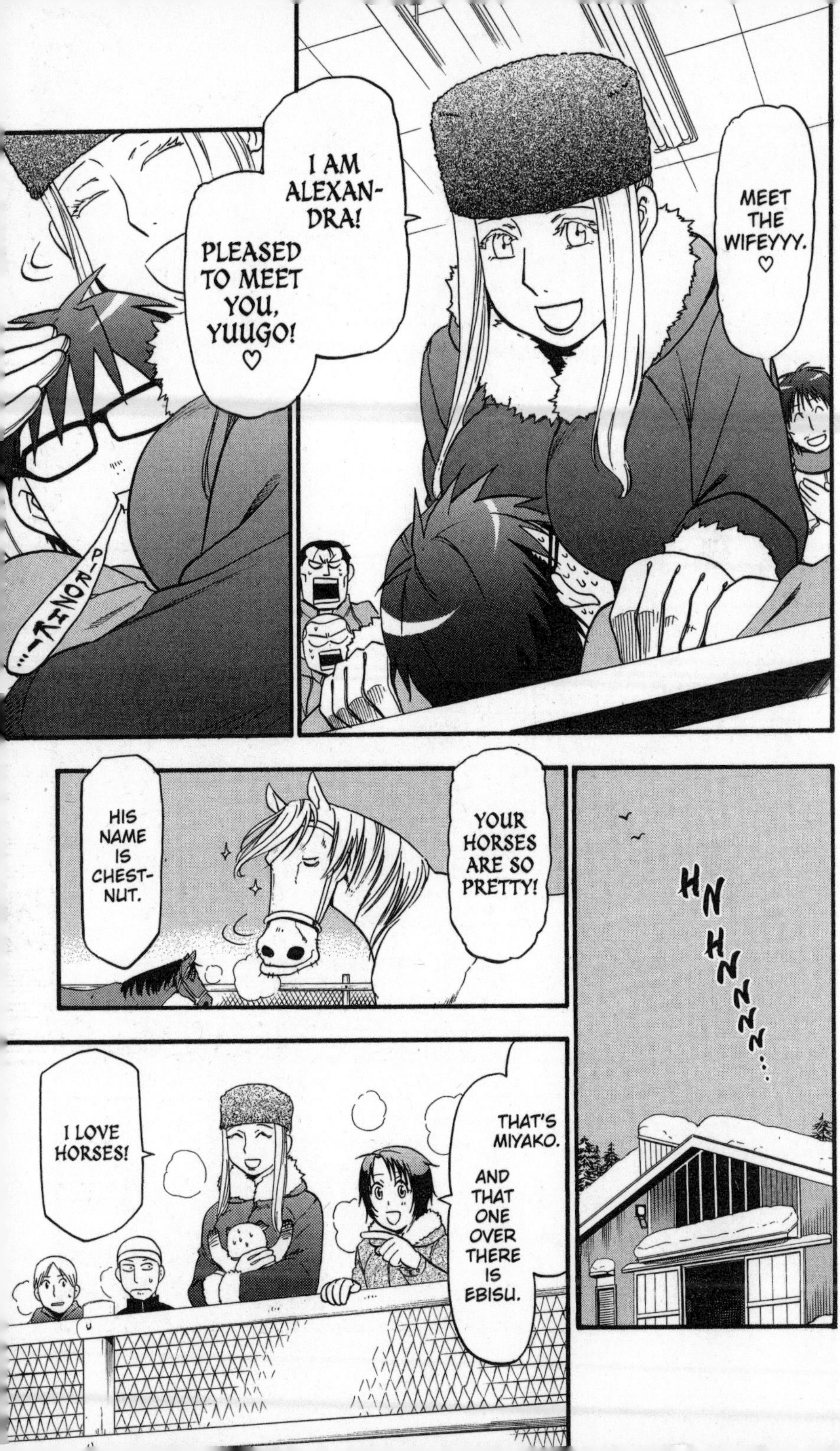
MEET THE WIFEYYY. ♡
I AM ALEXAN-DRA!
PLEASED TO MEET YOU, YUUGO! ♡
PIROSHKI...
HNHNNNN...
YOUR HORSES ARE SO PRETTY!
HIS NAME IS CHEST-NUT.
THAT'S MIYAKO.
AND THAT ONE OVER THERE IS EBISU.
I LOVE HORSES!

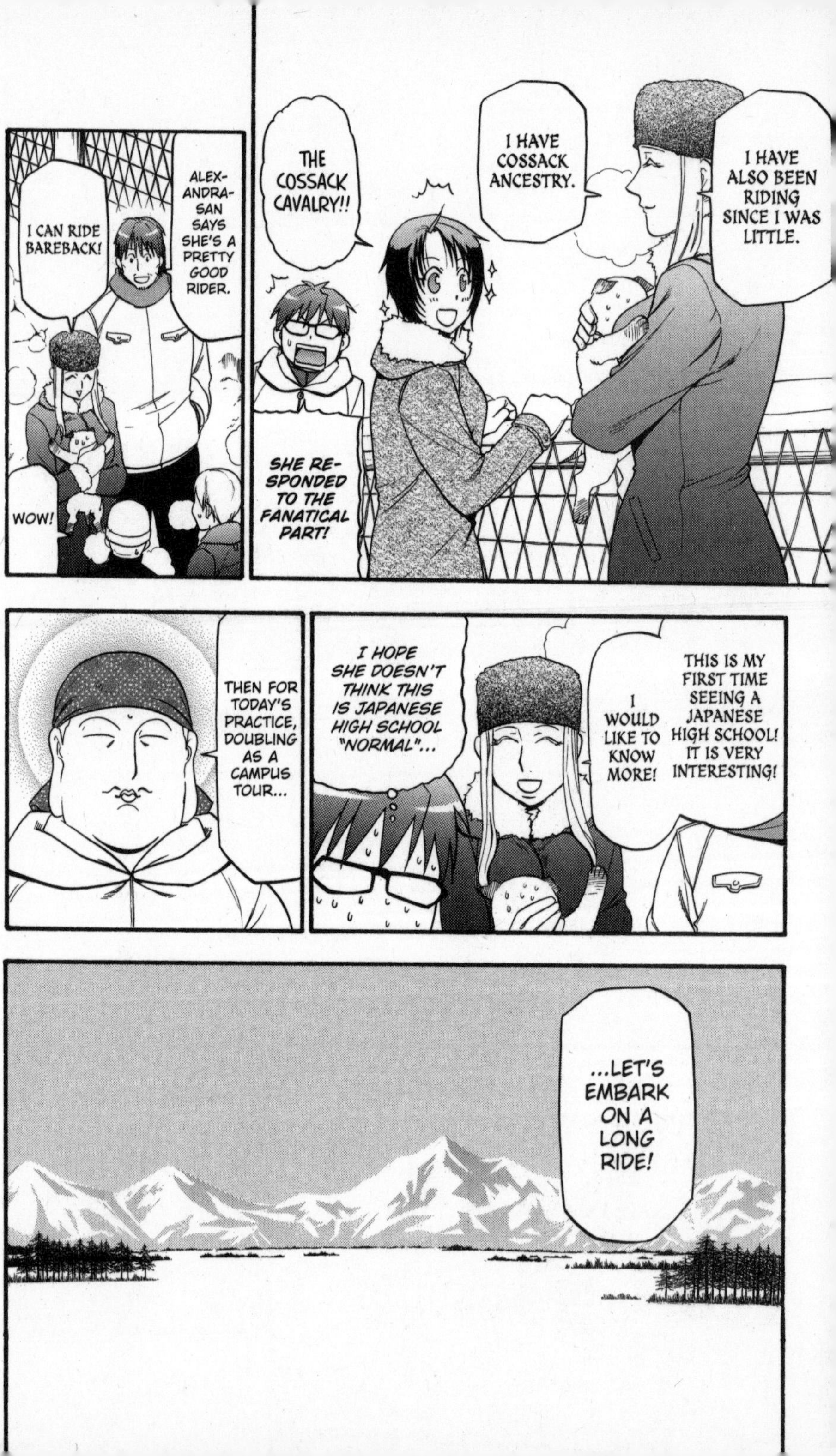
I HAVE ALSO BEEN RIDING SINCE I WAS LITTLE.
I HAVE COSSACK ANCESTRY.
THE COSSACK CAVALRY!!
SHE RESPONDED TO THE FANATICAL PART!
ALEXANDRA-SAN SAYS SHE'S A PRETTY GOOD RIDER.
I CAN RIDE BAREBACK!
WOW!
THIS IS MY FIRST TIME SEEING A JAPANESE HIGH SCHOOL! IT IS VERY INTERESTING!
I WOULD LIKE TO KNOW MORE!
I HOPE SHE DOESN'T THINK THIS IS JAPANESE HIGH SCHOOL "NORMAL"...
THEN FOR TODAY'S PRACTICE, DOUBLING AS A CAMPUS TOUR...
...LET'S EMBARK ON A LONG RIDE!

Silver Spoon

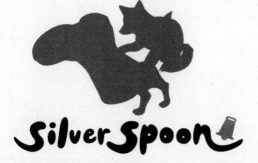

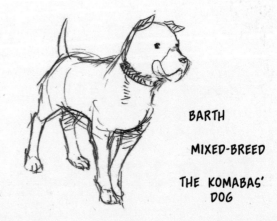

BARTH

MIXED-BREED

THE KOMABAS'
DOG

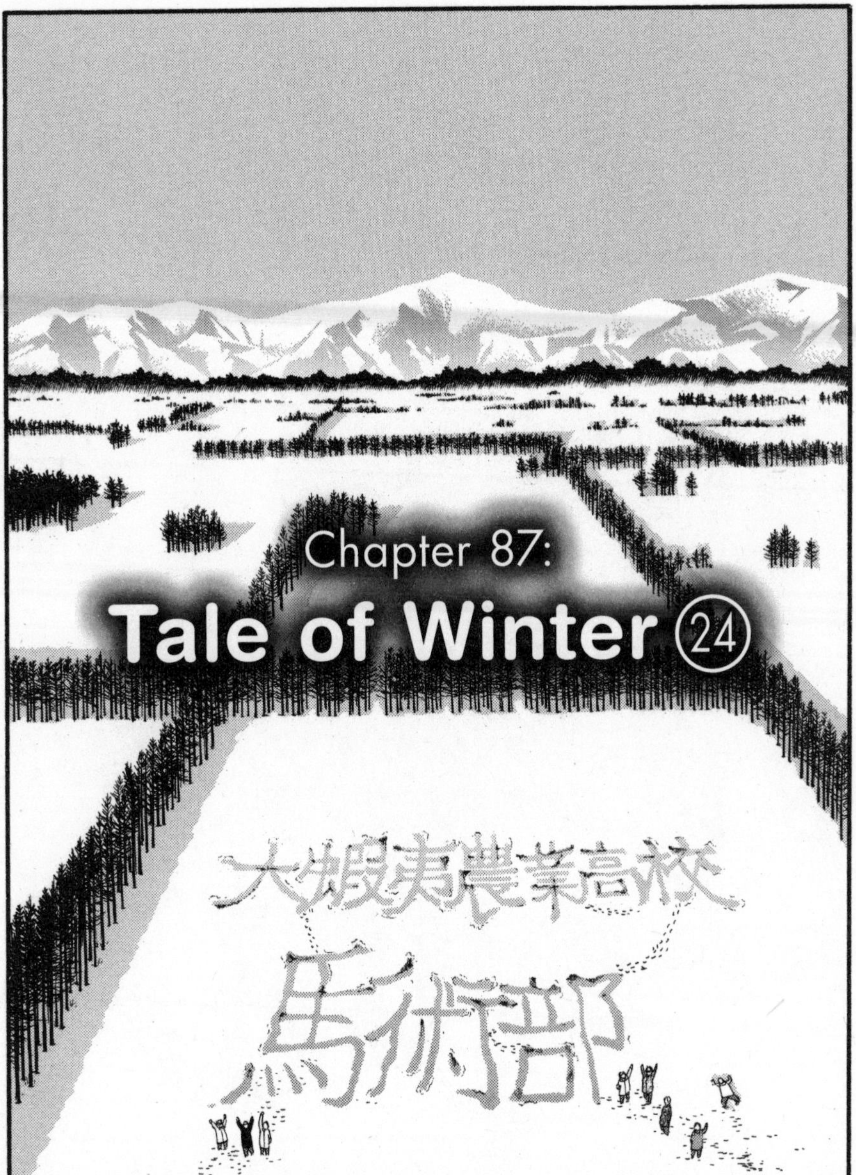
Chapter 87:
Tale of Winter ㉔
大蝦夷農業高校
馬術部

SNOW: OOEZO AG HIGH SCHOOL EQUESTRIAN CLUB

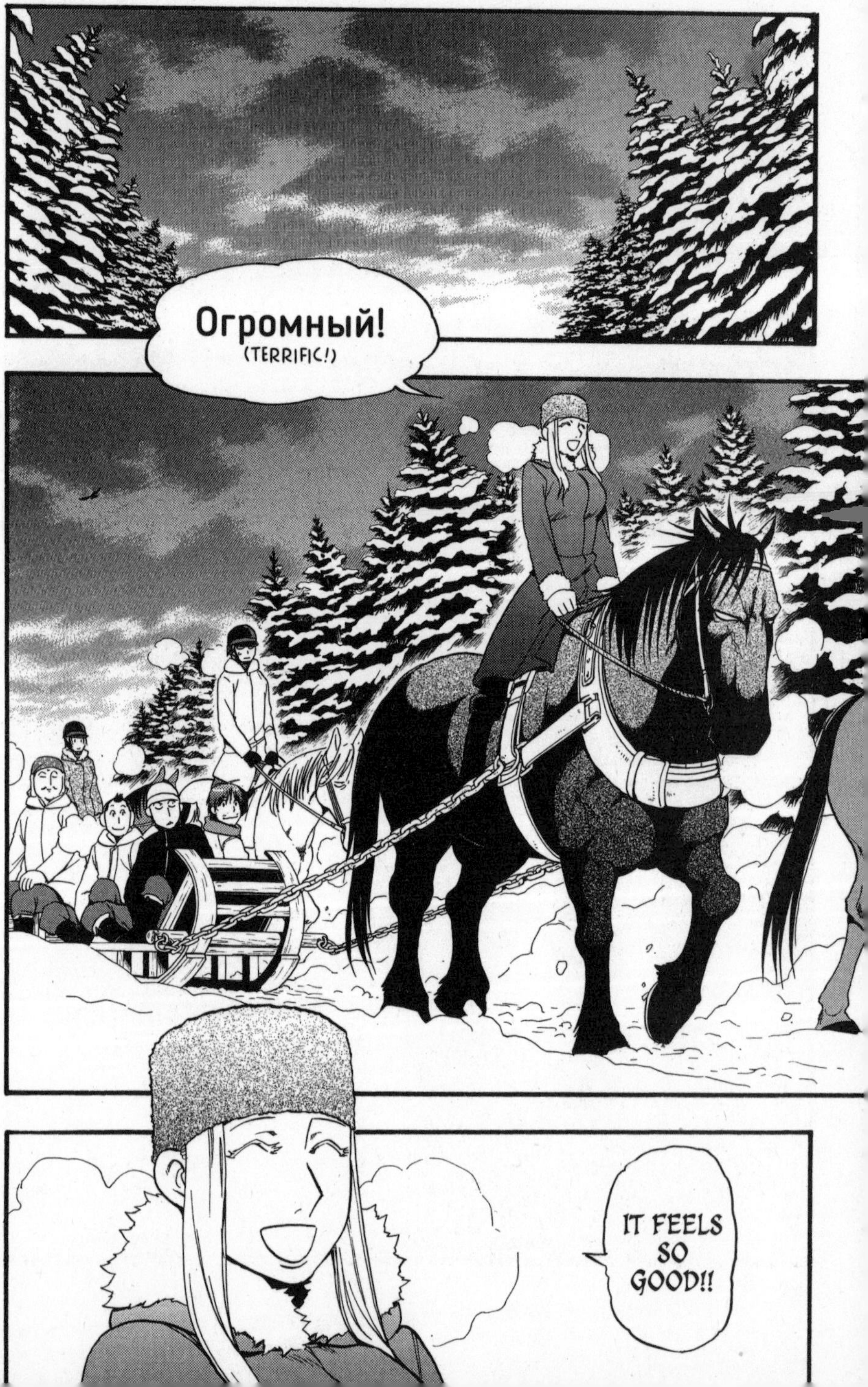
Огромный!
(TERRIFIC!)
IT FEELS SO GOOD!!

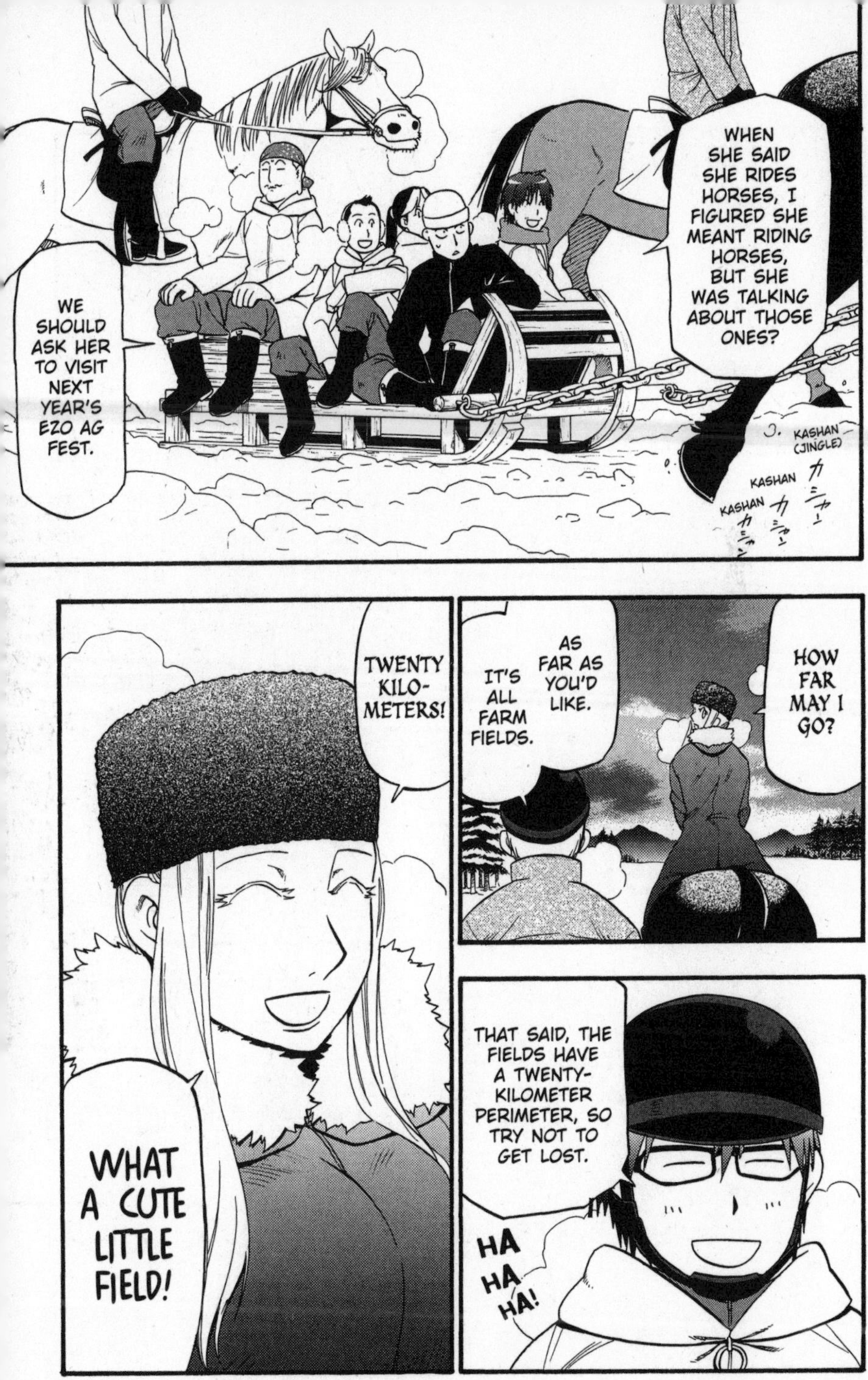
WHEN SHE SAID SHE RIDES HORSES, I FIGURED SHE MEANT RIDING HORSES, BUT SHE WAS TALKING ABOUT THOSE ONES?
WE SHOULD ASK HER TO VISIT NEXT YEAR'S EZO AG FEST.
KASHAN (JINGLE)
KASHAN
KASHAN
HOW FAR MAY I GO?
AS FAR AS YOU'D LIKE.
IT'S ALL FARM FIELDS.
THAT SAID, THE FIELDS HAVE A TWENTY-KILOMETER PERIMETER, SO TRY NOT TO GET LOST.
HA HA HA!
TWENTY KILOMETERS!
WHAT A CUTE LITTLE FIELD!

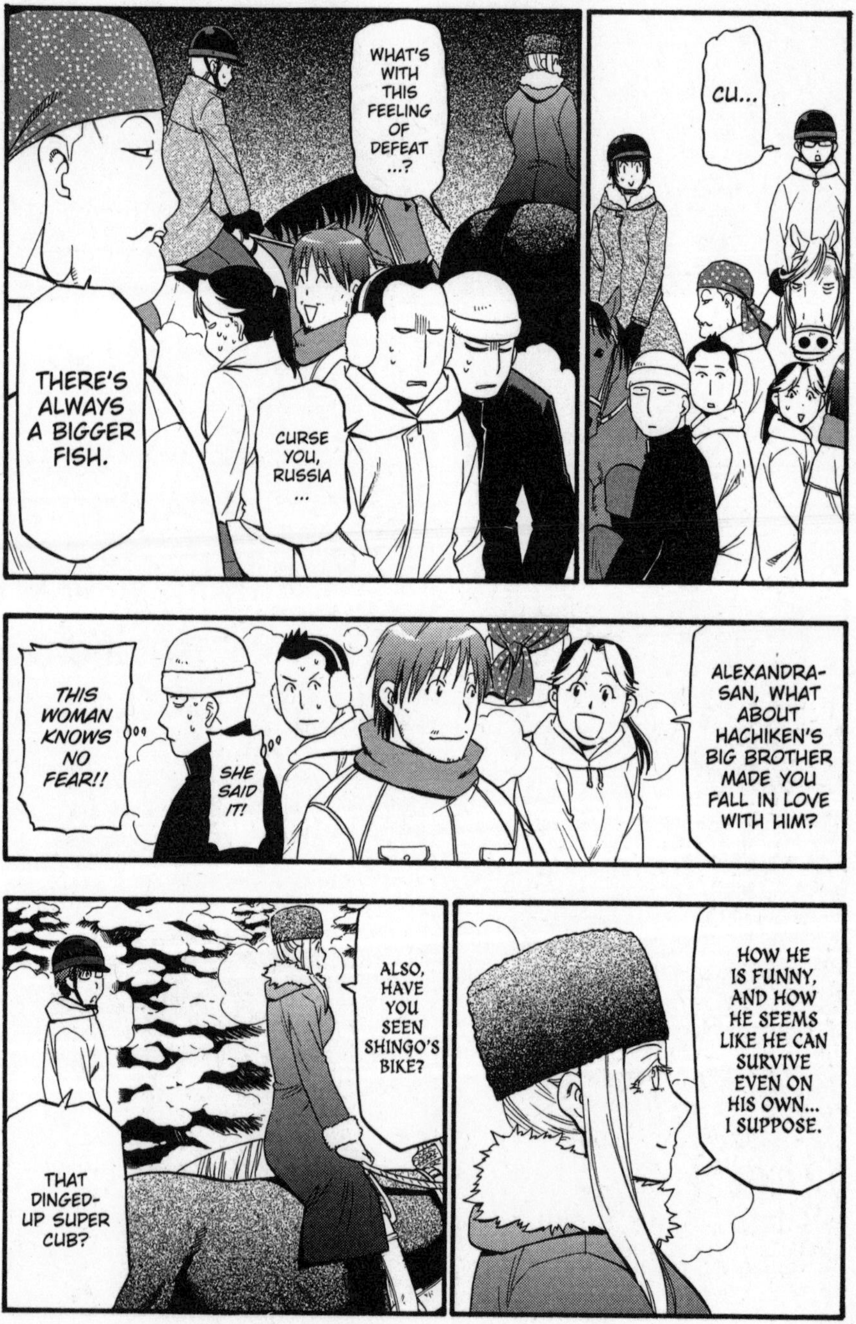
CU...
WHAT'S WITH THIS FEELING OF DEFEAT ...?
CURSE YOU, RUSSIA ...
THERE'S ALWAYS A BIGGER FISH.
ALEXANDRA-SAN, WHAT ABOUT HACHIKEN'S BIG BROTHER MADE YOU FALL IN LOVE WITH HIM?
SHE SAID IT!
THIS WOMAN KNOWS NO FEAR!!
HOW HE IS FUNNY, AND HOW HE SEEMS LIKE HE CAN SURVIVE EVEN ON HIS OWN... I SUPPOSE.
ALSO, HAVE YOU SEEN SHINGO'S BIKE?
THAT DINGED-UP SUPER CUB?

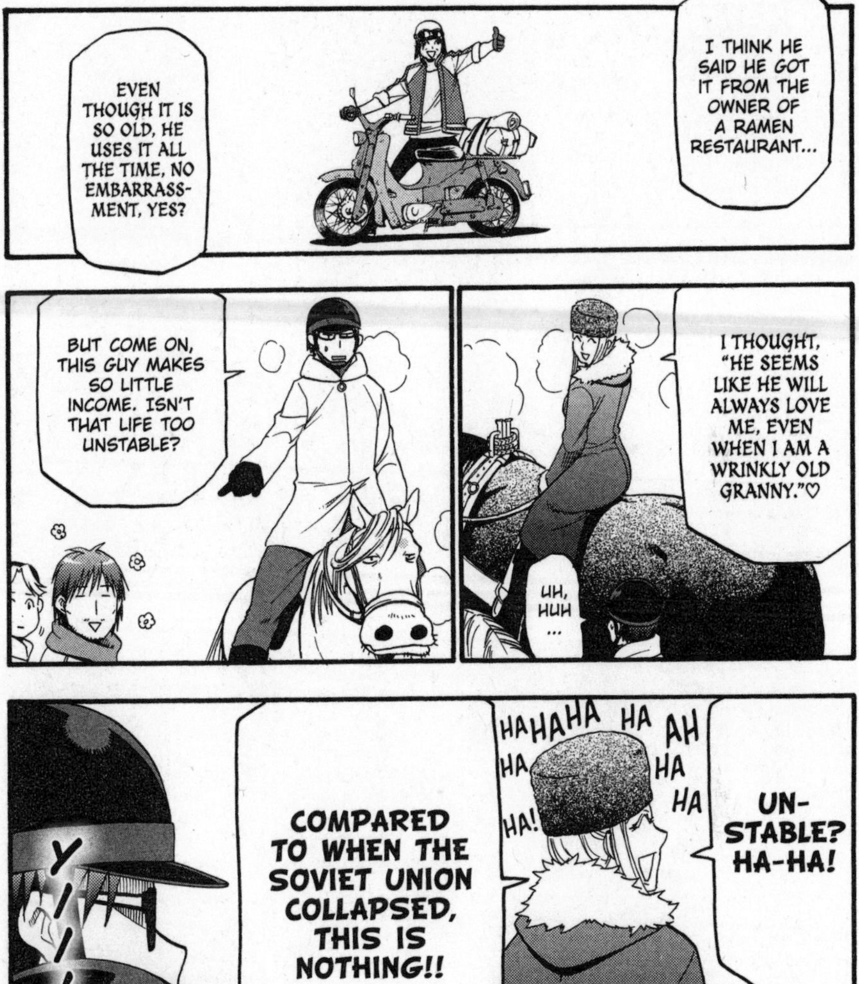
I THINK HE SAID HE GOT IT FROM THE OWNER OF A RAMEN RESTAURANT...
EVEN THOUGH IT IS SO OLD, HE USES IT ALL THE TIME, NO EMBARRASSMENT, YES?
I THOUGHT, "HE SEEMS LIKE HE WILL ALWAYS LOVE ME, EVEN WHEN I AM A WRINKLY OLD GRANNY."♡
UH, HUH ...
BUT COME ON, THIS GUY MAKES SO LITTLE INCOME. ISN'T THAT LIFE TOO UNSTABLE?
UN-STABLE? HA-HA!
HA HA HA HA AH HA HA HA HA HA!
COMPARED TO WHEN THE SOVIET UNION COLLAPSED, THIS IS NOTHING!!
YIIIKES...

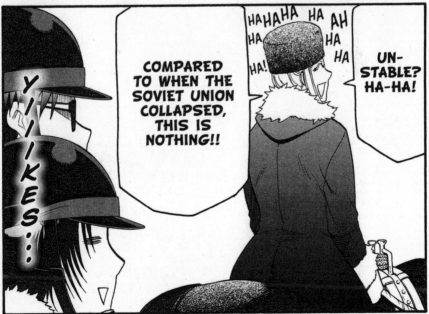

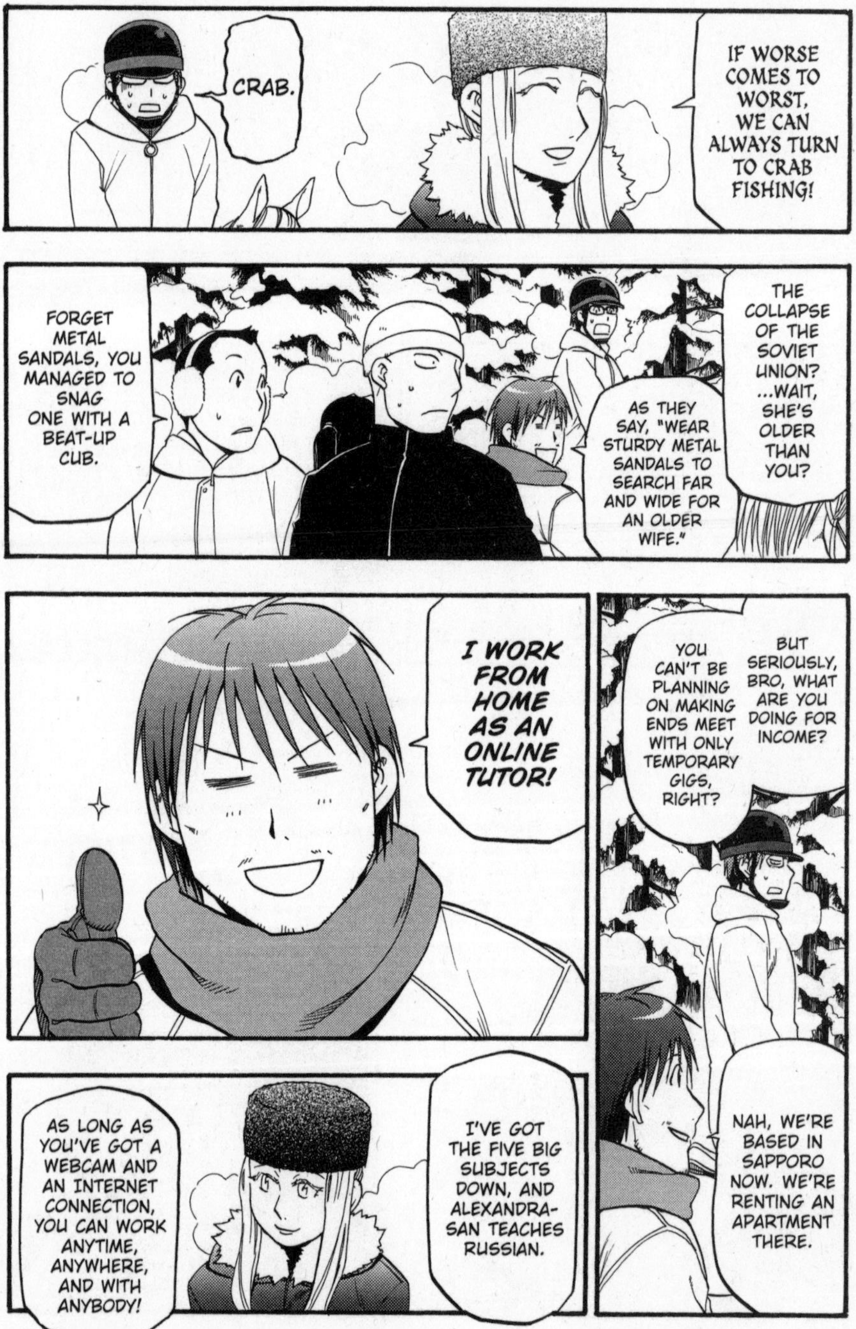
IF WORSE COMES TO WORST, WE CAN ALWAYS TURN TO CRAB FISHING!
CRAB.
THE COLLAPSE OF THE SOVIET UNION? ...WAIT, SHE'S OLDER THAN YOU?
AS THEY SAY, "WEAR STURDY METAL SANDALS TO SEARCH FAR AND WIDE FOR AN OLDER WIFE."
FORGET METAL SANDALS, YOU MANAGED TO SNAG ONE WITH A BEAT-UP CUB.
BUT SERIOUSLY, BRO, WHAT ARE YOU DOING FOR INCOME?
YOU CAN'T BE PLANNING ON MAKING ENDS MEET WITH ONLY TEMPORARY GIGS, RIGHT?
NAH, WE'RE BASED IN SAPPORO NOW. WE'RE RENTING AN APARTMENT THERE.
I WORK FROM HOME AS AN ONLINE TUTOR!
I'VE GOT THE FIVE BIG SUBJECTS DOWN, AND ALEXANDRA-SAN TEACHES RUSSIAN.
AS LONG AS YOU'VE GOT A WEBCAM AND AN INTERNET CONNECTION, YOU CAN WORK ANYTIME, ANYWHERE, AND WITH ANYBODY!

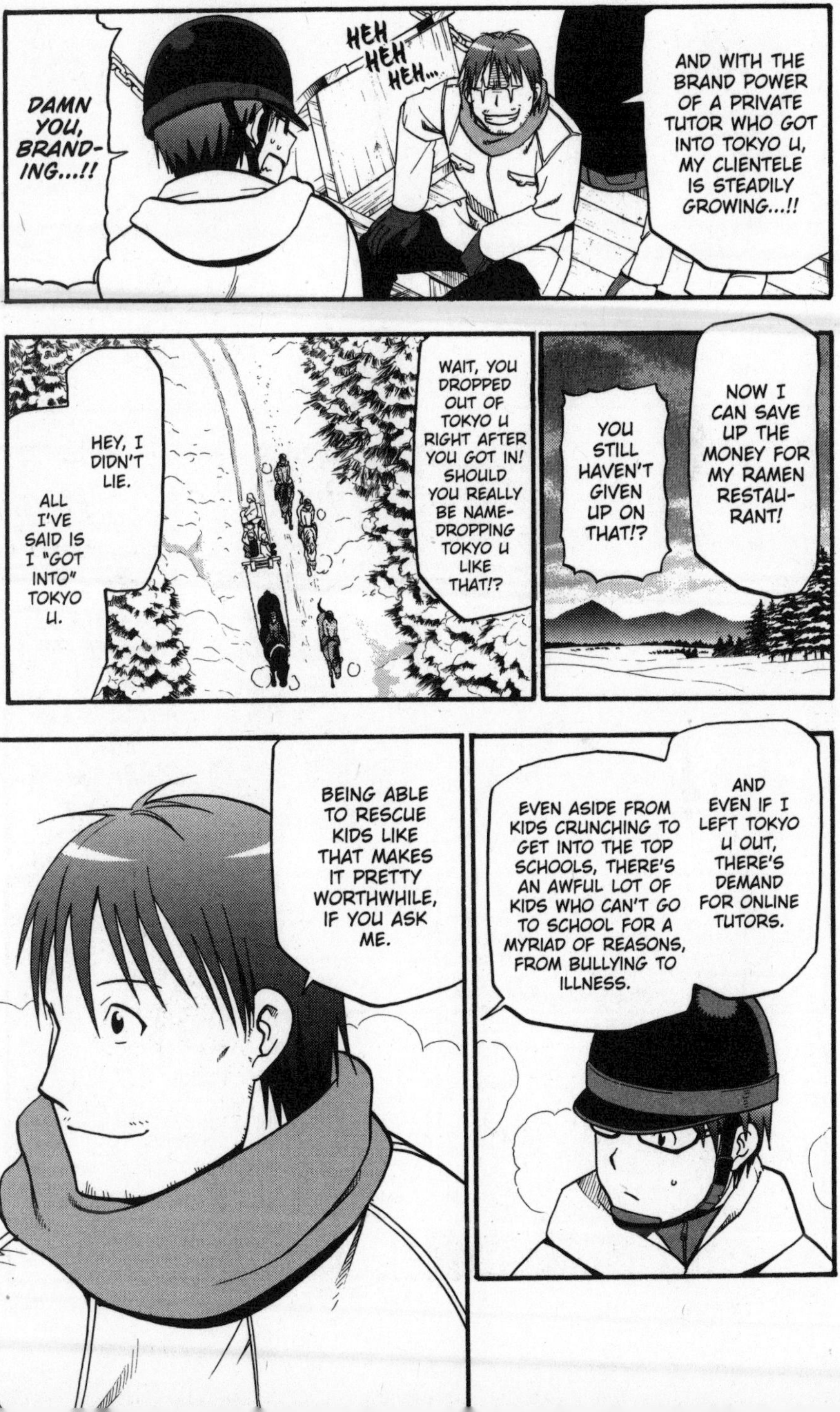
AND WITH THE BRAND POWER OF A PRIVATE TUTOR WHO GOT INTO TOKYO U, MY CLIENTELE IS STEADILY GROWING...!!
HEH HEH HEH...
DAMN YOU, BRANDING...!!
NOW I CAN SAVE UP THE MONEY FOR MY RAMEN RESTAURANT!
YOU STILL HAVEN'T GIVEN UP ON THAT!?
WAIT, YOU DROPPED OUT OF TOKYO U RIGHT AFTER YOU GOT IN! SHOULD YOU REALLY BE NAME-DROPPING TOKYO U LIKE THAT!?
HEY, I DIDN'T LIE.
ALL I'VE SAID IS I "GOT INTO" TOKYO U.
AND EVEN IF I LEFT TOKYO U OUT, THERE'S DEMAND FOR ONLINE TUTORS.
EVEN ASIDE FROM KIDS CRUNCHING TO GET INTO THE TOP SCHOOLS, THERE'S AN AWFUL LOT OF KIDS WHO CAN'T GO TO SCHOOL FOR A MYRIAD OF REASONS, FROM BULLYING TO ILLNESS.
BEING ABLE TO RESCUE KIDS LIKE THAT MAKES IT PRETTY WORTHWHILE, IF YOU ASK ME.

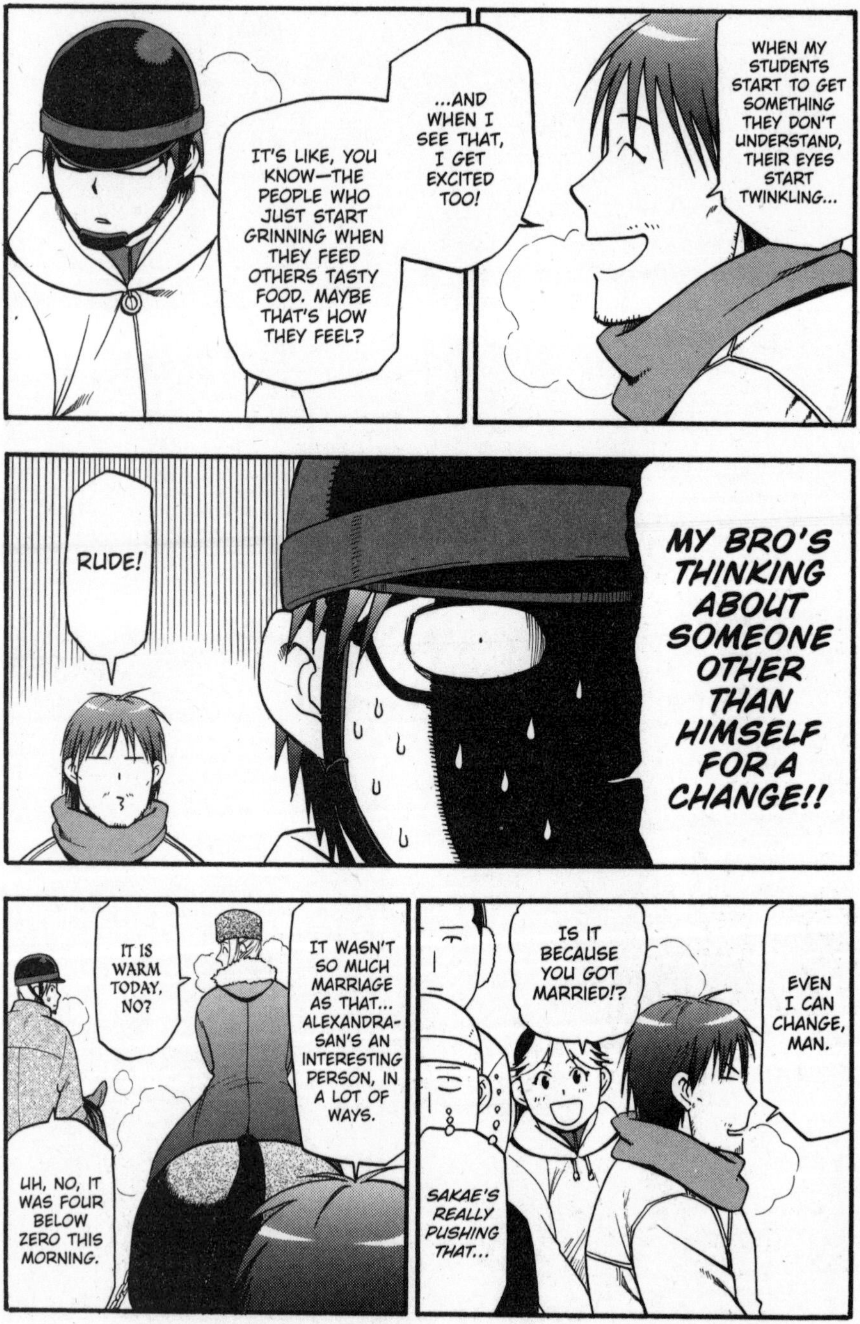
WHEN MY STUDENTS START TO GET SOMETHING THEY DON'T UNDERSTAND, THEIR EYES START TWINKLING...
...AND WHEN I SEE THAT, I GET EXCITED TOO!
IT'S LIKE, YOU KNOW—THE PEOPLE WHO JUST START GRINNING WHEN THEY FEED OTHERS TASTY FOOD. MAYBE THAT'S HOW THEY FEEL?
MY BRO'S THINKING ABOUT SOMEONE OTHER THAN HIMSELF FOR A CHANGE!!
RUDE!
EVEN I CAN CHANGE, MAN.
IS IT BECAUSE YOU GOT MARRIED!?
SAKAE'S REALLY PUSHING THAT...
IT WASN'T SO MUCH MARRIAGE AS THAT... ALEXANDRA-SAN'S AN INTERESTING PERSON, IN A LOT OF WAYS.
IT IS WARM TODAY, NO?
UH, NO, IT WAS FOUR BELOW ZERO THIS MORNING.

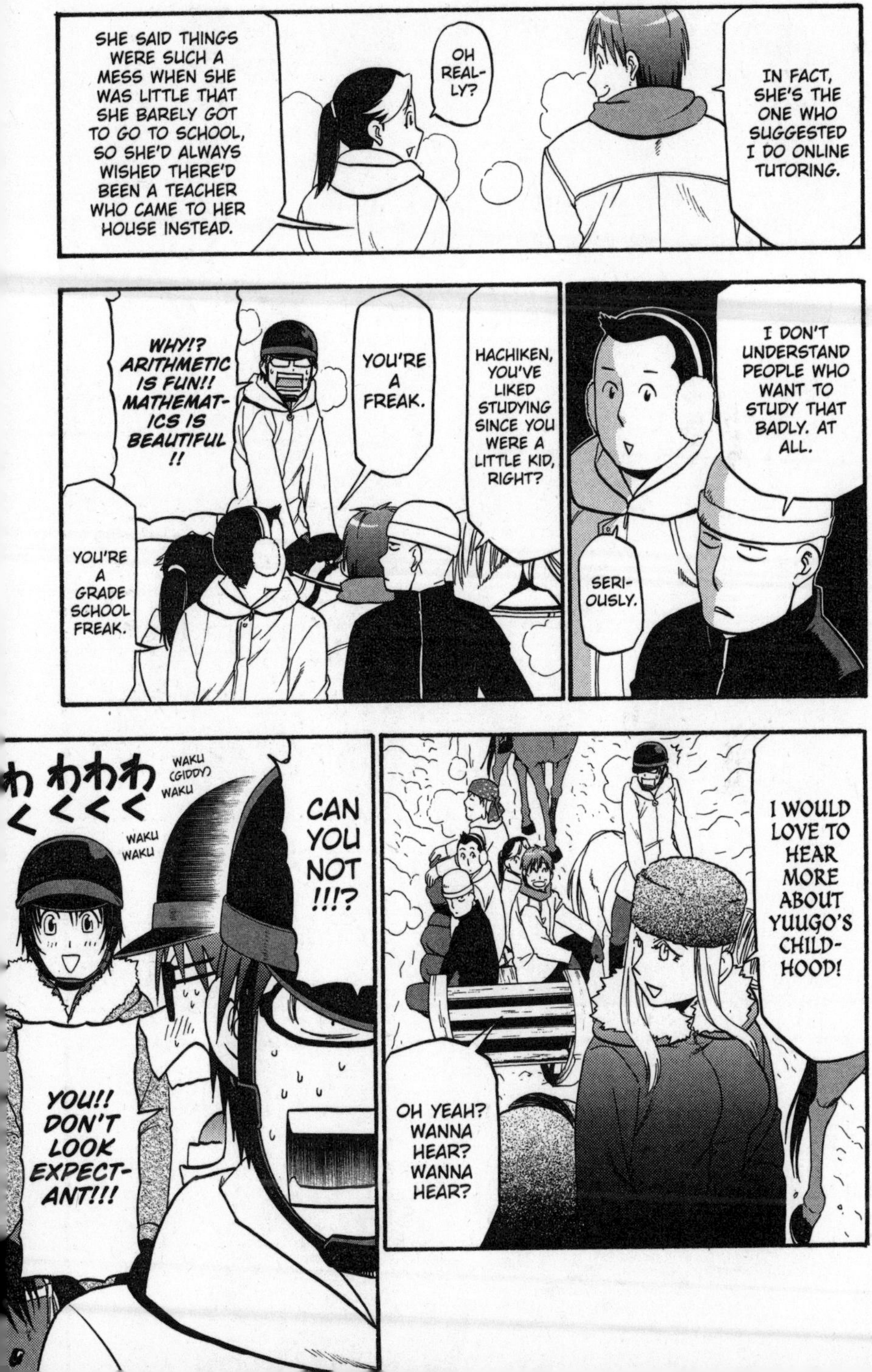
IN FACT, SHE'S THE ONE WHO SUGGESTED I DO ONLINE TUTORING.
OH REALLY?
SHE SAID THINGS WERE SUCH A MESS WHEN SHE WAS LITTLE THAT SHE BARELY GOT TO GO TO SCHOOL, SO SHE'D ALWAYS WISHED THERE'D BEEN A TEACHER WHO CAME TO HER HOUSE INSTEAD.
I DON'T UNDERSTAND PEOPLE WHO WANT TO STUDY THAT BADLY. AT ALL.
SERIOUSLY.
HACHIKEN, YOU'VE LIKED STUDYING SINCE YOU WERE A LITTLE KID, RIGHT?
YOU'RE A FREAK.
WHY!? ARITHMETIC IS FUN!! MATHEMATICS IS BEAUTIFUL!!
YOU'RE A GRADE SCHOOL FREAK.
I WOULD LOVE TO HEAR MORE ABOUT YUUGO'S CHILDHOOD!
OH YEAH? WANNA HEAR? WANNA HEAR?
CAN YOU NOT!!!?
わくわく
WAKU (GIDDY) WAKU
わくわく
WAKU WAKU
YOU!! DON'T LOOK EXPECTANT!!!

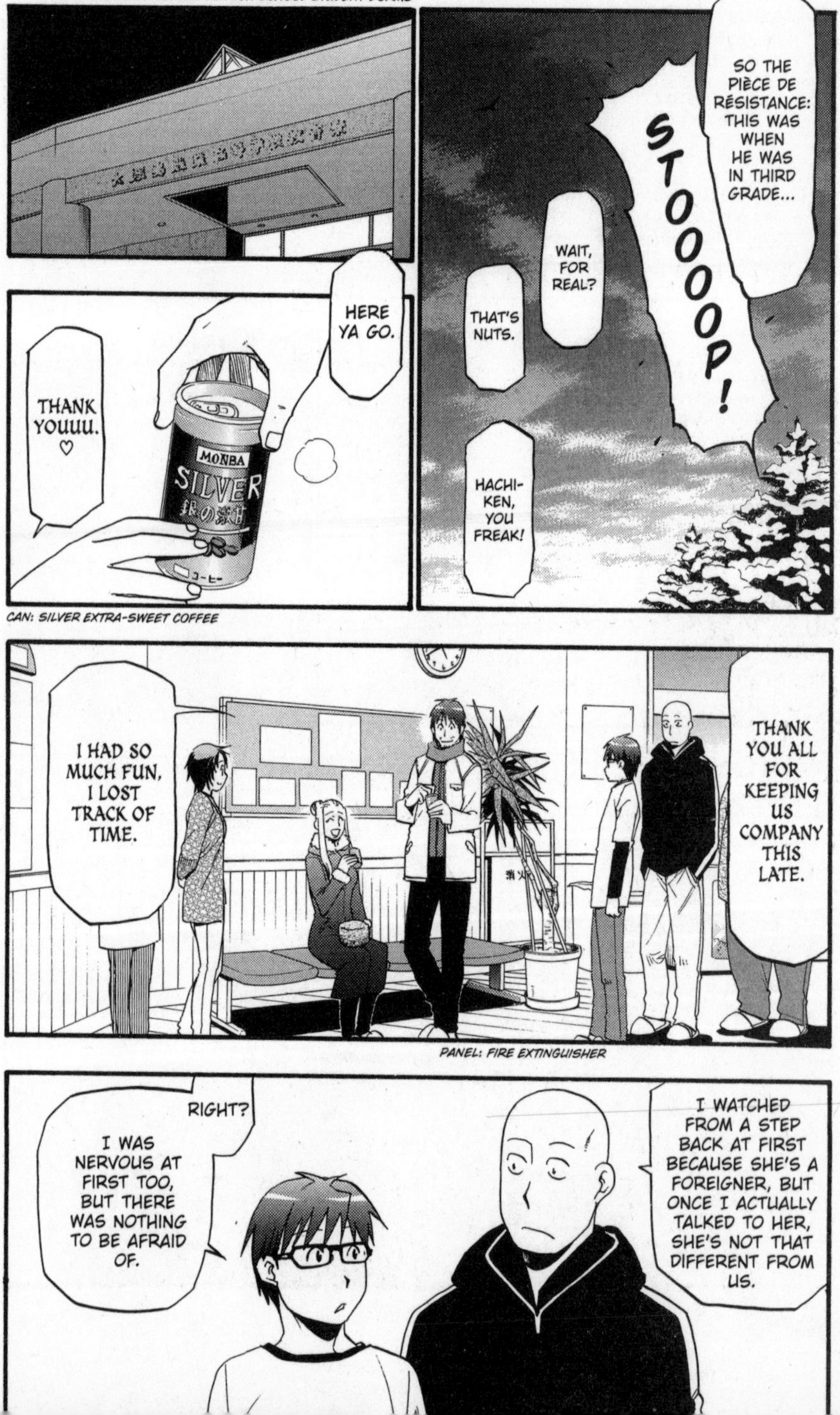
SO THE PIÈCE DE RÉSISTANCE: THIS WAS WHEN HE WAS IN THIRD GRADE...
STOOOOOP!
WAIT, FOR REAL?
THAT'S NUTS.
HACHI-KEN, YOU FREAK!
MONBA SILVER
HERE YA GO.
THANK YOUUU. ♡
THANK YOU ALL FOR KEEPING US COMPANY THIS LATE.
I HAD SO MUCH FUN, I LOST TRACK OF TIME.
I WATCHED FROM A STEP BACK AT FIRST BECAUSE SHE'S A FOREIGNER, BUT ONCE I ACTUALLY TALKED TO HER, SHE'S NOT THAT DIFFERENT FROM US.
RIGHT?
I WAS NERVOUS AT FIRST TOO, BUT THERE WAS NOTHING TO BE AFRAID OF.

SIGN: OOEZO AGRICULTURAL HIGH SCHOOL STUDENT DORMS

CAN: SILVER EXTRA-SWEET COFFEE

PANEL: FIRE EXTINGUISHER

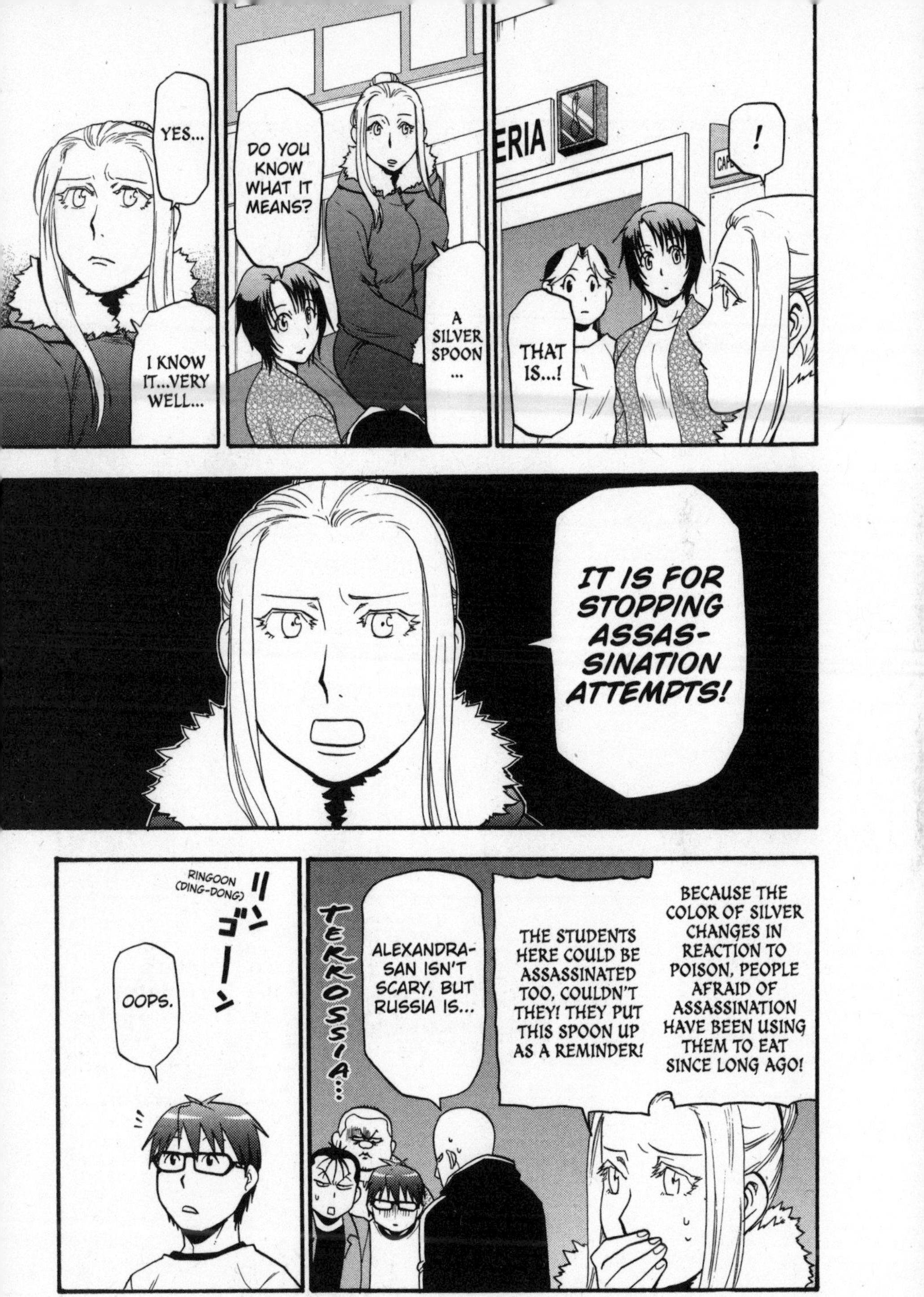
!
THAT IS...!
A SILVER SPOON ...
DO YOU KNOW WHAT IT MEANS?
YES...
I KNOW IT...VERY WELL...
IT IS FOR STOPPING ASSAS-SINATION ATTEMPTS!
BECAUSE THE COLOR OF SILVER CHANGES IN REACTION TO POISON, PEOPLE AFRAID OF ASSASSINATION HAVE BEEN USING THEM TO EAT SINCE LONG AGO!
THE STUDENTS HERE COULD BE ASSASSINATED TOO, COULDN'T THEY! THEY PUT THIS SPOON UP AS A REMINDER!
ALEXANDRA-SAN ISN'T SCARY, BUT RUSSIA IS...
TERROSSIA...
RINGOON (DING-DONG)
OOPS.

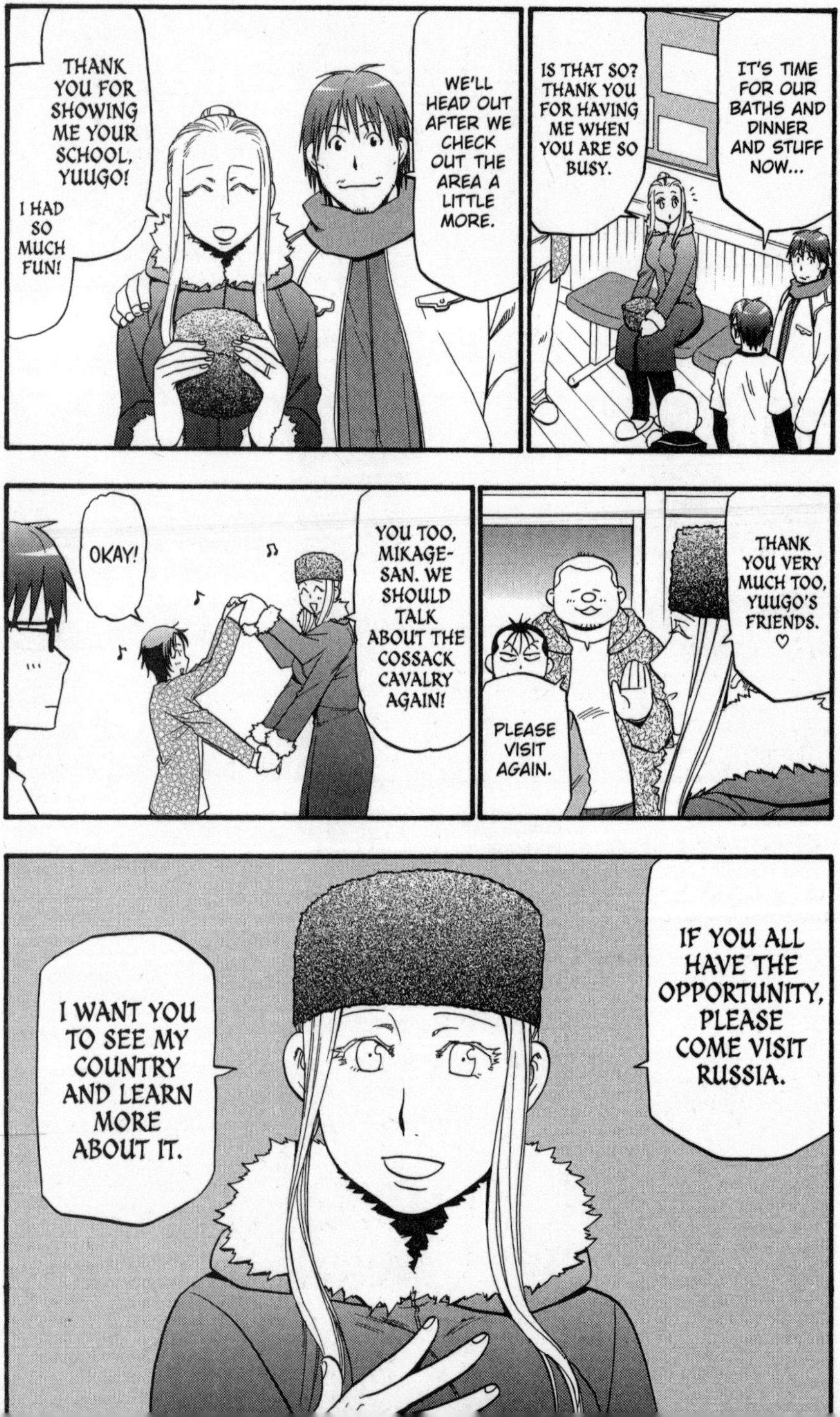
IT'S TIME FOR OUR BATHS AND DINNER AND STUFF NOW...
IS THAT SO? THANK YOU FOR HAVING ME WHEN YOU ARE SO BUSY.
WE'LL HEAD OUT AFTER WE CHECK OUT THE AREA A LITTLE MORE.
THANK YOU FOR SHOWING ME YOUR SCHOOL, YUUGO!
I HAD SO MUCH FUN!
THANK YOU VERY MUCH TOO, YUUGO'S FRIENDS. ♡
PLEASE VISIT AGAIN.
YOU TOO, MIKAGE-SAN. WE SHOULD TALK ABOUT THE COSSACK CAVALRY AGAIN!
OKAY!
...
IF YOU ALL HAVE THE OPPORTUNITY, PLEASE COME VISIT RUSSIA.
I WANT YOU TO SEE MY COUNTRY AND LEARN MORE ABOUT IT.

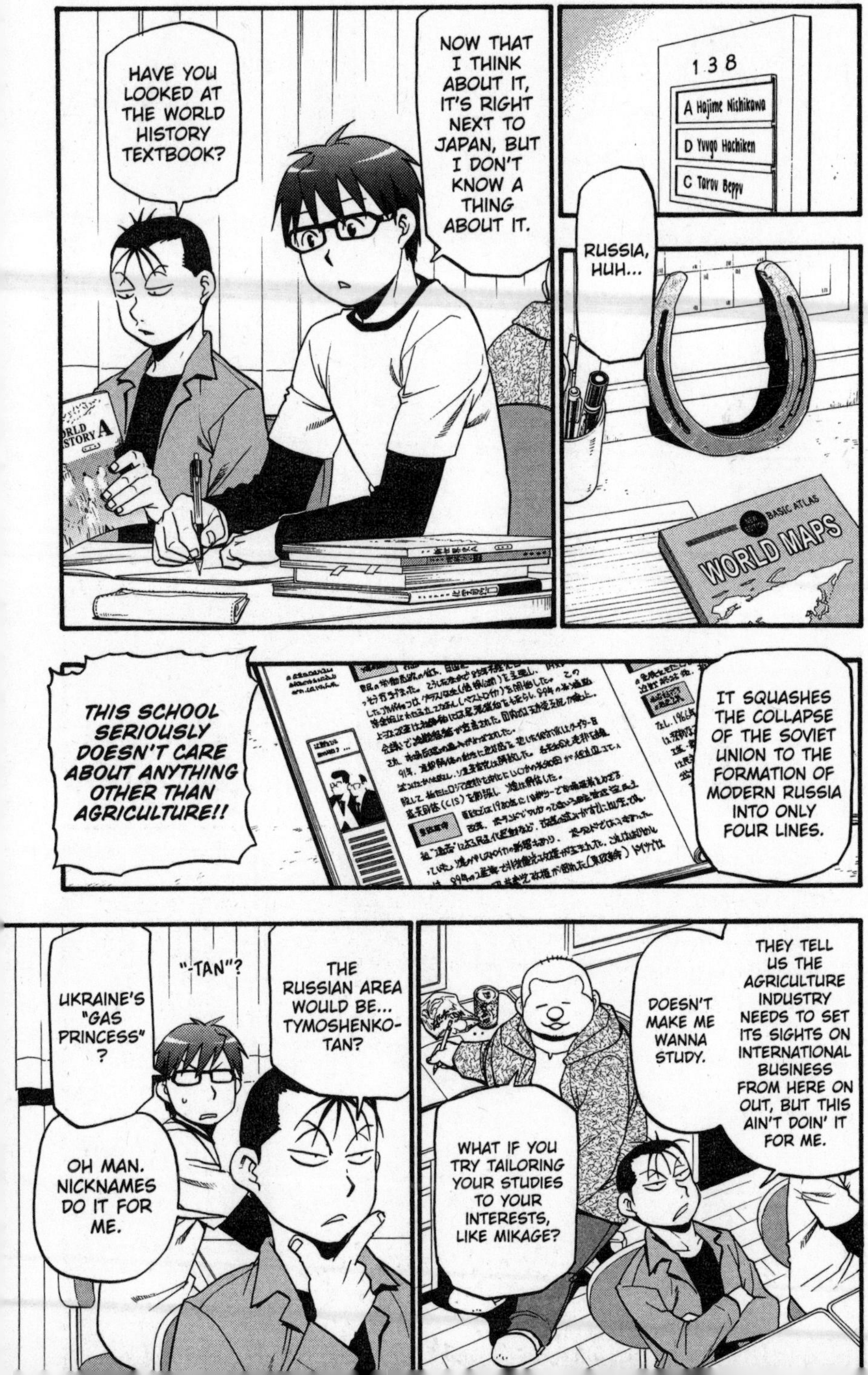
1 3 8
A Hajime Nishikawa
D Yuugo Hachiken
C Tarou Beppu
RUSSIA, HUH...
BASIC ATLAS
WORLD MAPS
NOW THAT I THINK ABOUT IT, IT'S RIGHT NEXT TO JAPAN, BUT I DON'T KNOW A THING ABOUT IT.
HAVE YOU LOOKED AT THE WORLD HISTORY TEXTBOOK?
IT SQUASHES THE COLLAPSE OF THE SOVIET UNION TO THE FORMATION OF MODERN RUSSIA INTO ONLY FOUR LINES.
THIS SCHOOL SERIOUSLY DOESN'T CARE ABOUT ANYTHING OTHER THAN AGRICULTURE!!
THEY TELL US THE AGRICULTURE INDUSTRY NEEDS TO SET ITS SIGHTS ON INTERNATIONAL BUSINESS FROM HERE ON OUT, BUT THIS AIN'T DOIN' IT FOR ME.
DOESN'T MAKE ME WANNA STUDY.
WHAT IF YOU TRY TAILORING YOUR STUDIES TO YOUR INTERESTS, LIKE MIKAGE?
THE RUSSIAN AREA WOULD BE... TYMOSHENKO-TAN?
"-TAN"?
UKRAINE'S "GAS PRINCESS"?
OH MAN. NICKNAMES DO IT FOR ME.

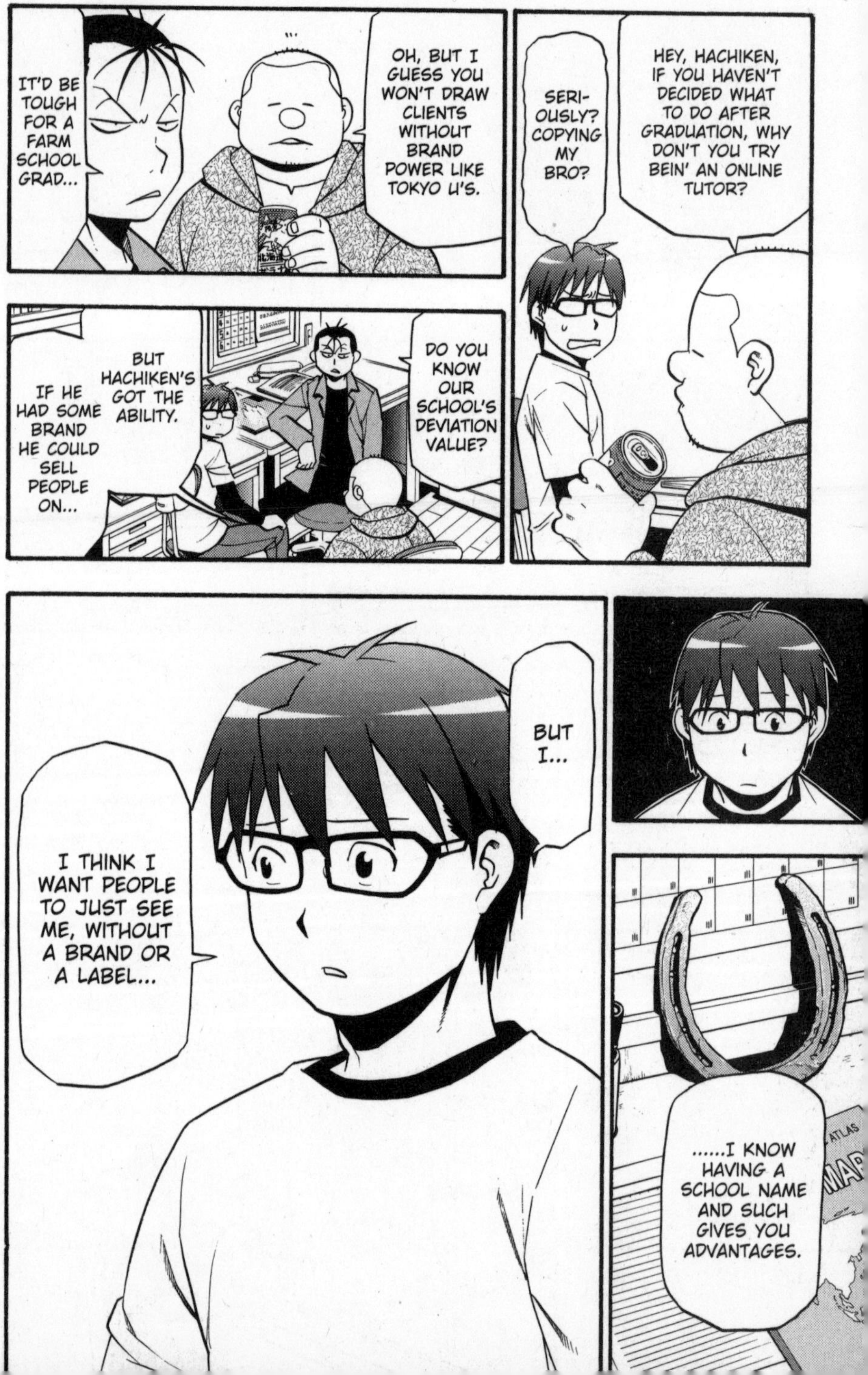
HEY, HACHIKEN, IF YOU HAVEN'T DECIDED WHAT TO DO AFTER GRADUATION, WHY DON'T YOU TRY BEIN' AN ONLINE TUTOR?
SERI-OUSLY? COPYING MY BRO?
...
OH, BUT I GUESS YOU WON'T DRAW CLIENTS WITHOUT BRAND POWER LIKE TOKYO U'S.
IT'D BE TOUGH FOR A FARM SCHOOL GRAD...
DO YOU KNOW OUR SCHOOL'S DEVIATION VALUE?
BUT HACHIKEN'S GOT THE ABILITY.
IF HE HAD SOME BRAND HE COULD SELL PEOPLE ON...
......I KNOW HAVING A SCHOOL NAME AND SUCH GIVES YOU ADVANTAGES.
BUT I...
I THINK I WANT PEOPLE TO JUST SEE ME, WITHOUT A BRAND OR A LABEL...

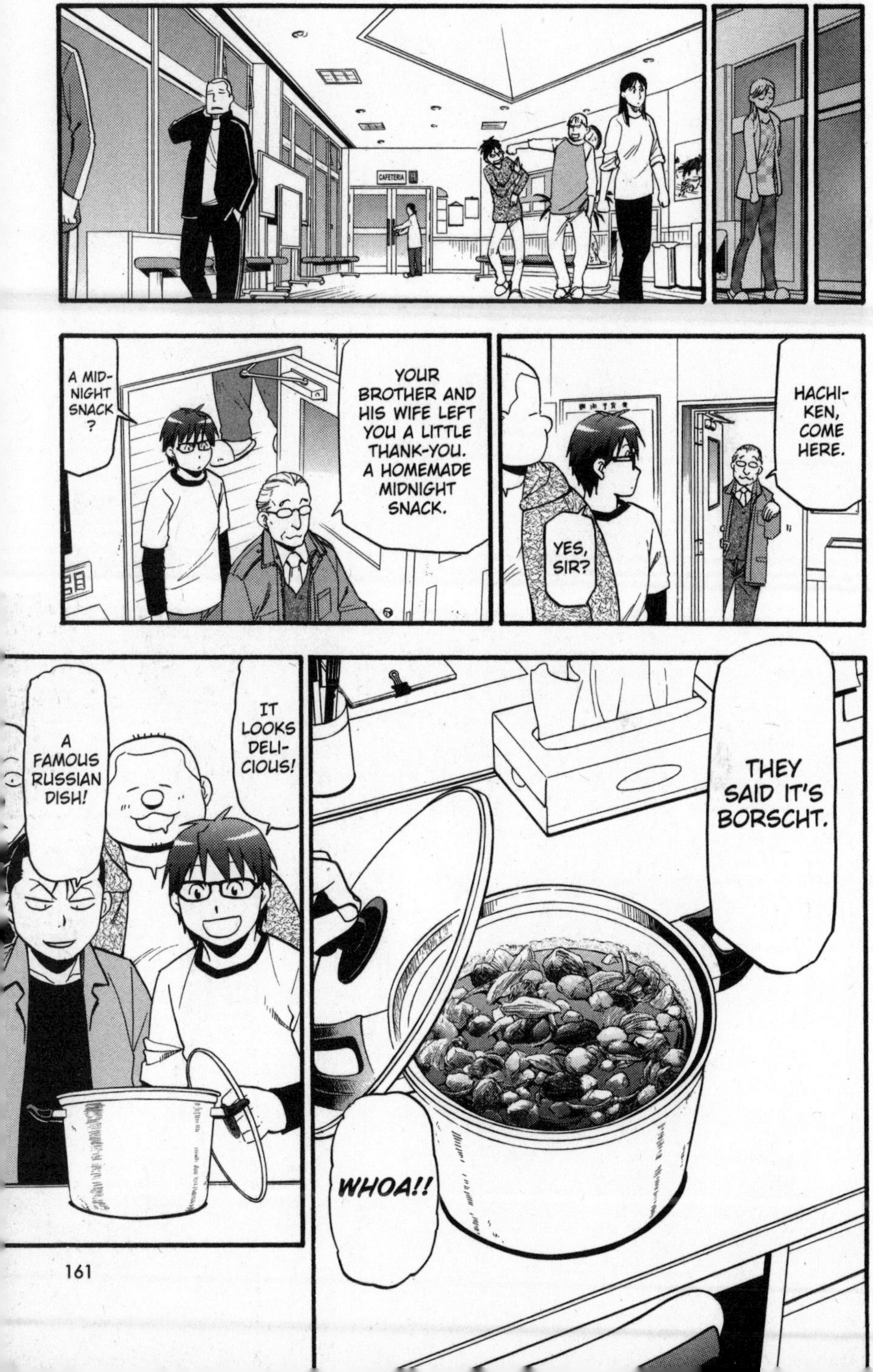

CAFETERIA
HACHI-KEN, COME HERE.
YES, SIR?
YOUR BROTHER AND HIS WIFE LEFT YOU A LITTLE THANK-YOU. A HOMEMADE MIDNIGHT SNACK.
A MID-NIGHT SNACK?
THEY SAID IT'S BORSCHT.
WHOA!!
IT LOOKS DELI-CIOUS!
A FAMOUS RUSSIAN DISH!

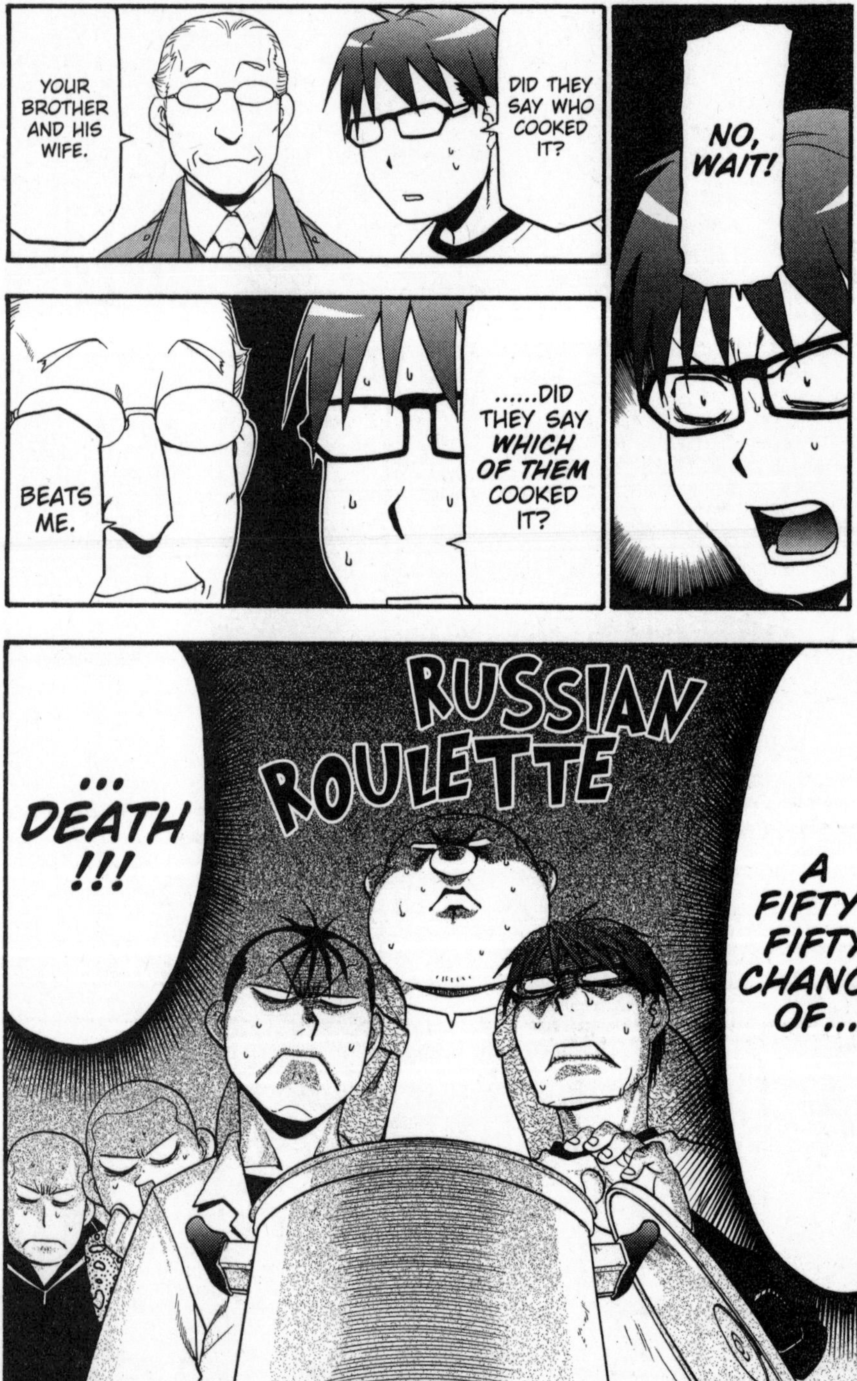
NO, WAIT!
DID THEY SAY WHO COOKED IT?
YOUR BROTHER AND HIS WIFE.
......DID THEY SAY WHICH OF THEM COOKED IT?
BEATS ME.
A FIFTY-FIFTY CHANCE OF...
RUSSIAN ROULETTE
...DEATH!!!

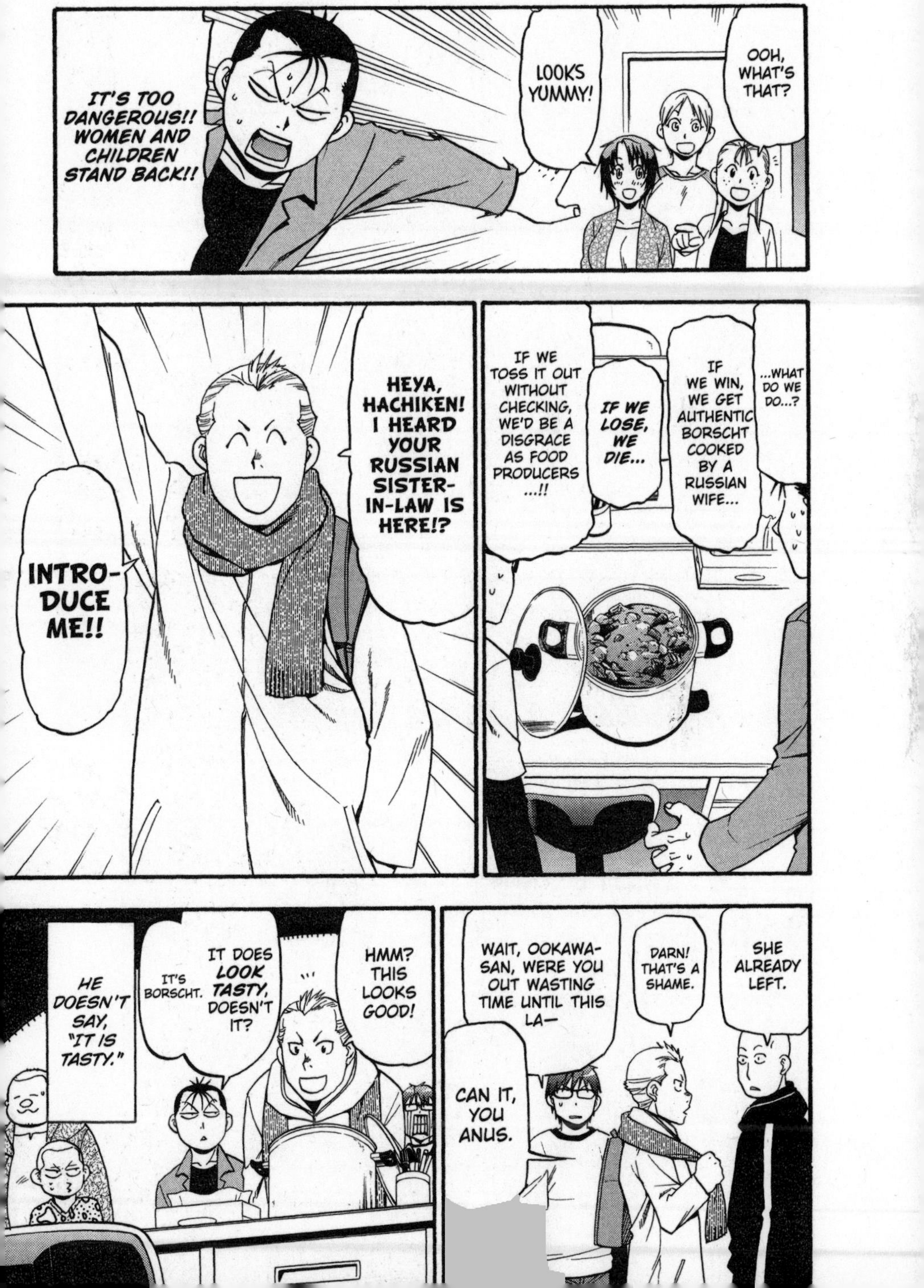
OOH, WHAT'S THAT?
LOOKS YUMMY!
IT'S TOO DANGEROUS!! WOMEN AND CHILDREN STAND BACK!!
...WHAT DO WE DO...?
IF WE WIN, WE GET AUTHENTIC BORSCHT COOKED BY A RUSSIAN WIFE...
IF WE LOSE, WE DIE...
IF WE TOSS IT OUT WITHOUT CHECKING, WE'D BE A DISGRACE AS FOOD PRODUCERS ...!!
HEYA, HACHIKEN! I HEARD YOUR RUSSIAN SISTER-IN-LAW IS HERE!?
INTRODUCE ME!!
SHE ALREADY LEFT.
DARN! THAT'S A SHAME.
WAIT, OOKAWA-SAN, WERE YOU OUT WASTING TIME UNTIL THIS LA—
CAN IT, YOU ANUS.
HMM? THIS LOOKS GOOD!
IT DOES LOOK TASTY, DOESN'T IT?
IT'S BORSCHT.
HE DOESN'T SAY, "IT IS TASTY."

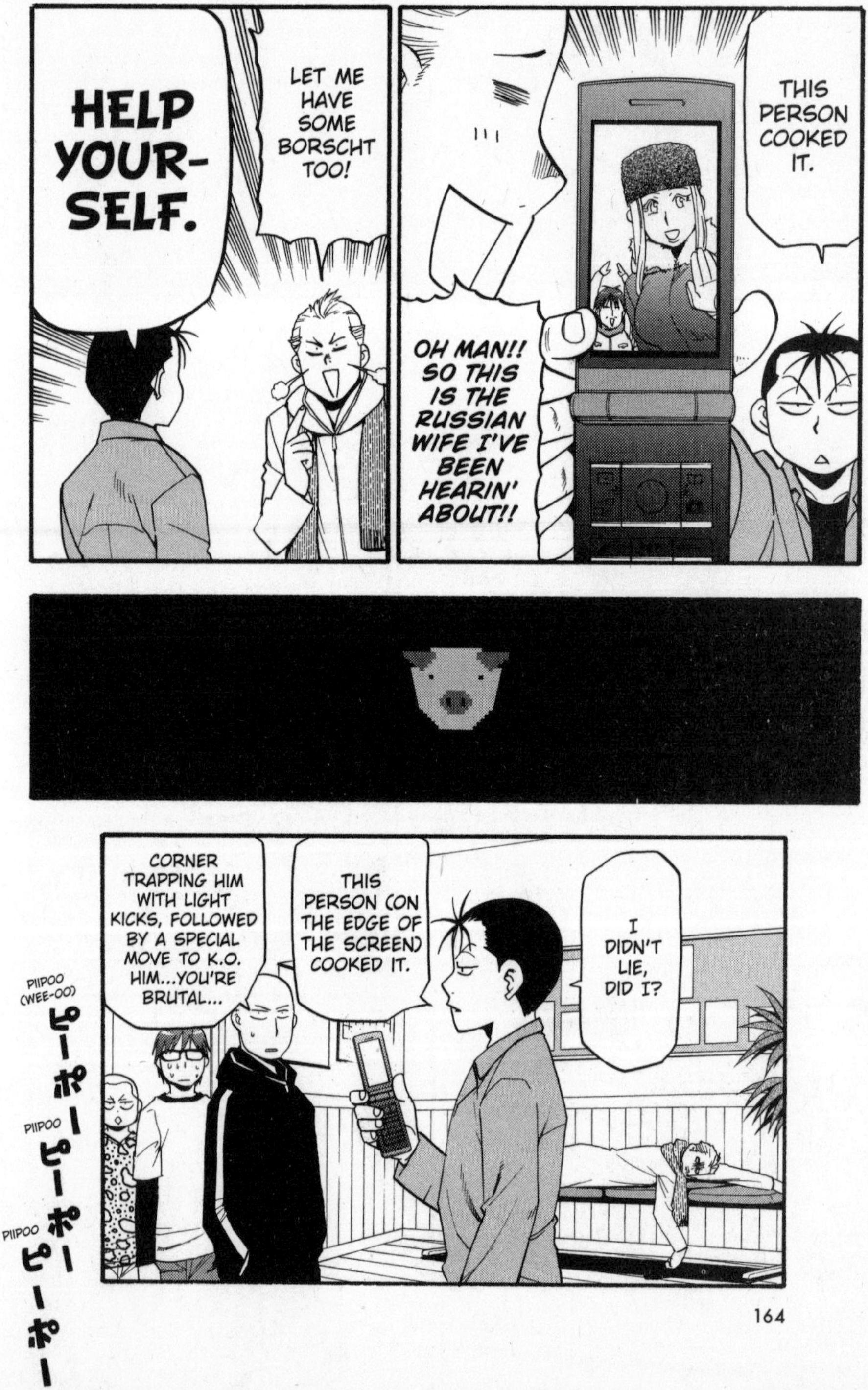
THIS PERSON COOKED IT.
OH MAN!! SO THIS IS THE RUSSIAN WIFE I'VE BEEN HEARIN' ABOUT!!
LET ME HAVE SOME BORSCHT TOO!
HELP YOURSELF.
I DIDN'T LIE, DID I?
THIS PERSON (ON THE EDGE OF THE SCREEN) COOKED IT.
CORNER TRAPPING HIM WITH LIGHT KICKS, FOLLOWED BY A SPECIAL MOVE TO K.O. HIM...YOU'RE BRUTAL...
PIIPOO (WEE-OO)
ピーポー
PIIPOO
ピーポー
PIIPOO
ピーポー

Silver Spoon

POCHI

DOBERMAN

THE INADAS'
DOG

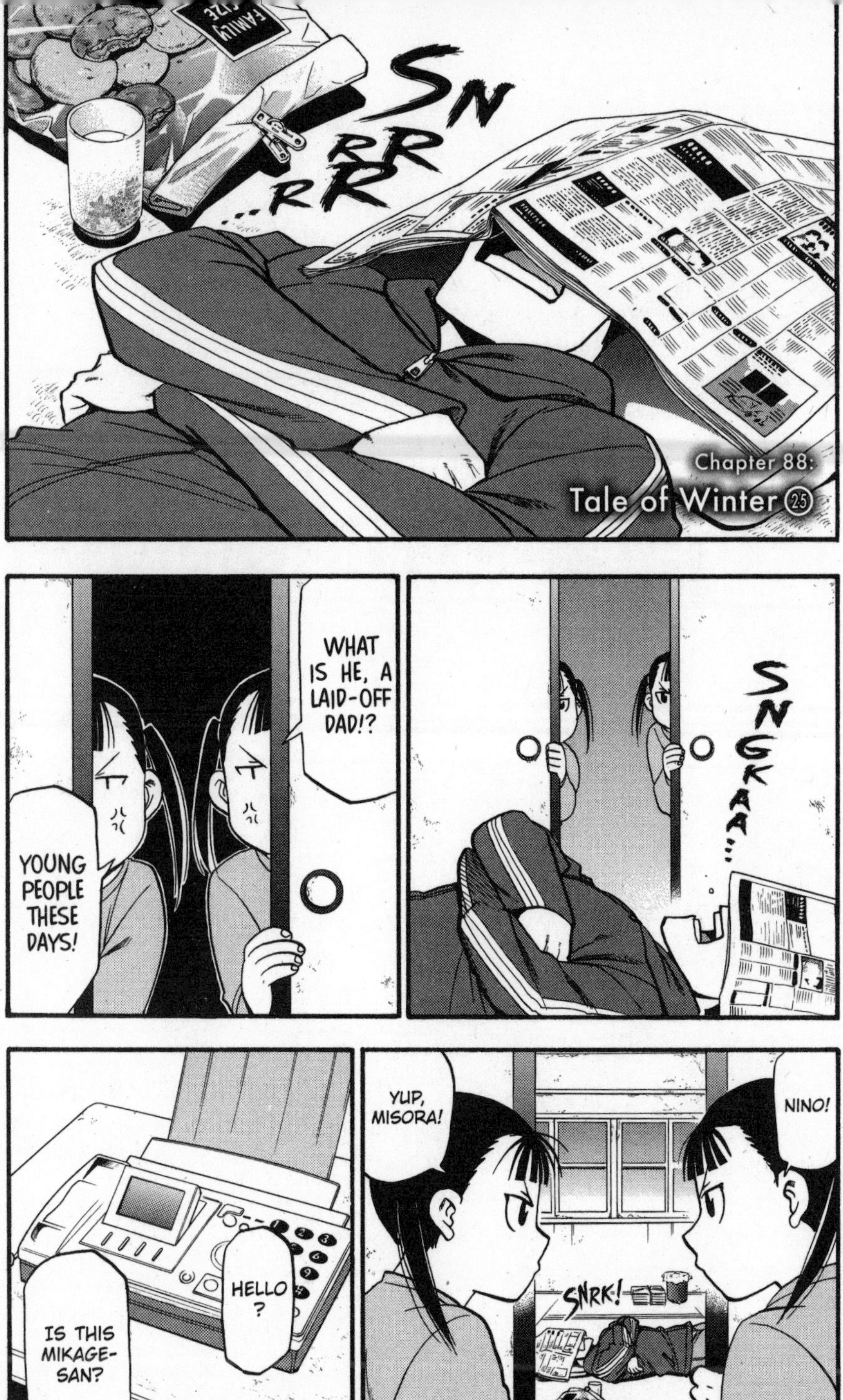

SN RRRR...
Chapter 88:
Tale of Winter ㉕
SNGKAA...
WHAT IS HE, A LAID-OFF DAD!?
YOUNG PEOPLE THESE DAYS!
NINO!
YUP, MISORA!
SNRK!
HELLO?
IS THIS MIKAGE-SAN?

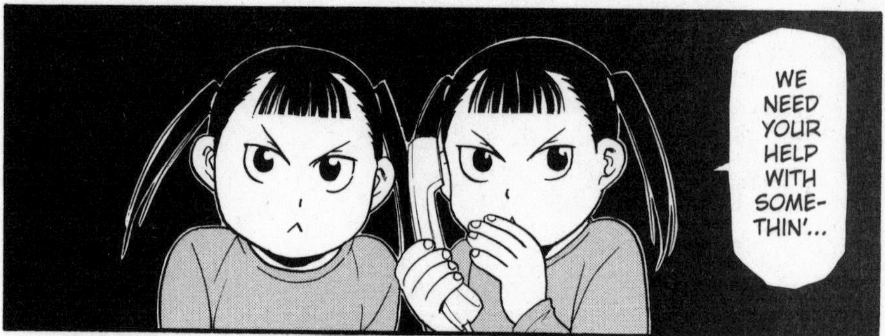
WE NEED YOUR HELP WITH SOME-THIN'...

Chapter 88:
Tale of Winter ㉕

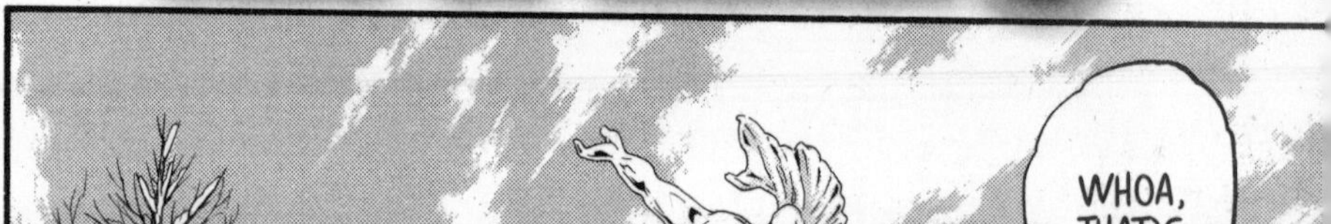
WHOA, THAT'S INCREDIBLE!
ANNUAL ICE SCULPTURE CONT

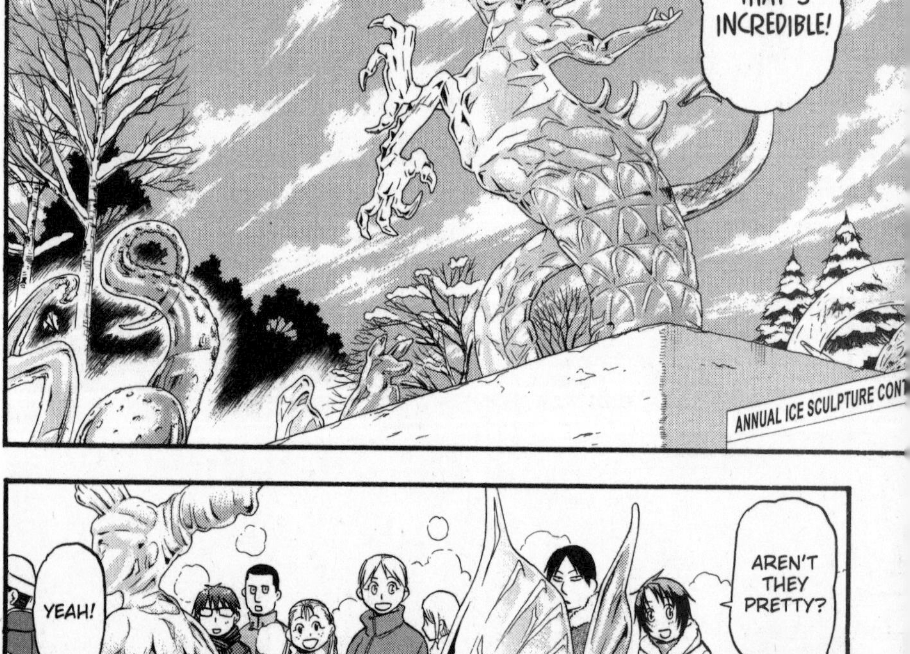
AREN'T THEY PRETTY?
YEAH!

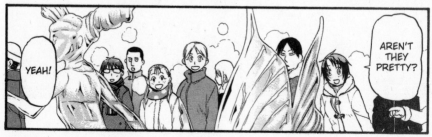

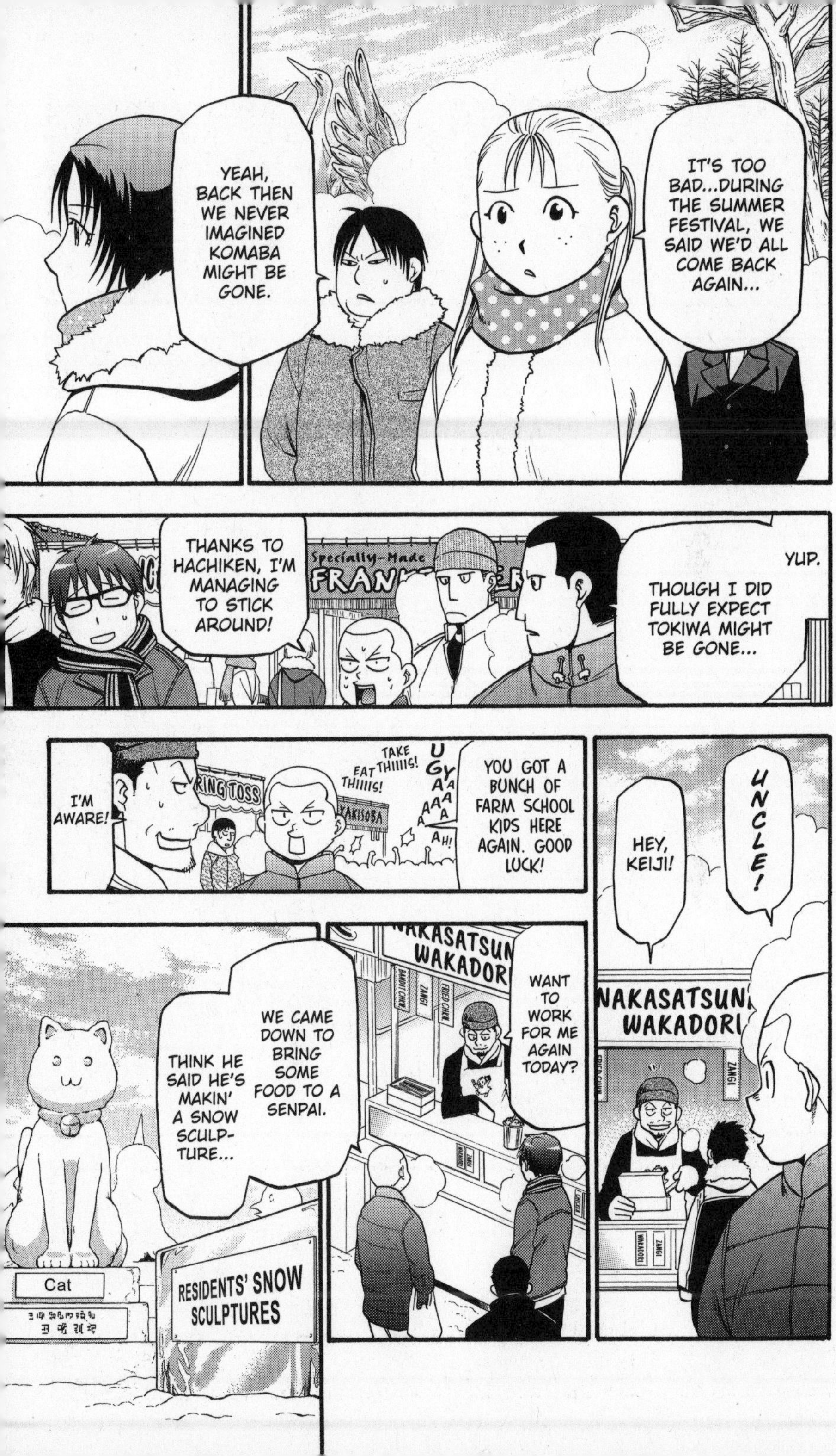
IT'S TOO BAD...DURING THE SUMMER FESTIVAL, WE SAID WE'D ALL COME BACK AGAIN...
YEAH, BACK THEN WE NEVER IMAGINED KOMABA MIGHT BE GONE.
YUP.
THOUGH I DID FULLY EXPECT TOKIWA MIGHT BE GONE...
THANKS TO HACHIKEN, I'M MANAGING TO STICK AROUND!
Specially-Made
UNCLE!
HEY, KEIJI!
YOU GOT A BUNCH OF FARM SCHOOL KIDS HERE AGAIN. GOOD LUCK!
UGYAAAAAAH!
TAKE THIIIIS!
EAT THIIIIS!
RING TOSS
I'M AWARE!
ZANGI
WANT TO WORK FOR ME AGAIN TODAY?
ZANGI
FRIED CHKN
WE CAME DOWN TO BRING SOME FOOD TO A SENPAI.
THINK HE SAID HE'S MAKIN' A SNOW SCULPTURE...
Cat
RESIDENTS' SNOW SCULPTURES

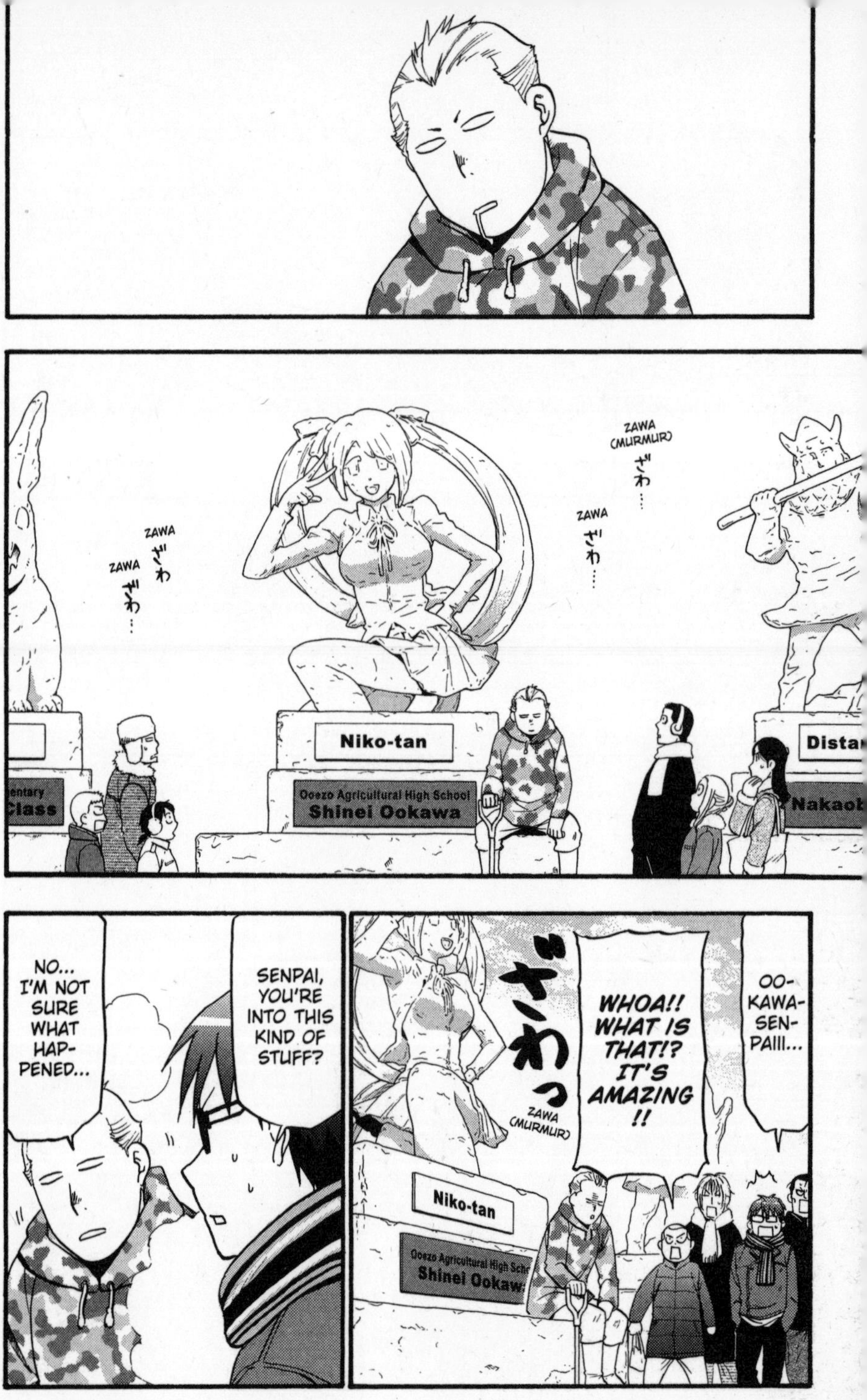
ZAWA (MURMUR) ざわ…
ZAWA ざわ…
Niko-tan
Ooezo Agricultural High School
Shinei Ookawa
ZAWA ざわ
ZAWA ざわ…
OO-KAWA-SENPAIII…
WHOA!! WHAT IS THAT!? IT'S AMAZING!!
ざわっ ZAWA (MURMUR)
Niko-tan
SENPAI, YOU'RE INTO THIS KIND OF STUFF?
NO… I'M NOT SURE WHAT HAPPENED…

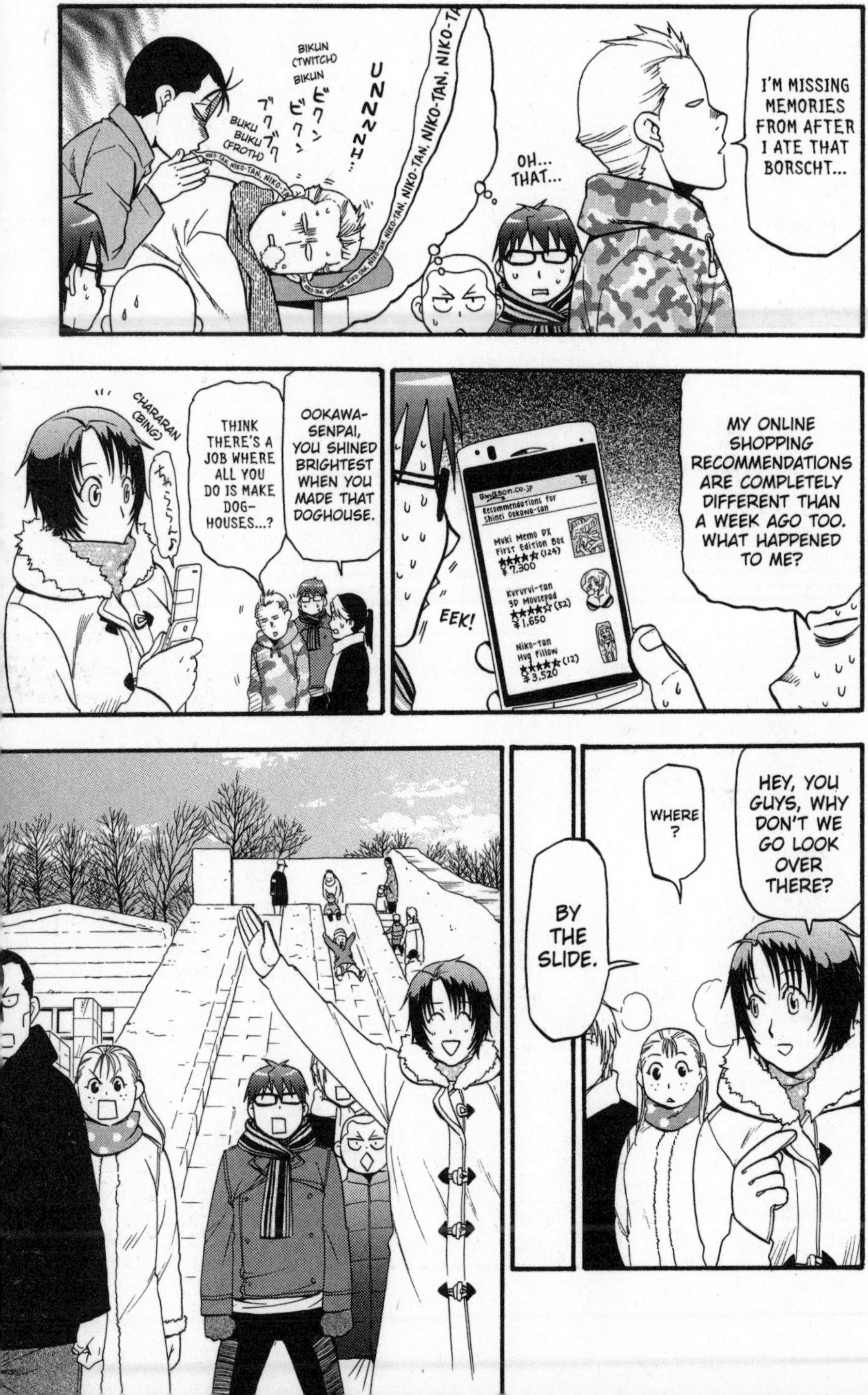
I'M MISSING MEMORIES FROM AFTER I ATE THAT BORSCHT...
OH... THAT...
NIKO-TAN, NIKO-TAN, NIKO-TAN, NIKO-TA
UNNNNNH...
BIKUN (TWITCH) BIKUN
ビクン ビクン
BUKU BUKU (FROTH)
ブクブク
NIKO-TAN, NIKO-TAN, NIKO-TA
MY ONLINE SHOPPING RECOMMENDATIONS ARE COMPLETELY DIFFERENT THAN A WEEK AGO TOO. WHAT HAPPENED TO ME?
Recommendations for Shinei Ookawa-san
Mvki Memo DX First Edition Box (124) ¥7,300
Kvrvrvi-tan 3D Mousepad (52) ¥1,650
Niko-tan Hug Pillow (12) ¥3,520
EEK!
OOKAWA-SENPAI, YOU SHINED BRIGHTEST WHEN YOU MADE THAT DOGHOUSE.
THINK THERE'S A JOB WHERE ALL YOU DO IS MAKE DOG-HOUSES...?
CHARARAN (BING)
ちゃららん♪
HEY, YOU GUYS, WHY DON'T WE GO LOOK OVER THERE?
WHERE?
BY THE SLIDE.

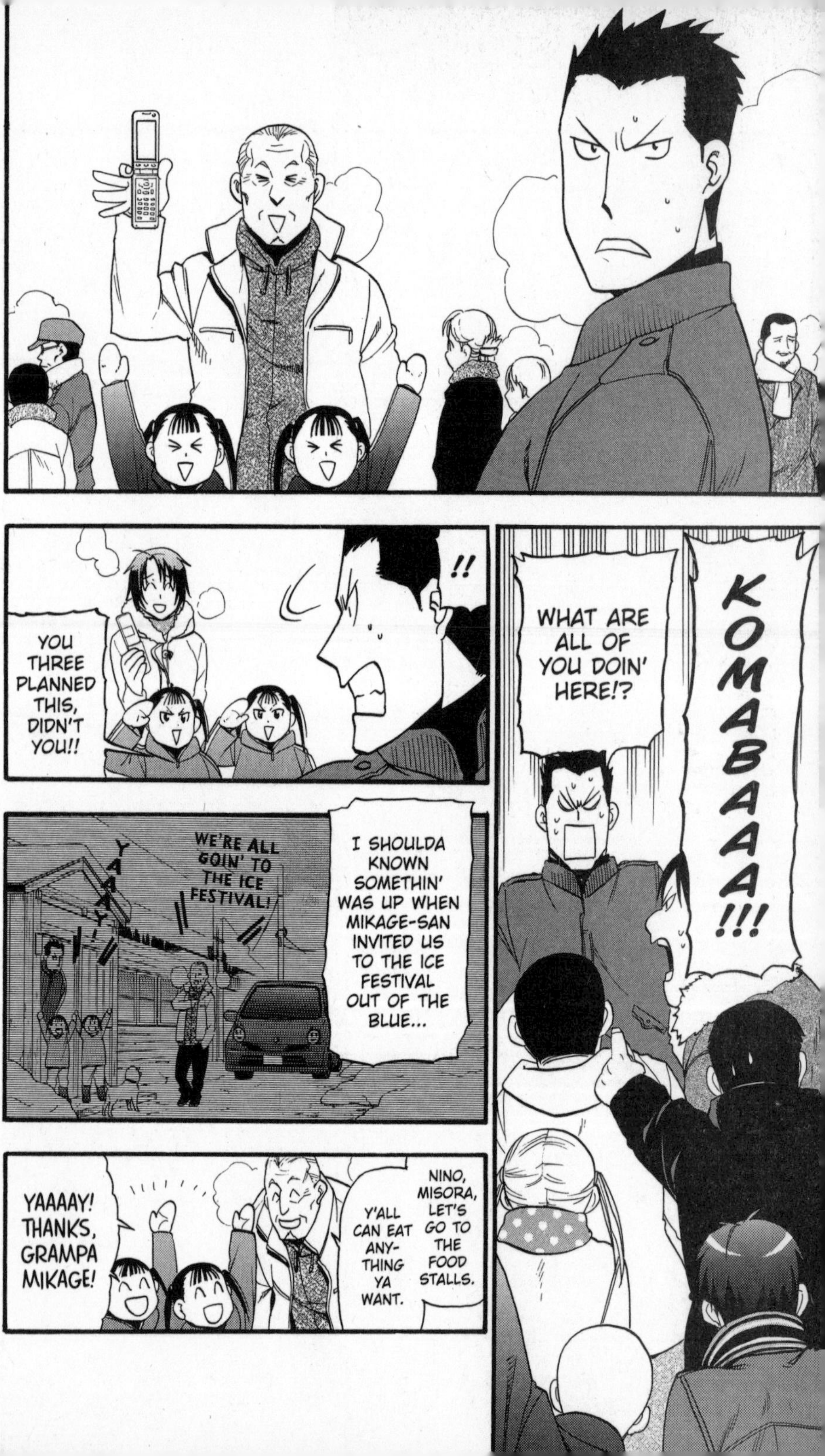
KOMABAAAA!!!
WHAT ARE ALL OF YOU DOIN' HERE!?
!!
YOU THREE PLANNED THIS, DIDN'T YOU!!
I SHOULDA KNOWN SOMETHIN' WAS UP WHEN MIKAGE-SAN INVITED US TO THE ICE FESTIVAL OUT OF THE BLUE...
WE'RE ALL GOIN' TO THE ICE FESTIVAL!
YAAAAY!
NINO, MISORA, LET'S GO TO THE FOOD STALLS.
Y'ALL CAN EAT ANY-THING YA WANT.
YAAAAY! THANKS, GRAMPA MIKAGE!

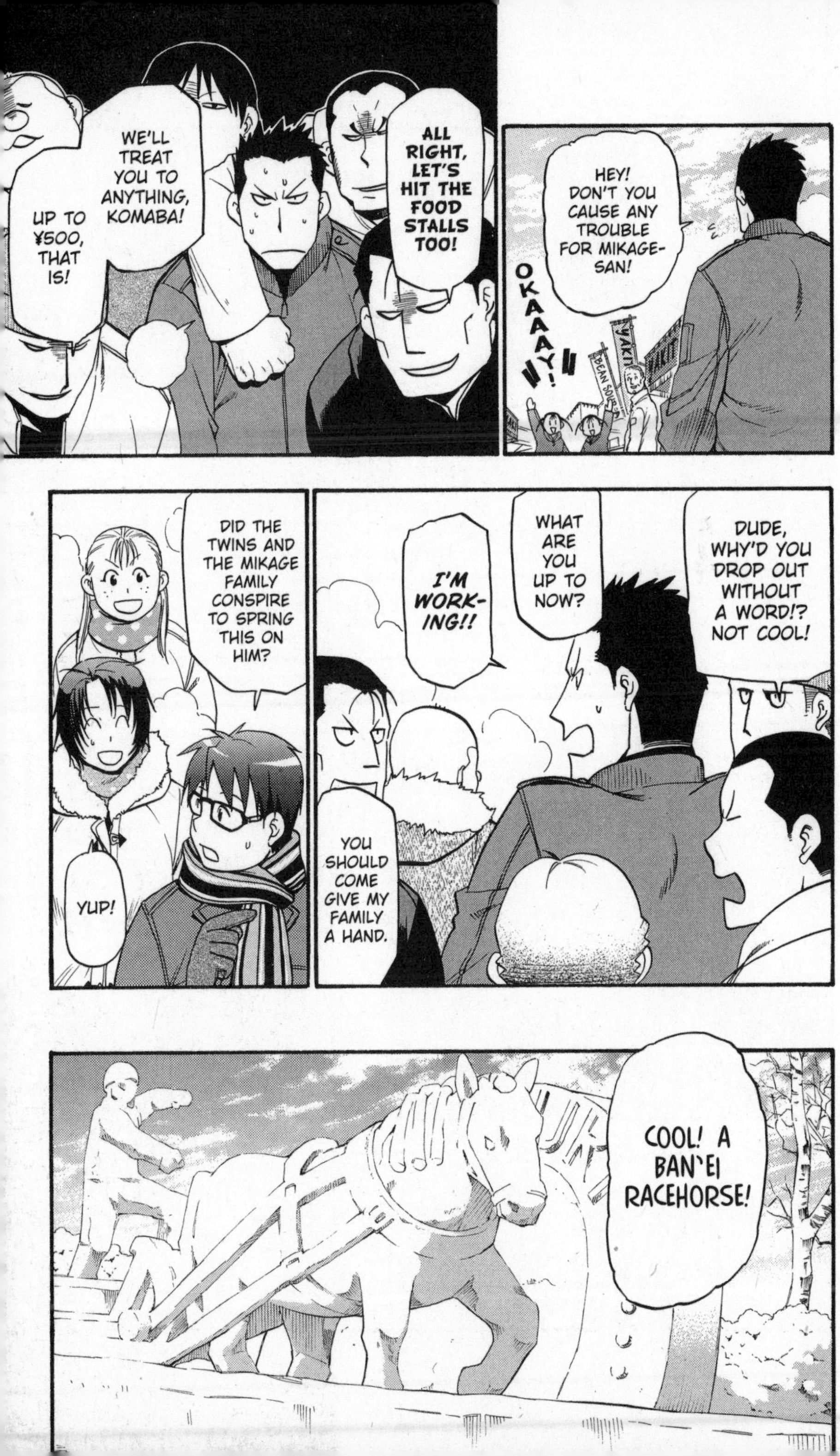
HEY! DON'T YOU CAUSE ANY TROUBLE FOR MIKAGE-SAN!
OKAAAAY!
BEAN SOUP
ALL RIGHT, LET'S HIT THE FOOD STALLS TOO!
WE'LL TREAT YOU TO ANYTHING, KOMABA!
UP TO ¥500, THAT IS!
DUDE, WHY'D YOU DROP OUT WITHOUT A WORD!? NOT COOL!
WHAT ARE YOU UP TO NOW?
I'M WORKING!!
YOU SHOULD COME GIVE MY FAMILY A HAND.
DID THE TWINS AND THE MIKAGE FAMILY CONSPIRE TO SPRING THIS ON HIM?
YUP!
COOL! A BAN'EI RACEHORSE!

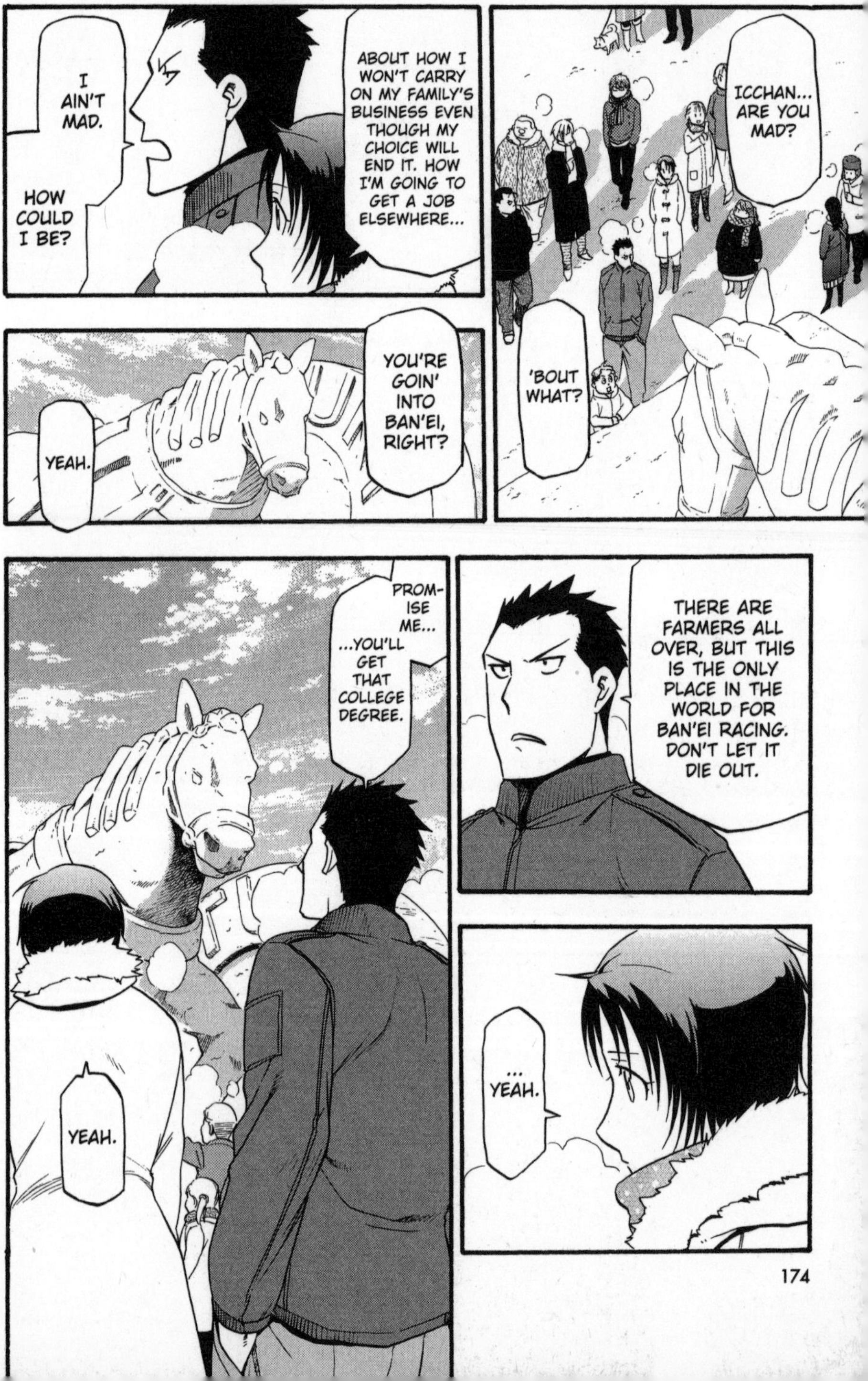
ICCHAN... ARE YOU MAD?
'BOUT WHAT?
ABOUT HOW I WON'T CARRY ON MY FAMILY'S BUSINESS EVEN THOUGH MY CHOICE WILL END IT. HOW I'M GOING TO GET A JOB ELSEWHERE...
I AIN'T MAD.
HOW COULD I BE?
YOU'RE GOIN' INTO BAN'EI, RIGHT?
YEAH.
THERE ARE FARMERS ALL OVER, BUT THIS IS THE ONLY PLACE IN THE WORLD FOR BAN'EI RACING. DON'T LET IT DIE OUT.
... YEAH.
PROM-ISE ME...
...YOU'LL GET THAT COLLEGE DEGREE.
YEAH.

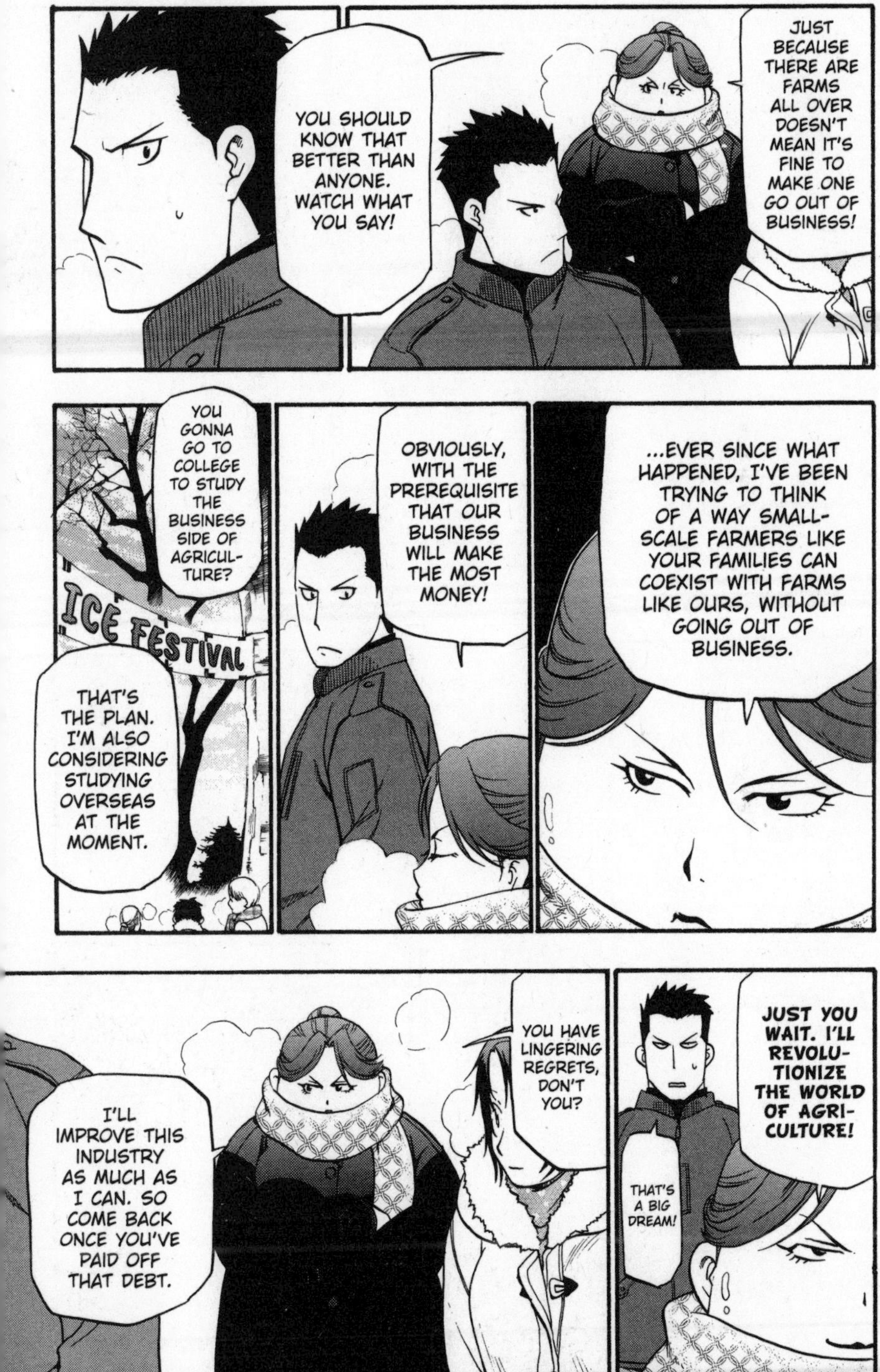
JUST BECAUSE THERE ARE FARMS ALL OVER DOESN'T MEAN IT'S FINE TO MAKE ONE GO OUT OF BUSINESS!
YOU SHOULD KNOW THAT BETTER THAN ANYONE. WATCH WHAT YOU SAY!
...EVER SINCE WHAT HAPPENED, I'VE BEEN TRYING TO THINK OF A WAY SMALL-SCALE FARMERS LIKE YOUR FAMILIES CAN COEXIST WITH FARMS LIKE OURS, WITHOUT GOING OUT OF BUSINESS.
OBVIOUSLY, WITH THE PREREQUISITE THAT OUR BUSINESS WILL MAKE THE MOST MONEY!
YOU GONNA GO TO COLLEGE TO STUDY THE BUSINESS SIDE OF AGRICUL-TURE?
ICE FESTIVAL
THAT'S THE PLAN. I'M ALSO CONSIDERING STUDYING OVERSEAS AT THE MOMENT.
JUST YOU WAIT. I'LL REVOLU-TIONIZE THE WORLD OF AGRI-CULTURE!
THAT'S A BIG DREAM!
YOU HAVE LINGERING REGRETS, DON'T YOU?
I'LL IMPROVE THIS INDUSTRY AS MUCH AS I CAN. SO COME BACK ONCE YOU'VE PAID OFF THAT DEBT.

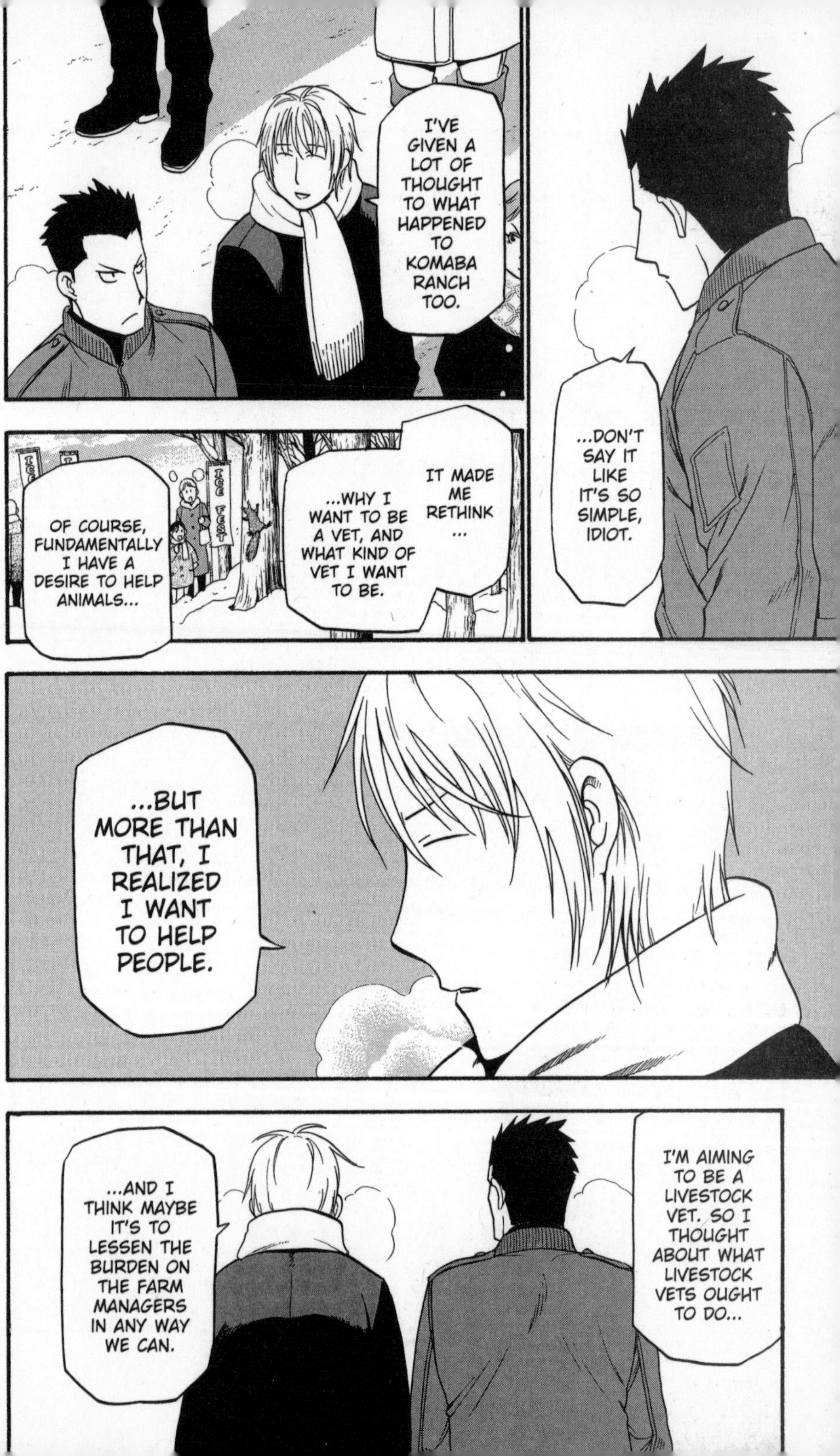
...DON'T SAY IT LIKE IT'S SO SIMPLE, IDIOT.
I'VE GIVEN A LOT OF THOUGHT TO WHAT HAPPENED TO KOMABA RANCH TOO.
IT MADE ME RETHINK ...
...WHY I WANT TO BE A VET, AND WHAT KIND OF VET I WANT TO BE.
ICE FEST
OF COURSE, FUNDAMENTALLY I HAVE A DESIRE TO HELP ANIMALS...
...BUT MORE THAN THAT, I REALIZED I WANT TO HELP PEOPLE.
I'M AIMING TO BE A LIVESTOCK VET. SO I THOUGHT ABOUT WHAT LIVESTOCK VETS OUGHT TO DO...
...AND I THINK MAYBE IT'S TO LESSEN THE BURDEN ON THE FARM MANAGERS IN ANY WAY WE CAN.

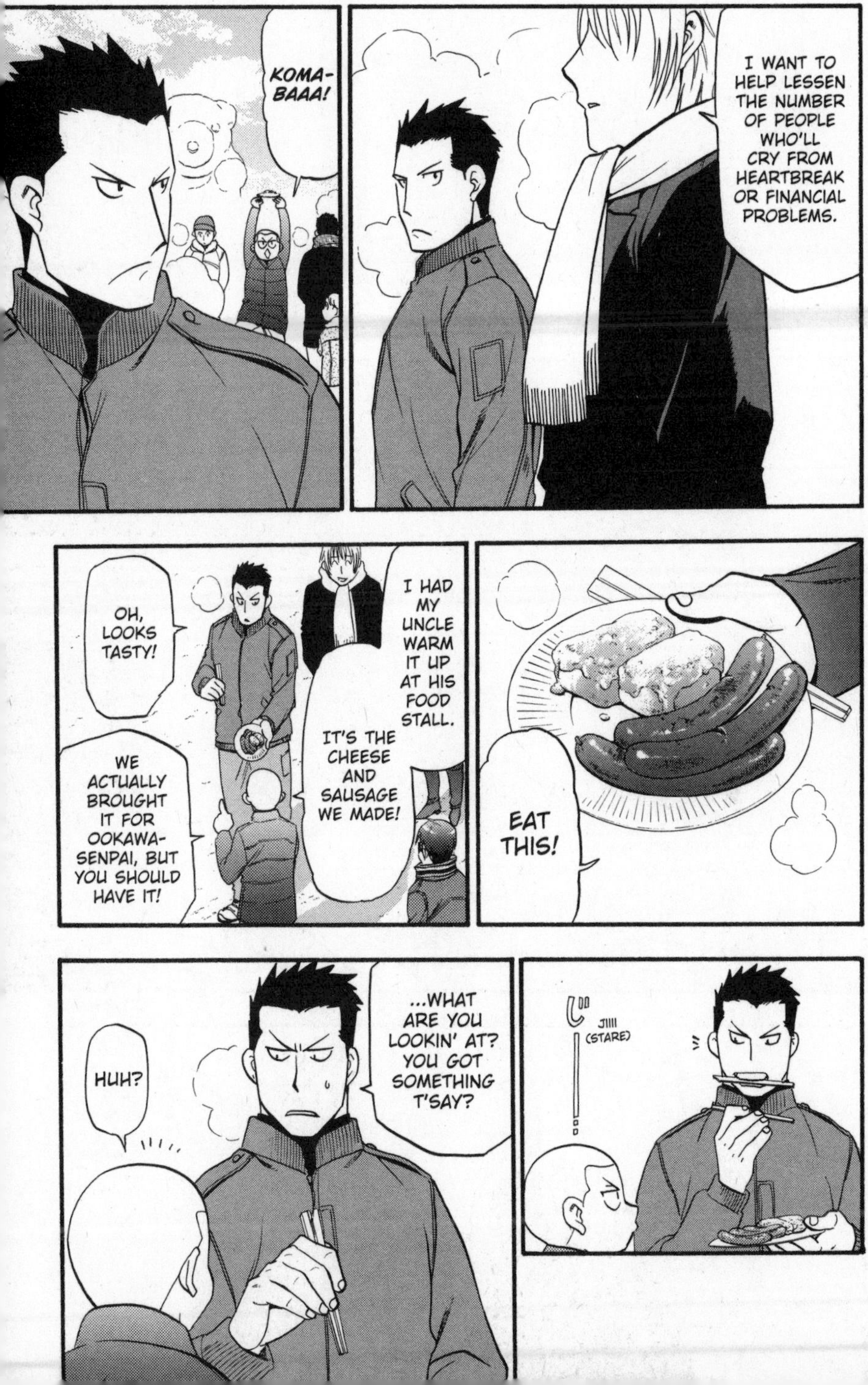
I WANT TO HELP LESSEN THE NUMBER OF PEOPLE WHO'LL CRY FROM HEARTBREAK OR FINANCIAL PROBLEMS.
KOMA-BAAA!
EAT THIS!
I HAD MY UNCLE WARM IT UP AT HIS FOOD STALL.
IT'S THE CHEESE AND SAUSAGE WE MADE!
OH, LOOKS TASTY!
WE ACTUALLY BROUGHT IT FOR OOKAWA-SENPAI, BUT YOU SHOULD HAVE IT!
じ
JIIII (STARE)
...WHAT ARE YOU LOOKIN' AT? YOU GOT SOMETHING T'SAY?
HUH?

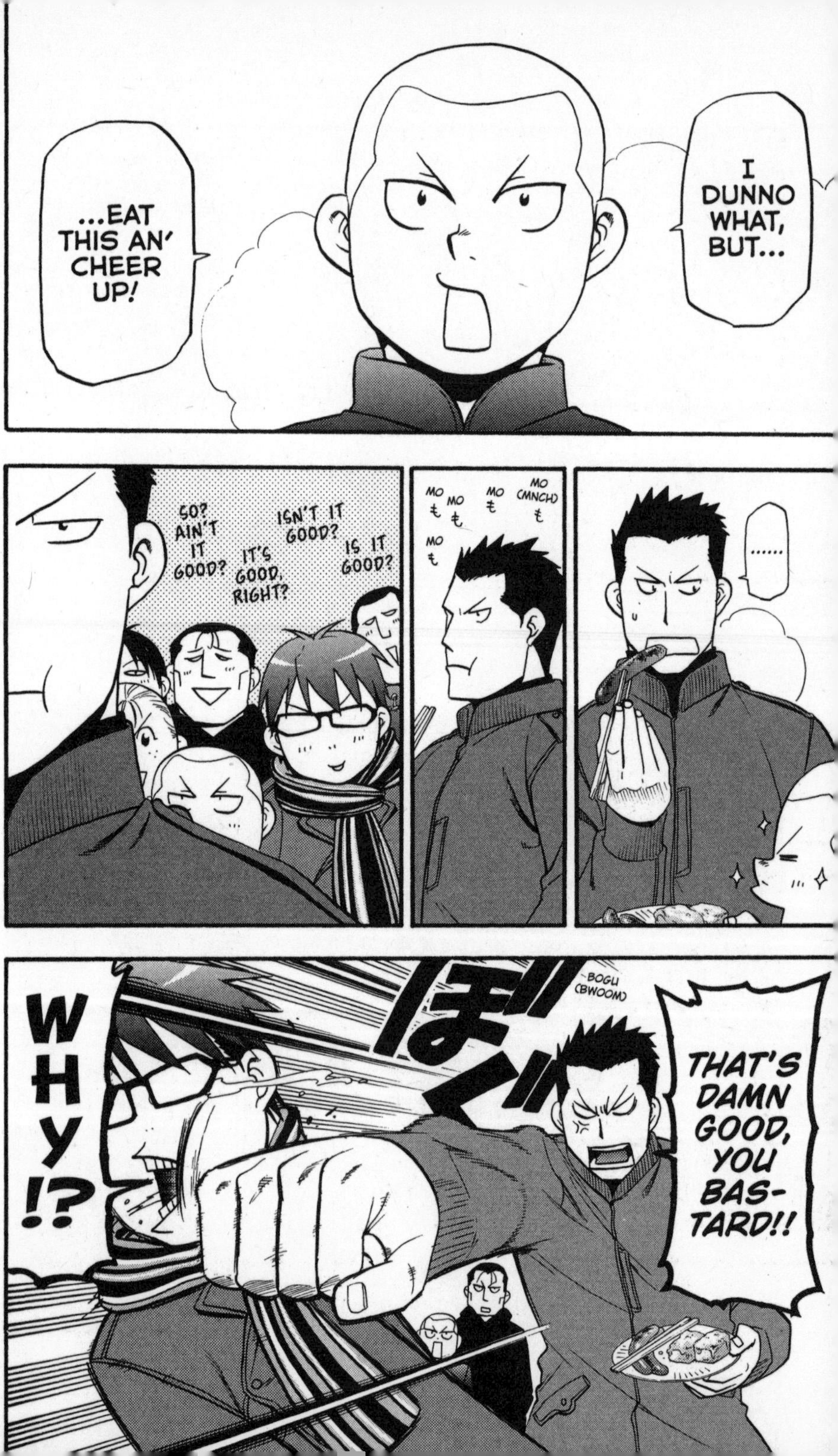
I DUNNO WHAT, BUT...
...EAT THIS AN' CHEER UP!
......
MO も MO も MO も MO (MNCH) も MO も
IS IT GOOD?
ISN'T IT GOOD?
IT'S GOOD, RIGHT?
SO? AIN'T IT GOOD?
THAT'S DAMN GOOD, YOU BAS-TARD!!
ぼぐ BOGU (BWOOM)
WHY!?

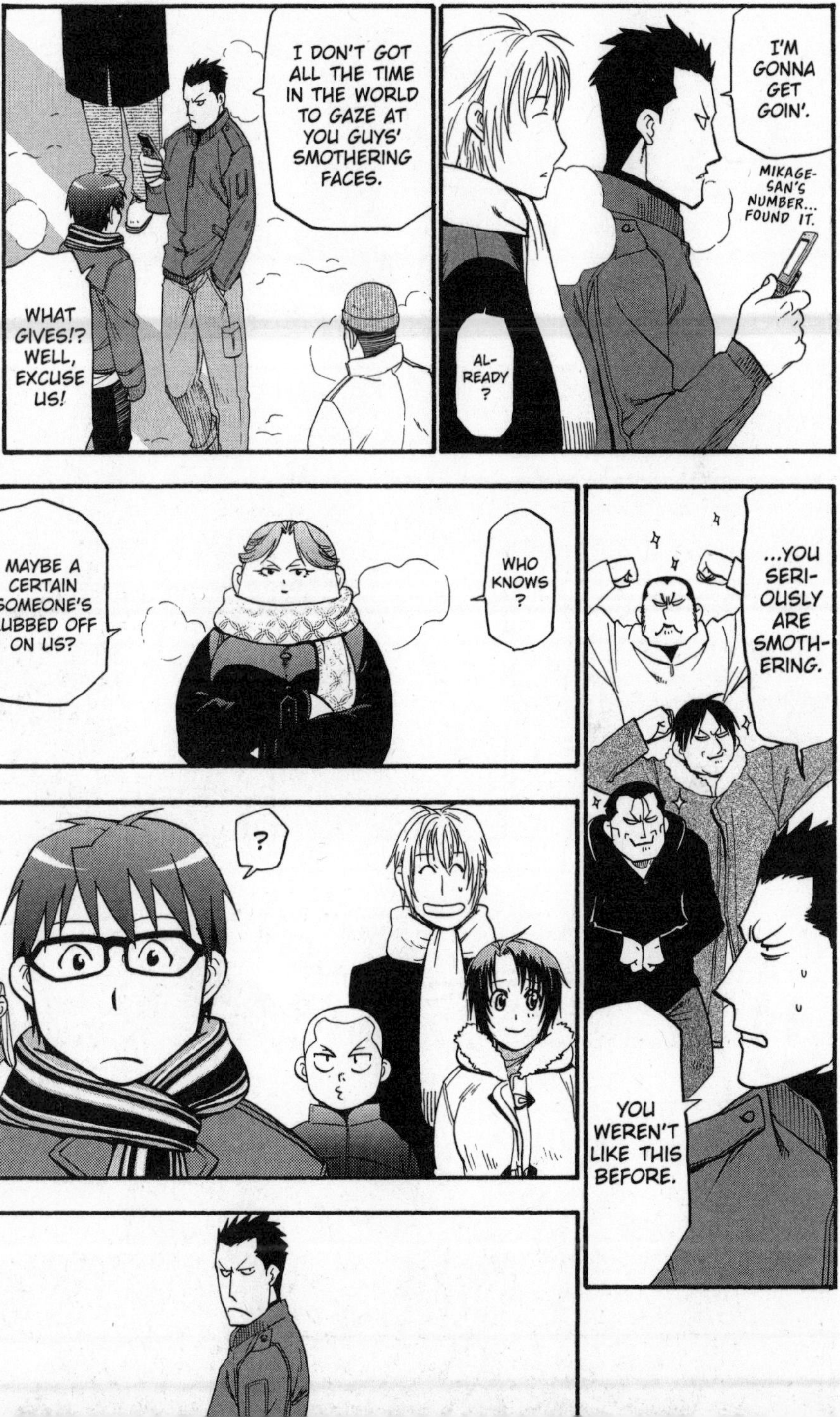
I'M GONNA GET GOIN'.
MIKAGE-SAN'S NUMBER... FOUND IT.
AL-READY?
I DON'T GOT ALL THE TIME IN THE WORLD TO GAZE AT YOU GUYS' SMOTHERING FACES.
WHAT GIVES!? WELL, EXCUSE US!
...YOU SERI-OUSLY ARE SMOTH-ERING.
YOU WEREN'T LIKE THIS BEFORE.
WHO KNOWS?
MAYBE A CERTAIN SOMEONE'S RUBBED OFF ON US?
?

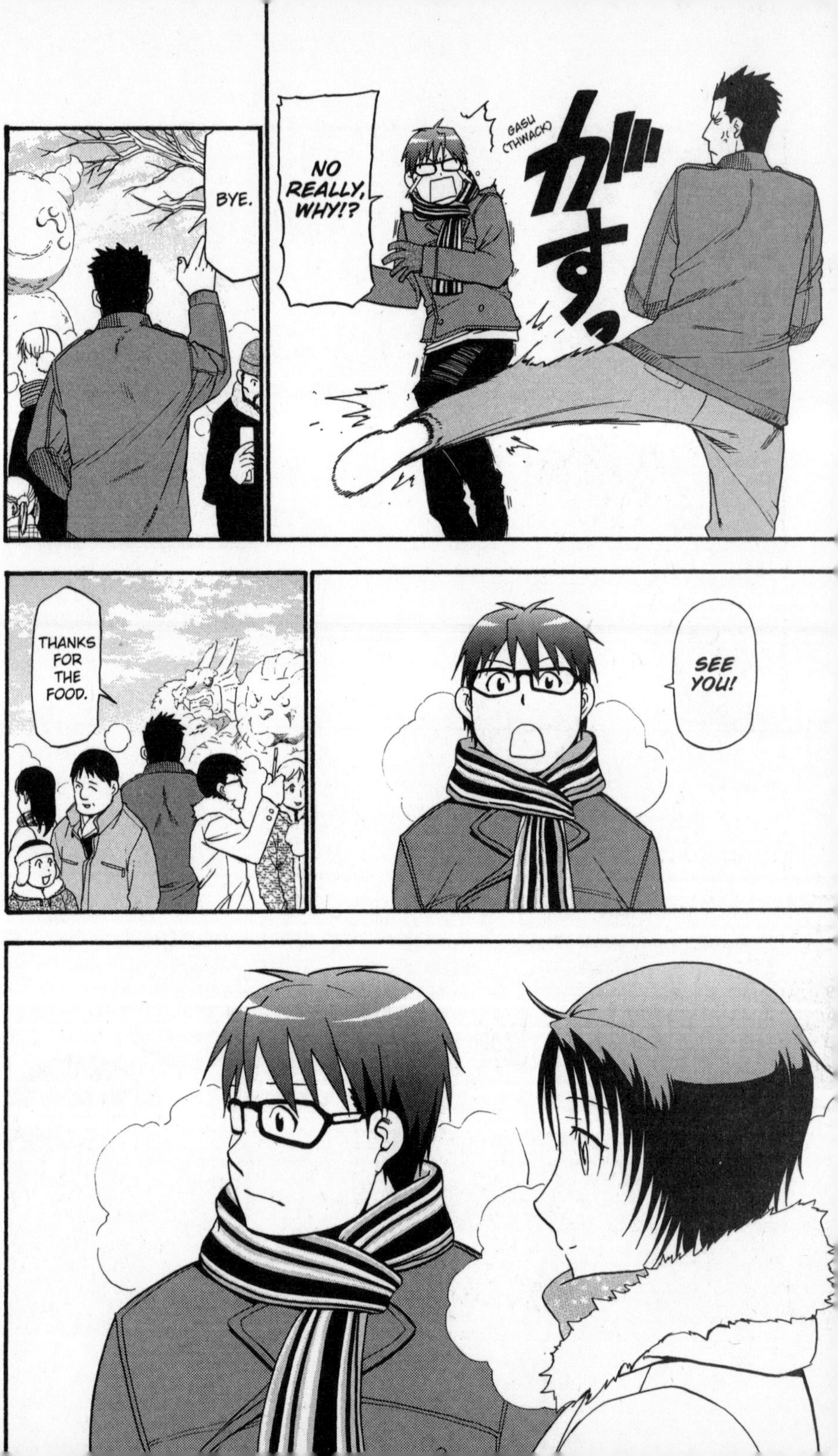

NO REALLY, WHY!?
がすっ
GASU (THWACK)
BYE.
SEE YOU!
THANKS FOR THE FOOD.

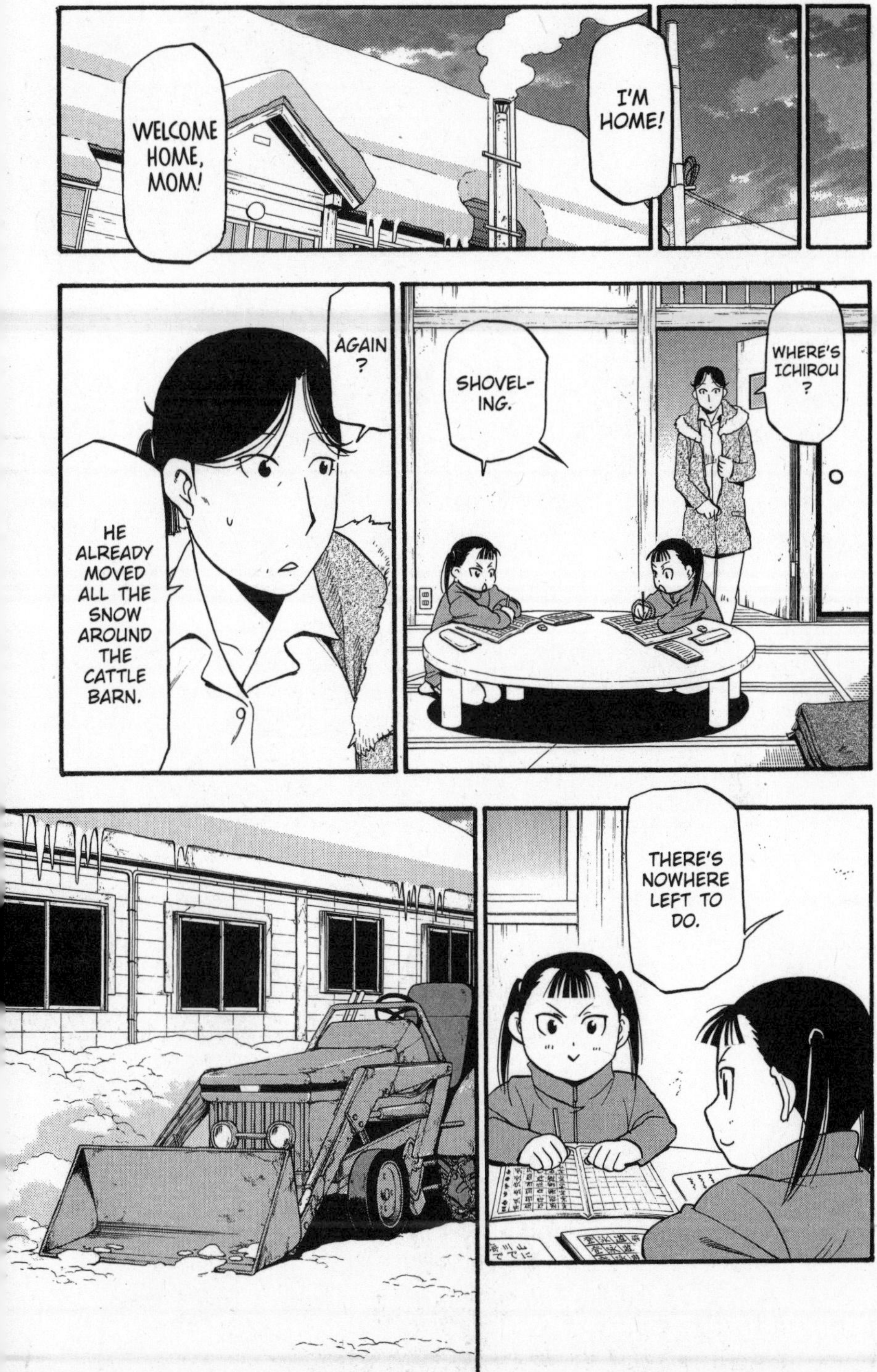
I'M HOME!
WELCOME HOME, MOM!
WHERE'S ICHIROU?
SHOVEL-ING.
AGAIN?
HE ALREADY MOVED ALL THE SNOW AROUND THE CATTLE BARN.
THERE'S NOWHERE LEFT TO DO.

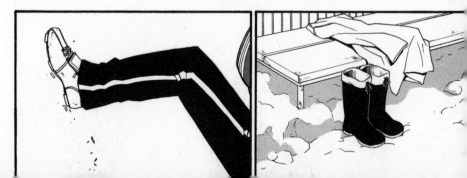

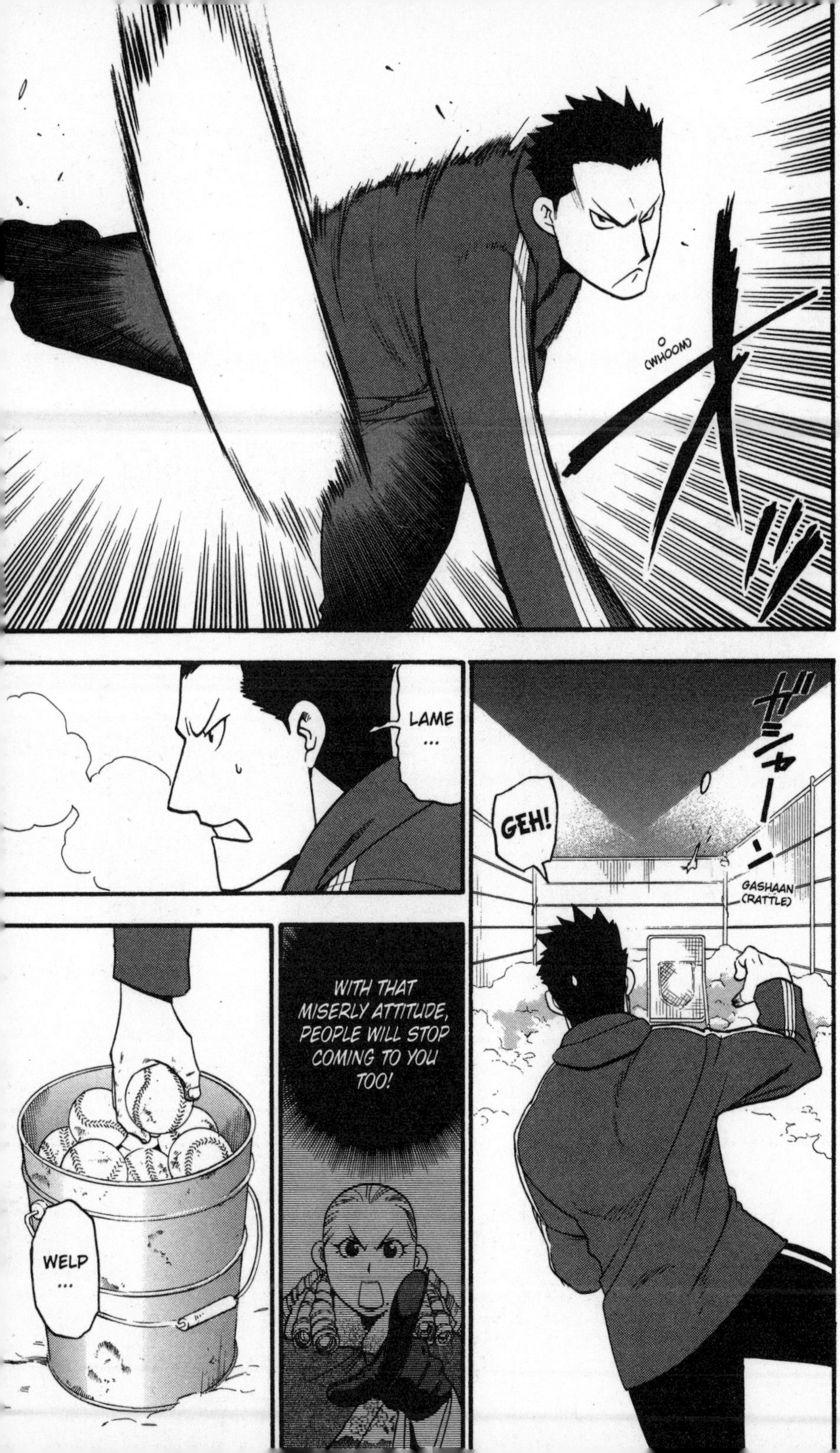

(WHOOM)
GEH!
GASHAAN (RATTLE)
LAME ...
WITH THAT MISERLY ATTITUDE, PEOPLE WILL STOP COMING TO YOU TOO!
WELP ...

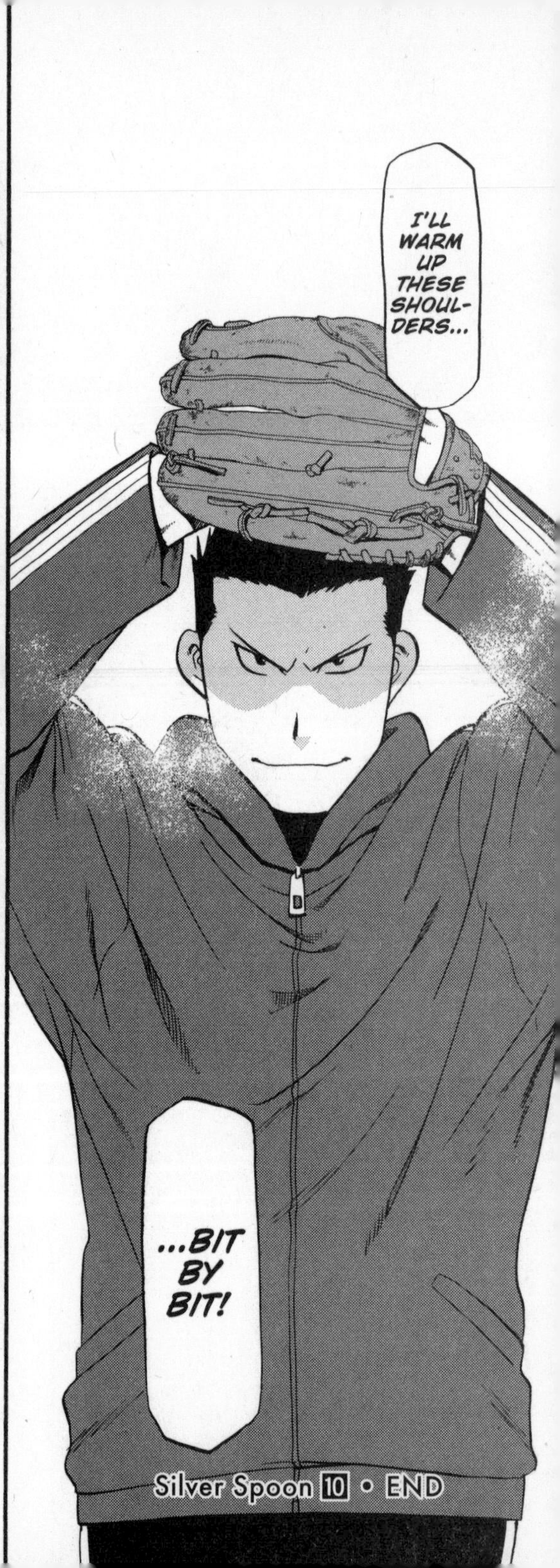
I'LL WARM UP THESE SHOULDERS...
...BIT BY BIT!
Silver Spoon 10 • END
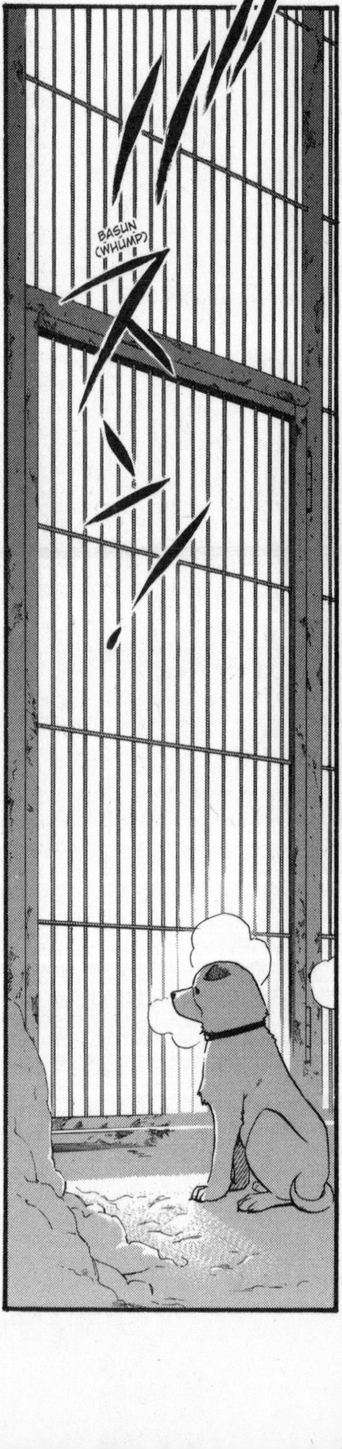
BASUN (WHUMP)

Silver Spoon

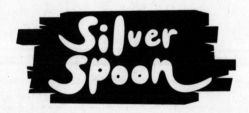

My Russian Sister-in-Law

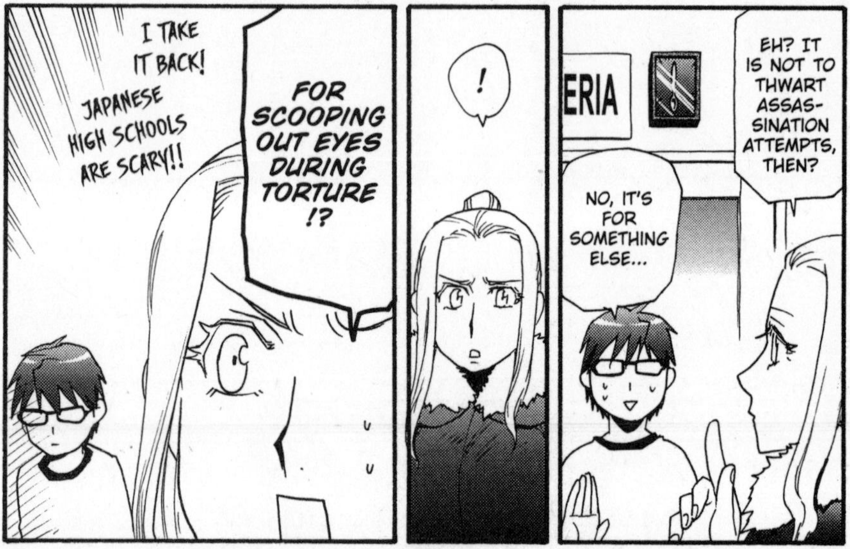
EH? IT IS NOT TO THWART ASSAS-SINATION ATTEMPTS, THEN?
ERIA
NO, IT'S FOR SOMETHING ELSE...
!
FOR SCOOPING OUT EYES DURING TORTURE !?
I TAKE IT BACK! JAPANESE HIGH SCHOOLS ARE SCARY!!

My Russian Wife

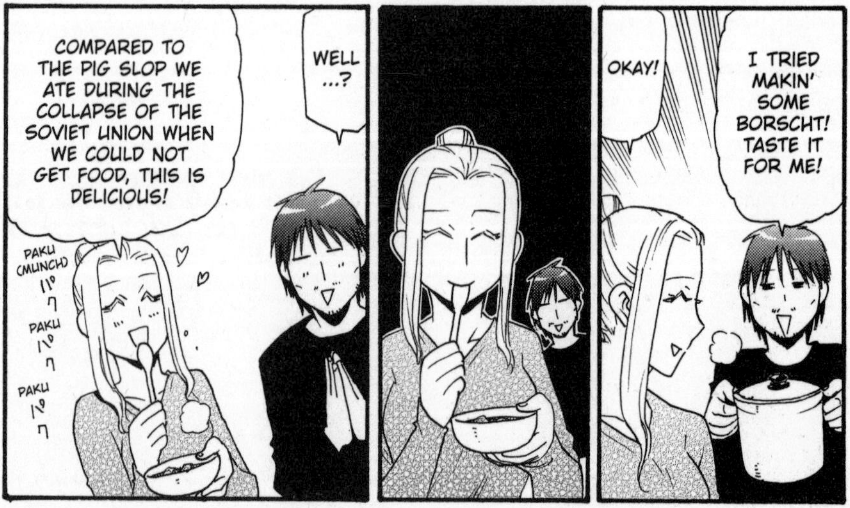
I TRIED MAKIN' SOME BORSCHT! TASTE IT FOR ME!
OKAY!
WELL ...?
COMPARED TO THE PIG SLOP WE ATE DURING THE COLLAPSE OF THE SOVIET UNION WHEN WE COULD NOT GET FOOD, THIS IS DELICIOUS!
PAKU (MUNCH) パク
PAKU パク
PAKU パク

Cow Shed Diaries: "At the Filming of the Film Adaptation" Chapter

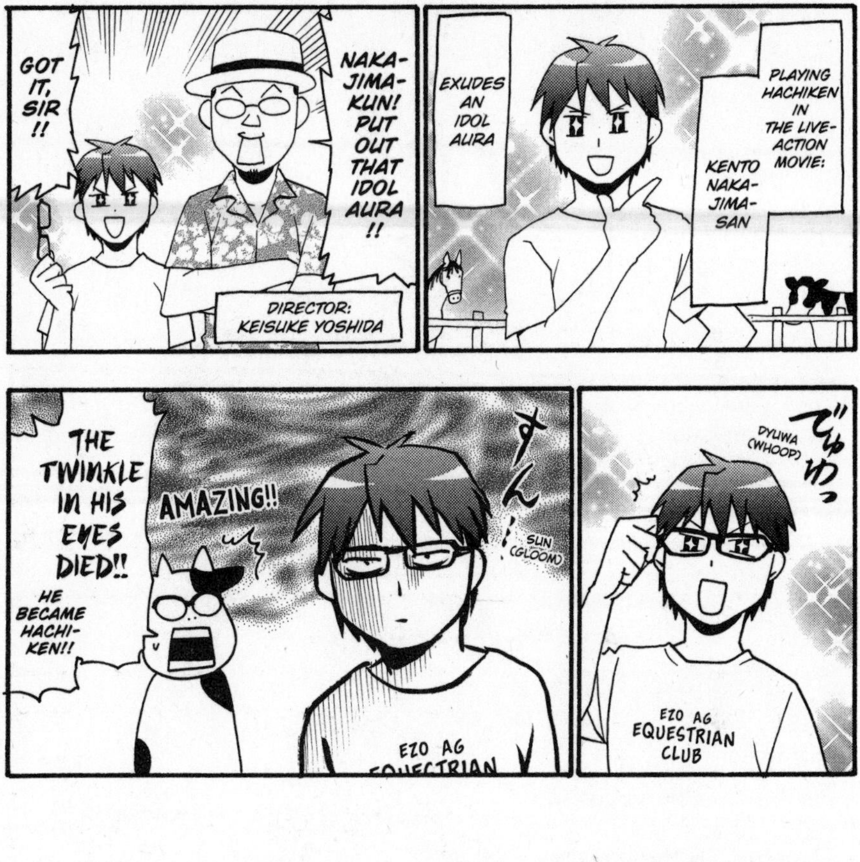
PLAYING HACHIKEN IN THE LIVE-ACTION MOVIE:
KENTO NAKAJIMA-SAN
EXUDES AN IDOL AURA
NAKAJIMA-KUN! PUT OUT THAT IDOL AURA!!
GOT IT, SIR!!
DIRECTOR: KEISUKE YOSHIDA
DYUWA (WHOOP)
EZO AG EQUESTRIAN CLUB
SUN (GLOOM)
AMAZING!!
THE TWINKLE IN HIS EYES DIED!!
HE BECAME HACHIKEN!!
EZO AG

Silver Spoon 10!
We've hit double digits!! I'm so grateful that the series has been able to continue so long so smoothly.
I'll keep doing my best.

あらかわひろむ
Hiromu Arakawa

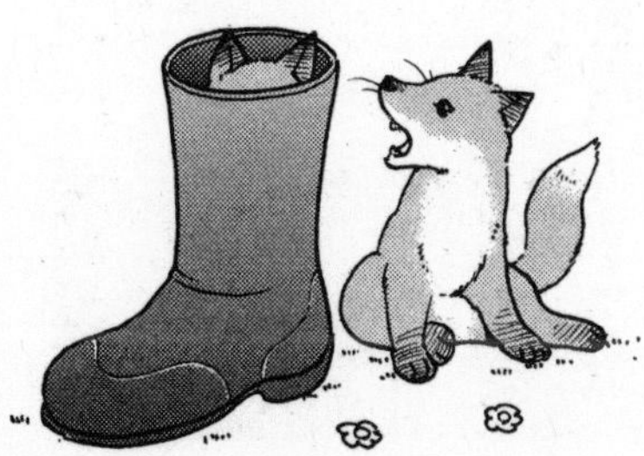

~ Special Thanks ~
All of my assistants,
Everyone who helped with collecting material, interviews, and consulting,
My editor, Mr. Tsubouchi, Mr. Yamada

AND YOU!!

COMMEMORATING VOLUME 10!!!

Made at Ezo Ag!

RECIPE UNVEILING!!!

The recipes in the *Silver Spoon* official guidebook were so popular, we've brought them back! Here are some of the mouthwatering dishes Hachiken and friends ate in volume 10, turned into fun recipes you can make at home!

SOBA Recipe Variations

These are some simple home-cooking variations on the Principal's soba. Introducing easy recipes substituting store-bought brands for the soba and grated yam, and chicken for the duck!

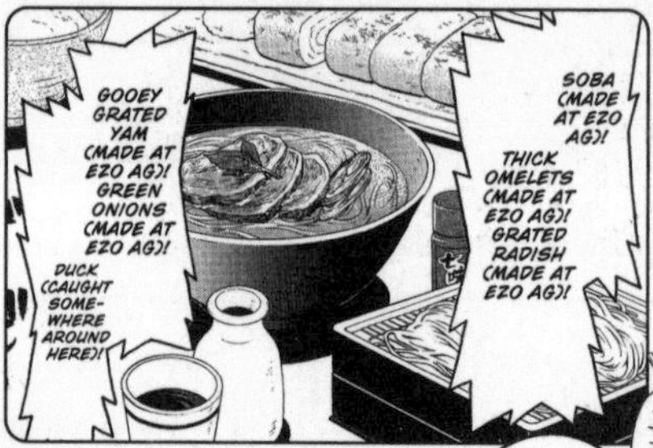

SOBA (MADE AT EZO AG)!
THICK OMELETS (MADE AT EZO AG)! GRATED RADISH (MADE AT EZO AG)!
GOOEY GRATED YAM (MADE AT EZO AG)! GREEN ONIONS (MADE AT EZO AG)!
DUCK (CAUGHT SOMEWHERE AROUND HERE)!

↑ Naturally, at Ezo Ag, everything from the side dishes and condiments to even the duck can be locally sourced! The grated yam soba is great either cold or hot!!

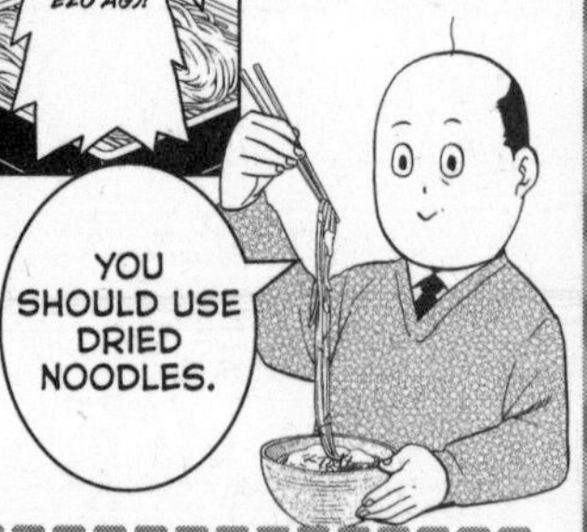

YOU SHOULD USE DRIED NOODLES.

BASIC INGREDIENTS (FOR 2)

1. 200g soba (2 bundles)
2. Noodle soup base (as desired)

VARIANT: CHICKEN NANBAN SOBA (FOR 2)

INGREDIENTS

1. Half a chicken thigh
2. 2 tbsp. each, soy sauce & mirin
3. 1/3 green onion

KEY POINTS

Cook the soba noodles as instructed on the package, and simply place the nanban on top! If you think the green onion will be too pungent, rinse it thoroughly with water before cutting it!

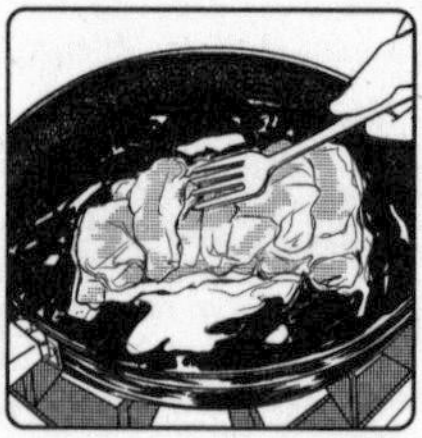

1 Cook skin-side first in a frying pan

Butterfly the chicken thigh. In an oiled frying pan, place chicken skin-side down and cook over medium heat.

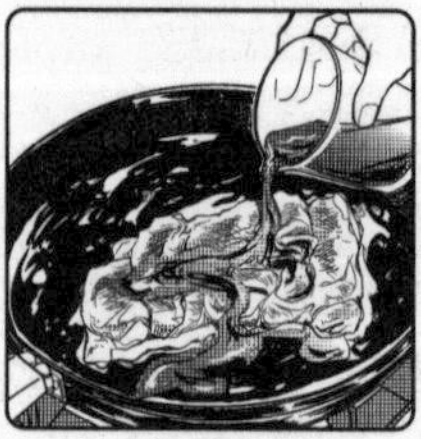

2 Dress with sauce

Turn the chicken over and cook as you drizzle it with the soy sauce and mirin sauce. Chop the green onion into thin slices. When the chicken is cooked through, top with green onion.

VARIANT: GOOEY GRATED YAM SOBA (FOR 2)

INGREDIENTS

1. 80–100g Chinese yams (or mountain yams)
2. 3–5 tbsp. noodle soup base (classic)

1 Grate the yam

Grate the peeled yam with a grater, with the yam held vertically.

2 Dilute with soup

Gradually add soup base to grated yam, diluting to taste.

MOCHI
Recipe Variations

On top of the classic mochi spread served at Ezo Ag, we're going to teach you two more recipe variations, original to these pages!!

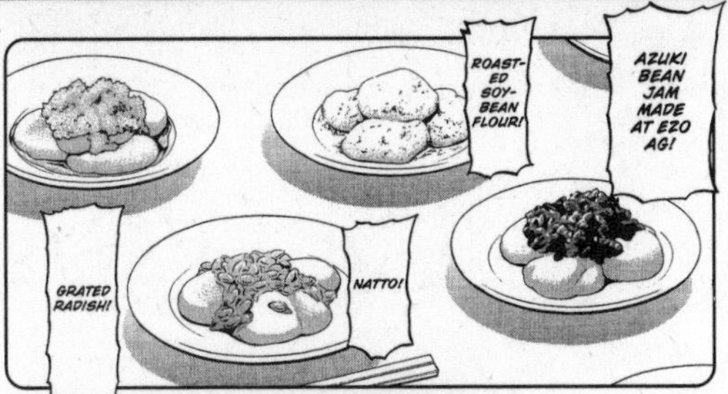
AZUKI BEAN JAM MADE AT EZO AG!
ROAST-ED SOY-BEAN FLOUR!
NATTO!
GRATED RADISH!

BASIC INGREDIENTS (FOR 1)

① 2 pieces *kirimochi* (round *marumochi* is fine too!)

↑ Ultra-fresh ingredients added to freshly-pounded mochi is an unbeatable mix. We're gonna recreate these with *kirimochi* (rectangular slices of dried mochi).

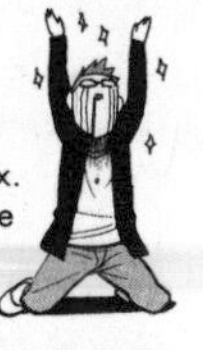

VARIANT KINAKO MOCHI (FOR 1)

INGREDIENTS

① 2 tbsp. *kinako* (roasted soybean flour)
② 1 tsp. sugar

Dip roasted mochi in water. Then cover the outside in kinako.

VARIANT ANKO MOCHI (FOR 1)

INGREDIENTS

① 2–3 tbsp. boiled azuki beans

Simply top your roasted mochi with boiled azuki beans. If you use canned azuki, warm it up first.

VARIANT OROSHI MOCHI (FOR 1)

INGREDIENTS

① 3–4 tbsp. grated radish
② 1 tsp. soy sauce

Place grated radish on top of roasted mochi, then top with a dollop of soy sauce.

VARIANT NATTO MOCHI (FOR 1)

INGREDIENTS

① 1 pack natto
② a sprinkle of green onions
③ a dash of mustard

Mix onion and mustard into natto before placing it on roasted mochi.

MADE IN EZONO RECIPE CARD

MAPLE & NUTS MOCHI

《INGREDIENTS FOR ONE》 ① 1 tbsp. butter ② 1 tbsp. mixed nuts ③ 2 tsp. maple syrup

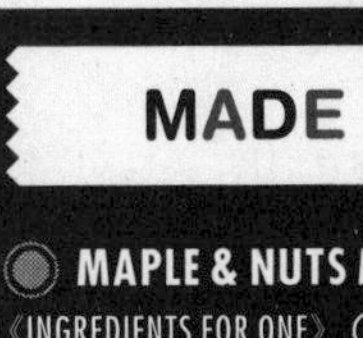

Top with syrup, nuts, and butter, then wait. When the butter starts to melt, it's ready to eat!

SESAME SOY SAUCE MOCHI

《INGREDIENTS FOR ONE》 ① 1 tbsp. sesame oil ② 1 tbsp. soy sauce ③ seven spice blend & green onion to taste

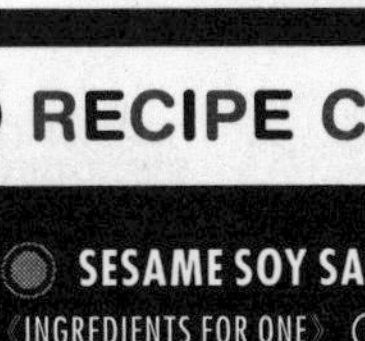

Mix the sesame oil and soy sauce into a sauce, then drizzle on roasted mochi. Add seven spice blend and green onion to taste.

HOT DOGS

How to make hot dog buns (yields 8 buns)

A simple home-cooking version of the mouth-watering hot dogs that had Hachiken and friends going crazy!

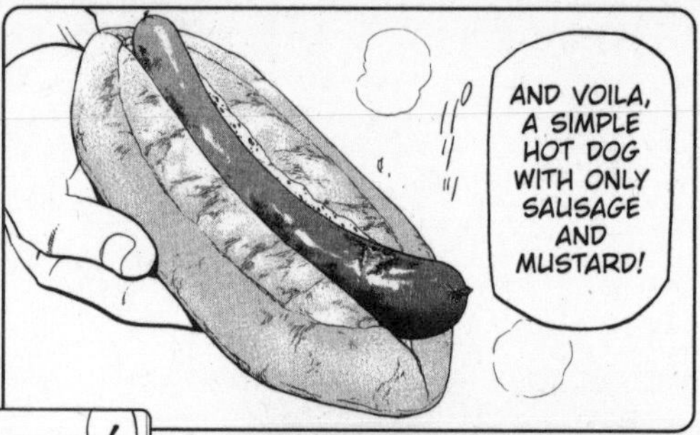
AND VOILA, A SIMPLE HOT DOG WITH ONLY SAUSAGE AND MUSTARD!

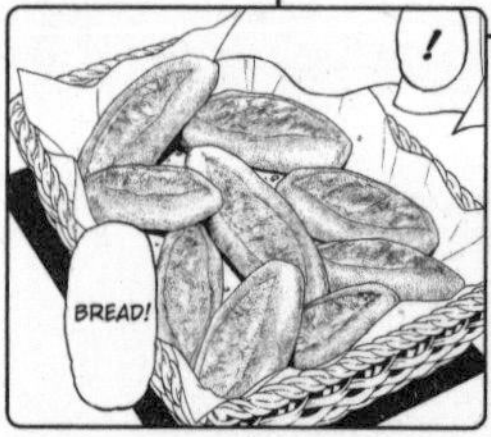
!
BREAD!

↑ Time to recreate these buns baked with a taste that fits sausage to a "T"!

INGREDIENTS

1. 8 sausage links
2. 300g bread flour
3. 100mL each water & milk
4. 20g butter (or olive oil)
5. 1 tsp. salt
6. 1½ tbsp. sugar
7. 1 tbsp. yeast

KEY POINTS

We're going to use store-bought sausage. Boil them, then brown them in a frying pan for crispy goodness!

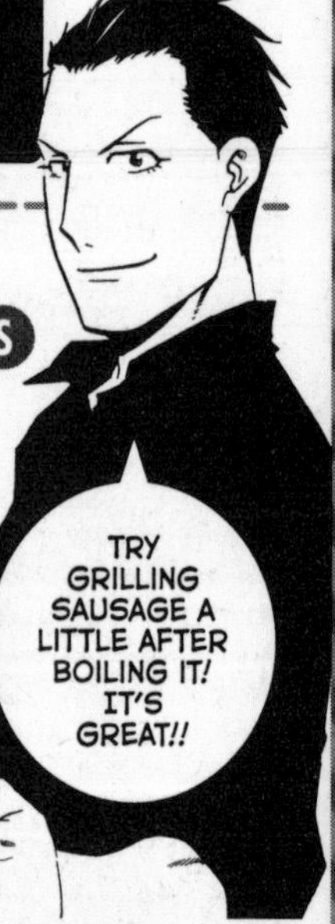
TRY GRILLING SAUSAGE A LITTLE AFTER BOILING IT! IT'S GREAT!!

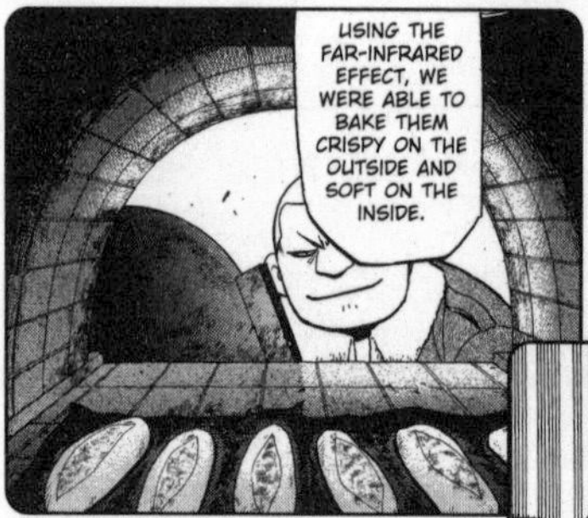
USING THE FAR-INFRARED EFFECT, WE WERE ABLE TO BAKE THEM CRISPY ON THE OUTSIDE AND SOFT ON THE INSIDE.

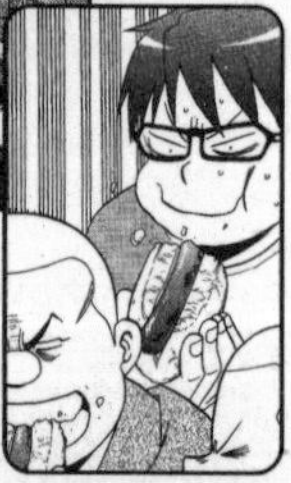

↑ At Ezo Ag, the students used a brick oven to bake the buns crispy on the outside, soft on the inside. We're going to substitute your standard home kitchen oven to bake some yummy bread!

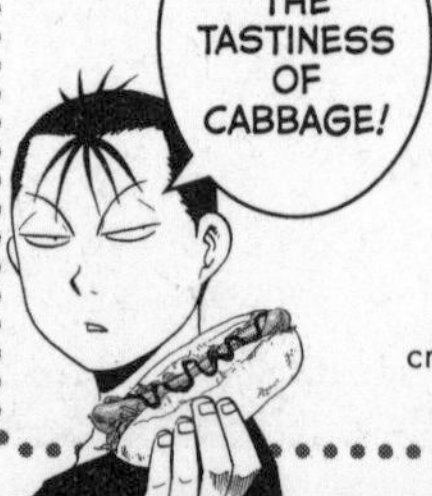
BEHOLD THE TASTINESS OF CABBAGE!

NISHIKAWA SPECIAL:

Healthy Dogs avec Cabbage!!!!!!!!!

Stuff plenty of shredded cabbage in that bun! The crisp feeling when you take a bite will have you hooked.

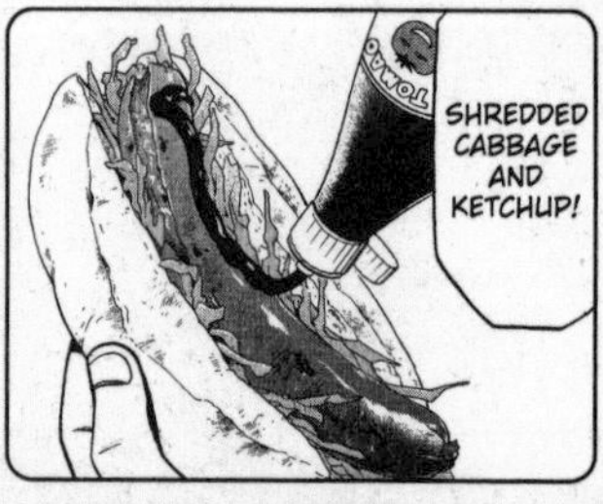
SHREDDED CABBAGE AND KETCHUP!

1 Add ingredients to bowl & knead

MILK

Measure flour into a large bowl. Add salt & butter to one area of the flour and sugar & yeast to a separate area. Add milk and water warmed to about 30°C, then knead for about ten minutes.

2 Wrap & let rise

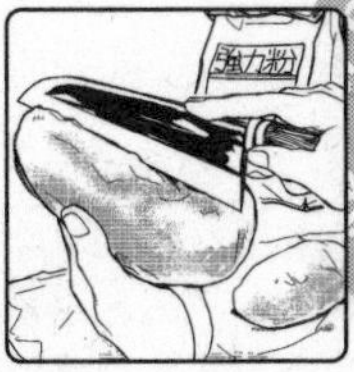

Form the dough into a ball. Place it into a lightly-oiled bowl and leave it in a warm place to rise for about 40 minutes. About 30°C is a good temperature.

3 Once it rises to twice its size, you're good to go!

Dough will be finished rising when it's reached twice its original size. Make sure you choose a large enough bowl for the risen dough to fit in for Step 2!

4 Divide & shape

Remove the dough from the bowl and divide it into eight equal balls. Shape each one into a narrow, oblong bun and space them evenly on a baking sheet lined with parchment paper.

5 Score and dust with flour

強力粉

Use a kitchen knife to score each piece of dough down the middle, so the buns will split open in the middle. Dust the surface with flour, and let the dough rest once more for about 15 minutes.

6 Bake in the oven

***Remember to preheat your oven in advance.**

IT'S DONE!

Bake for 13 to 15 minutes at 180°C. When it's done, add mustard and sausage as you like, and your hot dog is complete!

MADE IN EZONO RECIPE CARD

MAYONNAISE SCRAMBLE DOG

INGREDIENTS FOR TWO ① 2 sausage links ② 2 eggs ③ 2 tsp. mayonnaise ③ pepper to taste

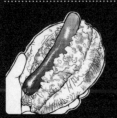

This recipe is simple but scrumptious! Adding mayo to the eggs makes your scrambled eggs come out fluffy, and it goes great with sausage. Great for breakfast or lunch!

1

マヨネーズ

Pour beaten egg on top of mayonnaise in a frying pan.

2

Mix coarsely and add pepper to taste.

●RECIPE WRITING ASSISTANCE / MIKA KANNO ●RECIPE ILLUSTRATIONS / YUUSUKE MATSUO

NEXT......
VALENTINE'S DAY
THE SCHOOL FINALLY STOPPED GETTING NEW GRADUATE RECRUITMENT REQUESTS. THEY DON'T HAVE A SINGLE ONE.
OH, I SEE... WAIT, WHOA!!
IN ONLY TWO MONTHS, THERE'LL BE NEW A NEW BATCH OF FIRST-YEARS!! KIDS ARE GONNA BE CALLING ME "HACHIKEN-SENPAI"!!
2012 2 FEBRUARY
WHOA!! I'M FROM A SCHOOL OUT IN THE COUNTRY, SO WE SKIPPED THE HONORIFICS AND JUST WENT WITH NAMES OR EVEN NICKNAMES!!
IF THEY CALL ME "SENPAI" I'LL FEEL ALL NERVOUS!!
SENPAI, WE CAN'T GROW CACAO AT EZO AG, RIGHT?
HUH?
ISN'T THAT A TROPICAL TREE?
ALSO, FOR THOSE OF YOU WHO HAVEN'T DECIDED WHETHER TO MOVE OVER TO THE UPPERCLASSMAN DORM FOR YOUR SECOND YEAR...
...TALK TO YOUR PARENTS AND MAKE A DECISION SOON!
YES, SIRRRRR.
HUH!? IF I LEAVE THE DORM...
WOW! LIVING ALONE! YOU'RE SO LUCKY!
COME ON IN!
...WOULD SHE COME OVER TO COOK FOR ME IF I ASKED!?
WELL, HACHIKEN-KUN SAID HE HAD A HANKERING FOR SOME CHOCOLATE.

**Milk, eggs, pork...
Wheat, all kinds of vegetables...
Even though Ezo Ag seems
to have everything, there
are a few things the school
doesn't make too, of course.
That something is cacao—
and February means...**

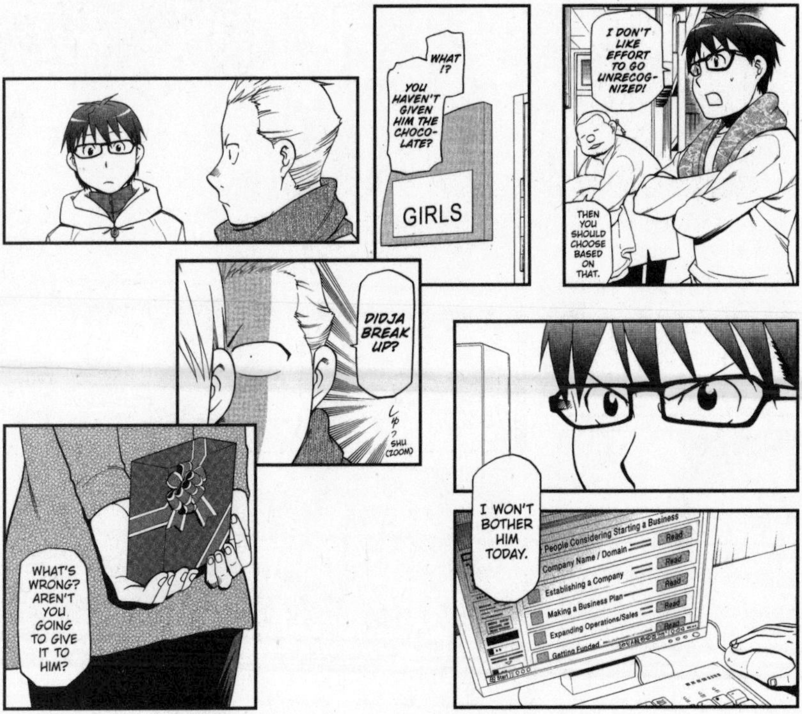
I DON'T LIKE EFFORT TO GO UNRECOG-NIZED!
THEN YOU SHOULD CHOOSE BASED ON THAT.
WHAT !?
YOU HAVEN'T GIVEN HIM THE CHOCO-LATE?
GIRLS
I WON'T BOTHER HIM TODAY.
People Considering Starting a Business
Read
Company Name / Domain
Read
Establishing a Company
Read
Making a Business Plan
Read
Expanding Operations/Sales
Read
Getting Funded
DIDJA BREAK UP?
SHU (ZOOM)
WHAT'S WRONG? AREN'T YOU GOING TO GIVE IT TO HIM?

...a celebration is about to unfold in the freezing cold... Valentine's Day!! It leaves boys bewildered, and girls hesitant... *Silver Spoon* 11, Coming Soon!!

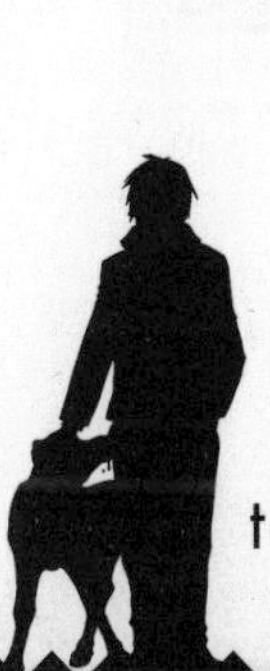

to be continued......

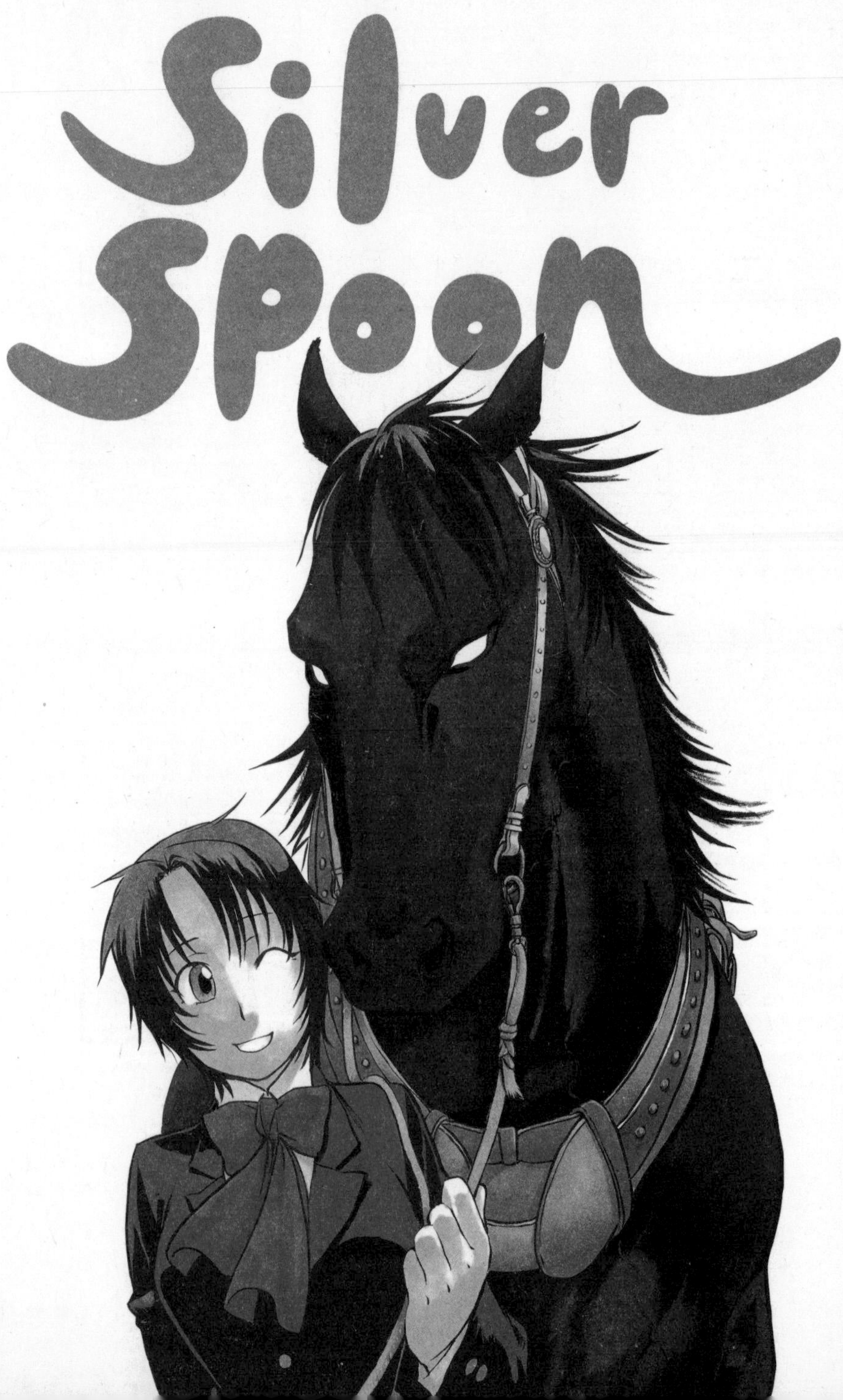
Silver
Spoon

IN NEPAL, YOGURT IS BELOVED AS A SACRED FOOD.
YOGURT FOR BIRTHDAYS. YOGURT FOR WEDDINGS TOO.
YOGURT IS VERY POPULAR IN INDIA AS WELL.
IN HINDUISM, IT'S A SACRED FOOD OFFERED TO THE GODS.
IT'S A SACRED FOOD.
BOYS' BATH YOGURT

Translation Notes

Common Honorifics

no honorific: Indicates familiarity or closeness; if used without permission or reason, addressing someone in this manner would constitute an insult.

-san: The Japanese equivalent of Mr./Mrs./Miss. If a situation calls for politeness, this is the fail-safe honorific.

-sama: Conveys great respect; may also indicate the social status of the speaker is lower than that of the addressee.

-kun: Used most often when referring to boys, this honorific indicates affection or familiarity. Occasionally used by older men among their peers, but it may also be used by anyone referring to a person of lower standing.

-chan: An affectionate honorific indicating familiarity used mostly in reference to girls; also used in reference to cute persons or animals of either gender.

-sensei: A respectful term for teachers, artists, or high-level professionals.

-niisan, nii-san, aniki, etc.: A term of endearment meaning "big brother" that may be more widely used to address any young man who is like a brother, regardless of whether he is related or not.

-neesan, nee-san, aneki, etc.: The female counterpart of the above, *nee-san* means "big sister."

Currency Conversion

While conversion rates fluctuate, an easy estimate for Japanese Yen conversion is ¥100 to 1 USD.

Page 7
In Japan, celebrating the new year is a big family holiday. Most people are expected to return home to visit the family for the festivities, so Hachiken staying behind at the dorm is surprising.

Page 9
New Year's soba (*toshikoshi soba*) is traditionally eaten on New Year's Eve. The long noodles symbolize a long life.

Page 15
A *kolkhoz* was a collective-owned farm in the Soviet Union. A *sovkhoz* was a state-owned farm in the Soviet Union. Kunashir, Iturup, Habomai, and Shikotan are all islands northeast of Hokkaido that the Soviet Union annexed at the end of World War II; they remain under territorial dispute between Japan and Russia.

Page 22
In Japan, viewing the first sunrise of the year (*hatsuhinode*) is believed to bring good luck.

Page 28
Mochi (sticky glutinous rice cakes) are a traditional New Year's treat. Mochi-pounding (*mochitsuki*) ceremonies are another part of the festivities, but are less common now than in the past.

Page 31
Zouni soup is a traditional New Year's Day soup containing mochi.

Page 32
In the Japanese, Tokiwa asks Hachiken how to read one of the *kanji* characters in his text message. Hachiken decides to text Tokiwa in all *hiragana* (the simpler, phonetic Japanese letters).

Page 35
Another Japanese New Year's tradition is *hatsumoude*—visiting a shrine for the first time in the new year. Shrines can be very crowded as everyone comes to pray for luck in the coming year.

Page 53
The smallest denomination banknote in Japan is ¥1,000 (about 10 USD), so Ayame is suggesting offering at least that much.

Page 70
The JSDF, or the Japanese Self-Defense Forces, is a national defense force created in Japan after World War II.

Page 76
If something is *moe*, it inspires feelings of affection. The otaku term is usually associated with cute characters, but you can be moe for anything that excites you.

Page 108
Nakajima-sensei's apron is a reference to the Buddha's last meal, *sukara maddava*. There's dispute over whether it means pork or truffles dug up by pigs.

Page 118
Wassamu is a small Hokkaido town famous for its pumpkin and cabbage.

Page 119
The story of Sai Weng and the horse begins when a horse belonging to an old man runs away. His friends and neighbors come to comfort him, but the old man says the loss of his horse could lead to good things. Sure enough, the horse later returns, bringing another, better horse with it. The old man's friends and neighbors come by to celebrate, only this time the old man says his windfall might lead to disaster. Sure enough, the old man's young son later falls off the new horse and breaks his leg. His friends and neighbors come to comfort him again, but the old man repeats what he said before: This misfortune may lead to good fortune. And he's right; when wartime comes, his son isn't drafted because of his injury.

Page 121
In Japanese, a carnivorous woman (*nikushokukei joshi*) is one who makes the first move when it comes to dating. In this case, though, it's literal...

Page 143
Pirozhki is a Russian puff pastry.

Page 159
Yulia Tymoshenko was the first woman appointed Prime Minister of Ukraine in 2005. She was nicknamed the "gas princess" in the 1990s when she was president of the company that was the main importer of Russian natural gas to Ukraine.

Page 166
Pochi is a stereotypical dog name equivalent to "Spot" or "Rover."

Silver Spoon

Translation: **Amanda Haley** Lettering: **Abigail Blackman**

This book is a work of fiction. Names, characters, places, and incidents are the product
of the author's imagination or are used fictitiously. Any resemblance to actual events,
locales, or persons, living or dead, is coincidental.

GIN NO SAJI SILVER SPOON Vol. 10
by Hiromu ARAKAWA
© 2011 Hiromu ARAKAWA
All rights reserved.
Original Japanese edition published by SHOGAKUKAN.
English translation rights in the United States of America, Canada, the United Kingdom,
Ireland, Australia and New Zealand arranged with SHOGAKUKAN
through Tuttle-Mori Agency, Inc.

English translation © 2019 by Yen Press, LLC

Yen Press
150 West 30th Street, 19th Floor
New York, NY 10001

Visit us at yenpress.com
facebook.com/yenpress
twitter.com/yenpress
yenpress.tumblr.com
instagram.com/yenpress

First Yen Press Edition: August 2019

Yen Press is an imprint of Yen Press, LLC.
The Yen Press name and logo are trademarks of Yen Press, LLC.

The publisher is not responsible for websites (or their
content) that are not owned by the publisher.

Library of Congress Control Number: 2017959207

ISBN: 978-1-9753-2765-1

10 9 8 7 6 5 4 3 2 1

WOR

Printed in the United States of America